OUR REASON FOR BEING

OUR REASON FOR BEING

An Exposition of Ecclesiastes on the Meaning of Life

T. F. LEONG

Foreword by C. Hassell Bullock

WIPF & STOCK · Eugene, Oregon

OUR REASON FOR BEING
An Exposition of Ecclesiastes on the Meaning of Life

Copyright © 2022 T. F. Leong. All rights reserved. Except for brief quotations in critical publications or reviews, no part of this book may be reproduced in any manner without prior written permission from the publisher. Write: Permissions, Wipf and Stock Publishers, 199 W. 8th Ave., Suite 3, Eugene, OR 97401.

Wipf & Stock
An Imprint of Wipf and Stock Publishers
199 W. 8th Ave., Suite 3
Eugene, OR 97401

www.wipfandstock.com

PAPERBACK ISBN: 978-1-6667-1706-8
HARDCOVER ISBN: 978-1-6667-1707-5
EBOOK ISBN: 978-1-6667-1708-2

AUGUST 2, 2022 8:10 AM

Unless otherwise indicated, Scripture quotations are the author's own translation.

Scripture quotations marked ESV are from The ESV® Bible (The Holy Bible, English Standard Version®), copyright © 2001 by Crossway, a publishing ministry of Good News Publishers. Used by permission. All rights reserved.

Scriptures marked GNB are from the Good News Bible © 1994 published by the Bible Societies/HarperCollins Publishers Ltd UK, Good News Bible© American Bible Society 1966, 1971, 1976, 1992. Used with permission.

Scripture quotations marked HCSB are taken from the Holman Christian Standard Bible®, Used by Permission HCSB ©1999, 2000, 2002, 2003, 2009 Holman Bible Publishers. Holman Christian Standard Bible®, Holman CSB®, and HCSB® are federally registered trademarks of Holman Bible Publishers.

Scripture quotations marked LSB are taken from the (LSB®) Legacy Standard Bible®, Copyright © 2021 by The Lockman Foundation. Used by permission. All rights reserved. Managed in partnership with Three Sixteen Publishing Inc. LSBible.org and 316publishing.com.

Scripture quotations marked NASB are taken from the (NASB®) New American Standard Bible®, Copyright © 1960, 1971, 1977, 1995, 2020 by The Lockman Foundation. Used by permission. All rights reserved. www.lockman.org.

Scripture quotations marked NIV are taken from THE HOLY BIBLE, NEW INTERNATIONAL VERSION®, NIV® Copyright © 1973, 1978, 1984, 2011 by Biblica, Inc.® Used by permission. All rights reserved worldwide.

Scripture quotations marked NJPS are taken from Tanakh: *The New Translation of the Holy Scriptures According to the Traditional Hebrew Text*. Copyright © 1985 by The Jewish Publication Society.

Scripture quotations marked NKJV are taken from the New King James Version®. Copyright © 1982 by Thomas Nelson. Used by permission. All rights reserved.

Scripture quotations marked NLT are taken from the Holy Bible, New Living Translation, copyright ©1996, 2004, 2015 by Tyndale House Foundation. Used by permission of Tyndale House Publishers, Carol Stream, Illinois 60188. All rights reserved.

Scripture quotations marked NRSV are taken from New Revised Standard Version Bible, copyright © 1989 National Council of the Churches of Christ in the United States of America. Used by permission. All rights reserved worldwide.

To YY and SY
my beloved children
raising them both
has enriched my reason for being

Contents

Foreword by C. Hassell Bullock | xi

Preface | xiii

Introduction to Ecclesiastes | 1

Apparent Pessimism | 2

Apparent Contradictions | 4

Coherent Message | 6

    Outline of Contents | 6

    Flow of Speech | 8

Exposition of Ecclesiastes | 15

Identification of Speaker (1:1) | 15

Announcement of Theme: "All Is Vanity" (1:2–3) | 17

Poem to Vivify Idea of Vanity (1:4–11) | 23

    Excursus to 1:4–11: Qoheleth's View of History | 28

Illustrations to Evoke Sense of Vanity (1:12–2:23) | 31

    Excursus to 2:1–11: Qoheleth's Experiment with Pleasure | 39

Admonition to Carefreeness in Light of Vanity (2:24–26) | 47

    Excursus to 2:24–26: Qoheleth's Admonishment about Enjoyment | 50

Poem to Amplify Sense of Vanity (3:1–8) | 55

Repetition of Theme: "What Profit is There?" (3:9) | 55

Explanation for Vanity and Sense of Eternity (3:10–15) | 59

    Excursus to 3:10–15: Qoheleth on Enjoyment and the Fear of God | 66

Observation to Reinforce Sense of Vanity (3:16–21) | 70

    Excursus to 3:16–21: Qoheleth on the Reality of God's Judgment | 74

    Admonition to Carefreeness in Light of Vanity (3:22) | 76

    Observations to Sustain Sense of Vanity (4:1–5:17) | 79

    Elaboration on Carefreeness (5:18–6:9) | 96

    Recapitulation of Theme and Sub-themes (6:10–12) | 105

    Deliberations on Life in Light of Vanity (7:1–11:6) | 108

        Excursus to 7:15–29: Qoheleth's View of Women | 124

        Excursus to 8:1–15: Qoheleth on the Certainty of God's Judgment | 131

    Admonition to Carefreeness in Light of Vanity (11:7–12:7) | 151

    Encapsulation of Theme: "All is vanity" (12:8) | 155

    Elaboration on Speaker and His Teaching (12:9–12) | 156

        Excursus to 12:9–12: Canonicity of the Book of Ecclesiastes | 159

    Conclusion and Call to Decision (12:13–14) | 167

TEACHING OF ECCLESIASTES | 173

    Encountering the Realities of Life | 174

        The Certainty of Death | 175

        The Uncertainties of Life | 176

        The Certainty of Judgment | 178

    Experiencing the Meaning of Life | 179

        Fulfilling the Purpose of Life | 180

        Perceiving Coherence in Life | 184

        Corroborating Empirical Evidence | 188

        Excursus: Secular Psychology on the Meaning of Life | 193

    Experiencing the Meaning of History | 195

        Contributing to the Purpose and Goal of History | 197

        Experiencing a Sense of Closure to History | 202

INTERPRETATION OF ECCLESIASTES | 207

    The Meaning of *Hebel* | 208

        Hebel as Vapor | 208

        The Transience of Vapor | 209

        The Insubstantiality of Vapor | 210

        The Semantics of Vanity | 214

        The Pragmatics of Vanity | 218

>   **The Meaning of "Under the Sun"** | 222
>> The Views of Leupold, Eaton and Heim | 222
>> The Views of Longman, Bartholomew and Weeks | 227
>
> **The Rhetoric of Ecclesiastes** | 231
>> The Interpretive Grid | 232
>> The Flow of the Argument | 234
>> "The End of the Matter" | 236
>> The Interpretation of Peter Enns | 238
>
> **Conclusion** | 241

Bibliography | 243

Foreword

GIVEN the myriad of interpretive labors expended on the book of Ecclesiastes through the centuries, we can say that Qoheleth has certainly contributed to the truth of his own avowal that "Of making many books there is no end, and much study is weariness to the body" (12:12), even though that was not his intent. Just think of the countless books that would be missing from modern libraries if Qoheleth had not written his book! And how much spiritual worth and emotional pessimism (whichever perspective one has derived from Qoheleth) would be lost! And Dr. Leong has added one more contribution—not a final one, but, I believe, an enduring one!—and he has accomplished that by working with, and even replicating, Qoheleth's methodology.

First, Leong calls attention to the literary style of the book to help unravel its mystery. That is, he recognizes Qoheleth's methodology to be cyclical, not linear, stressing that 1:2–12:8, by cyclical reasoning, prepares the readers for the decision mandated in 12:13–14: "fear God and keep his commandments, for this is (the essence of) every man. . . ." While this is not a new discovery, this author capitalizes on it with great benefit. In fact, Dr. Leong has executed his interpretation by engaging this methodology and showing how methodology and message are interdependent. Key to his exposition is one of the most powerful hermeneutical principles in biblical studies, and in any literary endeavor, for that matter, that readers must enter into Qoheleth's mind to understand his message, whether the readers agree with it or not—the latter is not the issue. The exegetical urgency involved in this interpretive principle and in Leong's study is the speaker's meaning, not the listener's response.

And as we have hinted, the structure of the commentary even reinforces that cyclical methodology. To explicate this point, after a quite thorough exposition of the text, Leong cycles back to give his readers an additional three sections where he approaches Qoheleth from different angles, enhancing and reinforcing the meaning of the text as he has read it in the exposition: "Teaching of Ecclesiastes," where he builds on and applies key themes that have already been discussed in some detail in the exposition; "Interpretation of Ecclesiastes," which is essentially a theological glossary defending and clarifying the meaning of key terms used in the exposition; and "The Rhetoric of Ecclesiastes," where he discusses the "interpretive grid" used in the exposition of Ecclesiastes. Even if Dr. Leong did not consciously intend this replication, I suspect what I believe the contents affirm, that he has followed his own directive so faithfully—to enter into the writer's mind—that his methodology is a virtual imitation of Qoheleth's. Even if readers do not put the same emphasis on methodology as Leong insists Qoheleth does, they would still be wise to recognize how methodology yields message and message presupposes methodology.

The arguments of Ecclesiastes are interrelated, one might even say overlapping. That is, Qoheleth presents a theme, for example, the beautiful poem of 3:1–8, then subsequently replicates it in other terms and with other metaphors, enhancing the theme and reinforcing the message. Methodologically he is looking back at arguments already introduced and forward to the major admonition of the "speech," as Leong calls it. Even though the methodology is cyclical, it produces a linear outcome. The movement of thought is from "All is vanity" to "Enjoy life" to "Fear God," which is the "end of the matter." Qoheleth's thought, Dr Leong insists (and I think correctly), involves a consideration of the certainty of death and the uncertainties of life, and those uncertainties are the goad that prods the readers onward to the fear of God, which is Qoheleth's goal after all is said and done. The latter precept, "Fear God and keep his commandments," is the means by which the joy is shaped and in which it is contained. The result of this argumentative style for readers is that it translates into a change of perspective, from Qoheleth the pessimist to Qoheleth the realist, thus providing one of the most powerful representatives of orthodoxy that we have in the Hebrew Bible.

A final word of commendation is Leong's personal translation of the Hebrew text. To his credit the translation is designed to capture the subtle nuances of the text that other translations have obscured and interpretive obsessions that have come to dominate some readers' conclusions. That is, the translation is not contrived but nuanced to the methodology which Qoheleth's arguments have engaged. In regard to all the readers and scholars who through the centuries have sought to understand Ecclesiastes, I personally commend their pursuits, which have been as intense, personal, and sincere as Qoheleth's long and passionate search for life's meaning. Now T. F. Leong's noble effort stands alongside them, and is worthy of an enduring place among them to direct and redirect his readers' into Qoheleth's mind and his compelling book of wisdom.

C. Hassell Bullock
Franklin S. Dyrness Professor of Biblical Studies Emeritus
Wheaton College
Wheaton, IL 60187

Preface

Human nature and human life are such that we all have a deep-seated desire to make sense of life—to find a meaning to life. For what is the point of being born into a world filled with woes to live a life full of cares and then die, leaving behind everything we have ever gained through our toils? Indeed, "the urge to understand the point of our existence is deep and pervasive, and is indicative of qualities of mind that are arguably central to being human."[1] What then is our reason for being?

A meaningless existence in itself is a painful experience. So our heart cries out for the purpose of our transitory existence in this seemingly hostile world. The biblical book of Ecclesiastes teaches that there is a God-given purpose for humanity, and that God so works in this world that humanity should live according to this purpose. Hence there is such a thing as *the* purpose *of* life, and thus, *the* meaning *of* life. And therefore, life will not make adequate sense until and unless we live according to this purpose.

Even renowned psychiatrist Viktor Frankl, the founder of the well-known school of psychotherapy called Logotherapy, recognized the reality of the meaning of life. To him "Life has meaning not only in specific situations but also in one's existence as a whole. The ultimate meaning of one's life, in Frankl's belief, is found in the spiritual dimension of human beings."[2] However, "Although Frankl believed in ultimate meaning and purpose, he chose to focus on specific meanings for concrete situations in psychotherapy."[3] But if the purpose and the meaning of life exist, is it then adequate just to live for *a* purpose *in* life and thus experience only *a* meaning *in* life?

This book is an interpretation and exposition of Ecclesiastes on the meaning of life, which goes beyond the purpose of life. It is amazing how relevant this ancient piece of wisdom literature is to contemporary thinking and living. Ecclesiastes addresses our need for the meaning of life in a rather comprehensive, coherent and compelling manner. It has a deeply meaningful message that we desperately need to hear.

---

1. Wolf, "Meaning of Life."
2. Wong, "Logotherapy," 622.
3. Wong, "Logotherapy," 622.

However, Ecclesiastes is also the most difficult biblical book to interpret coherently as authoritative Scripture. So, on the one hand this present book is written in such a way that one need not be a scholar to appreciate it, and on the other hand the exposition grapples with the interpretation of Ecclesiastes in its parts, and as a whole, based on scholarly exegesis of the Hebrew text. And in order to give Ecclesiastes the breadth and depth of coverage that it deserves, this book has four distinct parts.

I. The *Introduction to Ecclesiastes* introduces a fresh approach to the interpretation of Ecclesiastes. Contrary to the dominant view in contemporary scholarship, this part presents Ecclesiastes as a coherent speech that is neither pessimistic nor contradictory. It also outlines and surveys the contents of Ecclesiastes to show how it can be read as a coherent speech with a careful argument that stretches from the beginning to the end of the speech.

II. The *Exposition of Ecclesiastes* that follows forms the major bulk of this book. It is an expositional commentary of Ecclesiastes on the meaning of life. This exposition follows the linear flow of the text as outlined in the *Introduction*. It is a straightforward exposition of the message of Ecclesiastes with some discussion on issues that affect a coherent interpretation of the book as a whole. As will be explained at the beginning of this part, extra discussions that grapple with the interpretation of crucial verses are included to ground the exposition of Ecclesiastes not only on a coherent interpretation of the book but also on solid exegesis of crucial verses, which in turn support the coherent interpretation.

III. Following the linear exposition is a topical exposition on the *Teaching of Ecclesiastes* taken as a coherent whole. It complements the linear exposition in helping us see more coherently and thus more clearly the teaching of Ecclesiastes on the meaning of life. It builds on the exposition of the relevant texts in the *Exposition*. Unlike the linear exposition, this topical exposition allows us to make full use of clues in Ecclesiastes to extend the exposition to cover the meaning of history so as to present a more comprehensive and accurate understanding of the meaning of life. This part is an adaptation and expansion of chapter 34 of *Our Reason for Hope: An Exposition of the Old Testament on the Meaning of History*.[4] The expansion also incorporates relevant insights from philosophy, psychology, sociology as well as narratology. Most significant is the inclusion of real-life empirical evidence that corroborates the teaching of Ecclesiastes on the meaning of life.

IV. An essay on the *Interpretation of Ecclesiastes* forms the final part. It undertakes elaborate exegetical spadework to break new grounds in order to present and defend the interpretation adopted in this book against the array of conflicting scholarly interpretations, most of which assume Ecclesiastes contains self-contradictory and unorthodox statements. Thus they render the book, except for the last few verses, useless in terms of authoritative teaching. In the process of defending our interpretation, this part presents a deeper, richer and more nuanced understanding of Ecclesiastes

---

4. Leong, *Our Reason for Hope*.

as authoritative Scripture. It is placed at the end of the book because it is advisable for readers who are not yet familiar with the intricate issues involved in interpreting Ecclesiastes to read at least parts of the *Exposition* first.

Each of the four parts looks at the book of Ecclesiastes from a different but complementary angle so as to understand the book as much as possible in order to unlock the treasures of wisdom embodied in this marvelous text. Since all four parts are looking at the same text, a minimal repetition of materials is inevitable.

The genesis of the interpretive approach to Ecclesiastes taken in this book is my master's thesis written at Wheaton College in the summer of 1989. My supervisor-cum-first reader was the late Dr. Herbert Wolf. I appreciate his willingness to accept my thesis proposal knowing full well that I would be walking into an interpretive minefield. Otherwise, this book will likely not be written. Dr. Hassell Bullock, my other Old Testament professor, was the second reader. I appreciate his taking the time to write the foreword to this book. A special thanks to him for making the effort to capture the distinguishing features of the book. Appreciation is also due bibliographer William Hupper, who facilitated my research in alerting me to relevant published materials and even supplying articles that I did not have access to.

Introduction to Ecclesiastes

The book of Ecclesiastes has been called the "black sheep of the Bible."[1] It is "universally acclaimed as one of the most enigmatic in the Hebrew Scriptures. Aside from agreement on this point, however, almost every facet of the book has been a matter of contention among scholars and commentators."[2] And it is not just a matter of different interpretations of the book among scholars and commentators; this happens to every book of the Bible. Peter Enns captures the problem very well:

> Indeed, perhaps no other book of the Hebrew Scriptures has had the history of counterunderstandings as Ecclesiastes. Of nearly any other biblical book, one can make coherent statements as to its basic content and purpose that would find general agreement.... If any ten knowledgeable readers of Genesis were asked what Genesis is about, one might get ten diverse answers, but those answers would likely still accent legitimate and generally agreed upon aspects of the book.... But no one capable of coherent thought would say that Genesis is about God's destruction of the universe, his blessing of the tower of Babel project, or his rejection of Abraham.
>
> Yet Ecclesiastes ... is a book that is amenable to conflicting and even contradictory interpretations, and so respected interpreters throughout history have struggled with the basic message of the book. Is Qohelet ["the Preacher"] coherent or incoherent, insightful or confused? Is he a stark realist or merely faithless? Is he orthodox or heterodox? Is he an optimist or a pessimist? Is the ultimate message of the book, "Be like Qohelet, the wise man," or "Qohelet is wrong, make sure you don't fall into his trap"?[3]

How can all this be true of a book of the Holy Scripture? Is the problem with Ecclesiastes itself, or with its interpreters? Since our concern is the interpretation and exposition of Ecclesiastes as authoritative Scripture, we will approach the book without assuming that the problem is with the book itself. However, we do recognize that

---

1. Wright, "Interpretation of Ecclesiastes," 133.
2. Garfinkel, "Qoheleth," 51.
3. Enns, *Ecclesiastes*, 3–4.

any interpreter or expositor who considers Ecclesiastes as Scripture inspired by God encounters two glaring problems: apparent pessimism and apparent contradictions.

Apparent Pessimism

Consider the theme of the book, traditionally rendered as, "All is vanity (profitless)" (1:2; 12:8). If everything is profitless, what then is the point of living? The pessimism is only apparent. A proper understanding of "all is vanity (profitless)" will show that it is not pessimistic at all. As we shall see, what it means is that everything we gain in this temporal world will ultimately be profitless because we have to die and, when we die, we have to leave everything behind. This is simply realism and not pessimism.

The *New International Version* (NIV), a popular English translation of the Bible, accentuates the apparent pessimism by rendering the theme outrightly as, "Everything is meaningless." Why would a Bible translation as conservative as the (original) NIV deviate from the traditional rendering and accentuate the apparent pessimism?

According to J. Stafford Wright the theme "All is vanity" does not mean that life is profitless in the sense that life is not worth living (pessimism), but only that we cannot, and God will not help us, find "a meaning to life, to see it as a [coherent] whole."[4] Such an interpretation is possible. For people do not find meaning to life for two basic reasons: they do not have a worthwhile purpose to live for, or they cannot see life as a coherent (meaningful) whole, or both. Hence the expression "Everything is meaningless" can mean either life is purposeless or life is incoherent, or both.

Therefore according to Wright's interpretation, the view of life ("All is vanity") presented in Ecclesiastes is that life is "meaningless" not because it is purposeless (pessimism) but because we cannot see how every aspect of life, especially the painful ones, fit into a coherent (meaningful) whole. Thus life does not make sense. He says this view of life is not pessimism.

In the context of interpreting Ecclesiastes and applying its teaching, we need to understand "pessimism" in terms of reality. A "pessimistic" view of life is one that perceives life as worse than what life really is, and thus is inconsistent with (worse than) reality. An "optimistic" view of life is one that is better than reality. And a "realistic" view of life is one that is consistent with reality even when the reality is one that we may find unpleasant and undesirable, such as the reality that we have to die and leave behind everything.

Is the view that "Everything is meaningless"—in the sense that we will never be able to see life as a coherent (meaningful) whole—then realistic or pessimistic? Ecclesiastes teaches that human wisdom will not be able to piece together life as a meaningful whole especially since there is "innocent" or undeserved suffering in this world. How can this enigmatic and painful aspect of life fit coherently into any worthwhile

---

4. Wright, "Interpretation of Ecclesiastes," 140.

purpose of life? The biblical book of Job confirms that human wisdom *on its own* has no answer.

So if God does not exist, we are certainly all on our own and we can never see life as a meaningful whole. This means if God does not exist, "Everything is meaningless" is realistic and not pessimistic because it is consistent with the reality that we can never see life as a meaningful whole. Wright's interpretation of Ecclesiastes is that God, who alone holds the key to the meaning of life, will not give it to us.[5] Thus, even though God exists, we still can never see life as a meaningful whole. If his interpretation is correct, one can believe in God and yet recognize that "Everything is meaningless" is non-pessimistic.

Hence in view of Wright's interpretation of Ecclesiastes, the NIV translation "Everything is meaningless" can be understood to express a non-pessimistic view of life. This may in fact be what the NIV translators intended. For it is unlikely that the NIV would interpret Ecclesiastes as presenting a pessimistic view of life. Nevertheless, even if Wright's interpretation is correct and the NIV translation is indeed based on his interpretation, few readers of the NIV would actually understand "Everything is meaningless" in a non-pessimistic sense. This then means that the (unnecessary) attempt by the NIV to mitigate the apparent pessimism resulted in the unintended consequence of actually aggravating it. So it is not surprising that the commentaries of Duane Garrett[6] and Iain Provan,[7] though based on the NIV itself, have explicitly rejected this translation of the theme of Ecclesiastes.

Is Wright's interpretation of Ecclesiastes correct to begin with? We shall see that interpreting Ecclesiastes as a coherent speech will show that God has already revealed in Ecclesiastes (together with Job) how life is a coherent and meaningful whole even in light of the reality of undeserved suffering.

The *New Living Translation* (NLT) also translates the theme of Ecclesiastes as "Everything is meaningless." This is evidently due to the influence of Tremper Longman, who is one of the translators for Ecclesiastes as well as the senior translator for the wisdom books as a whole. Based on the commentaries of Longman,[8] "Everything is meaningless" is outrightly pessimistic. Why would a Bible translation as conservative as the NLT present the theme of Ecclesiastes as pessimistic? It has to do with Longman's interpretation of Ecclesiastes as a whole. Like most commentators, Longman distinguishes the speaker (1:2—12:8) from the "frame narrator," who appended the "epilogue" (12:9–14) to the speech.[9] The speaker is unorthodox—he has a

---

5. Wright, "Interpretation of Ecclesiastes," 140.

6. Garrett, *Proverbs, Ecclesiastes, Song of Songs*, 282–83.

7. Provan, *Ecclesiastes/Song of Songs*, 51–52.

8. Longman, *Ecclesiastes*; Longman, "Ecclesiastes."

9. Even though 1:1 explicitly says that what follows are the "words of the Preacher," Longman attributes 1:2–11 and 12:8 to the frame narrator as well. In any case, since these two texts are still considered words that express the Preacher's thought (Longman, *Ecclesiastes*, 58), for all practical purposes they are still the words of the Preacher just as 1:1 says that they are.

pessimistic view of life—but the frame narrator is orthodox. Longman supposes that the orthodox frame narrator uses the unorthodox speech as a foil, a teaching device, in order to instruct his audience concerning the dangers of speculative and doubting wisdom in Israel represented by the unorthodox speaker.[10]

In other words, although almost the entire book of Ecclesiastes (1:2—12:8) is unorthodox, the book taken as a whole is not and thus overall can still be considered the inspired word of God. Longman uses the unorthodox speeches in the book of Job as an analogy to justify the inclusion of the supposedly unorthodox speech of Ecclesiastes in Holy Scripture.[11] However, the three friends of Job are in a *dialogue* addressing Job and vice-versa like in a debate; the speaker in Ecclesiastes is in a *monologue addressing the reader like in a sermon*. And in the epilogue of Job, God declares the speeches of the three friends unorthodox (Job 42:7); in the "epilogue" of Ecclesiastes the supposed frame narrator affirms that the speech of the speaker is *orthodox* (12:9–12)![12] So the analogy is not valid. In any case, Longman's interpretation renders almost the entire book of Ecclesiastes practically useless to preachers.

This is not the place to directly engage Longman's interpretation of Ecclesiastes. Suffice it here to say that Longman's supposition—an orthodox frame narrator is using the speech of an unorthodox speaker as a foil—is apparently an afterthought to solve the problem of a supposedly pessimistic book in Holy Scripture. As indicated above, it will be shown in this book that the speech is not pessimistic—there is no need for Longman's supposition. And it will be shown below that when Ecclesiastes is interpreted as a coherent book from beginning to end, the rhetoric of Ecclesiastes flows consistently from 1:2 all the way to 12:14—there is also no room for Longman's supposition.

Apparent Contradictions

As for the question of apparent contradictions, we need to recognize the nature of wisdom literature. Wisdom is about putting knowledge of truth into practice. When we apply the same truth in different contexts, we may apply it in even opposite directions. The best example is found here: "Do not answer a fool according to his folly, lest you also be like him yourself. Answer a fool according to his folly, lest he will be wise in his own eyes" (Prov 26:4–5).

The contradiction is only apparent. The truth about the fool is the same in both cases—he is right in his own eyes and he brings harm to himself and others (Prov 12:15; 13:20; 18:6–7). In one context, because the fool is right in his own eyes, there is no point responding to him—he "has no delight in understanding, but only in

---

10. Longman, *Ecclesiastes*, 38.
11. Longman, *Ecclesiastes*, 37.
12. Longman reads against the grain of 12:9–12 in order to deny that the frame narrator affirms 1:2—12:8 as orthodox (see "Exposition of Ecclesiastes" under "Excursus to 12:9–12").

expressing his own opinion" (Prov 18:2). It would be foolish to do so—"he will despise the wisdom of your words" (Prov 23:9)—and thus become like him. In another context, because he brings harm to himself and others, we need to respond and show him and others that he is foolish (cf. Prov 18:17). As Longman puts it, whether to answer a fool or not "depends on the nature of the fool with whom one is engaged in conversation. In other words, the wise person must assess whether this is a fool who will simply drain one's energy with no positive results or whether an answer will prove fruitful to the fool or perhaps to those who overhear. The wise not only know the proverb but also can read the circumstances and the people with whom they dialogue."[13]

In fact, this phenomenon of apparent contradiction is not limited to wisdom literature and can be observed when truth is wisely applied in different contexts. Moses commanded the Israelites: "You shall not put the LORD to the test as you tested him at Massah" (Deut 6:16). At Massah they "tested the LORD, saying, 'Is the LORD among us or not?'" (Exod 17:7). However, in a different context, the LORD himself commanded the Israelites: "Test me now in this . . . (and see) if I will not open the windows of heaven for you and pour down for you a blessing until there is not enough room for it" (Mal 3:10).

Though the Hebrew word for "test" is different in each case, both are about testing whether God is faithful (this is precisely why Jesus cited Deut 6:16 in Matt 4:7). The same truth—God is faithful—is applied in opposite directions. In one context, it is about testing God's faithfulness in *disobedience* to him whereas in the other context it is about testing God's faithfulness in *obedience* to him.

Thus wisdom, because it is application centered, is context bound. We need to evaluate every application of truth in its context and make sense of it in that context. When we bear this in mind, we will see that there is no contradiction in Ecclesiastes. For instance, 6:3–5 says a stillborn child, who has never "seen the sun" (been alive in this world), is better off than a rich man who cannot enjoy his wealth. This means it is not good for this rich man to "see the sun." However, 11:7 says "it is good for the eyes to see the sun." A superficial reading will see contradiction in the two passages. But if we bear in mind how the truth is applied in the respective contexts, we will see no contradiction.

The truth is, according to Ecclesiastes, because "all is vanity," to make sense of life we need to enjoy what we have (2:24–26). So in the context of the rich man who cannot enjoy what he has though he has so much that "his soul lacks nothing that he desires" (6:2), his life is meaningless. A meaningless life is not worth living. Thus it is better off for that rich man not to have been alive. However, if we are able to enjoy what we have, life is worth living and it is good to be alive. Note that 11:7–10 is about how a young man can have enjoyment "in the days of your youth" (11:9).

---

13. Longman, *Proverbs*, 464.

COHERENT MESSAGE

This brings us to the question of whether Ecclesiastes can indeed be interpreted coherently from beginning to end. Most commentators, including some who accept Ecclesiastes as inspired Scripture, deny that it can be done at all. Many even assume that not only 1:2–12:8 (almost the entire book) has perspectives contradictory to that of 12:9–14 (the "epilogue"), there are also contradictory perspectives within 1:2–12:8 itself. This assumption is due mainly to a failure to see the flow of the argument of Ecclesiastes.

Now Ecclesiastes, which from beginning to end dwells relentlessly on the theme that all is vanity because of the certainty of death and the uncertainties of life (1:2–12:8), concludes with, "(when) all has been heard: fear God and keep his commandments" (12:13). In other words, it is a speech designed to persuade the audience that because "All is vanity" (theme of the book), they should therefore "Fear God and keep his commandments" (conclusion of the book). But how does the speaker come to this conclusion?

The flow of the argument is found in 1:2–12:8, but since Ecclesiastes is a speech and not a treatise, the train of thought need not move forward linearly from beginning to end like in the book of Romans. When this is recognized, the flow of the argument can be readily discerned. We need to pay attention to the repetitions of the theme and the sub-themes and consider how they develop the argument from the theme to the conclusion. We will then discover that the argument actually moves forward cyclically and not linearly.

Outline of Contents

The standard way to outline a book of the Bible is to label the content of each section (a paragraph or group of paragraphs) in terms of its topic. When Ecclesiastes is outlined this way, the outline will be seen as a list of disconnected topics randomly juxtaposed together without a coherent structure that unifies the content and unfolds the flow of the book from the beginning to the end. Can this be true of a book of the Bible, especially one with an explicit theme and conclusion? Certainly not. According to Sibley Towner,

> Every piece of literature, down to and including one's laundry list, has a plot. That is to say, it moves according to some logic. It aims at some end and follows some structure in order to reach that end. Certain essays and books display their plots prominently, while others conceal them in elaborate ways. . . . The same is true of biblical texts. They all have internal emphases, main points, punch lines, and the like. . . . Either the book of Ecclesiastes has one of the

most tortuous plots of any book of the Hebrew Bible, or else it has an extremely minimal one.[14]

How then should Ecclesiastes, a persuasive speech with a flow of argument that is presented cyclically and not linearly, be outlined? Since the book is designed to persuade the audience to make a decision on the basis of what has been presented in the speech, the argument in the speech should be able to prepare the audience adequately to make that decision. Otherwise, the "Preacher," the speaker of Ecclesiastes, is an incompetent preacher.

Consider the practice of Billy Graham, the Christian evangelist who preached to more people than anyone who ever lived. At the end of his evangelistic sermons he would call his audience to respond by making a decision to accept Jesus Christ. In a training session for evangelists on preaching evangelistic sermons, Graham said:

> The call to decision—the invitation—is therefore not something just added to the end of an evangelistic sermon as an afterthought. . . . Everything we say in our sermon should, directly or indirectly, point toward the call for decision we will make. . . . I have often found it helpful to confront people with the call to decision throughout the sermon. . . . Throughout the sermon, therefore, I often try to make it clear that the Gospel demands decision involving intellect, emotion, but primarily the will. The whole sermon should reinforce that fact and point toward the invitation.[15]

Evidently this is also the approach of Ecclesiastes, but better. The argument in 1:2–12:8 prepares the audience for the call to decision in 12:13–14. To outline the book, it is not enough to just ask: What is this section talking about (topic)? We need to also ask: What is this section doing here (purpose)? How does it elaborate on the theme, "All is vanity," to help prepare the audience intellectually, emotionally, as well as volitionally for the conclusion, "Fear God and keep his commandments"? We then outline the book in terms of the purpose and not the topic of each of the sections.

Below is the outline upon which the exposition of Ecclesiastes will be based. The coherence of Ecclesiastes in terms of the outline is reflected in how each of the sections contributes to the purpose of the speech toward achieving the goal that the audience would fear God and keep his commandments. The italics in the outline highlight that the speech keeps returning to the theme, indicating that the flow of the argument is cyclical, and not linear.

Identification of Speaker (1:1)
Announcement of Theme: "All Is Vanity" (1:2–3)
Poem to Vivify Idea of Vanity (1:4–11)
Illustrations to Evoke Sense of Vanity (1:12—2:23)

14. Towner, "Book of Ecclesiastes," 276.
15. Graham, "Evangelist's Appeal for Decision," 173–74.

　　　　Vanity of Wisdom (1:12–18)
　　　　Vanity of Pleasure (2:1–11)
　　　　Vanity of Success (2:12–23)
　　Admonition to Carefreeness in Light of Vanity (2:24–26)
　　Poem to Amplify Sense of Vanity (3:1–8)
　　Repetition of Theme: "What Profit Is There?" (3:9)
　　Explanation for Vanity and the Sense of Eternity (3:10–15)
　　Observation to Reinforce Sense of Vanity (3:16–21)
　　Admonition to Carefreeness in Light of Vanity (3:22)
　　Observations to Sustain Sense of Vanity (4:1–5:17)
　　　　Oppression in General (4:1–3)
　　　　Competition for Advancement (4:4–6)
　　　　Addiction to Advancement (4:7–8)
　　　　Admonition to Cooperation (4:9–12)
　　　　Vanity of Power and Popularity (4:13–16)
　　　　Admonition to Fear God (5:1–7)
　　　　Oppression in High Places (5:8–9)
　　　　Addiction to Money (5:10–14)
　　　　Repetition of Theme: "What Profit Is There?" (5:15–17)
　　Elaboration on Carefreeness in Light of Vanity (5:18–6:9)
　　　　Enjoyment of Prosperity (5:18–20)
　　　　Non-Enjoyment of Prosperity (6:1–9)
　　Recapitulation of Theme and Sub-themes (6:10–12)
　　Deliberations on Life in Light of Vanity (7:1–11:6)
　　　　Proverbial Wisdom in Light of Uncertainties of Life (7:1–14)
　　　　Admonitions in Light of Human Wickedness (7:15–8:15)
　　　　　　Fear God and Be Moderate (7:15–29)
　　　　　　Fear God and Be Carefree (8:1–15)
　　　　Elaboration on Uncertainties of Life (8:16–9:6)
　　　　Admonition to Carefreeness (9:7–9)
　　　　Admonition to Carefulness (9:10–11:6)
　　Admonition to Carefreeness in Light of Vanity (11:7–12:7)
　　Encapsulation of Theme: "All is Vanity!" (12:8)
　　Elaboration on Speaker and His Teaching (12:9–12)
　　Conclusion and Call to Decision (12:13–14)

Flow of Speech

As we now flesh out the flow of the speech outlined above to show how each section contributes to the purpose of the speech, we will also highlight the cyclical flow of the argument embedded in the speech. Hence we will also see the coherence of Ecclesiastes in terms of the flow of thought from beginning to end.

The book begins with identifying the speaker (in the third person), indicating that what follows is a speech (1:1). The speaker, or "Preacher," takes the persona of King Solomon, who is uniquely qualified to speak on the subject. Hence it gives the speech an aura of authority right from the beginning. Since the speech concludes with a call to decision (12:13), it is a persuasive speech. We will survey the contents of the speech based on the outline from the perspective of a Preacher like Billy Graham—everything he says in his sermon (persuasive speech) should, directly or indirectly, point toward the call for decision he will make at the end.

The speech begins abruptly by announcing the theme—"All is vanity" (Everything is profitless), which is also phrased as "What profit is there?" (There is no profit). This undoubtedly captures the attention of the audience. The poem that follows then makes vivid the idea that there is nothing new under the sun (1:4–11), which means, there is no net gain (profit) in this temporal world. The idea that all is indeed vanity will then naturally surface in the mind of the audience.

The Preacher then uses his past experiment with wisdom, pleasure, and success to illustrate the reality of vanity so that the audience begins to feel it (1:12–2:23). Having thus spoken to the heart and mind of the audience and hence persuaded them to some extent that all is vanity, he presents the sensible response by admonishing them to enjoy what they have instead of trying to pursue more of the things of this world and in the process fail to enjoy what they have (2:24–26). But to be able to enjoy what they have and thus make sense of life they must be pleasing to God. This is a crucial sub-theme.

The speech then returns (cycles back) to the theme with another poem on vanity (3:1–8). This poem deepens the feeling that all is vanity by reminding the audience that while death is certain, and thus we will eventually lose everything we have, life is uncertain. Thus we may lose everything we have even before we die and we may die young. So "What profit is there?" (3:9). Note that when the theme is first announced, both forms "All is vanity" and "What profit is there?" are used. The theme is formally repeated here and two more times later only as "What profit is there?" (3:9; 5:16; 6:11). In the final formal repetition, it returns to "All is vanity," thus encapsulating the theme (12:8).

When the theme is first announced, it is not (yet) explicit that it is because of the certainty of death that "All is vanity (profitless)"—we will *ultimately* lose everything we gain in this world—which means the theme is realistic and not pessimistic. Actually the Preacher has this in mind all along. For the poem that follows the first announcement begins with, "A generation goes and a generation comes" (1:4). And while illustrating vanity from his experiment with success, the Preacher says *ultimately* a wise man has no advantage over a fool because he also has to die and leave behind all the fruit of his labors (2:14–17). We will again see death highlighted in the remaining formal repetitions of the theme.

Coming back to the second poem, because of the uncertainties of life and the reality of vanity, human beings, with their God-given sense of "eternity," feel insecure about the future and thus want to know the future and if unfavorable, change it; but it is neither possible to know nor change the future (3:10–11, 14a, 15). It is reiterated that, in view of vanity, one should instead have enjoyment (3:12–13). This time, instead of saying that only those who are pleasing to God can have enjoyment, the audience is admonished to "do good in their lifetime." Hence to be pleasing to God is to do good in one's lifetime.

Why does God give humanity the sense of eternity and yet not let them find out the uncertain future and if unfavorable, change it so as to ease their sense of insecurity about the future? "God so works that men (people) should fear him" (3:14b). This means the sense of insecurity is intended to drive us to acknowledge and fear God. For to ease the sense of insecurity we need to acknowledge a God who is watching *over* us. And we cannot do that without first believing in a God who is *watching us*, and thus fear him and do good in our lifetime.

In other words, in view of the certainty of death and the uncertainties of life, one needs to fear God and do good in one's lifetime so as to be pleasing to God in order to ease the sense of insecurity and have enjoyment. If enjoyment is the sensible response to vanity, the fear of God is the sensible way to live. Thus the admonition to have enjoyment is actually an admonition to fear God, which is the solution to vanity. So the argument has now moved forward cyclically from "All is vanity" all the way to "Fear God."

What then is the reason "God so works that men should fear him"? If this is a coherent speech, we expect to hear the answer by the end of the speech. It is obvious by now that the Preacher has been preparing his audience intellectually, emotionally and volitionally to make a commitment to fear God and keep his commandments. Knowing how difficult it is to get a deep and lasting commitment from them, the Preacher seeks to reinforce this basic message in the rest of the speech. To reinforce the feeling that all is vanity, the Preacher highlights the observation that life is so uncertain that even in a court of law, the last bastion for justice, there may be miscarriage of justice (3:16–21). This further drives home the need to have enjoyment (3:22), and thus fear God.

The Preacher then cycles back (again) to the theme of the speech (4:1–5:17). Earlier he illustrated the reality of vanity using his own experience. This enables him to speak with credibility and authority on the subject. But the audience may not be able to identify fully with him because of his unusual personal experience. Now he needs more illustrations from observable human experience which his audience can better identify with. Having just reinforced the sense of vanity through the observation of injustice in the court of law, a form of oppression, he now moves on to an observation of oppression in general to sustain the sense of vanity (4:1–3).

And since oppression is about the abuse of power, he continues with observations on rivalry in the pursuit of power in the form of socio-economic advancement (4:4–6), which can become addictive (4:7–8). He declares repeatedly that this also is "vanity," which confirms that his observations are illustrations of vanity. He then interposes his observations on the rivalry for power with an admonition on the benefits of cooperation (4:9–12). With this and other sensible advice, he wins the trust of his audience as one who knows what he is talking about and so can better persuade them to fear God. He concludes his observations on the pursuit of advancement with the vanity of the ultimate advancement—the vanity of the power and popularity of the king (4:13–16).

Since "God so works that men should fear him," with the natural conclusion of this series of observations on vanity (of power), the Preacher returns to the subject of fearing God (5:1–7). Before (directly) admonishing (for the first time) his audience to fear God, he talks about a matter in their religious life (the making and keeping of vows). This is to ensure that they will not misunderstand what he means by fearing God, which is not merely about observing prescribed religious rituals, but doing what is right (according to God's commandments) even when no one, except God, is watching or holding one accountable—such as keeping one's vows to God (cf. Deut 23:21–23). Thus the argument moves forward again by pointing out implicitly that to fear God is to keep his commandments, which will be spelled out explicitly only at the end of the speech (12:13).

Having clarified what it means to fear God, the Preacher returns to the depressing subject of oppression in the form of corruption in government and talks about it in a way that will arouse anger at corruption (5:8–9). This puts his audience in the right mood to hear him out on a subject that would otherwise not get through to them—the love of money (5:10–14). For, if they are feeling angry with corruption, which is about the love of money, they would be more open to hear him talk about the dangers of loving money—it brings self-imposed cares. He ties this discussion on the misery of loving money to the theme of the speech "What profit is there?" (5:15–17) by highlighting that just as we came into this world with nothing, we will leave this world with nothing. Thus he reinforces his message that, because of the certainty of death, all is vanity and so it makes no sense to love money and be miserable. Instead one needs to respond accordingly, which is to have enjoyment.

So in response to the vanity of loving money, he returns again to the sub-theme of enjoyment. This time he elaborates on this subject and begins to clarify why fearing God is needed to have enjoyment. To be able to have enjoyment, one needs to be relatively free from the cares of this world (5:18–20). For how can one have enjoyment when one is full of cares? This explains why we have labeled the sub-theme of enjoyment in terms of "carefreeness." And to be relatively carefree, one must be free from not only the sense of insecurity but also covetousness. For a covetous heart, such as one that loves money, is a restless heart filled with self-imposed cares (6:1–9). And covetousness violates the last of the Ten Commandments. To overcome covetousness, one has to fear God, for only God watches even what is in the heart. This further clarifies that to fear God is to keep his commandments *from the heart*.

In the previous cycle the connection between "All is vanity" and "Fear God" was already affirmed: Vanity—Enjoyment—Fear God. And the reason for connecting Enjoyment to Vanity was already given, but it is only now that the reason for connecting Enjoyment to Fear God is explained: Vanity—Enjoyment—*Carefreeness*—Fear God. In this sense the cyclical argument has progressed even more.

By now the audience should be adequately moved to seriously consider fearing God and keeping his commandments. To ensure that they would actually make the commitment to do so, the Preacher deliberates on the uncertainties of life. But before he does that, he recapitulates (cycles back to) the theme and the sub-themes (6:10–12). And again the reality of death is highlighted—our life is fleeting like a shadow and we do not know what is going to happen in this world after we are gone.

The Preacher's deliberations on the uncertainties of life take up almost half of the speech (7:1–11:6). No wonder he recapitulated the theme and sub-themes so that his audience will not lose sight of the overall message while he deliberates on the uncertainties of life. Evidently, he spends so much time on the uncertainties of life because it is far more effective than the certainty of death (the focus of the first half of his speech) in bringing (especially young) people to take the vanity of life seriously and so be ready to commit to the most sensible thing to do—fear God so that they can have enjoyment.

The deliberations begin with a list of proverbs (7:1–14) like those in the book of Proverbs. The Preacher thus takes on the role of a wise man and the wisdom displayed not only is relevant to how one should live in light of the uncertainties of life but also demonstrates that he is indeed a man of wisdom.

Since most uncertainties in life, like the oppression of innocent people, are due to human wickedness, the Preacher has much to say about how one should live in light of this reality. Ironically life is so uncertain that the wicked may even be seen to prosper while the righteous suffer (7:15–8:15). Why does this happen? It has already been answered—"God so works that men should fear him" (3:14), that is, this enigmatic reality is so that people would *truly* fear God. Hence the advice is to fear God and be moderate (7:15–29) and thus be carefree so as to have enjoyment (8:1–15).

In case his audience thinks that to be carefree is to be complacent and careless, he elaborates on the uncertainties of life (8:16–9:6) in such a way that to make sense of life one should not only have enjoyment, especially with loved ones (9:7–9), but also be careful. To be careful does not mean to be full of cares as one is to be carefree as well (9:10–11:6). His deliberations on how to live a careful life will make clear that it is not a life full of cares. All this teaches his audience how to live in the various contexts of life in view of uncertainties, and further establishes himself as a wise and trustworthy person.

Before he concludes his argument, he repeats for the last time his admonition to have enjoyment (11:7–12:7). This time he targets young people (which explains the need to deliberate at length on the uncertainties of life) and makes a more direct connection between enjoyment and fearing God by keeping his commandments (11:9–12:1; cf. 12:13–14; see below). Then, immediately following a poem on old age leading to death (12:1–7), he encapsulates the theme with a final formal repetition in the form "All is vanity" (12:8). It serves not only to remind the audience of the sensible connection between the vanity of life and the enjoyment of it, but also makes it unmistakable that 1:2 all the way to 12:8 is about the vanity of temporal life in view of the certainty of death.

This then formally connects the theme "All is vanity" (1:2; 12:8) with the conclusion and call to decision (12:13–14). For following the encapsulation, the very next thing the Preacher says (in the first person) is: "The end (conclusion) of the matter, (when) all has been heard: fear God and keep his commandments" (12:13a). Before sounding this call to decision, there is an elaboration on the Preacher (in the third person). It spells out that he is a wise and trustworthy person to assure the audience that what they have just heard is indeed the truth; and his speech has in fact been prodding them to make a decision (12:9–12).

Sure enough, following this call to decision, the answer to why "God so works that men should fear him" (3:14b) is provided. And it is because, to "fear God and keep his commandments" is God's purpose for humanity (12:13b) and God will one day judge everyone on this basis (12:14). In other words, God is helping everyone to be ready for that final judgment. This is how the speech ends and it shows how closely knit the Preacher's argument is, from the theme of the speech (1:2–12:8) to its conclusion (12:13–14). This shows how coherent the speech is.

In fact, integral to the Preacher's argument in preparing his audience to make the decision to commit to fearing God, he has also been sounding out the reality of God's judgment (whether within or beyond this life) throughout the speech. In the context of the observation on the miscarriage of justice in the courts of law, he assures the audience that God will one day judge both the righteous and the wicked to make things right (3:17). When giving his admonition to fear God in the context of making vows, he warns that one would otherwise face adverse consequences from God (5:6).

And before admonishing his audience to (fear God and) have enjoyment in the face of the enigma that the righteous may suffer and the wicked may prosper (8:14–15), he warns that though the wicked may seem to get away with their evil deeds, it would not go well with them because they do not fear God (8:11–13). Finally, in admonishing young people to have enjoyment, he cautions that they must do so without violating any commandment of God, for God "will bring them to judgment" in how they enjoy themselves (11:9–10; cf. 12:13–14). This further demonstrates how coherent Ecclesiastes is, from the very first verse to the very last verse.

This concise survey of the contents of the speech is to help us see Ecclesiastes as a coherent whole so that we will not miss the "forest" when we get immersed in the "trees." However, it does not do justice to the profound teaching and rhetorical power of the speech. For that, we need to turn to the exposition of Ecclesiastes.

Exposition of Ecclesiastes

THE Old Testament book of Ecclesiastes is essentially a speech. More specifically, it is a persuasive speech. We are told that the words of the speaker are like goads (12:11). They provoke us in order to persuade us. The speaker is helping us to make sense of life by prodding us to come to terms with the certainty of death and the uncertainties of life. What follows is a section-by-section translation of the original Hebrew text accompanied by an exposition. The exposition attempts to recapture the meaning of the ancient speech as well as recreate its persuasive force.

In some sections, there are discussions that are more thorough and technical in nature. These more elaborate analyses address peculiarities or difficulties in the Hebrew text that are significant to the interpretation of not only the respective section but also the book as a whole. They provide firm exegetical support for the translation of the text as well as probe deeper into the meaning of the section. These additional discussions are in the form of excursuses. As in the main exposition, no knowledge of Hebrew is assumed.

Identification of Speaker (1:1)

> 1:1 *The words of Qoheleth, the son of David, king in Jerusalem:*

The author of Ecclesiastes, whoever he is, introduces the book as "the words of Qoheleth." Hence "Qoheleth" is identified as the speaker of the speech from 1:2 up to at least 12:8. In case anyone argues that "the words of Qoheleth" do not stretch all the way to 12:8, the strategic position of "says Qoheleth" at the very beginning (1:2), somewhere in the middle (7:27), and at the very end (12:8), should settle the matter for us.

In Ecclesiastes, Qoheleth is a persona, that is, "a character through whom an author speaks."[1] And it is not a personal name. This Hebrew word most likely means someone who convenes and speaks in a meeting. It has been translated as "the Preacher" or "the Teacher." And he is "the son of David." In the Old Testament this phrase most often, but not always, refers to Solomon. It can refer to any male descendant of

---

1. Fox, *Time*, 372.

King David. This male descendant of David was also a king. Like all Davidic kings he reigned in Jerusalem. Who is Qoheleth?

Qoheleth has to be King Solomon. He is the most obvious choice. In 1:12 the speaker says, "I, Qoheleth, have been king over Israel." Though all Davidic kings reigned in Jerusalem, only Solomon reigned over Israel. Israel was divided into Judah and Israel after Solomon died and thus all subsequent Davidic kings reigned over Judah only. A descendant of David who reigned over Israel must then be Solomon. Thus Qoheleth could not be anyone else except Solomon. Also, the rest of the autobiographical description in 1:12–2:23 matches Solomon perfectly.

Now who would write Ecclesiastes, speaking through a persona that matches the person of Solomon? Traditionally it is believed that it is Solomon himself. So the persona referred to in the book is also the person who wrote it. But based on some technical reasons, most (but not all) scholars today reject the idea that Solomon wrote Ecclesiastes.[2] But for our purpose, it does not matter whether Solomon himself actually wrote Ecclesiastes. So we will not get bogged down here. Even scholars who deny that Solomon wrote the book claim that someone impersonated him. For instance, Choon-Leong Seow denies that the author is Solomon but affirms, "clearly the author intends to equate himself with Solomon."[3] We can then liken the author to a ghostwriter who wrote a rather personal speech for a well-known figure who would deliver it as his own. This figure is so well known and his speech so personal that his identity is unmistakable even though he is not explicitly named.

So for all practical purposes we can assume that the speech comes from Solomon. After all, whether he is the author of Ecclesiastes or not, the speaker is a persona that can only be him, referred to as Qoheleth. This is important. No one else has the kind of credibility and authority that Solomon has to say the things said in the speech. In fact, if Solomon was not the author, this would be the most plausible explanation why anybody would write this particular speech and identify the speaker with a persona that can only be Solomon. For no other human being was (and is) so blessed with temporal and material things like Solomon. He was powerful as king of Israel at her political peak. He was world famous because of his outstanding and incomparable wisdom. He was extremely wealthy. And on top of it all, he had seven hundred wives and three hundred concubines. When someone who has had what he had and says what he says in the next two verses and in the rest of the speech, we listen. We had better!

---

2. For a succinct defense of Solomonic authorship, see Garrett, *Proverbs, Ecclesiastes, Song of Songs*, 254–67.

3. Seow, *Ecclesiastes*, 119.

Exposition of Ecclesiastes

Announcement of Theme: "All Is Vanity" (1:2–3)

> 1:2 "Vanity of vanities," says Qoheleth. "Vanity of vanities, all is vanity!" 1:3 What profit does man have in (exchange for) all his labor which he toils under the sun?

Without warning, Qoheleth grabs our attention with a disturbing assertion (1:2) and then a haunting question (1:3). These two verses are both saying the same thing in two different ways. "Indeed v. 3, a rhetorical question, functions as a response to the assertion of v. 2."[4] Thus the rhetorical question, "What profit does man have in (exchange for) all his labor? [None!]," is an emphatic way of saying, "All is vanity (profitless)!" Like "holy of holies" (the most holy), "vanity of vanities" is the Hebrew way of expressing the superlative. This superlative expression is uttered twice for emphasis. And we already know that these are the words of Qoheleth. So the phrase "says Qoheleth" is redundant in terms of adding information. But not so in terms of adding weight to the claim being made. All this gives the assertion "all is vanity" a force that no attentive audience can miss. It also increases the force of the sentiment implied in the rhetorical question: "There is no profit—*whatsoever!*—under the sun."

These twin verses forcefully announce the theme of the speech. We know 1:2 expresses the theme because it is repeated verbatim in 12:8. The only difference is that "vanity of vanities" is uttered only once there. Besides, the phrase "all is vanity" is repeated exactly several times in the speech (1:14; 2:11, 17; 3:19). As James Crenshaw puts it, "this unforgettable refrain unifies the entire book: from first to last nothing profits those who walk under the sun."[5] Also, the alternative expression of the theme in 1:3 is repeated thrice in the same form, "What profit does man (or the laborer) have?" (3:9; 5:16; 6:11). It is repeated once plainly as, "There is no profit under the sun" (2:11). We have not even mentioned the many instances when a specific item, such as wealth, is labeled as "vanity."

What then is the meaning of the theme? Is it pessimistic as assumed by most interpreters? The Hebrew word translated "vanity" is *hebel*. Its basic meaning is breath (Isa 57:13). It can also refer to the fleeting vapor that we see when someone breathes into cold air (Prov 21:6); it appears and disappears. Qoheleth is saying that everything we work for in this life is vaporous—fleeting! Why then do we translate *hebel* as "vanity," in the sense of "profitless"?

In some contexts in Ecclesiastes the word is best left translated as "fleeting." These are the two clearest examples: "all the days of your *fleeting* life" (9:9) and "the prime of life is *fleeting*" (11:10). In these contexts, the brevity of the prime of life or of life itself is presented as a matter of fact. The focus is on the transitoriness of life or the prime of life, thus calling us to make the most of life, and especially the prime of life, because it will soon be over.

---

4. Horne, *Proverbs-Ecclesiastes*, 383.
5. Crenshaw, *Ecclesiastes*, 35.

In 1:2–3, however, "all is vapor" answers the question, "What profit does man have in (exchange for) all his labor? [None]" Thus "all is vapor" here means "all is profitless." Qoheleth is thus saying that everything is profitless because everything is transitory. How is this so?

The Hebrew word *yitrôn*, translated here as "profit," is a term referring to net gain.[6] The root meaning of the word is "excess over." When used in the context where two items are compared, that is, one has an "excess over" the other, the meaning is "(has) advantage or excel (over)" (2:13; 5:9; 7:12; 10:10, 11). When no such comparison is made, as is the case here, the "excess over" refers simply to net gain or profit (also 2:11; 3:9; 5:16). Profit refers to the net gain over expenditures made over a period of time, often called the fiscal year. An organization may be recording a profit if it balances its accounts in the middle of the fiscal year. But it may be bankrupt by the end of it.

Qoheleth has in mind a "fiscal year" that lasts from our birth all the way to our death when he asks, "What profit does man have?" Commenting on 1:2–3, Crenshaw says, "the author must imply something in these two verses that will come to explicit expression later: the finality of death. Implicit within the word *hebel* is the sense of transience. Perhaps the word *yitrôn* points to this direction, for one cannot calculate the profit or loss of individual activity until it ceases. Prior to this final closure all judgments of expenditures and receipts are necessarily provisional."[7]

That the finality of death is implied can be inferred from the very next verse (1:4): "a generation goes (death) and a generation comes (birth) . . . ." It is confirmed by 12:7, "and the dust returns to the earth as it was, and the (life) breath returns to God who gave it" (cf. Gen 2:7 and 3:19), which explicitly puts death as the context for asserting (again) "Vanity of vanities, all is vanity" in 12:8. When we balance our accounts after we die, what will we have gained from all our labors since the day of our birth? Nothing. In fact, Qoheleth spells out that just as we all came naked into this world, we will all go naked into the next world (5:15). There is no net gain. Death confiscates everything we have ever gained in this world. "So what is the profit to him who toils for the wind?" (5:16).

In other words, Qoheleth is not denying that there is *immediate* (transitory) profit to our labors. Otherwise we will have no reason to labor at all. But in light of death there is no *ultimate* (eternal) profit. Thus in 2:13–14 and elsewhere in the speech (7:12, 19; 8:1; 10:10), he acknowledges the value of wisdom and the advantage of laboring with wisdom. A wise man will be more successful in life than a foolish one. But the wise man must die like the fool and leave behind all the fruit of his labors. So he asserts that even wisdom is (ultimately) profitless (2:14–17).

The translation "labor" (or "toil") captures the idea inherent in the Hebrew word *'āmāl*: human work can be physically or emotionally burdensome, or even both.

6. Cf. Fox, *Time*, 112–13.
7. Crenshaw, *Ecclesiastes*, 60.

In 2:22–23 the man's "labor" is described as a "painful and grievous" task that he "strives" at; "even at night his mind does not rest." If *yitrôn* is the profit, *'āmāl* is the "investment."[8]

Note that in the context of 1:2–3, "*all* is vanity," in the sense that everything is (ultimately) profitless, does not refer to literally *everything* in this world—this would indeed be pessimism. The Hebrew literally reads "*the* all is vapor," and thus the "all" is limited to something "specific and identifiable" from the context.[9] The first time "the all" occurs in the Hebrew Bible the text says, "You shall put *the* all on the palms of Aaron . . ." (Exod 29:24). It refers to everything mentioned in the previous two verses and is most often translated "all these." Here it refers to all that is gained through human effort (1:3)—there is nothing that we gain in this world from our birth to our death that can be taken with us to the next world. This is realism not pessimism.

The phrase "under the sun" refers to the realm of human life and activities in this world as opposed to the hereafter. This is clear from Qoheleth's description of the living as "those who move about *under the sun*" (4:15) and of the dead as those who "will no longer have a share in all that is done *under the sun*" (9:6). However, interpreters and preachers who recognize Ecclesiastes as Scripture inspired by God tend to give it a different meaning, which affects the meaning and application of the book. They resort to such an approach only because they believe "all is vanity" expresses pessimism. So if "under the sun" refers to life in this world, it would mean Ecclesiastes is teaching a pessimistic view of life in this world. Hence they give "under the sun" a different meaning such as when one leaves God out of one's life,[10] which enables them to avoid attributing a supposed pessimistic view of life to inspired Scripture. This is unnecessary as "all is vanity" is not in itself pessimistic (for a discussion on the meaning of "under the sun" and how it has been understood by commentators who give it a different meaning, see "Interpretation of Ecclesiastes" under "The Meaning of 'Under the Sun'").

Seow is undoubtedly correct when he argues that "under the sun" does not have the exact same meaning as "under the heavens," which is very common in the Old Testament but occurs only three times in Ecclesiastes (1:13; 2:3; 3:1).[11] Both phrases mean "this world." But "under the sun" refers to "this (temporal) world," as opposed to the netherworld, whereas "under the heavens" refers to "this (geographical) world,"[12] with

---

8. As indicated in our translation of the phrase "in (exchange for) all his labor" (1:3), the Hebrew preposition which usually means "in," here has the nuance of "in exchange for" (Holmstedt et al., *Qoheleth*, 53). So it can be translated as "for." It has also been translated as "from" (cf. Schoors, *Preacher*, 193). Whether it is "in exchange for" or "from" does not change the meaning of the verse significantly, but "in exchange for" (better than "for") makes a greater emotional impact: there is no ultimate profit *in exchange for* our burdensome investments under the sun!

9. Holmstedt et al., *Qoheleth*, 51.

10. Eaton, *Ecclesiastes*.

11. Seow, *Ecclesiastes*, 104–5.

12. There is a specific purpose in using "under the heavens" instead of "under the sun" in the three

no reference to the hereafter. Thus "under the sun" does not just indicate the realm (of the living) in which everything is ultimately profitless; it also makes reference to the transitoriness of human life in this world.

Qoheleth's distinct preference for this phrase over "under the heavens" is surely not accidental. So "under the sun" further clarifies that Qoheleth has death and ultimate profit in mind when he asks rhetorically, "What profit does man have?" How then do we feel about our burdensome investments (*'āmāl*) under the sun? The rhetorical question of 1:3 prods us to ask whether the transitory profits we *laboriously* pursue after in *this* world is really worth it. But we tend to evade this unpleasant question to avoid the inconvenient truth. In this speech Qoheleth wants us to face it honestly for our own good.

We can now see that translating "all is *hebel*" (1:2; 12:8) as "all is vanity" is appropriate. It forcefully sounds out the warning that everything we gain under the sun is ultimately profitless, and so living for the things of this world is futility. Hence the theme of Ecclesiastes in and by itself is certainly not pessimistic. For to say that all our labors are futile, in the sense that we take nothing with us when we die, is not being pessimistic but simply realistic.

Michael Fox argues that in Ecclesiastes *hebel* means absurd or absurdity, thus making the theme pessimistic. He summarizes his argument as follows: "In other words, 'toil' may be futile [objective reality], but *the fact that* toil is futile is absurd [subjective reaction]."[13] So he himself recognizes that *hebel* (when applied to toil) in and of itself does not mean "absurd," but rather "futile." But *the fact that* toil is futile evokes the reaction that it is absurd. Why is there such a reaction? Because the reality that toil is futile is not acceptable. This happens, we acknowledge, in individuals whose expectations in life are sorely let down by this reality.

Such individuals would include people who put their hopes in the things of this temporal world, who are then bound to pursue after them. In contemporary societies they would do so even to the detriment of their marriage, family and their own health. Thus they do not expect and cannot accept the reality that what they are doing is, in the final analysis, futile as the fruit of their labors is ultimately profitless. So it evokes in them the sense that everything is absurd or meaningless. Hence they react *pessimistically* to the reality that "all is vanity." Given the unprecedented obsession with temporal success in recent history, it is not surprising that the world today is characterized by a prevalent sense of meaninglessness. This may explain why there is

---

contexts it occurs. In 1:13 it spells out that the geographical scope of Qoheleth's investigation covers "everything that has been done under the heavens"—the kind of things that happen *everywhere in this world*. In 2:3 Qoheleth sought to discover "what is good" for humanity "to do" *anywhere in this world* during their fleeting lifetime. And 3:1 introduces a poem about the things that happen *everywhere in this world*. It is crucial to recognize that Qoheleth's investigation and thus the observations he referred to in Ecclesiastes were not limited to what happened in Israel.

13. Fox, *Qoheleth*, 31.

a tendency in recent years to translate "all is *hebel*" as "everything is meaningless (or absurd)."

According to William Brown, the "notion of the absurd is forged not only from a collision between [a man's] expectations and [realities in] the world, but also from a collision within himself."[14] Philosopher Thomas Nagel explains why this internal collision occurs: "Humans have the special capacity to step back and survey themselves, and the lives to which they are committed, with that detached amazement which comes from watching an ant struggle up a heap of sand."[15] The "detached amazement" becomes "attached disillusionment" when we realize that we are that ant, and its futile and senseless struggle up a heap of sand is a reflection of ours.

As affirmed by even atheist philosopher Paul Edwards in his classic essay on the meaning and value of human life,[16] our temporal life will make sense only if and when there is a worthwhile purpose to live for (see further "Teaching of Ecclesiastes" under "Fulfilling the Purpose of Life"). Philosophers may have different theories about what constitutes a worthwhile purpose. But given the painful realities of life under the sun, can a life that is given to the pursuit of vaporous things be experienced as meaningful?

According to renowned psychiatrist Viktor Frankl, "For too long we have been dreaming a dream from which we are now waking up: the dream that if we just improve the socioeconomic situation of people, everything will be okay, people will become happy. The truth is that as the *struggle for survival* has subsided, the question has emerged: *survival for what*? Ever more people today have the means to live, but no meaning to live for."[17] To substantiate, he reports that a former assistant of his at Harvard University could show that "among graduates of that university who went on to lead quite successful, ostensibly happy lives, a huge percentage complained of a deep sense of futility, asking themselves what all their success had been for."[18] He then asks, "Does this not suggest that what today is so often referred as 'mid-life crisis' is basically a crisis of meaning?"[19]

Thus many people do actually experience futility and meaninglessness. But Fox has wrongly assumed that every human being must have the same expectations. There are people, even if they are a minority in contemporary societies, who do not put their hopes in temporal things. Therefore they have different expectations. The reality that "all is futility" need not evoke in them the sense that everything is meaningless or absurd. These are people who have intellectually as well as emotionally come to terms with the reality that all is vanity. They know and accept that when they die, they cannot take with them anything from the fruit of their labors. So the most sensible

---

14. Brown, *Character in Crisis*, 132.
15. Nagel, "Absurd," 720; cited in Brown, *Character in Crisis*, 132.
16. Edwards, "Meaning of Life."
17. Frankl, *Unheard Cry for Meaning*, 21.
18. Frankl, *Unheard Cry for Meaning*, 21.
19. Frankl, *Unheard Cry for Meaning*, 21.

thing to do is to enjoy what they have when they still have them. They recognize that it is meaningless to crave after the "good things" of this world. For they know this will cause them to pursue after them in such a way that they cannot enjoy what they already have, whether marriage, family, or even material luxuries. Thus they respond *realistically* to the reality that everything is futility.

As we shall see, this is actually Qoheleth's own response and is a central teaching of Ecclesiastes. So neither Ecclesiastes the book nor Qoheleth the speaker is being pessimistic just because many people react to the theme of the speech pessimistically. It is true that the rhetorical question in 1:3 comes with a somber tone. It can easily be misinterpreted as conveying pessimism. But it is no more pessimistic than the somber rhetorical question that Jesus Christ asked, "What profits a man to gain the whole world and forfeit his soul?" (Mark 8:36).

In fact Jesus has commanded his followers: "Do not lay up for yourselves treasures on earth. . . . But lay up for yourselves treasures in heaven. . . . For where your treasure is, there will your heart be also" (Matt 6:19–21). So there is such a thing as spiritual and eternal profits ("treasures in heaven") which one can lay up while still living under the sun. Even if Qoheleth was aware of it, he ignored this kind of profit in his speech. He spoke exclusively about material and temporal profits ("treasures on earth") even when he was considering the profits of righteousness (see exposition of 8:14–15). Hence when he declared, "there is no profit under the sun," he was not ruling out "treasures in heaven."

However, followers of Jesus who are committed to obey this command face a major obstacle. For, being human and living in a covetous world, they are under pressure to conform to the rest of humanity in the pursuit of "treasures on earth." This must have led Henry Martyn, a nineteenth century missionary known for "forsaking all for Christ,"[20] to pray: "May I have Christ here with me in the world; not substituting imagination in the place of faith; but seeing outward things as they really are, and thus obtaining a radical conviction of their vanity."[21] For "a radical conviction" concerning the vanity of the things of this world would set his heart free to obey the command of Jesus to lay up "treasures in heaven."

Qoheleth's persuasive speech is designed to cultivate just such a conviction. People like Henry Martyn would see Ecclesiastes as God's answer to their prayer. They will thus respond *optimistically* to the reality that "there is no profit under the sun." To them "all is vanity" is actually most meaningful! And of course this optimistic response and the realistic response admonished by Qoheleth—to have enjoyment in life—are not mutually exclusive. So according to the Bible, it is possible to "have the best of both worlds," this and the next!

We can now conclude what "all is *hebel* (vanity)" means: In the light of death everything we gain in this world is transitory and is thus ultimately profitless and

---

20. Henry, *Forsaking All for Christ*.
21. Sargent, *Henry Martyn*, 227–28; cited in Bridges, *Ecclesiastes*, 7.

worthless even though items that come under this sweeping conclusion, such as wisdom and wealth, may have temporal profit and worth. Hence the pursuit of the things of this world is ultimately futile. (For an elaborate essay showing that in Ecclesiastes *hebel* can carry not only this but also other nuances of "profitless" as well as mean "futile," and thus is best translated as "vanity" when it does not mean "fleeting," see "Interpretation of Ecclesiastes" under "The Meaning of *Hebel*." That essay provides the linguistic basis for our interpretation and translation of *hebel* in our exposition of Ecclesiastes).

Therefore "all is vanity" is realism and not pessimism. However, to one who, for whatever reason, is not able or willing to come to terms with this reality, it is pessimism. But this is a listener's response and not the speaker's meaning. Since different listeners can respond differently to the speaker's meaning, any translation that reflects only one possible response is misleading. This includes, "everything is meaningless" even though it strikes a responsive chord in the hearts of very many people today.

Distinguishing Qoheleth's intended meaning and the listener's individual response is crucial to the understanding of not only the theme but also the rest of the speech. But is it really possible to recover Qoheleth's intended meaning? This present writer believes that at least some, if not most, readers of this exposition are able to follow his trend of thought. Otherwise, why bother to write at all? He is thus confident that those who can make coherent sense of his exposition do recover at least the essence of his own intended meaning. On this basis he is assuming that if we could make coherent sense of Qoheleth's speech as a whole, we would have recovered essentially not only the intended meaning of the speech, but also its persuasive force. After all, Qoheleth expects his audience to understand at least the essence of his speech and feel some of its persuasive force. For in 12:13 he summarily exhorts them to make a decision based on the speech.

POEM TO VIVIFY IDEA OF VANITY (1:4–11)

> *1:4 A generation goes and a generation comes,*
>   *Yet the world remains as ever.*
> *1:5 The sun rises and the sun sets,*
>   *Panting (back) to the place where it rises.*
> *1:6 Blowing to the south,*
>   *Turning to the north,*
>   *Round and round the wind blows,*
>   *On (account of) its rounds the wind returns.*
> *1:7 All the streams flow to the sea,*
>   *Yet the sea is never full.*
>   *To the place where the streams flow,*
>   *There they flow again.*

Our Reason for Being

> *1:8 All things are wearying,*
>   *A man is not able to speak,*
>   *An eye is not sated by seeing,*
>   *An ear is not filled by hearing.*
>
> *1:9 Whatever has happened, that is what will happen; whatever has been done, that is what will be done; there is nothing new under the sun. 1:10 Is there something of which one might say, "See this. It is new"? It has already happened in the ages which were before us. 1:11 There is no remembrance of those in the past; and also, there will be no remembrance of those in the future among those who will come after them.*

Having forcefully announced the theme of his speech, Qoheleth recites a poem. Verses 1:4–8 present the poem proper. The meaning is spelled out in 1:9—(in spite of constant activity) "there is nothing new under the sun," that is, there is nothing added and thus there is no net gain. The different cycles of activity graphically present this idea in different ways. Verses 1:10–11 then explain and defend why this conclusion is true. Hence the assertion in 1:2–3 that there is no profit under the sun is immediately followed by a poem that makes vivid the idea that under the sun there is nothing new and thus there is no net gain.

The poem begins with the proclamation that though there is a continuous cycle of one generation of people being replaced by the next—the "going" (death) of one generation and the "coming" (birth) of another generation—the world remains the same.[22] Thus there is nothing new and there is no net gain.

However, like most sweeping statements, the claim that there is nothing new in this world is not to be taken without qualifications. A basic principle behind linguistic communication is that the listener cooperates with the speaker. The listener is often expected to supply the qualifications, especially when the speaker is making a sweeping statement. If a newspaper headline reads, "History Repeats Itself," a fair-minded reader would not find fault by highlighting exceptions to falsify the statement. He would, as is expected of him, seek to determine from the context in what sense the statement is true.

From the context of the speech, we see that Qoheleth is not saying there is nothing new under the sun in terms of technological inventions. Specifically, he is saying that what has happened will happen again and what has been done will be done again (cf. 3:15). This covers both human activities and natural phenomena. This means humanity and the natural (as opposed to man-made) conditions in which humans live do not change. The result is that there is nothing new in what humans basically

---

22. Our interpretation of the second half of 1:4—the world of humanity as we know it remains the same—differs from that of most Bible translations, which interpret it to mean the physical earth remains forever. The basis for our interpretation and why we prefer it is discussed below (Excursus to 1:4–11).

experience, and in how and why they typically act or react. In this narrow sense history repeats itself.

Even new technological inventions are ultimately just different means to meet the same old unchanging needs. A spaceship, as a means for transport, is not really new. A boat, whether made of steel or of reed, has been a means for transport since time immemorial. The difference is in degree (how fast and how far one can travel in it) and not in kind. Hence the world has not really changed. To interpret otherwise and find fault with Qoheleth is to be uncooperative.

The regularity of natural phenomena (as illustrated by the sun, the wind and the streams) is obvious. In the human realm, we observe that in our own capitalistic society people are motivated by competition to toil and succeed. As Qoheleth tells us later, he had observed that, "every toil and every skillful work is due to a man's rivalry with his neighbor" (4:4). The form may be different but the essence is the same. That was more than two thousand years ago.

Thus, despite the constant replacement of one generation by the next, human nature and human behavior have not changed. And despite undeniable economic and technological advancement, many today are asking, "Why has progress failed?" To the rest who are still optimistic about "progress," Christopher Lasch has written a scholarly book to answer a simple question: "How does it happen that serious people continue to believe in progress, in the face of massive evidence that might have been expected to refute the idea of progress once and for all?"[23] Therefore, despite constant movement there is no net gain, as there is nothing really new.

So the poem stimulates our imagination in order to vivify the idea of vanity in our minds. It is significant that Qoheleth says, "a generation *goes* and a generation *comes*," and not the reverse as expected. He is thinking of a constant cycle of one generation being replaced by the next. And by highlighting the *going* of the older generation, Qoheleth provides the broader context for his sweeping claim that (in light of death) everything is (ultimately) profitless (1:2–3).

The sun, the wind and the streams vividly illustrate the idea that in this world there is no net gain despite endless toils. Sunrise and sunset is depicted as the sun panting from the place it rises to the place it sets and then to the place from where it rises all over again (1:5). This conjures the image of constant tiresome activity with no net gain. Similarly, the wind is pictured as going in rounds with no net gain (1:6).[24]

---

23. Lasch, *True and Only Heaven*, 13.

24. We have translated the Hebrew preposition in 1:6, which usually means "on (its rounds)," as "on account of (its rounds)." With Seow we have followed Ellermeier, who argues that the preposition here indicates purpose, thus meaning "on account of" or "for the sake of" (Seow, *Ecclesiastes*, 108; Ellermeier, *Qohelet*, 200–201). Even Schoors, who does not prefer this view, admits that "this is an attractive variant" (Schoors, *Preacher*, 201). Both translations fit the context and do not change the meaning of the verse significantly. We prefer Ellermeier's variant because it highlights the idea of constant activity without net gain more vividly: the wind returns again and again not because there is any gain to be got. So whenever we feel the wind blowing, we are told that it is doing so simply *for the sake of* its endless rounds.

As for the streams, though they continuously pour water into the sea, the sea is never "full" (1:7), in the sense that "the sea can always take more water."[25] This is the most vivid depiction of endless toils with no net gain.

"All things," as illustrated by the endless activities of the sun, wind and streams, says Qoheleth, "are wearying" (1:8) both to them and to the observer. Qoheleth is in effect making the claim that everything that is done under the sun (in this temporal world)—the constant toiling without net gain—is wearying, that is, wearisome to both participant and observer. And in the last two lines of 1:8, he forcefully presents two phenomena within humanity which vividly exemplify endless activity without net gain that parallel that of the unfilled sea: the eyes are never sated with seeing and the ears are never filled with hearing. As is common in Hebrew poetry, the two corresponding ideas in the parallel lines ("not sated" and "not filled"), though the second refines the meaning of the first, are saying the same thing: the eyes and ears are constantly receiving stimuli and yet they are never "sated" by being "filled"; like the unfilled sea, they can always take in more and more.

Since this poem illustrates the futility of human toil, the statement "all things are wearying" focuses our attention on the wearying human labor (*'āmāl*) expended to gain temporal profit (*yitrôn*) that does not last.[26] Hence the poem vivifies not only the idea of "no net gain" but also the laboriousness of the toil involved. Qoheleth then graphically describes the human response: "A man is not able to speak," that is, it leaves us "speechless";[27] Duane Garrett notes that the verb "to speak" in this verbal form can occur without an object (Gen 24:15; Job 1:16; 16:4, 6); supplying an object like "it" distorts the meaning of the verse.[28]

Then 1:9 simply spells out what is implicit in the poem: since what happens and will happen has happened before, there is nothing new, and thus no net gain, under the sun. What is left to be said in 1:10–11 is to answer possible objections to this

---

25. Fox, *Time*, 166. Our interpretation of 1:7b is the same as that of ESV, HCSB, NASB, and NRSV, but differs from that of NIV, NKJV, NLT, and NJPS—*circular* flow of the water: "To the place the streams come from, there they return again" (NIV). Both interpretations are possible grammatically (Holmstedt et al., *Qoheleth*, 60). However, contextually, the poem is about *observable* phenomena. The NIV interpretation assumes 1:7 describes a phenomenon that cannot be directly observed: "*although* all the rivers flow into the sea, the sea does not overflow *because* the water returns to its source through evaporation" (Whybray, *Ecclesiastes*, 43). In either case, the basic meaning of the verse is clear: though the rivers are constantly pouring water into the sea, there is no net gain to the sea.

26. Seow's analysis on the word translated "wearying" shows that "the distinction 'weary' (being worn out) and 'wearisome' is one made in English, not Hebrew" (Seow, *Ecclesiastes*, 109). So the translation "all things are *wearying*" preserves the ambiguity, leaving it to the context to determine whether it is "weary" or "wearisome," or even both, as is the case here. Fox objects to the translation "all *things* are wearying" because the Hebrew word "*dabar* ['word' or 'thing'] is nowhere used of physical entities" (Fox, *Time*, 167) and so "all things" cannot refer to the sun, wind and streams. But we are not saying that "all things (lit., all-the-things)" refers to the sun, wind and streams, but to their activities as in: "Then the servant told Isaac all-the-things (everything) that he had done" (Gen 24:66).

27. Whybray, *Qoheleth*, 44.

28. Garrett, *Proverbs, Ecclesiastes, Song of Songs*, 287.

conclusion. The most likely objection is that there are happenings that we can genuinely say are new because we have neither seen nor heard of them before. Qoheleth preempts this by insisting that they have happened before. He further insists that we are not aware of them because the remembrance of them and of those who committed them have not been passed down to us. In 1:11 there is ambiguity over whether the lack of "remembrance" is about things that happen, people who do them, or the ages (times) in which these things happen.[29] In our translation we have left the options open: "There is no remembrance of those (things/people/ages) in the past . . . those (things/people/ages) in the future." This makes sense because in reality the three options cannot be separated—Qoheleth is saying there is no remembrance of the things people do during their times (ages).

It is difficult to argue with Qoheleth. Consider Karl Polanyi, an economic historian who claims that the supply-and-demand price-fixing mechanism that characterizes our modern market economy is something new and did not operate in a premodern economy. This view is widely accepted even by those who have never read him. Economist Morris Silver challenges Polanyi's position "by confronting his factual assertions with available evidence."[30] For instance, Polanyi asserts that even the Assyrian trading station in Anatolia (ancient Turkey) carried on an ample international trade without price-making markets.[31] Based mainly on the work of Assyriologist K. R. Veenhof,[32] Silver concludes,

> The evidence on price formation at the Assyrian trading station in Anatolia is fully consistent with the operation of market forces of the usual kind. The thousands of business documents from the station refer to changes in the demand for the supply of the main import goods (tin and textiles) and to the effects of seasonality and emergency, and they record price changes. The price changes, including a change of more than 20 percent in the price of tin over a short period, are inconsistent with Polanyi's position.[33]

We are talking about international trade at about 1800 BC, more than three thousand years before the rise of our modern market economy! Also, as pointed out by Silver, the phrase "at the going (market) price" occurs frequently in Babylonian texts of about the same time.[34] Polanyi claims, "See this. It is new!" Silver counterclaims: "It has already happened in the ages which were before us." Now those Assyrian and Babylonian documents were once lost and forgotten and were rediscovered by modern archaeology. This echoes eloquently, "There is no remembrance of those

---

29. Cf. Longman, *Ecclesiastes*, 75; Whybray, *Ecclesiastes*, 46.
30. Silver, *Economic Structures of Antiquity*, 95.
31. Silver, *Economic Structures of Antiquity*, 96.
32. Veenhof, *Old Assyrian Trade*; Veenhof, "Prices and Trade."
33. Silver, *Economic Structures of Antiquity*, 98.
34. Silver, *Economic Structures of Antiquity*, 99.

in the past; and also, there will be no remembrance of those in the future among those who will come after them."

Garrett sums it all up succinctly, "For us . . . , as for our ancient predecessors, the sun rises and sets; the rivers run their courses; people continue their endless quest for fame, power, and happiness even as they move steadily toward death."[35] There is nothing new under the sun. All is vanity. Thus the first eleven verses of Ecclesiastes lead us to ask, what then is the point of living? What is the meaning of life?

Excursus to 1:4–11: Qoheleth's View of History

Graham Ogden, though he acknowledges that "most commentators" adopt the view that the first half of 1:4 refers "to generations of humankind replacing one another on the earth," prefers the view that the verse "contrasts a circular movement within nature with the steadfast and immovable earth."[36] Even then he notes that "Seow has pointed out that *dôr* ['generation'] in combination with the verbs [sic] *hlk* 'go', speaks of death, thus the coming and going of the generations speaks of the cycle of life as one generation replaces another."[37] Since "generation" (of people) makes so much sense in this context, "There is no reason to depart from the accepted interpretation."[38]

And since most translators render the second half of 1:4 differently as "but the (physical) earth remains (lasts) *forever*" instead of "yet the earth (the world) remains *as ever* (does not change)," we need to address this possibility. As Fox puts it, 1:4 "is commonly understood to contrast the permanence of the [physical] earth with the ephemerality of the generations."[39] He objects to this dominant interpretation because "the permanence of the physical earth has no relevance to the individual life."[40] This may not be true, especially in the context of a poem, where experience and not reason is the focus. Alister McGrath recognizes that for some people, "when contemplating the starlit heavens . . . , the lonely pinpoints of light against the dark velvet of the night speak of loneliness and pointlessness. Those same stars have witnessed generations rising and falling. Human empires rise and fall, the same stars shone down on them all. The same stars shone while generation after generation flourished, and passed into the dust. . . . The heavens thus heighten our sense of transience, forcing us to ask whether this life is all that we can hope for."[41]

Thus it is possible to live with the apparently incongruent contrast that Fox points out. The verse then graphically paints the picture of the transitoriness ("All is vapor")

---

35. Garrett, *Proverbs, Ecclesiastes, Song of Songs*, 288.
36. Ogden, *Qoheleth*, 35.
37. Ogden, *Qoheleth*, 35; Seow, *Ecclesiastes*, 106.
38. Schoors, *Preacher II*, 355.
39. Fox, *Time*, 166.
40. Fox, *Time*, 166.
41. McGrath, *Glimpsing the Face of God*, 6, 8.

introduced in 1:2 that results in ultimate profitlessness ("What profit is there?") in 1:3. However, it is possible to avoid contrasting the transitoriness of human generations with the permanence of the physical earth altogether. Fox has pointed out that the Hebrew word for "earth" in a number of contexts means (figuratively) "humanity." A very good example is in Gen 11:1, "Now the whole *earth* [i.e., humanity] used the same language and the same words." Another unmistakable example is in Ps 33:8, "Let the *earth* fear the LORD; Let the *inhabitants of the world* stand in awe of him." In this context, the word "earth" not only must include humanity, it is clearly paralleled in meaning to "inhabitants of the world."

Since not only the generations of humanity, but also the natural phenomena experienced by humanity, are said to be moving in cycles (1:5–7), we have translated 1:4 as "a generation goes and a generation comes, yet the *world* remains as ever." And since humanity and its world and not the physical earth is in mind, the translation "(the world) *remains* as ever"[42] is preferred to "(the earth) *stands* (remains) forever." This translation is valid because the Hebrew verb *'āmad* ("stand") can mean "remain unchanged," as in Lev 13:5; Ps 33:11; 102:26 [Heb. v. 27]; Jer 32:14; 48:11.[43] Therefore, despite one generation being repeatedly replaced by another (1:4a), there is no change or net gain in this world (1:4b). We have adopted this interpretation in the translation of 1:4 because it fits better the theme of the poem that this verse introduces—there is nothing new and thus there is no net gain under the sun.

As pointed in the exposition above, this means history repeats itself in some sense. Craig Bartholomew, who assumes that Ecclesiastes was written against a Greek background,[44] claims that "this poem expresses, on the basis of observation, a [cosmic] cyclical view of history, in contrast to the OT's cyclical *and linear* view."[45] In other words, history repeats itself in a cosmic sense. It is believed that this (cyclical) view of history has "origins . . . in the dim past in the cultures of Mesopotamia and Egypt. These origins are related to observations of the birth-death cycle of life, the cyclic shedding of the skin by the serpent, and the cycles of the sun and moon. Man the thinker and inventor of hypotheses soon developed philosophical ideas of cosmic cycles which became the typical view of history in the great civilizations especially of India and Greece; also in China this notion is found in a unique and indigenous form."[46]

Hence the view that history repeats itself in "cosmic cycles" was the prevalent view of history in the ancient world. Consider this ancient Greek view of how history repeats itself: "the same events, the same things, and the same persons under the same

---

42. Seow, *Ecclesiastes*, 106.
43. Seow, *Ecclesiastes*, 106.
44. Bartholomew, *Ecclesiastes*, 54–59.
45. Bartholomew, *Ecclesiastes*, 145.
46. Cairns, *Philosophies of History*, xvi.

circumstances would everlastingly recur in every cycle."[47] In other words, "history has no beginning and would have no end; and in the eternal cyclical pattern of the universe, Socrates would drink the hemlock again and again."[48] And thus Hitler would return to repeat the Second World War to perpetuate the cosmic cycles of history.

It is tempting to attribute this ancient view to Qoheleth. For in this poem he recounts not only the death-birth cycle, but also the cycles of the sun. However, since Qoheleth was an Israelite and Ecclesiastes is canonized in the Old Testament, we need to be cautious in jumping to such a conclusion, which renders him unorthodox. Actually the Greek cyclical view of history as presented above is not the only form of cyclicism. And it is hard to imagine a modern person subscribing to this form. A form that we find in modern times "restricts cyclicism to the rise and fall of nations and civilizations . . . [and thus] history is repetitive but each subsequent repetition is different in important ways."[49] Such repetitions can indeed be observed in ancient as well as in modern times. The question is whether there is an end to this cyclical flow of history.

In the context of 1:2–11, it is clear that Qoheleth's purpose in reciting this poem is to illustrate that, since there is nothing new under the sun, there is no net gain or profit under the sun. There is no evidence that he philosophized his observations of the death-birth cycle and the cycles of nature to a view of history that contradicts the biblical view. Since he alludes to the creation and fall of humanity (7:29; cf. Genesis 1–3) and thus affirms a beginning to history, there is evidence that he subscribes to the Old Testament view of history.

Now Bartholomew himself notes that the Old Testament view of history is not only linear—with a beginning moving toward a goal at the end—but also cyclical.[50] This is most explicitly described in the book of Judges and is summarized in Judges 2:11–19. Thus the Old Testament does observe a cyclical dimension to the flow of history. Hence there is room within the Old Testament view of history for a poem that highlights the cyclical dimension of history to illustrate a point. In fact this poem makes a crucial contribution to the biblical view of history by *explicitly* qualifying that the biblical view of history is not a straight-line kind of "linear" flow from the beginning to the end. Rather, it is a linear-cyclical flow. For though history is moving toward a goal, there are repetitions along the way that can be observed.

However, Qoheleth makes it clear that the repetition is not that of the same persons returning to repeat history to perpetuate the cycles of history, but that of one generation replacing another to "repeat" history to continue the flow of history to its goal. We have already indicated above in what (narrow) sense "history repeats itself" (see further the discussion on 3:15 in Excursus to 3:10–15). It is important to clarify

---

47. Cairns, *Philosophies of History*, 206.
48. Montgomery, *Shape of the Past*, 42.
49. Nash, *Meaning of History*, 32.
50. Cf. Montgomery, *Shape of the Past*, 41–45.

Qoheleth's view of history because, if his view is "cyclical" without end and not linear-cyclical toward a goal, his view of the meaning of life will be very different from what is presented in this exposition (see "Teaching of Ecclesiastes" under "Experiencing the Meaning of History").

ILLUSTRATIONS TO EVOKE SENSE OF VANITY (1:12–2:23)

Vanity of Wisdom (1:12–18)

> 1:12 I, Qoheleth, have been king over Israel in Jerusalem. 1:13 I set my heart to inquire and to explore by wisdom everything that has been done under the heavens. It is a grievous preoccupation (that) God has given to the children of man with which to be occupied. 1:14 I observed all the deeds that have been done under the sun, and look! all is vanity and a pursuit after wind.
> 1:15 What is made crooked cannot be straightened;
>   What is lacking cannot be counted.
> 1:16 I said to myself, "Look! I have increased greatly in wisdom beyond all who were over Jerusalem before me." Now my heart has seen much wisdom and knowledge. 1:17 But when I set my heart to know wisdom and to know stupidity and folly, I realized that even this is a pursuit after wind.
> 1:18 For in much wisdom is much vexation;
>   And an increase in knowledge is an increase in pain.

Qoheleth now begins to speak conversationally. Though this passage is not the actual beginning of the speech, it is here that Qoheleth begins to recount how he came to the conclusion expressed in 1:2–11, which functions more like a prologue to the speech proper.

The phrase in 1:12 translated "I have been king" is often translated "I was king" because the Hebrew verb, as Seow points out, "is commonly taken to indicate a past fact."[51] But the grammatical form of this verb used here "need not indicate past realities [and] may also indicate an existing state, a reality that began in the past but continues into the present."[52] Translating it as "I was king" rules out Solomon as the author of Ecclesiastes since he remained king until his death. But this translation is questionable. Seow rejects this translation even though he does not accept Solomonic authorship. For even if the dominant view that an anonymous author impersonated Solomon using the persona Qoheleth is correct, he would not have made Qoheleth say "I was king" since Solomon died while he was still king. While translating the phrase as "I have been king" does not necessarily indicate Solomonic authorship, it does leave the option open.

---

51. Seow, *Ecclesiastes*, 119.
52. Seow, *Ecclesiastes*, 119.

In the same vein, even though before Solomon there was only one Israelite king (David) who ruled over Jerusalem, Qoheleth's boast that he was wiser than "all (the kings) who were over Jerusalem before me" (1:16) does not rule out Solomon as the author. Based on similar language in Akkadian literature, Seow concludes that, "This is a stock phrase in royal boast.... Hence, even though Qohelet is assuming the role of Solomon, there is no need to ask if he had slipped in the plural reference to his predecessors in Jerusalem . . . or if he was referring to pre-Israelite kings. Qohelet is adopting the language and style of royal propagandistic literature."[53]

In this section Qoheleth reveals that he had committed himself ("set his heart") to a comprehensive (philosophical) investigation into human experience ("to inquire and explore with wisdom everything that has been done") everywhere in this world ("under the heavens"). What was he trying to achieve? What did he want to know about human experience everywhere in this world? Why did he make his investigation comprehensive? The goal of any comprehensive investigation of what we observe or experience in this world is not just to understand the parts but also to make sense of the whole. That is how the human mind works.

Hence it is not surprising that an introductory book on philosophy, which is a comprehensive rational investigation based on "raw material [that] comes directly from the world [observations under the heavens] and our relation to it [experience under the sun]" is entitled *What Does It All Mean?*[54] Qoheleth was thus seeking a comprehensive understanding of human experience to make sense of human life as a whole. He was trying to answer the question: "What is human life all about? What does it all mean?" He was thus searching for the meaning of life.[55]

As we have seen, the most important ingredient of the meaning of life is a worthwhile overall purpose. For without such a purpose life does not make sense. And philosopher Keith Ward adds, "When people complain that life is meaningless, they often mean they cannot see how the events that happen to them fit into any overall pattern. To see the meaning of a human life would be to see how its various elements fit into a unique, complex, and integrated pattern."[56] Thus, to have a truly meaningful life we must not only have a worthwhile purpose to live for but we must also be able to see how the different aspects of our life, especially the painful ones, contribute to that overall purpose (see further "Teaching of Ecclesiastes" under "Perceiving Coherence in Life").

As we shall see from his speech, Qoheleth's comprehensive study covers both these ingredients of the meaning of life. He was trying to find meaning and purpose to different human experiences as well as to human life as a whole. He first made philosophical evaluations of his own personal experiences (1:12–2:26) as well as

53. Seow, *Ecclesiastes*, 124.
54. Nagel, *What Does It All Mean*, 4.
55. Cf. Bartholomew, *Ecclesiastes*, 123.
56. Ward, "Religion and Meaning," 22.

his personal observations (3:16–8:15). And based on these evaluations he made the philosophical conclusion that life as a whole is vanity (1:14). As he recounts his findings in this speech, he also seeks to show how this philosophical conclusion fits into a bigger coherent picture, one that presents the meaning of life. We will piece this picture together as we move along (for a concise presentation of this coherent picture as a whole, see "Introduction to Ecclesiastes").

In a sense the present passage (1:12–18) is the actual beginning of the speech proper. Here Qoheleth begins to recount his experiences and later his observations, interspersed with evaluations and admonitions, before finally concluding with the exclamation, "Vanity of vanities! All is vanity" in 12:8. Thus the announcement of the theme (1:2–3) and the vivification of it (1:4–11) can be viewed as the conclusion of the deliberations that begin at 1:12 and go all the way to 12:7.

This is why we did not hesitate to use in advance examples of vanity from the later parts of Qoheleth's speech when we explicated the meaning of his philosophical conclusion, "all is vanity," first announced in 1:2. He is not saying that this conclusion itself constitutes the meaning of life. But, as just pointed out, even as he shows how he came to this conclusion, he also shows how this conclusion fits into a bigger coherent picture that presents the meaning of life. He can do this, and quite early in the speech (see exposition on 3:1–15), because he has already announced and vivified the conclusion beforehand (1:2–11).

The philosophical conclusion is simply an observable reality that would and should cause us, as it did Qoheleth, to search further for the meaning of life. For if everything is vanity, what is the point of living? How does this painful reality fit into the overall purpose of life? How then shall we live? But many today would just react to this reality with pessimism and conclude that life is meaningless. They would rather accept and endure this pessimism than to search further. Some do not even try perhaps because they do not want to consider or reconsider how they should then live, or they do not know where to begin. Others have tried before but found the attempt itself even more meaningless. Perhaps Qoheleth can help all of them. He speaks with the authority that comes from a comprehensive investigation as well as incomparable wisdom and experience.

Recall that when he announced "All is vanity" as the theme of his speech (1:2–3), he used a poem to vivify the idea of profitlessness (1:4–8). Now, as he illustrates various pursuits of vanity (1:12–6:9), he continues to vivify the idea of futility (of the pursuits): every human endeavor under the sun is like pursuing or chasing after wind (1:14; also, 2:11, 17, 26; 4:4, 6, 16; 6:9). He is out to persuade us. We may not grasp the far-reaching implication of the theme of his message unless we first grasp it vividly in our minds. Then, as we now see, Qoheleth builds on it by evoking the sense of vanity in our hearts. For if his message does not also move our emotion, how can he move our volition?

His illustrations of vanity from his own experience (1:12–2:23) start the ball rolling in speaking to our hearts as well. In this first illustration (1:13–18) he confesses that the very intellectual effort that led him to recognize that everything is vanity (profitless) is itself vanity (futile)! For having concluded that everything is vanity (1:14), he also realized that human knowledge and wisdom could not do anything about it (1:15; see below). Death will certainly confiscate whatever profits we may have gained under the sun. But in the mind of Qoheleth, death is not the only reason for the impermanence of human gains. He will soon highlight that our temporal profits can be lost even before we die (3:1–9). They may be lost immediately through calamities or crimes, if not through our own carelessness or foolishness. We live under the constant threat that whatever we value, including life itself, will not only be lost ultimately but may also be lost immediately. And this reality cannot be changed.

Qoheleth was an exceptionally wise man—he has "seen much wisdom and knowledge" and thus "greatly increased in wisdom" (1:16). Yet even *he* feels helpless. He captures this sentiment proverbially: "What is made crooked [qualitative deficiency] cannot be straightened; what is lacking [quantitative deficiency] cannot be counted" (1:15). In other words, human nature and human experience cannot be reordered so as to remove the constant threat and the certain reality of suffering loss. It is again very difficult to argue with Qoheleth. To fault him we are required to show that human knowledge and wisdom are able to prevent aging and death as well as calamities and sicknesses, and also overcome the moral, social, economic, and political problems in human society by removing the selfish and criminal inclinations that characterize humanity (7:29).

The truly knowledgeable and wise will recognize more clearly the problem and realize more acutely the lack of solution. Thus, "in much wisdom is much vexation; and an increase in knowledge is an increase in pain" (1:18). In other words, human wisdom does not even have immediate profit when it comes to solving the problem of the vanity of life.

It is in this sense that he declares in 1:17 that his intellectual effort "to know (experience the truth about) wisdom and to know (experience the truth about) stupidity and folly"[57] is itself a pursuit after wind. This verse gives us a preview of Qoheleth's investigation into his own experiences (cf. 2:12): the truth about the pursuit of pleasure ("stupidity and folly") in terms of the satisfaction it fails to bring (2:1–11), and the truth about wisdom in terms of the (temporal) success it does bring (2:13–23). Having known the truth about each of them and the vanity that comes with it, there is nothing he could do about it. What is expressed is again realism and not pessimism.

---

57. The Hebrew word we translate here (and in 2:12; 7:25; 9:3; 10:13) as "stupidity" is most often translated as "madness." We prefer "stupidity" because, based on how the word is used in Ecclesiastes, it seems "to denote a state of ignorance or stupidity, rather than madness in the modern sense of the word" (Schoors, *Preacher II*, 443; cf. Ogden and Zogbo, *Handbook*, 48).

The comprehensive philosophical investigation that Qoheleth undertook, which we inferred above is the search for the meaning of life, is said to be "a grievous preoccupation that God has given to the children of man with which to be occupied" (1:13). But most people would not personally undertake such an investigation. How then could he say that this is a preoccupation God has given to human beings?

We need to look at the ultimate goal of Qoheleth's investigation—to find the meaning of life—rather than the specific means he used to achieve it. In other words, his philosophical investigation is only a specific expression of the more basic "God-given" preoccupation: the "relentless quest for meaning" propelled by the innate drive to "make sense of the world."[58] In his book, *The Unheard Cry for Meaning*, psychiatrist Viktor Frankl attests, "Man is always reaching out for meaning, always setting out on his search for meaning."[59] His idea that, "Man's search for meaning is the primary motivation in his life,"[60] has been developed into a flourishing meaning-oriented approach to psychology that involves "empirical research on meaning of life and its vital role in well-being, resilience, and psychotherapy."[61]

Actually, the Hebrew word translated "preoccupation" here basically means, "task, business, affair, [which] is used only in Ecclesiastes (see also 2:23, 26; 3:10; 4:8; 5:2, 13; and 8:16). From the occurrences it seems to carry a negative connotation (i.e., disagreeable work, unhappy business)."[62] In this particular context, since it refers to the God-given "innate drive" to search for the meaning of life, the "unhappy business" is a "(grievous) preoccupation."

For most people, the means they use (often unconsciously) to express this preoccupation would be through the pursuit of pleasure and leisure (2:1–11), or of wealth and success (2:12–23), which may include power and popularity (4:13–16), or a combination of these. All these laborious pursuits are found to be futile in terms of finding the meaning of life. No wonder Qoheleth declares that humanity's search for meaning is a "*grievous* preoccupation." No matter how one expresses this preoccupation, sooner or later he realizes the grievous reality about human existence and earthly experiences. He is forced to come to terms with the inevitability of vanity under the sun. How then should he proceed? In this speech Qoheleth shares with us an answer that he has found.

Vanity of Pleasure (2:1–11)

> 2:1 I said to myself, "Come now, I will let you experiment with (try out) pleasure so that you see good (have enjoyment)." But look! this also is vanity. 2:2 I said

---

58. McGrath, *Glimpsing the Face of God*, 11, 13.
59. Frankl, *Unheard Cry for Meaning*, 31.
60. Frankl, *Man's Search for Meaning*, 121.
61. Wong, "Introduction," xxvii.
62. Holmstedt et al., *Qoheleth*, 73.

> of laughter, "It is stupidity," and of pleasure, "What does it accomplish?" 2:3 I explored with my mind how to cheer my body with wine—my mind still guiding me with wisdom—and how to lay hold of folly until I could see what is good for the children of man to do under the heavens during the few days of their life.
>
> 2:4 I enlarged my estate: I built houses for myself, I planted vineyards for myself. 2:5 I made gardens and parks for myself, and I planted in them all kinds of fruit trees. 2:6 I made pools of water for myself from which to irrigate a forest of growing trees. 2:7 I bought male and female slaves, and I had home-born slaves. I also had a great possession of cattle and sheep, more than anyone who was before me in Jerusalem. 2:8 I also accumulated for myself silver and gold, and the treasure of kings and provinces. I got for myself male and female singers, and the delights of men—many concubines.
>
> 2:9 So I became great and surpassed all who were before me in Jerusalem. My wisdom also stood by me. 2:10 And whatever my eyes asked for I did not withhold from them. I did not restrain my heart from any pleasure; my heart indeed found pleasure from all my wealth, and this was my lot from all my toil. 2:11 Then I turned (to consider) all the activities that my hands had engaged in and the wealth that I had so labored to acquire; and oh! all is vanity and a pursuit after wind, and there is no profit under the sun.

Qoheleth previously mentioned that "he set his heart to know (experience the truth about) wisdom and to know (experience the truth about) stupidity and folly" (1:17). This turns out to involve the evaluation of his own experience in experimenting with (trying out) pleasure. The question is whether the "experiment with pleasure" is successful in reaching its goal—"see good (have enjoyment)."[63] To make sense of the experiment and Qoheleth's response to the outcome, we need to recognize what is implicit in the text—"enjoyment" is differentiated from "pleasure." Pleasure is any form of pleasant sensation; it may or may not satisfy. Enjoyment is pleasure that satisfies. For unless we are satisfied with an experience, no matter how pleasurable, we cannot really say we enjoyed it. And we are not in direct control over whether pleasure satisfies or not (see below on 2:24–26).

Even before describing what the experiment with pleasure consisted of, Qoheleth gives us the conclusion of his evaluation: "this also is vanity." He even asked rhetorically, "What does it accomplish?" This means he did not enjoy the pleasure, the goal of his experiment. The pleasure was profitless as it failed to satisfy and the experiment was thus futile as it failed to reach its goal. He was so disappointed that he would in retrospect label the experiment as stupidity (2:2) and folly (2:3). It is important to note that Qoheleth did not consider pleasure in and of itself stupidity or folly, but only the pursuit of it. For he was evaluating pleasure when pleasure is the focus of attention to

---

63. Our translation, "I will let you experiment with (try out) pleasure so that you see good (have enjoyment)," is unusual and is crucial to understanding what Qoheleth is doing here. The exegetical basis for this translation is elaborated below (Excursus to 2:1–11).

"see" whether such an activity "is good (worth it) for the children of man (humanity) to do under the heavens (anywhere in this world)" (2:2–3). Furthermore, very soon we will hear him admonishing us to "see good (have enjoyment)" in our labor through enjoying its fruit (2:24). So he could not be saying that pleasure in and of itself is stupidity and folly.

Qoheleth tells us that throughout this evaluation, even when he was experimenting with the pleasure of wine, which is associated with drunkenness, his mind was still guiding him with wisdom (2:3). Also, throughout the wealth-acquiring activities described in 2:4–8, which made him greater than others before him in Jerusalem, his wisdom "stood by him" (2:9). This has two implications.

Firstly, his pursuit of pleasure was not wanton and he avoided gross indulgence. The Hebrew word behind the phrase translated "many concubines" in 2:8 occurs only here in the Hebrew Bible. Its meaning is disputed. After a lengthy discussion, Schoors concludes that "It is hard to decide whether 'cup-bearers, waitresses' or 'concubines' should be preferred, since both have good credentials."[64] He prefers the first alternative. Though "cupbearers, waitresses" does fit the context of pleasure through drinking and feasting, "concubines" fits even better since it refers to the "delights of men." And as Longman puts it, "It would have been surprising in the extreme if this aspect of his [Solomon's] life went unmentioned."[65] But whichever the case, it is not about gross indulgence. For having concubines was a "normal" royal practice, widely accepted in the ancient world. A wise man like him does not need to discover that gross indulgence is stupidity and folly; it is obvious enough that it serves no purpose except self-destruction.

Secondly, though his evaluation is experience based, it is philosophical in nature. We are thus reminded that this is part of the comprehensive philosophical investigation he talked about in 1:13–18. What exactly was he trying to do? Oliver Rankin answers succinctly:

> "Solomon" turns to the task of testing [evaluating] whether perchance pleasure may be a worthwhile object of human effort, the good which is completely satisfying. Wine, women, and song, the gathering of riches, the enjoyment of luxury, the acquisition of rare and special products and commodities derived from foreign rulers and countries through trade, gift or tribute, the prosperity fostered by successful projects of agriculture and afforestation, the magnificence of his buildings, of his gardens and parks and vineyards—all this "Solomon" briefly indicates in describing the means he used to find out by test and trial whether pleasure provided a soul-satisfying purpose of life.[66]

---

64. Schoors, *Preacher II*, 455.
65. Longman, *Ecclesiastes*, 92.
66. Rankin, "Book of Ecclesiastes," 34; cited in Schoors, *Preacher II*, 365–66.

Needless to say, Qoheleth's evaluation of human effort in this particular context cannot be applied to people who are struggling just to "make ends meet." He was evaluating whether the pursuit of what we call "the good life" is worth it. Again, he is not evaluating the good life in and of itself, but only when it becomes "an object of human effort." He reports that "my heart indeed found pleasure from all my wealth."[67] Thus his wealth gave him pleasure and a pleasurable (luxurious) lifestyle. And he declared, "this was my *lot* from all my toil" (2:10b). The idea of "lot" implies that what his labor gave (allotted) him was pleasure from his wealth and nothing more (the meaning of "lot" is further discussed in the exposition of 3:22). A poignant way of putting it would be: "And that was all I got out of my wealth" (NJPS). He got only pleasure but no satisfaction from all his labor. But the goal of the experiment was to have enjoyment ("see good") and not just pleasure, which was only the means. So he concludes that his pursuit of the good life "is vanity and a pursuit after wind."

When pleasure fails to satisfy, it does not even have immediate profit. Hence when pleasure is pursued, whether through "wine, women and song," or through the accumulation of wealth, or both, it is profitless, and the pursuit is thus futile. Psychiatrist Frankl observed that, "pleasure is, and must remain, a side-effect or a by-product, and is destroyed and spoiled to the degree to which it is made a goal in itself."[68] In Qoheleth's case, "the degree to which it is made a goal in itself," can be seen from his tenacity in pursuing pleasure: "whatever my eyes asked for I did not withhold from them. I did not restrain my heart from any pleasure" (2:10). No wonder he labeled it "stupidity and folly."

But why does pleasure not satisfy when it is pursued? We need to consider why Qoheleth pursued pleasure in the first place. It was part of his quest for the meaning of life. People pursue pleasure to find happiness so as to experience the meaning of life. Happiness is the state of (well-)being characterized by an overall sense of satisfaction with life. So if the pleasure is satisfying, it can contribute to happiness and thus the meaning of life.

However, psychologists have discovered that the "feeling that one's life has meaning, in the sense of purpose and value, is a centrally important aspect of happiness, seeming to affect one's satisfaction with almost every aspect of life [and not just pleasure]."[69] That means, pleasure does not satisfy and cannot contribute to happiness if one's life already lacks meaning. Yet it is when life lacks meaning that one feels the need to pursue after pleasure. In other words, pleasure does not satisfy when it is pursued because it is pursued to meet a need (the meaning of life) that pleasure cannot satisfy.

It is no accident that when Qoheleth sought to find what was worth doing in this fleeting life (that is, beyond meeting survival needs), he began with evaluating

---

67. See below (Excursus to 2:1–11) on translating "my wealth" instead of "my labor/toil."
68. Frankl, *Man's Search for Meaning*, 145.
69. Baumeister, *Meanings of Life*, 215.

whether pleasure is worth pursuing (2:3). For whether we realize it or not, the motivation behind virtually every human effort beyond making a living is to find happiness and the meaning of life through pleasure.

Note that, as assumed above, Qoheleth's pursuit of pleasure included the accumulation of wealth, which is pleasurable though we do not usually think of it as the pursuit of pleasure. So by evaluating the pursuit of pleasure, which includes the pursuit of wealth, Qoheleth had "turned (to consider) *all* the activities that my hands had engaged in and the wealth that I had so labored to acquire" (2:11a). By doing this he evaluates every human undertaking which is motivated (usually unconsciously) by the need to make sense of life, whether as part of work or leisure.

Today this would cover most activities associated with the pursuit of "the good life." The result of his investigation so far begins to substantiate his overall conclusion about human activities already presented in 1:14: "all is vanity and a pursuit after wind, and there is no profit under the sun" (2:11b). Living for pleasure or "the good life" cannot be "a soul-satisfying purpose of life." It is also vanity. Since it does not heal, but only numb, the pain of meaninglessness, it can only cause one to become addicted to some form of pleasure, which could even be something as "innocent" as keeping up with what is in vogue.

Though Qoheleth's evaluation excludes illicit indulgence, we can extend the insights gained to evaluate it. For every act of indulgence, by the very nature of the impulse behind it, is an act of seeking pleasure as a goal in itself. That means we can expect indulgence, illicit or not, though pleasurable, to be not satisfying. The saying, "stolen water is sweet, and bread eaten in secret is pleasant" (Prov 9:17), which refers to illicit pleasure, particularly illicit sex, is true. However, this only means illicit sex may be exciting in terms of sheer momentary pleasure but not deeply satisfying. In fact, illicit sex often leaves one feeling empty, if not guilty as well. On the other hand, it is possible to "have enjoyment with the wife of your youth. . . . Let her breasts satisfy you at all times; be intoxicated always with her love(-making)" (Prov 5:18–19).

Excursus to 2:1–11: Qoheleth's Experiment with Pleasure

The exposition above rests on our translation, "I will let you experiment with (try out) pleasure so that you see good (have enjoyment)" (2:1), which is unusual. Thus it needs to be adequately substantiated exegetically. Unlike almost all Bible translations, we have rendered the second half as a purpose or result clause: "*so that* you see good (have enjoyment)." This is because the verb in the first half—"I will let you experiment (with pleasure)"—is a cohortative and the verb in the second half is an imperative: "(and) see good (have enjoyment)!" Grammatically the sequence of two volitives (a cohortative and an imperative in this case) joined by the conjunction "and" expresses purpose or result, that is, goal.⁷⁰ This interpretation is adopted by a recent (2021) Bible translation: "I will test you with gladness, *so that* you shall see good things" (LSB; italics added).

The word translated "pleasure" (*śimḥāh*) can mean pleasure or enjoyment, which is a form of pleasure. We need to discern from the context which nuance is intended. Here *śimḥāh* is contrasted with "see good," which Schoors has shown means to "enjoy pleasure,"⁷¹ that is, enjoy oneself through "enjoy[ing] good things."⁷² Since "see good" (goal of experiment) means "have enjoyment," *śimḥāh* (object of experiment) in this verse (and throughout 2:1–11) has to mean "pleasure." This is because we can experiment with (give ourselves an experience of) pleasure (within our control) but not with enjoyment (beyond our control).

Also, unlike the Bible translations, we have rendered the Hebrew verb in the first half as "I will *let you* (Qoheleth) *experiment*" instead of "I will *test you* (Qoheleth)." The near consensus in the translation of the word here cannot be correct because if anything is tested, it is pleasure and not Qoheleth (cf. "I will make a test of pleasure" NRSV), for the conclusion is that (the pursuit of) pleasure is vanity. A survey of how the word is used in the Hebrew Bible shows that it may or may not have the nuance of test. Moshe Greenberg has shown that the basic meaning of the word, depending on the context, is either "to have an experience of" or "to give X an experience of."⁷³ We will now show that whether the word refers to an experience that involves a test or not depends on the purpose of having or giving the experience.

A person or nation may be given an experience of something with a specific purpose or goal in mind. In the case of God "testing" Abraham (Gen 22:1), the purpose of God asking him to sacrifice Isaac was to "test" what was in Abraham's heart, whether he truly feared God. In the case of God "testing" Israel in the wilderness (Exod 16:4) by giving them manna with the stipulation that they were to gather only enough for the day, the purpose was to "test" whether they would follow God's instructions. In the case of God "testing" Israel at Mount Sinai (Exod 20:20) by manifesting before them in thunder, lightning, trumpet sound and smoke, the purpose was *not* to "test" them on anything; it was to achieve the goal that they would fear God and obey him.

The Hebrew word can also refer to having an experience that involves trying out something: "Let me test (try out) just once more with the fleece" (Judg 6:39). In this case the trying out (experiment) has the purpose of testing. In the case of the delicate woman who would not "try out" (usually translated "venture") touching the ground with the sole of her foot (Deut 28:56), there is no purpose of testing. Beyond 2:1, the word occurs in Ecclesiastes one other time: "All this I have tested (examined) with

---

70. Waltke and O'Connor, *Syntax*, §§34.5.2b, 34.6a.

71. Schoors, *Preacher II*, 61–62.

72. Schoors, *Preacher II*, 218–19. In three contexts, "see good" parallels "have enjoyment" (see our translation of 2:24–25; 3:12–13; 5:18–19).

73. Greenberg, "נסה," 275, 276; cf. Schoors, *Preacher II*, 365–66.

wisdom" (7:23). In that context, the experience has the purpose of "testing" in the sense of probing or examining something.

In the context here, since the word can carry the nuance "try out," the verse is about Qoheleth giving himself an experience of experimenting with (trying out) pleasure with the goal of having enjoyment (cf. "Come on, let's try pleasure" NLT). So the purpose is not to test himself but to achieve a goal for himself. In the context of 2:1–11, Qoheleth was trying out not just pleasure but the pursuit of pleasure. The pursuit is an "experiment" like that of youths when they "experiment" with (try out) drugs with the goal of having ecstatic pleasure. But unlike the case of the youths who mindlessly indulge in drugs, Qoheleth's experiment amounts to a "test" concerning pleasure because, with his wisdom guiding him, he was at the same time *evaluating* whether his experiment with pleasure "is good . . . to do" (2:3). In other words, he was trying out the pursuit of pleasure with the goal of having enjoyment so as to test (evaluate) whether the pursuit of pleasure is worth it.[74]

As highlighted in the exposition above, Qoheleth's experiment with pleasure also involved the pursuit of wealth. This is made explicit through our translation of 2:10b as "my heart indeed found pleasure from all *my wealth*, and this was my lot from all my toil." The Hebrew word (*ʿāmāl*), which usually means "toil" or "labor" occurs twice, and we have rendered the first occurrence as "wealth." As Thomas Krüger notes, the word "can designate both the *process* and the *result* of the work (the latter meaning is clear from 2:18[–21])."[75] That the word can mean the product of labor or "wealth" is clear from 2:18 because the first occurrence of the word there in the phrase "the *labor* which I labored" (literal translation) has to refer to the product of labor as it is something that can be left behind to an heir.[76]

So in the first occurrence of the word here in 2:10, it "may refer to the immediate source of pleasure, namely Qohelet's wealth, or to the further source, namely his toil."[77] It is preferable to understand it as wealth as it makes better sense for Qoheleth to say that his lot is the pleasure derived from his wealth rather than from the stressful labor expended to acquire it (2:22–23). Also, in 2:11 Qoheleth talks about looking at

---

74. The *NET Bible* interprets 2:1 in a way similar to how we interpret it. It recognizes not only that the sequence of volitives indicates purpose or result, but also that Qoheleth was trying out pleasure and so it was pleasure and not him that was being tested. However it interprets the verse itself to mean that Qoheleth was testing whether (self-indulgent) pleasure was worthwhile. As we have just indicated, in view of 2:3, the experiment does amount to this, but it is not the meaning of 2:1 itself. The *NET Bible* reads "see (what is) good" in 2:1 to mean "see (discover) what is good (worthwhile)," and not "have enjoyment." The *Dictionary of Classical Hebrew* specifically defines "see good" in 2:1 as "enjoy" (Clines, *Dictionary* VII, 352, 7a; cf. Koehler et al., *Lexicon*, 1159, 13b; Brown et al., *Lexicon*, 908, 8a.5). And it recognizes that "see" carries the nuance "ascertain, find out [discover], determine," but only when this verb is followed by an indirect question as in 2:3—"see (discover) what—which?—is good" (Clines, *Dictionary* VII, 341, 11; 356, 11.9). This is not the case with "see (what—that which—is) good" in 2:1.

75. Krüger, *Qoheleth*, 58.

76. Cf. Garfinkel, "Qoheleth," 55–57.

77. Fox, *Time*, 180.

"all the works my hands have done" as well as "the labor which I have labored to do" (both phrases literally translated). Since the word for "labor" can mean product of labor, it makes so much sense to translate the second phrase as: "the *wealth* that I had so *labored* to acquire."[78] This supports the translation in 2:10b and in turn is supported by it.

Also, unlike most Bible translations, we have rendered 2:10b as "my heart *indeed* found pleasure . . ." instead of "*for* my heart found pleasure . . . ," which gives the impression that the reason Qoheleth did not restrain his heart from any pleasure was that he did find pleasure in his wealth. However, the reason he did not restrain his heart from any pleasure was because he was experimenting with the pursuit of pleasure to see if it was worth it; restraining his heart from any pleasure would defeat the purpose. So though the particle concerned most often means "for (because)," it makes better sense to translate it as "indeed."[79] Thus, in Qoheleth's unrestrained pursuit of pleasure he did indeed find pleasure (but only pleasure, and nothing more, and thereby failed to achieve the goal of having enjoyment).

Vanity of Success (2:12–23)

> 2:12 So I turned to consider wisdom as well as stupidity and folly. For what can the man who comes after the king do except what has already been done? 2:13 Then I saw that wisdom has advantage over folly as light has advantage over darkness. 2:14 The wise person has his eyes in his head, but the fool walks in darkness. But I also realized that one fate befalls both of them. 2:15 Then I said to myself, "As is the fate of the fool, it will also befall me. So why then have I been excessively wise?" Thus I said to myself that this also is vanity. 2:16 For there is no lasting remembrance of the wise as with the fool, seeing that in the days to come both will have already been forgotten. And how the wise dies just like the fool! 2:17 So I hated life because the work that is done under the sun was grievous to me, for all is vanity and a pursuit after wind.

Earlier Qoheleth discovered that wisdom could not solve the problem of the vanity of life (1:12–18). Then he applied wisdom in his experiment with the pursuit of pleasure, which included the pursuit of wealth (2:1–11). He evaluated that pursuit and concluded that it is also vanity ("stupidity and folly"). Now he returns to consider (evaluate) wisdom as well as stupidity and folly again, this time focusing on its advantage over stupidity and folly in bringing temporal and material success. He is doing this because "what can the man who comes after the king do except what has already been done?" (2:12b).[80]

---

78. Cf. Whitley, *Koheleth*, 23.

79. Thus Ogden and Zogbo, *Handbook*, 62; cf. Kautzsch, *Grammar*, §15; Waltke and O'Connor, *Syntax*, §39.3.4e.

80. The Hebrew text of this clause is problematic. It can be read literally as: "For what can the

In other words, after having considered the philosophical value of wisdom (1:12–18) and the existential value of pleasure (2:1–11), by turning now to consider the practical value of wisdom, he would have considered all the categories of the means people tend to use to seek (in vain) for the meaning of life. So his successor or anyone else would have nothing to add to what he had already discovered. What is left to be done is to take heed of what he is going to say in response to what he has discovered, especially in 2:24–26 (see below).

Qoheleth recognizes that the wise person does have real advantage over the foolish one (2:13–14). Wisdom cannot solve the problem of the vanity of life, but wisdom enables a person to do better in daily life. For a wise person (who "has eyes in his head") is more able to avoid getting into trouble, and to advance in society easier, than a foolish one (who "walks in darkness"). One who sees clearly in the light certainly has distinct advantage over one who gropes cautiously in the dark. So wisdom has *immediate* profit under the sun.

Today, the pursuit of wisdom for the purpose of success often takes the form of a pursuit for higher education. A university degree is seen as the passport to "the good life." But no wise or educated person, no matter how successful, can avoid death. Thus both the wise and the fool have the same final outcome ("fate")—death. Hence *ultimately* the wise is no different from a fool. So success is vanity because all that we gain from our successful endeavors is transitory. Not only that. Since human life itself is transitory, whether one is wise or foolish, one will eventually be forgotten—there is no lasting remembrance—after one has departed from this world; as the saying goes, "out of sight, out of mind" (cf. 1:11).

Qoheleth therefore questioned the point of being so wise. Even when it is used to gain immediate profits, wisdom is also vanity (ultimately profitless) in light of death. He was expressing the feeling that whatever profits he gained from acting wisely would all be left behind when he dies (2:18). His disappointment with this reality is well captured in his exclamation: "And how the wise dies just like the fool!" So he says he "hated life." This was because "the work that is done under the sun," that is the work of gaining temporal profits like wealth, was "grievous" to him. This in turn is because "all is vanity and a pursuit after wind." Why was the work "grievous" just because "all is vanity"? He realized that not only "all is vanity," but also that this reality cannot be changed (1:14–15).

---

man (do) who comes after the king that which already has been done?" (cf. Murphy, *Ecclesiastes*, 20; Schoors, *Preacher*, 156–57). Gordis helpfully remarks: "In spite of the textual difficulties, the idea is quite clear. Koheleth, in his assumed role as Solomon, wishes to assure the reader that he has experienced the ultimate in both wisdom and pleasure and that there is no need for any one else to repeat the experiment" (Gordis, *Koheleth*, 221; for a technical linguistic analysis in support of this interpretation, see Holmstedt et al., *Qoheleth*, 99–100). Unfortunately, this remark limits what Qoheleth is saying here to only his experience with wisdom in 1:12–18 and with pleasure in 2:1–11. Qoheleth is here saying that in addition to those experiences, what he is going to do next (2:13–17) would render any future attempt to repeat what he has done redundant.

It is painful to be toiling away when you are aware that it will one day amount to nothing, and nothing can be done about it. People suppress this awareness to avoid the pain, and this is one reason death is a taboo subject. But Qoheleth had to face it, and face it long enough, to evaluate what is worth living for. So he "hated" life. This expression of despair must be seen in the light that the more one has accumulated in terms of wealth and the higher one has attained in terms of prestige, the more grievous it is to realize that one has to leave this world empty-handed. Nonetheless, this reaction was pessimistic. But was he still pessimistic about life when he recounted this painful experience in this speech? We shall see.

> 2:18 And I hated all my wealth for which I toiled under the sun, because I must leave it to the man who will come after me. 2:19 And who knows whether he will be wise or a fool? Yet he will have control over all my wealth for which I toiled and used my wisdom under the sun. This also is vanity. 2:20 So I gave my heart to despair over all the wealth for which I toiled under the sun. 2:21 For it happens that a man whose wealth is (acquired through toiling) with wisdom, knowledge and skill must leave his estate to one who did not toil for it. This also is vanity and a great affliction. 2:22 For what is there for a man in (exchange for) all his toiling and striving of his heart which he does under the sun? 2:23 For all his days are full of pain and his work is a vexation. Even at night his heart does not rest. This also is vanity (meaningless).

It is now revealed that Qoheleth "hated" life (2:17) also because it dawned on him that all the wealth for which he had labored had to be left to his heir, and this led him to "hate" all his wealth (2:18). Qoheleth is here highlighting the wealth which he acquired through labor (cf. 2:4–8). He acquired this wealth with wisdom but, as is unmistakable even in the English translation, it was not without toiling. When we have to toil to acquire something, in somber moments, we ask whether it is all worth it. Qoheleth did not think it was worth it because he had to leave everything to his heir. So he says "This also is vanity" (2:19) and even "despaired" over his wealth (2:20).

However, since his wealth would benefit his heir, why did he consider leaving it to him as something so grievous that he would "hate" and "despair" over it? Qoheleth's explanation: he had to give everything he gained through laboring wisely into the hands of an heir who may be foolish (2:19) and who did not labor for it (2:21). The implication is that he feared that this heir would not have what it takes to make good use of the inheritance. This is most obvious if the heir is foolish. He will simply squander the wealth away.

Worse still, it is a common observation that wealth that falls on one's lap, whether through inheritance or other means, often destroys the recipient in one way or another. And having wealth to leave behind in and of itself may ruin one's family due to inheritance disputes when "unequal estate distributions, parental disinheritance or simple disagreements over 'who gets what' reignite 'old issues of sibling rivalry and dominance."[81] Some disputes are driven purely by economic consequences of a lost inheritance; but in many instances, it is the fact that specific bequests are viewed as posthumous representations of 'love, validation, and importance'[82] between parent and child that is the real problem."[83]

Even if Qoheleth's heir is wise, but because he did not labor for it, he may still lack what it takes to manage the level of wealth acquired through his father's level of wisdom and experience. We translate the last clause of 2:21 as, "who did not toil *for it*," as do most Bible translations because it is more idiomatic in English. However, it is possible, in fact more plausible grammatically, to translate it as, "who did not toil *with it*." A translator's handbook on Ecclesiastes actually advocates this interpretation.[84]

The verse is then saying that Qoheleth's wealth (estate) is acquired by toiling[85] "*with* wisdom and *with* knowledge and *with* skill" (literal translation of the Hebrew phrase), but he had to leave everything to one who did not toil "*with* it" (same Hebrew preposition), that is, one who did not toil with wisdom, knowledge, nor skill. To capture this meaning, the clause has been translated as, "who has not labored *with them*" (NASB 1995; italics added). This translation makes explicit Qoheleth's fear that his heir may not have what it takes to handle the wealth he had acquired because his heir did not work "for it."

Qoheleth's fear is not unfounded. The well-known Chinese proverb, "Wealth never survives three generations" has an American counterpart: "From shirtsleeves-to-shirtsleeves in three generations."[86] And this theme is not limited to the Americans and the Chinese. "According to studies, only 30 percent of family businesses built by one generation are passed on to their children, and only 10 percent of those businesses ever reach a third generation."[87] So whether Qoheleth's heir is wise or foolish, the wealth that took such a toll on him to create will not likely last beyond the third generation.

---

81. Folberg, "Mediating Conflicts," 8.
82. Accettura, *Blood and Money*, 2.
83. Conway and Stannard, "Emotional Dynamics," 240.
84. Ogden and Zogbo, *Handbook*, 76.
85. The first part of 2:21 reads literally, "For there is a man whose labor (is) with wisdom . . ." (cf. NKJV). Evidently to make sense of the clause, we "must reconstruct an appropriate semantic value for the copula ['is . . .'], in this case 'made, accomplished, achieved'" (Holmstedt et al., *Qoheleth*, 110; cf. Delitzsch, *Song of Songs and Ecclesiastes*, 250); it is similar to "And his return to Ramah" (1 Sam 7:17)—"Then *he would make* his return to Ramah" (NASB). Our reconstruction for 2:21—". . . a man whose wealth is (acquired by toiling) with wisdom . . ."— is in line with the discussion above that "labor" means "wealth" when it refers to something that is to be left behind (here it refers to Qoheleth's "estate"). The verse has also been rendered as, "For a man comes to possession with wisdom . . ." (Krüger, *Qoheleth*, 57). Most Bible translations render "labor" here as a verb, but it does not change the meaning of the verse.
86. Alberts, *Passing the Torch*, xiv.
87. Alberts, *Passing the Torch*, xiv.

And it is even more tragic if in the process of transferring wealth across generations, families become ruined in one way or another. Humans are basically acquisitive. In an age of "economic progress" this acquisitiveness is unleashed in a manner unseen before. People are aware that they have to leave their acquisitions behind. But the idea that they can leave their wealth to their children may have given some an illusive purpose or meaning to their frantic pursuit of wealth. Qoheleth's confession is that, "This also is vanity and a great affliction" (2:21).

This confession is a warning applicable to everyone who labors like him because verses 2:22–23, which explain why "This also is vanity and a great affliction," are in the third person. Verse 2:22 reiterates the theme of Ecclesiastes: "what [profit] is there for a man in (exchange for) all his toiling and striving of his heart which he does under the sun." Verse 2:23 clarifies what "all his toiling and striving of his heart" involves: the work is "full of pain (physical) and vexation (emotional)" to the extent that "Even at night his heart does not rest."

This is not true of everyone even in modern times let alone in the ancient world of Qoheleth. R. N. Whybray is correct that "Like the previous verses, this is not a comment on the human condition in general" but only on the kind of person like Qoheleth himself, who "is possessed by a restless ambition to achieve something—whatever it may be—for himself . . . and who puts this 'business' (work) above everything else."[88]

However, today many people in affluent societies take for granted that this is the way to live. They call it "pursuing a career." They do not question the wisdom—or the lack of it—of living this way. Ecclesiastes teaches that it is because our life lacks meaning that we are driven to join the rat race to try to fill the vacuum created by the sense of meaninglessness. Since we do not find the meaning of life in this race, we may not realize that this is what we are actually running after. And we may not welcome this realization as not many of us would admit even to ourselves that we are actually chasing after wind.

Qoheleth's labor to accumulate wealth was already "grievous" just because he had to leave everything behind (2:17–18), what more when the labor itself was physically and emotionally grievous as expressed in 2:22–23? So we see why he says it is not only "vanity" but also "a great affliction." This explains more fully why he hated and despaired over his wealth. Qoheleth uses the term *hebel* ("vanity") four times within 2:12–23. Now that we have seen all that Qoheleth has to say about how he felt about his pursuit of vanity, especially in view of the "pain," "vexation" and lack of sleep involved in the pursuit, the fourth time he says "This also is *hebel*" (2:23) may be better translated "This is indeed meaningless."

The meaning of *hebel* here is still "vanity," but in this particular context it has the connotation of "meaningless." This captures more adequately what Qoheleth is saying. For Qoheleth, who hated and despaired over his wealth, would himself find his grievous pursuit of wealth not only vanity but also meaningless (for a discussion on the

88. Whybray, *Ecclesiastes*, 62.

connotations of *hebel* in Ecclesiastes and how they affect the translation of this word in a particular context, see "Interpretation of Ecclesiastes" under "The Pragmatics of Vanity").

To sum up, the pursuit of pleasure and success is vanity. The pursuit of knowledge and wisdom to solve the problem of vanity is itself vanity. How then shall we live?

Admonition to Carefreeness in Light of Vanity (2:24–26)

> *2:24 There is nothing good for man except that he should eat and drink and let his soul see good (have enjoyment) in his labor. And this I have seen, that it is from the hand of God. 2:25 For who can eat or who can have enjoyment apart from him? 2:26 For to a man who is good in his sight he has given wisdom, knowledge and joy, but to the sinner he has given the business of gathering and collecting in order to give to one who is good in God's sight. This also is vanity and a pursuit after wind.*

Qoheleth's expressions of despair and pessimism in the previous passage are in the context of recounting his past experiences, especially his experience of pursuing temporal success through laboring with wisdom. He is sharing how he felt when he evaluated those experiences and realized the vanity of them all. But does he still feel this way at the time of recounting them in the speech? We need to look at the purpose of this recounting.

The passage before us introduces a major sub-theme of the speech. Qoheleth here admonishes us to have enjoyment in life. This admonition is repeated several times later in the speech (3:12–13, 22; 5:18; 8:15) with slight variations in expression (as to why we have entitled 2:24–26 and the following passages "Admonition to Carefreeness," see exposition of 5:18–20). Then in 9:7–9, and finally in 11:7–10, the admonition takes the form of an outright instruction.

He is in fact presenting it as the proper response to the vanity of life. For every time this admonition occurs it is in the context of how we should respond to the vanity of life, whether in light of what he personally experienced as is the case here, or (later) in light of what he personally observed, or both. That means Qoheleth is recounting his past experiences as a personal testimony on how not to live in order to persuade us how then to live. So he must have learned from his past pessimism and departed from it. As we now take a closer look at the admonition, it will become clear that he has indeed moved on to embrace a wholesome form of realism.

Qoheleth pursued after pleasure to find out "what is good . . . to do" (2:3). Even with his wisdom guiding him, he found the experience disappointing. For the pursuit could only give pleasure but not enjoyment because it did not satisfy. Even then, the material things that gave pleasure, which were acquired through laboring with wisdom, would one day be taken away (2:12–23). So "what [then] is *good . . . to do*?" Qoheleth presents his answer in the form of an admonition. "There is *nothing good* except," Qoheleth says, "that he should eat and drink" so as to "let his soul see good (have enjoyment) in his labor."[89]

The soul is the seat of desire. For the soul to "see good," the desire must be satisfied.[90] This was the goal of the failed experiment, which Qoheleth is now addressing. This means "what is good . . . to do" is to find satisfaction in and through the fruit of our labor and thus have enjoyment of food and possessions. In fact Qoheleth later spells it out: "Look! What I have seen is good, what is fitting, is to eat and drink and to see good (have enjoyment) in all of one's labor in which he toils under the sun the few days of his life that God has given him, for this is his lot" (5:18). This is a sharp contrast and a direct response to the lack of satisfaction and thus of enjoyment in the experiment with pleasure to find out what is good. We have retained the Hebrew phrase "see good" (have enjoyment) in the translation of 2:1 and 2:24 so that we can see even better that 2:24–26 is a direct response to that failed experiment in 2:1–23.

However, the repeated admonition to have enjoyment is not as if Qoheleth "were saying that enjoyment of food and possessions is the goal of life. In this context he is talking about how one should view life with respect to labor and the fruit of labor."[91] It is only the proper (realistic) response, and not exactly the solution, to vanity. In other words, if the laborious pursuits of pleasure and success, even when boosted by wisdom, are in reality futile as the objects of pursuit are profitless, how then should we live? What role should labor and its fruit play in our life? Qoheleth's answer is that we should enjoy the fruit of our labor. Let us explore the implications of this answer.

As we have discussed in our exposition of 2:1–11, we will find satisfaction and have enjoyment only if we are not trapped in pursuing after pleasure or the things that give pleasure. Most often people do not even realize this is what they are doing. So we must stop and evaluate our goals in life. This brings us back to the insight of psychiatrist Frankl that pleasure must not be made a goal in itself but instead remain a side-effect.

What then is the goal of labor if it should not be pleasure, whether the pleasure associated with success or the luxury it brings? Qoheleth affirms that people pursue after pleasure, success and even wisdom in order to satisfy the need to make sense of life (see exposition of 1:13). And he presents his admonition to have enjoyment not only as the sensible response to the vanity of life, but also as the alternative to these pursuits, stressing that besides it, "there is nothing good." That means his admonition must in some ways address the basic question of the meaning of life. And it would also give a hint on the proper goal of labor.

Qoheleth has testified to the vanity of wisdom, pleasure and success in such a way that when he says that there is nothing good except to have enjoyment, our

---

89. Our translation "There is nothing good except . . . (have enjoyment)" rather than "There is nothing better . . . than (having enjoyment)," is grounded exegetically below (Excursus to 2:24–26).

90. Cf. Schoors, *Preacher II*, 218–19.

91. Garrett, *Proverbs, Ecclesiastes, Song of Songs*, 296.

conscience will not argue with him. For when we labor, consciously or unconsciously, it is in order to find satisfaction. So it does not make sense that all that our labor brings is possession that does not last or pleasure that does not satisfy. Therefore the most realistic and sensible thing to do is to enjoy what we have and not pursue more temporal things and in the process fail to enjoy even what we already have. And how can life as a whole be meaningful if we are not doing the most sensible or meaningful thing in light of its vanity? In this way, enjoyment helps us make sense of life, and thus contributes to the meaning of life. Qoheleth's response to the vanity of life at the time of the speech is thus realistic. But his is not a godless form of realism.

For when Qoheleth presents the response to the vanity of life for the very first time, he brings God into the picture. He spells out that the ability to have enjoyment "is from the hand of God"—it is in fact "a gift from God" (3:13; 5:19). And God gives this ability only to those who "are good in his sight." This may sound outrageous to contemporary ears. Here Qoheleth does not explain why this is so. But he will develop and defend this idea later on (especially in 5:18–6:9 and 11:7–10). Let us then give him the benefit of the doubt for now so that we can move on and see what he is trying to say.

This is not difficult because, if we have been following his arguments and feeling his (past) frustrations, we would have realized that though we can pursue after pleasure and success, we cannot ensure that we enjoy life. It implies that we may need help beyond ourselves. Qoheleth's ancient audience would have been rather receptive to this idea, which we may find repulsive today. Even if we do not believe in God, we can still understand, "who can have enjoyment without him," as a figure of speech to mean that the ability to find satisfaction in life is beyond self-determination.

After all, this does not mean that this ability is beyond human initiative. Recall that psychiatrist Frankl has observed that "pleasure [and thus enjoyment] is, and must remain, a side-effect or a by-product." He does not say the side-effect or by-product of what. Qoheleth says that God will allow us to enjoy life if we are "good in his sight," a condition we can do something about. In other words, the ability to find satisfaction is a side-effect or a by-product of being "good in his sight." Who then is considered "good in his sight"?

We are told that such a person is given "knowledge, wisdom and joy." In Old Testament wisdom teaching, the "fear of God" is the "beginning" of *knowledge* (Prov 1:7) and of *wisdom* (Prov 9:10). So to say that God has given to those who are good in his sight knowledge and wisdom is indirectly saying they fear God. We shall see that one who "fears God" is basically a conscientious person with an upright heart. He would then have *joy* in his heart because of his upright ways (Prov 12:20). Hence one who is "good in God's sight" is one who seeks to live an upright life, and is here aptly contrasted with "the sinner," or the wicked, whose self-destructive way of life betrays a lack of knowledge and wisdom, and whose joy is therefore only "momentary" (Job 20:5).

Later Qoheleth acknowledges that the wicked may also become prosperous. Here he points out in advance that they would not be able to enjoy their prosperity (an idea elaborated in 6:1–6). They are "given the business of gathering and collecting (wealth) in order to give to one who is good in God's sight." For the sinner, this "business" without doubt "also is vanity and a pursuit after wind" (2:26). What then does "in order to give to one who is good in God's sight" mean? It can be understood in light of 6:2, where Qoheleth talks about a man who is not able to enjoy his wealth, but instead a "stranger" will enjoy it. This "stranger" is someone who is "good in God's sight."

In other words, those who are not upright can only be busy "gathering and collecting" wealth but not enjoy it. And since they have to leave their wealth behind (2:12–18), it can benefit others. But since their heirs may not enjoy it because they may not have what it takes to handle the wealth (2:19–23), in the end, as the wealth scatters, it will only benefit "strangers" who are "good in God's sight." In this sense, the sinner is storing up wealth to be "given" to the upright (cf. Prov 13:22b). In a world in which the wicked may seem to get away with their ill-gotten wealth, this teaching helps us make sense of life as we see it.

If, just for the sake of understanding Qoheleth better, we grant him that it is indeed a real and not a figurative God who gives the ability to enjoy life, what difference does it make? It will give us a transcendent purpose to labor and to the enjoyment of life. Labor enables us to meet our material needs, without which we can have no life let alone enjoyment of life. And when we recognize that it is God who enables us to enjoy the fruit of our labor, we can thank and praise him wholeheartedly. This ability to thank and praise God then contributes to the meaning of life. For as C. S. Lewis puts it, "all enjoyment spontaneously overflows into praise . . . and we delight to praise what we enjoy because the praise not merely expresses but completes the enjoyment; it is its appointed consummation . . . ; the delight is incomplete until it is expressed [in praise]. It is frustrating . . . to come suddenly, at the turn of the road, upon some mountain valley of unexpected grandeur and then to have to keep silent because the people with you care for it no more than for a tin can in the ditch."[92]

In other words, without a real God to thank, we can only "thank goodness," and so even the enjoyment of an exceptionally good fortune serves no transcendent, and thus no deeply satisfying or truly meaningful, purpose.

Excursus to 2:24–26: Qoheleth's Admonishment about Enjoyment

The Hebrew text of 2:24 literally reads: "There is nothing good *in* man that he should . . . (have enjoyment)." The literal translation does not make good sense unless we accept Herbert Leupold's interpretation that "in man" means "(inherent) in man."[93] Qoheleth is then saying, "There is nothing good *inherent in* man that he

---

92. Lewis, *Reflections on the Psalms*, 94–95.
93. Leupold, *Ecclesiastes*, 74; followed by Barrick, *Ecclesiastes*, 58.

should . . . (have enjoyment)." This means no human being in and of himself would be able to have enjoyment. This fits the immediate context as Qoheleth goes on to say, "For who can eat and who can have enjoyment apart from him?" But in the context of the sub-theme of Qoheleth's admonition to have enjoyment, "in man" cannot mean "(inherent) in man." For in 3:12, "in them," which refers to humanity within whose heart God has put eternity (3:11), clearly cannot mean "(inherent) in them"; even Leupold translates it as "among men."[94]

It has long been recognized that based on 8:15 and 6:12, where the preposition is actually "for" and not "in," the "in" in 2:24 and 3:12 has the force of "for."[95] Actually, the preposition "in" of both 2:24 and 3:12 has a force stronger than merely "for." For in both verses the "in" means "in regard to," as in Lev 6:2 [Heb. 5:22]: "When a person sins and acts unfaithfully against the LORD by deceiving his neighbor *in regard to* a deposit, or *in regard to* a security, or *in regard to* a robbery, or defrauds his neighbor . . . ."[96] This means Qoheleth is saying "There is nothing good *in regard to* humanity that he should . . . (have enjoyment)." To better bring out the force, it can be translated: "As for man there is nothing good (except) that he should . . . (have enjoyment)." But for the sake of consistency with 8:15, where the preposition is "for" and not "in," we follow most translations in rendering "in man" (2:24) as "for man" and "in them" (3:12) as "for them."

We saw that our translation of 2:24, "There is *nothing good* for man *except* that he should . . . (have enjoyment)," is crucial in helping us see the flow of thought from 2:1–23 to 2:24—"there is *nothing good* . . . except" (2:24) answers the question "what is *good* . . . to do" (2:3), which is what 2:1–23 is about. We now need to establish this translation on firm exegetical ground though it requires an elaborate discussion, especially since the Hebrew text is problematic and our translation is unusual.

Evidently something is missing from the Hebrew text of 2:24—"there is nothing good for man <???> that he should . . . (have enjoyment)"—due to scribal error. The Hebrew phrase "there is nothing good" occurs three other times in Ecclesiastes, all in the context of Qoheleth's admonition to have enjoyment (3:12, 22; 8:15). Hence the meaning of 2:24 as a whole is to be determined in light of these other texts. What is missing in 2:24 can be inferred from 3:12, 8:15 or 3:22. We shall see that, by comparing the Hebrew texts and bearing in mind the kind of errors that scribes are likely to make, what is missing is to be restored from 3:22—the preposition "from" so that 2:24 should read: "there is nothing good for man <*(apart) from*> that he should … (have enjoyment)."

Almost all Bible translations and commentators render not only 3:22 and thus 2:24, but also 3:12 and 8:15, along the line: "There is *nothing better* for man *than* that

---

94. Leupold, *Ecclesiastes*, 78.

95. Ginsburg, *Coheleth*, 300; cf. 10:17, where the last two occurrences of "in" also have the force of "for."

96. Waltke and O'Connor, *Syntax*, §1.2.5e.

he should . . . (have enjoyment)." This virtual consensus is not on sound exegetical ground. First of all, it is clear that 3:12 and 8:15 have to be rendered not in terms of "nothing better . . . than" but instead "nothing good . . . except" (cf. NJPS).[97] For the Hebrew conjunction (literally "that if") that connects "there is nothing good" with "to have enjoyment" (3:12) or with "to eat and drink" (8:15) introduces an exceptive clause:[98] "there is nothing good . . . *except* to have enjoyment/eat and drink." And virtually all Bible translations render the same conjunction in 5:11 [Heb. v. 10] as "except." Both Christian Ginsburg[99] and Seow[100] are inconsistent; they render 3:12 in terms of "nothing good *except*," but 8:15 in terms of "nothing *better than*" though the same exceptive conjunction is used in both cases. Hence interpreting and translating 3:12 and 8:15 in terms of "nothing good except" should not be controversial.

What really needs discussion is how 3:22 should be rendered—"there is nothing good *from* that man should have enjoyment in his labors." The question here is how the preposition "from" should be interpreted. It often introduces a comparison. If applicable to this case, the clause would read, "there is nothing better (*more* good) *than* . . . have enjoyment," which is how most Bible translations and commentators interpret it. However this would require the word "good" to be an adjective.[101] But the word "good" in 3:22 and the other three texts on enjoyment *functions* as a noun.[102]

Technically speaking, in and by itself the Hebrew word "good" in "There is nothing *good*" (2:24; 3:12, 22; 8:15) is an adjective and not a noun. It modifies a "phonologically null noun."[103] This means it is the adjective ("good") of a noun phrase where the noun is not pronounced or written (represented by ϕ): "good ϕ." The phrase means "good thing." Thus, strictly speaking we should translate the four instances as: "There is *no good thing*." However, since the adjective represents a noun phrase in these four instances and practically functions as a noun, for convenience, like Schoors[104] we will treat it as a noun.

How then does one get the adjective "better" (more good) from the noun "good"? Hence none of the four "nothing good" instances can be rendered in terms of "nothing better than." We need to interpret 3:22—"there is nothing good *from* that man should have enjoyment"—in light of 3:12 and 8:15. If the phrase "nothing good *from*" does not mean "nothing better (*more* good) *than*," how then do we make sense of it?

Since in 3:12 and 8:15 we clearly have "nothing good except," can the preposition "from" in 3:22 also carry the nuance "except"? It is known that this preposition,

---

97. Also, Holmstedt et al., *Qoheleth*, 130, 243.
98. Kautzsch, *Grammar*, §163; Clines, *Dictionary* IV, 390a.
99. Ginsburg, *Coheleth*, 311, 405–6.
100. Seow, *Ecclesiastes*, 158, 276.
101. Kautzsch, *Grammar*, §133.
102. Cf. Schoors, *Preacher II*, 39.
103. Miller-Naudé and Naudé, "Adjective Distinct," 8.
104. Schoors, *Preacher II*, 39.

with the basic meaning of "separation," can mean "separated or free from," that is, "without"[105] as in, "their homes are safe (free) *from* [without] fear" (Job 21:9). This means the preposition can easily carry the separative nuance "apart from." Thus 3:22 can be translated as "there is nothing good *apart from* [that is, *except*] that man should have enjoyment." Therefore, in terms of form, what is missing in 2:24 is to be restored from 3:22—the preposition "(apart) from"—but in terms of meaning ("except") it does not matter whether it is restored from 3:12, 8:15 or 3:22, as it amounts to the same thing.

Now the Hebrew of the last clause of 2:3 reads literally: "until I could see (discover) *what is good* for the sons of man, *which they should do* under the heavens . . . ."[106] However, like the Bible translations and most commentators, we have rendered the clause in more idiomatic English as "until I could see (discover) *what is good* for the sons of man *to do* under the heavens . . . ." Either way, "what is good" is the object of the verb ("should do"/"to do"). Thus it refers to *something* good to be done. So 2:3 is about discovering "what is the good *thing* . . . to do."[107] Therefore "there is *no good thing* except . . . have enjoyment" (2:24) is clearly a direct response to "what is *the good thing* . . . to do" (2:3).

Ogden[108] takes for granted that the four instances of "nothing good except" are to be rendered in terms of "nothing better than" even though he recognizes that the word "good" in these four instances is functioning as a noun and not an adjective. In a different work, he explains, "The adjective better is actually a noun meaning 'good things.' From the point of view of sentence structure, the Hebrew uses a comparative ['better than'] form, but the sense is an *exclusive* one. That is to say, Qoheleth believes that this is the best or *only* thing to do."[109] What is intriguing is that, though the form is supposedly comparative (which is questionable), the sense is still exclusive (or exceptive)—enjoyment is the "only thing to do," that is, there is *nothing good except* enjoyment.

It must be added that even if we accept the popular "nothing better than" translation, we must not lose sight of the fact that Qoheleth's admonition to have enjoyment in 2:24-26 is a response to the question that arose in his experiment with pleasure (and success)—"what is *good* . . . to do" (2:3). For to say that there is nothing "better" than enjoyment is to say there is nothing "more *good*" than enjoyment. Thus "nothing more good" responds to "what is good."

---

105. Kautzsch, *Grammar*, §119w; Clines, *Dictionary* V, 341c.
106. Cf. Holmstedt et. al., *Qoheleth*, 84, 87–88. The interrogative pronoun translated "what" most often means "where" outside of Ecclesiastes but here the sense is "what (is good)" and in 11:6 it is "which (will succeed)" (Schoors, *Preacher*, 57–58; cf. Koehler et al., *Lexicon*, 38, 2d).
107. Cf. Schoors, *Preacher II*, 40–41.
108. Ogden, "'Nothing is Better'-Form," 340–41.
109. Ogden and Zogbo, *Handbook*, 79 (italics added).

To better appreciate what Qoheleth has to say about enjoyment, we also need to take a closer look at the translation of 2:25—"For who can eat or who can have enjoyment apart from him?" Though this translation is the most widely accepted, we still need to establish that this is the correct translation because there are two technical issues that affect how this verse should be translated. Firstly, the word translated "can have enjoyment" is from a verb that occurs only once in the Hebrew Bible and its meaning is disputed. According to Crenshaw, by appealing to various verbs in cognate languages, "Scholars have suggested the following: (1) enjoy; (2) be anxious, fret; (3) refrain; (4) eat; and (5) consider."[110]

Secondly, in the Hebrew text the word translated "from him" is actually "from me." It has often been assumed that the word "from me" in the Hebrew text is a scribal error and thus emended to "from him." However, Charles Whitley argues that the emendation is unnecessary; he shows evidence that the form of the word as it is in the Hebrew text can still be read as "from him."[111] Either way, is it then legitimate to assume that, based on the context, Qoheleth intended to say "from him"?

The best way to solve these two technical problems is to look at 2:25 as a whole in its context. This verse is preceded by an affirmation on what is good—to eat and drink so that one's soul "see good" (*enjoy* pleasure) in (the fruit of) one's labor, adding that (when one is able to do this) it is a gift *from the hand of God* (2:24). And it is followed by an affirmation that to those who are "good in his (God's) sight," *God has given* "joy" (*śimḥāh*). So in the context of 2:24–26, what translation can be better than, "For who *can eat* or who *can have enjoyment* apart from *him*?" No wonder this is the most accepted translation.

The question then arises: Why did Qoheleth not use *śimḥāh* in 2:25 to mean enjoyment instead of the unfamiliar word, the meaning of which is now disputed? It is unfamiliar to us but may not be to the original audience. Evidently, he chooses this word because he has used *śimḥāh* in 2:1 to refer to pleasure that is pursued and hence does not satisfy. Here he is referring to enjoyment, pleasure that satisfies, as a gift of God (not something to be pursued)—a sharp contrast to the pleasure just discussed earlier. The change of word helps to avoid confusion. Also, in the next verse (2:26) he uses *śimḥāh* to refer to the joy as a consequence of upright living.

Even though virtually all Bible translations render *śimḥāh* in 2:26 as "joy," Fox[112] argues that the Hebrew word *śimḥāh* in Ecclesiastes can only mean "pleasure" or "enjoyment" and not "happiness" or "joy." Thus Fox translates "*śimḥāh* of his heart" in 5:20 [Heb. v. 19] as "his heart's pleasure."[113] Now the text there says that "he will not much call to mind the days of his life, since God is keeping <him> occupied with his heart's pleasure" (Fox's own translation). This reminds us of how Jacob felt in

---

110. Crenshaw, *Ecclesiastes*, 90.
111. Whitley, *Koheleth*, 29.
112. Fox, *Time*, 113–15; followed by Schoors, *Preacher II*, 176–80.
113. Fox, *Time*, 238.

anticipation of marrying Rachel: "So Jacob served seven years for Rachel but they seemed a few days to him because of his love for her" (Gen 29:20). It is not difficult to imagine that at the least "(his heart's) pleasure" (5:20) is gladness. If śimḥāh can mean "gladness" in Ecclesiastes, why not "joy" when used in a context associated with the fear of God and upright living as in Prov 12:20 and Job 20:5, where even Fox[114] himself renders śimḥāh as "joy"?

In 2:24–26 we find a sudden shift from the topic of pleasure that does not satisfy to the sub-theme of enjoyment as the appropriate (realistic) response to vanity, including the vanity of pursuing pleasure. After this transition, Qoheleth begins to use the noun śimḥāh or a verbal form of the same root to refer to enjoyment (see 3:12–13 and 5:18–20, where these terms parallel "see good," which we have seen means "have enjoyment").[115] It will be elaborated in our exposition of 5:18–6:9 how the God-given gladness or joy in the heart enables one to enjoy the fruit of one's labor and why one must be good in God's sight to have this gladness or joy.

Poem to Amplify Sense of Vanity (3:1–8)

Repetition of Theme: "What Profit is There?" (3:9)

> 3:1 There is a season for everything,
>   and a time for every matter under the heavens:
> 3:2 A time to be born, and a time to die;
>   a time to plant, and a time to uproot what is planted;
> 3:3 A time to kill, and a time to heal;
>   a time to tear down, and a time to build up;
> 3:4 A time to weep, and a time to laugh;
>   a time to mourn, and a time to dance;
> 3:5 A time to throw away stones, and a time to gather stones;
>   a time to embrace, and a time to refrain from embracing;
> 3:6 A time to search, and a time to give up as lost;
>   a time to keep, and a time to throw away;
> 3:7 A time to tear apart, and a time to sew together;
>   a time to keep silence, and a time to speak;
> 3:8 A time to love, and a time to hate;
>   a time for war, and a time for peace.
> 3:9 What profit has the worker in (exchange for) all that he toils?

At the end of the previous section, we noted that we could understand Qoheleth better if we would grant him his assumption concerning God. Now to understand this present passage and the rest of the speech, if we do not share his assumptions about God,

---

114. Fox, *Proverbs 10–31*, 556.

115. However, "house of śimḥāh" (7:4) obviously means "house of pleasure" and not "house of enjoyment" as such a place can only provide pleasure but cannot ensure that it will become enjoyment.

we need to hear him out as if we do. Mortimer Adler warns of two common mistakes in reading a piece of writing built on dogmatic principles: (1) "refuse to accept, even temporarily, the articles of faith that are the first principles of the author. As a result, the reader continues to struggle with these first principles, never really paying attention to the book itself"; (2) "assume that, because the first principles are dogmatic, the arguments based on them, the reasoning they support, and the conclusions to which they lead to are all dogmatic in the same way."[116] We do well to heed these warnings so that we can understand Qoheleth's message. After all, having understood his message on his terms, we can still reject it if we have valid reasons to reject his assumptions. Otherwise we will not understand him, and if we reject what we *think* he is saying, we will not know what it is that we are really rejecting.

In the previous passage Qoheleth has presented the appropriate response to the vanity of life. In this passage he returns to the theme of vanity (3:9). He sought to vivify the idea of vanity in our minds through the earlier poem (1:4–8). Using illustrations from his past experiences (1:12–2:23), he sought to recreate the sense of vanity in our hearts. Now through another poem he seeks to amplify this sense of vanity.

Why do we say so? We know 3:1–8 is a poem about vanity from the rhetorical question of 3:9, which is basically the same as that of 1:3. Just as "Vanity of vanities; all is vanity" (1:2) is the expected answer to "What profit does man have . . . ?" (1:3), this poem is the answer to that same question expressed in 3:9. Thus the poem embodies the idea of "Vanity of vanities; all is vanity." And poetry by design evokes imagination (as in 1:4–8) and most often (as in this case) emotion as well.

This poem is not saying, as is commonly misunderstood, that there is a time permitted for us to do this or that thing listed in the poem. The Hebrew word translated "season" in 3:1 means appointed time,[117] and the word translated "matter" has the root meaning of "desire" and in this context means "desired or purposed event."[118] In view of 3:11–15 (see below), it is clear that 3:1 refers to events purposed and appointed by God.

The poem is then saying that the nature and timing of everything that happens everywhere in this world ("under the heavens"), whether good or bad, such as what is listed in the poem, are purposed and appointed by God. Qoheleth takes for granted that God has sovereign control over everything in this world. So every "matter," including human activities, is either directed or permitted by God. Everything that happens in this world is thus "God's work" (see further exposition on 8:17). This is not to say that Qoheleth had a fatalistic view of life, the view that everything is fated or predetermined so that we cannot be held responsible for whatever we do or fail to do.

This passage follows immediately that which introduces for the first time God's sovereignty (over who may have enjoyment). That very passage also highlights human

---

116. Adler, *How to Read a Book*, 292.
117. Seow, *Ecclesiastes*, 159.
118. Cf. Talley, "חפץ," 233–34.

responsibility (to be good in God's sight as a condition to having enjoyment). Thus God's sovereignty is not to the exclusion of human responsibility, which then implies human freedom of choice.[119]

In fact, Qoheleth later admonishes us to be prudent in light of life's uncertainties (11:1–6). He assumes the biblical teaching of not only divine sovereignty but also human responsibility. But how can it be true that God has sovereign control over everything that happens and yet human beings have freedom to choose and thus be held responsible for their actions? We cannot understand it. But our inability to comprehend does not mean that it cannot be true. Scientists affirm that light is both wave and particle even though they cannot understand how it can be so. They have to accept the paradoxical nature of light to make sense of physical phenomena that we observe.[120] The modernist assumption that the human mind can understand and explain everything in the universe has long been obsolete.

Later we shall see why and how the paradoxical teaching of divine sovereignty and human responsibility is necessary for making sense of human experience. For now, we take note that the sovereign God "makes everything [including misfortunes] appropriate in its time," for a purpose (3:11). The purpose of misfortunes happening at "appropriate" times in the world or in our life involves evoking in us the sense of vanity. As pointed out in our exposition of 1:12–18, the poem of 3:1–8 highlights that even before we die, our temporal profits can be lost through calamities or crimes if not through our own carelessness or foolishness. So by reminding us of the misfortunes of life, Qoheleth is seeking to further evoke or amplify the sense of vanity in us. Let us now consider how he does this.

The poem presents fourteen pairs of opposite things that happen in this world. The first pair, "a time to be born, and a time to die," reaffirms the certainty of death. It echoes "a generation goes [death] and a generation comes [birth]" (1:4). The rest reminds us of the uncertainties of life. As poetry teases our imagination, what is named in the pairs may represent different events beyond the named event itself. For example, "a time to weep" refers to not only weeping itself, but also the different painful events that make us weep. And "a time to dance" covers not just dancing, but also all sorts of events that cause us to rejoice. So the fourteen pairs taken together cover every conceivable event under the heavens (3:1).[121]

---

119. Cf. Rudman, *Determinism in Ecclesiastes*, 33, 149.

120. See for instance, Stannard, "Wave/Particle Paradox."

121. Technically speaking, the first thirteen pairs of events should be translated: "a time for birthing . . . for dying . . . for weeping . . . for dancing . . . for loving . . . for hating" (Seow, *Ecclesiastes*, 160). We have followed most Bible translations in rendering them into more idiomatic English. However it is disputed whether "for birthing" is to be read as "to give birth" (active sense) or "to be born" (passive sense). The grammatical form is "neutral with respect to voice, namely the active form may be passive in force" (Joüon and Muraoka, *Grammar*, §124t). Thus in Jeremiah 25:34, "your days *for slaughtering* have come" means "the days for you *to be slaughtered* have come." Most Bible translations render "for birthing" in 3:2 as "to be born" (cf. Fox, *Time*, 207). We have opted for this translation because it captures the intention of the poem regardless of whether the sense is active or passive. For

The last pair, "a time for war, and a time for peace," aptly summarizes the poem. The image of war helps us capture the range of the negative experiences represented. For when there is war, people get killed and there is weeping and mourning; stones are gathered as weapons[122] and clothes get torn apart; buildings get torn down and plants are uprooted, adding to the destruction; refugees throw their belongings away and there is no time to search for what is missing; in grief people keep silence and refrain from embracing for cordiality, only for empathy; the war was nurtured by a lack of love, the war then breeds hatred all over.

Qoheleth is saying that whatever fortunate event we experience between birth and death has an unfortunate counterpart that may or may not happen as well. If it happens, it cancels out the profit gained.[123] The intended effect of the poem (3:1–8) is to impress upon us the uncertainties of life and thus the sense that whatever profit we gain under the sun may be lost even before we die. The image of war is particularly effective in helping us capture the sense of suffering loss. And the certainty of death means that even if we do not lose everything before we die, we will lose them all eventually. So all is vanity and there is no profit under the sun (3:9). We have to come to terms with not only the certainty of death but also the uncertainties of life. Iain Provan puts it eloquently: "The universe has a flow and a regularity to it that is beyond any human control and renders futile all attempts at 'profit.' The wise person lives life in the light of this massive truth."[124]

The theme of the speech as expressed here is thus more nuanced than the outright assertion in 1:2–3. For it not only affirms, as in 1:2–3, that the *ultimate* profitlessness of all temporal gains is certain, but also that the *immediate* futility of all earthly pursuits is possible. This is unsettling even for people who smugly think and feel that they can live with the unpleasant reality that death will finally confiscate all that they have. Hence the sense of vanity evoked by this poem not only strengthens but is stronger than that evoked by the illustrations from Qoheleth's personal experiences. Why does God appoint events such that we experience vanity even before we die? Why does Qoheleth use this reality to unsettle our feelings? As we continue to hear him out, we will find the answers to these vexing questions.

---

even reading it in the active sense, the pair "a time for birthing" and "a time for dying" is "an allusive reference to the beginnings and the endings of life" (Holmstedt et al., *Qoheleth*, 122). For it is referring to the events of birth and death in general; "a time to give birth, and a time to die" is not about any particular individual (cf. Seow, *Ecclesiastes*, 160). So the pair is about "a time (for mothers) to give birth" and "a time (for people) to die." Now "a time (for mothers) to give birth" is the same as "a time (for people) to be born," which contrasts with "a time (for people) to die." In other words, there is "a time to be born, and a time to die"—a time for life to begin (a generation comes) and a time for life to end (a generation goes).

122. Dunham, "Time to Throw Away Stones," 331–35.
123. Cf. Crenshaw, *Ecclesiastes*, 96.
124. Provan. *Ecclesiastes/Song of Songs*, 87.

Explanation for Vanity and Sense of Eternity (3:10–15)

> *3:10 I have seen the preoccupation that God has given to the children of man to be occupied with. 3:11 He makes everything appropriate in its time. He has also put eternity in their heart, yet so that man will not discover what God does from the beginning to the end. 3:12 I know that there is nothing good for them except to have enjoyment and to do good in their lifetime; 3:13 and also that (in the case of) every man who eats and drinks and sees good (has enjoyment) in all his toil, it is a gift of God. 3:14 I know that everything God does cannot be changed; nothing can be added to it, nor anything taken from it. For God so works that men should fear him. 3:15 Whatever comes to be, has already been; that which will come to be, already has been; for God seeks what has gone by.*

This passage is one of the most important and perhaps the most profound in Ecclesiastes. It not only answers the vexing questions raised above, it also begins to give us a coherent picture of the meaning of life. As we now proceed to consider its message, let us be reminded that if we do not share Qoheleth's assumptions about God, for the sake of understanding what he has to say, we need to accept them temporarily.

And, as previously discussed, Qoheleth assumes that God has control over everything that happens and yet human beings have the freedom to choose. So to Qoheleth, whatever happens in this world, including what human beings experience or "freely" choose to do, is the work of God. That means, when he uses phrases like "what God does" or "God so works," he is simply talking about what we experience or observe, without necessarily implying what is called a "supernatural intervention."

What then does the "preoccupation" (3:10) that "God has given to the children of man to be occupied with" refer to? We saw in 1:13a that human beings have a God-given preoccupation to make sense of life. In that context this preoccupation was expressed in Qoheleth's intellectual investigation of the meaning of life. Similarly, the preoccupation here refers to the human impulse to make sense of life. But we need to consider, in this context, how this preoccupation is expressed in human life.

Note that this passage flows logically from the preceding one (3:1–9), and they form one inseparable thought unit. So the force of the rhetorical question, "What profit has the worker in (exchange for) all his toils" (3:9), which was asked in light of the somber reality embodied in the poem—the certainty of death and the uncertainties of life—must be carried over to the reading of this passage, especially 3:10. We can then infer that the preoccupation or impulse to make sense of life referred to in 3:10 is triggered by the sense of vanity evoked by that somber reality captured by the fourteen pairs of opposites. For when it dawns on us that what we gain in this world will not only be left behind when we die but may also be lost even before we die, we need to come to terms with this realization in order to make sense of life.

In the next verse, when Qoheleth says, "He makes everything appropriate in its time" (3:11), he is referring back to the fourteen pairs of opposite things listed in the poem, such as "a time for war, and a time for peace" (3:8). For, like in 1:2, the Hebrew word translated "everything" is literally "the all," which refers to things that are specific and can be identified from the context, which in this case is the poem of 3:1–8. There he affirmed that each of these things happens according to its "season" or appointed time (3:1). Here he adds that it is God who appoints these times, and that he makes each of those things "appropriate in its time" (NASB, HCSB).[125] Thus the triggering of the impulse to make sense of life is by God's design.

In other words, God has made this world and sustains it in such a way that human beings are driven to seek for the meaning of life. We now explore, in this particular context, how this God-given preoccupation is expressed in human life.

As he continues in the same verse, Qoheleth says that God "has also put eternity in their heart." In view of how the Hebrew word translated "eternity" is used elsewhere in Ecclesiastes (1:4, 10; 2:16; 3:14; 9:6; 12:5) as well as in the context of 3:1–11, Krüger is on solid ground when he says that "the interpretation of [the word] as a time concept has the greatest probability."[126] Whatever "eternity" means here, the phrase "eternity in their heart" at the least refers to the human ability to transcend the present to look back into the past as well as think about the future.[127] The clause has even been translated as, "moreover he has put a sense of past and future into their minds" (NRSV).[128]

We shall see that this interpretation makes perfect sense in light of what follows in the rest of the verse: "(yet so that) man will not discover what God does from the beginning to the end." For since "what God does" means whatever happens, the verse as a whole is affirming this: God not only makes the opposite things listed in the poem "appropriate in its time," thus evoking the sense of vanity, he has *also* given humanity the sense of past and future, "yet so that" they will not find out what will happen in this world. This profound statement deserves special attention. The logical connection between "He has also put eternity in their heart" and "yet so that man will not discover what God does" (3:11)[129] is not immediately obvious. To capture it, we need

---

125. The Hebrew word translated "appropriate" basically means "beautiful." Thus translating the phrase as "beautiful in its time" (ESV, NIV, NKJV) is technically correct, but obscures the meaning. Since it refers to something happening according to its appointed time to fulfill a purpose, it is "beautiful" in the specific sense that it is "fitting" or "appropriate" (cf. Schoors, *Preacher II*, 257). This nuance is more clearly seen in 5:18—"What I have seen is good, what is *fitting* (literally, "beautiful"), is to eat and drink and to see good (have enjoyment)." There the Bible translations generally render it as either "fitting" (ESV, NASB, NKJV) or "appropriate" (HCSB, NIV).

126. Krüger, *Qoheleth*, 80; cf. Schoors, *Preacher II*, 221–25.

127. Cf. Whitley, *Koheleth*, 32.

128. Cf. Holmstedt et al., *Qoheleth*, 128.

129. Though Krüger recognizes that the Hebrew word (*māṣā'*) translated "discover" literally means "find out," on the basis of 8:17, he translates it as "comprehend" (a few Bible translations have "fathom" or "fully understand") instead of "find out" or "discover" (Krüger, *Qoheleth*, 80, 163). We shall see that in 8:17 the three occurrences of the word there have to mean "discover." There is no reason to deviate from the literal meaning "find out" in 3:11 or 8:17.

to imagine what it is like to live in a world as pictured in the poem and have eternity in our heart, that is, the ability to look backward and forward in time. When we look into the past, we see that the poem is telling the truth—bad things do happen to even good people. So when we think of the future, we worry about what might happen, and thus want to find out what will happen.

Hence the sense of eternity in our heart aggravates the sense of vanity with the effect that we want to find out about future events. So in this context this is how the preoccupation to make sense of life is expressed. In fact, the standard Jewish English translation of the Hebrew Bible, having rendered the clause as "He also puts eternity in their mind," paraphrases it (in a footnote) as "He preoccupies man with the attempt to discover the times of future events" (NJPS).

Thus "He [in addition to making everything appropriate in its time to evoke in the human heart the sense of vanity] has also put [the sense of] eternity in their heart" means that God has created humanity in such a way that they will, in response to vanity, be occupied with wanting to find out what God does (what will happen), *"yet so that* man (humanity) will not discover what God does from the beginning to the end (of history)." In other words, God has given humanity the ability to think about the past and the future, which causes them to want to find out about the future, but not the ability to discover what will happen throughout their lifetime.

Why then did God create humanity in such a way that, in response to vanity, they will seek to know the future yet he will not allow them to discover it? How then should human beings respond? And how have human beings responded? As we continue to look at the passage, we will answer these questions, but not necessarily in that order.

According to 3:14a, even if we can somehow discover what will happen, we cannot avoid it, as "everything God does cannot be changed; nothing can be added to it, nor anything taken from it," which means, whatever is going to happen will surely happen. Of course in certain circumstances if we knew what would happen, we could do something about it. For instance, if we discovered that a massive bomb would soon go off in our office building, we could warn as many people as possible as we rush out. But by "everything God does" Qoheleth is referring to what will actually happen, such as whether we managed to get out of the doomed building in time or not. We can change what could have happened but not what will actually happen.

Why does Qoheleth point out something so obvious? People living in a premodern world practice divination and sorcery (magic). They use divination to discover what is supposedly fated to happen. Fated events "will actually happen" and thus cannot be avoided by natural means. But they believe that ill-fated events could be nullified through magic, the supposed manipulation of supernatural forces. Qoheleth is here discrediting both divination and magic. His original audience would have understood what he was getting at.

The widespread practice of divination and magic, or their equivalents, attests to the universal human impulse to come to terms with the certainty of death and the uncertainties of life. Divination and magic are intended to satisfy the human need to know about, and then to escape from, misfortunes that are supposedly fated to happen. In this way, divination and magic soothe the deep-seated feeling of insecurity that the sense of eternity, coupled with the sense of vanity, evoke in us. This helps to give some meaning to life. But Ecclesiastes teaches that this and other man-made means to soothe the sense of insecurity only replace it with a false sense of security. These are actually human attempts to evade God's purpose in appointing the events represented in the poem and in putting eternity in our heart (3:11, 14a).

Qoheleth then spells out this purpose: "For God so works (in order) that men (people) should fear him" (3:14b).[130] But what does it mean to "fear God"? Building on 3:14b, Qoheleth makes it clear in 5:1–7 what it means to "fear God." In our exposition of 5:1–7 we will derive this working definition: *to fear God is to do what is right and not what is wrong (even) when no one, except God, is watching or holding us accountable.* It usually works through the conscience (Rom 2:14–16). A God-fearing person, who may even be one who professes to be an atheist, is a conscientious person. For such a person seeks to do what is right and not what is wrong (according to his conscience) even when no one (except God) is watching or holding him accountable.

Actually, here in 3:14b Qoheleth uses the Hebrew phrase "fear before God" (also in 8:13) rather than "fear God" as in 5:7 (also in 7:18; 8:12; 12:13). However, as Whybray points out, "in 8:12, 13, he uses the two forms interchangeably."[131] Hence we take "fear before him" as synonymous to "fear him." Also, Whybray adds, "the idea that Qoheleth's concept of 'the fear of God' is essentially different from its usual meaning in the Old Testament . . . is an idea derived from a particular interpretation of Qoheleth's thought in general rather than from his actual use of the phrase."[132] And in the Old Testament, fearing God and keeping his commandments are inseparable (see especially Deut 10:12–13). So whenever Qoheleth talks about fearing (before) God, keeping his commandments is implied; this is confirmed in 12:13, where this implication is spelled out. All this is clear from our exposition of the verses where the concept occurs whether explicitly or implicitly.

In the context of 3:10–15, "God so works that men should fear him," means God so works in the world, such as through the sense of vanity aggravated by the sense of eternity resulting in a sense of insecurity, so that people should and would acknowledge him and seek to live a God-fearing or conscientious life. How then does this happen?

Given the certainty of death and the uncertainties of life as depicted in the poem (3:1–8), the only way to feel secure about the future is to be able to trust in one who is in control of what will happen and who is just. Qoheleth presents God as such a

---

130. In this context, the Hebrew particle *še-* translated "that" clearly "expresses purpose, 'so that, in order that'" (Whitley, *Koheleth*, 34; cf. Schoors, *Preacher*, 143).

131. Whybray, *Ecclesiastes*, 75.

132. Whybray, *Ecclesiastes*, 75.

one: he is all-powerful and is thus in control of whatever happens, in fact he "makes all things appropriate in its time" (3:1–11), and he is all-just and thus upholds justice (3:17; 8:12–13; 12:14). Hence no bad things can happen to us unless he allows it. And when he allows it, it is for a good cause as he is just.

This means if we trust in God to watch over us, we can feel secure about the future. In fact there is no other option. God so works that we need to trust in him to watch over us. But if we trust in God to *watch over us*, we must first wholeheartedly believe in the existence of an all-powerful and all-just God who is *watching us* (Prov 15:3). And if we wholeheartedly believe in the existence of such a God, we will fear him (Job 37:22–24)—do what is right and not what is wrong even when no one, except God, is watching or holding us accountable. Hence God so works that we should—need to—fear him.

But since human beings have the freedom to choose, many have sought to evade this purpose of God that we should fear him as in the case of people who practice divination and magic. This explains why Qoheleth has to remind us of the somber reality captured in the poem to unsettle our feelings and having done that, explain God's purpose in the way he works in this world. By doing this he puts those who have not yet yielded to God's purpose into the mood to reconsider their chosen path, as well as encourages those who have already done so. Knowing how difficult it is to get people to change their way of thinking and living, Qoheleth has crafted a speech with exceptional persuasive power. In this exposition we can only partially recreate this force as part of our attempt to recapture his rhetoric.

We have seen how, after he has captured our attention with the forceful assertion that everything is vanity (1:2–3), he engages our imagination by using a poem to vivify the idea of vanity (1:4–11), and then speaks to our emotion through illustrations from his personal experience to recreate the sense of vanity (1:12–2:23). When we are thus ready to begin reconsidering how we should then live, he appeals to our intuition by admonishing that, in light of the reality that everything is vanity, the most meaningful thing to do is to have enjoyment of life (2:24–26). For otherwise life does not make sense. Now having amplified the sense of vanity through another poem (3:1–8), and in the context of explaining God's overall purpose (3:10–15), Qoheleth returns to the subject of enjoyment (3:12–13). Here he admonishes having enjoyment of life, instead of seeking to know and possibly change the future (3:11, 14a), as the proper response to the uncertainties of life (3:1–9) in order to make sense of life (3:10). How does his admonition to have enjoyment relate to God's purpose that we should fear him (3:14b)?

In 2:24–26 Qoheleth affirmed that the ability to have enjoyment is "from the hand of God." That means "it is a gift of God" (3:13), which he gives to those who are "good in his sight."[133] The meaning of 3:12–13 should be clear in light of our exposition

---

133. The Hebrew of 3:13 reads literally, "and also, every man who eats and drinks and sees good in his labor it (is) a gift of God." No matter how 3:13 is translated, since 2:24–26 says that the ability

of 2:24–26 as it says essentially the same thing. The only difference is that instead of saying those who are able to have enjoyment are those who are "good in God's sight," here it is replaced with an admonition "to do good in their lifetime."[134] Thus he spells out that those who are "good in God's sight" are those who "do good in their lifetime," that is, do what is right and not what is wrong (even) when no one, except God, is watching or holding them accountable. This means to have enjoyment, one needs to "fear God." Since God so works that people need to have enjoyment to make sense of life, we again see that God so works that they should fear him. As to why fearing God is necessary to have enjoyment, it will be elaborated in 5:18–6:7 and then 11:7–10.

In other words, since one cannot have enjoyment apart from the fear of God, undergirding the admonition to have enjoyment is the admonition to fear God and thus be good in his sight by doing what is (morally) good. Hence, though Qoheleth presents enjoyment as the sensible response to vanity, enjoyment is not itself the solution to vanity. The solution is the more basic response to vanity: fear God.

Therefore "God so works" in two ways "that we should fear him." Firstly, our sense of insecurity due to the uncertainties of life prods us to trust in God to watch over us. This requires us to first believe in the existence of an all-powerful and all-just God who is watching us, and thus fear him. Secondly, our sense of futility due to the certainty of death prods us to have enjoyment while we are still alive. This requires us to be good in God's sight and thus do good in our lifetime, that is, fear him.

Only the fear of God enables us to replace the sense of insecurity with a deep-seated sense of security so that we can truly have enjoyment in the face of the uncertainties of life. We saw that when we fear God, who watches us, we can trust in him to watch over us. Though he allows adversities, his purpose is for our well-being, enabling us to truly enjoy life. That means, God makes everything appropriate in its time to accomplish his good purpose for humanity. Qoheleth's speech is designed to prod us to recognize this work of God and thus feel secure about the future.

---

to "see good" (have enjoyment) in one's labor is (a gift) from the hand of God given only to those who are "good in his sight," the "gift of God" (ability to have enjoyment) here has to be limited to some people—those who "fear God" (3:14) and thus "do good" (3:12). To make this implication clear we have added "in the case of (every man)" in our translation of 3:13. HCSB does it by adding "whenever": "It is also the gift of God whenever anyone eats, drinks, and enjoys all his efforts" (also NJPS; NASB does not make the implication clear). Most Bible translations render the verbs with a modal sense ("should") as in NKJV: "and also that every man should eat and drink and enjoy the good of all his labor—it *is* the gift of God" (NIV has "may" not "should"; NRSV does not make sense). This rendering does not make the implication clear. In giving the verbs a modal sense, it reads the relative particle "who" (which would be qualifying "every man") as "that," which "is [then] introducing the fact of enjoyment": "every person, that one should eat . . ." (Seow, *Ecclesiastes*, 164). Whether the relative particle is read as "who" or "that," 3:13 echoes 2:24–26 that the ability to have enjoyment is a gift of God. But to truly echo 2:24–26, a translation should also make the implication clear that not everyone receives this gift.

134. For a discussion that here "to do good" retains its plain sense and normal meaning—"to do (moral) good"—and is not synonymous to "see good (have enjoyment)" as claimed by most commentators, see below (Excursus to 3:10–15).

The technical term for this work of God is "providence." But most people today would dismiss this belief in divine providence as "a crutch for the weak." Throughout his speech, Qoheleth tries to help us see, by making us feel, that we are all weak and that we all need a reliable crutch. In view of the uncertainties of life we need to recognize that we cannot really live, as John Calvin puts it, without "the knowledge of the providence of God; because, without it, we would be harassed with doubts and fears, being uncertain whether or not the world was governed by chance. . . . [Now] what can be more awfully tormenting than to be constantly racked with doubt and anxiety? And we will never be able to arrive at a calm state of mind until we are taught to repose with implicit confidence in the providence of God."[135]

Actually, every society has its crutches. In a premodern (and segments of a postmodern) society, the dominant crutch has been some form of divination and magic. Strictly speaking, divination is about gaining knowledge of the world through observing the workings of fate, the supposed impersonal cosmic force believed to be running the world. Magic involves the use of techniques to manipulate this force to our benefit. Hence divination is the premodern counterpart to modern science and magic is the premodern counterpart to modern technology. And modern science and technology have confirmed Qoheleth's view that divination and magic are sheer superstitions.

In a modern society, the dominant crutch is (or was) the idea of "progress." As a balm to soothe the deep-seated sense of insecurity "progress" promises not just material, but also emotional, comforts. The incredible material comforts brought about by modern science and technology lend credibility to this idea. But "progress" has failed miserably in terms of emotional comforts, which matter more than material comforts. So beginning with the second half of the twentieth century, even modern people began to consider the idea of "progress" a modern superstition. Prominent American writer Walker Percy asked, "Why does man feel so sad in the twentieth century . . . when, more than in any other age, he has succeeded in satisfying his needs and making over the world for his own use?"[136] By the end of the century, this is how Oxford historian Felipe Fernandez-Armesto summed up the century, striking a responsive chord in the hearts of many today: "It was the best of times. It was the worst of times. . . . It promised so much and betrayed so many. . . . Why did progress fail?"[137]

Trust in "progress" is essentially trust in human potential to solve every human problem. As British historian David Bebbington puts it, "Man, according to the idea of progress, has advanced not just in matters like technology and its improvement of material conditions. There has been progress also in the use of man's intellect and, in many versions, in his moral capacity. Human history is therefore the account of the improvement of the human condition from barbarism to civilization."[138] In light of

---

135. Calvin, *Commentary on the Psalms*, 265.
136. Percy, *Message in the Bottle*, 3.
137. Fernandez-Armesto, "Century of Paradox."
138. Bebbington, *Patterns in History*, 68.

the deep-seated sense of insecurity, modern people need the assurance that things are getting better. But as the twenty-first century unfolds, the more knowledgeable and wiser one becomes, the more one despairs over whether the human race would survive another century.

As if anticipating this faith in progress as a crutch to evade God's purpose that we should fear him, Qoheleth in the next breath says, "Whatever comes to be, has already been; that which will come to be, already has been; for God seeks what has gone by" (3:15). This verse basically reiterates the sub-theme introduced in 1:9, which is summarized there as, "there is nothing new under the sun." As we have seen, this idea is embodied in Qoheleth's first poem (1:4–8), which begins with this line: "a generation goes and a generation comes, yet the world (including humanity) remains as ever." Thus 3:15, which begins with "a time to be born [a generation comes], and a time to die [a generation goes]," reaffirms that there can be no real progress in the human condition.

Also, here in the context of the second poem (3:1–8), "there is nothing new under the sun" means the reality depicted in the poem—the certainty of death and the uncertainties of life—will not change and thus remains with us to the very end of human history. Since the proper response to this somber reality is to fear God, 3:15 reinforces the teaching of 3:14, which indirectly admonishes us to fear God.

Though there has been no real progress in the human condition, it does not mean that history has no progress in the sense that it is not moving toward a goal. For that would mean history has no purpose and hence no meaning. Qoheleth's belief in divine providence implies that history has purpose and goal and thus meaning (see further "Teaching of Ecclesiastes" under "Experiencing the Meaning of History"). It is pertinent here to note that, "the idea of progress, according to a widely accepted interpretation, represents a secularized version of the Christian belief in providence."[139] This means the (outmoded) belief in "progress" is an implicit, if not explicit, rejection of providence and thus of God's purpose in his providence that we should fear him.

Now given the options based on modern science and technology, or their pre-modern counterparts, how then can one come to terms with the certainty of death and the uncertainties of life? Would it not be wise to listen carefully and without prejudice to what Qoheleth has to say to us?

Excursus to 3:10–15: Qoheleth on Enjoyment and the Fear of God

The above exposition of 3:10–15 on enjoyment and the fear of God is crucial to the flow of thought of Ecclesiastes. The text deserves a more thorough exegetical study. We first need to establish our translations of 3:11 and 3:14 on firm exegetical ground because they differ at least in part from most Bible translations. The verb ʿāśāh ("to

---

139. Lasch, *True and Only Heaven*, 40; see further Nash, *Meaning of History*, 78–79.

do or make") occurs twice in 3:11 and once in 3:14b in the Hebrew perfective form, which is usually translated in the past or past perfect tense, as well as once in 3:14a in the Hebrew imperfective form, which is usually translated in the future tense. All four occurrences of the verb describe God's work in this world, and to make coherent sense of 3:10–15, all four must have the same tense. In 3:11b we have the phrase "what God *does/did/has done* from the beginning to the end." If the tense is the past ("did") or past perfect ("has done"), it means Qoheleth is saying that whatever happens in this world (as represented in the poem) has been predetermined by God in the fatalistic sense even before the beginning of the world.

However there is virtually no dispute that the occurrence of the verb ʿāśāh in 3:14a is to be translated in the present tense—"I know that everything God *does*"—as the imperfective form here clearly "has a frequentative force or express the habitual."[140] And not only the imperfective but also the perfective form can have the "present/habitual significance."[141] So the three occurrences of ʿāśāh in the perfective form in 3:11, 14 are to be translated also in the present tense:[142] "He *makes* everything appropriate" (3:11a); "what God *does* from the beginning" (3:11b); "For God so *works*" (3:14b). We do not translate "He also *puts* eternity in their heart" (3:11b) though the verb "put" is also in the perfective form because it refers to a characteristic of humanity that God *has put* in them when he created humanity and not to God's present (habitual) activity in the world.

The phrase translated "(everything God does) cannot be changed" (3:14a) is literally "it shall be forever" and is usually rendered along this line. But what does it mean by "everything God does shall be forever"? In view of the qualifying clause, "nothing can be added to it, nor anything taken from it," the sense is that everything God does cannot be modified or changed, or as one Bible translation renders it: "whatever God does *is final*" (NLT; italics added).

As for the connecting phrase "yet so that" (3:11), it translates a negating particle often translated "without" followed by a conjunction meaning "that," which occur together only this once in the Hebrew Bible and thus the meaning is not certain and must be determined from this context itself.[143] What is certain is that together they connect "He has also put eternity in their heart (so they want to find out what will happen)" and "they will not discover what God does (what will happen)." We know from 8:17 that though "man may toil to seek, but he will not discover [what God does]." Hence 3:11 is saying: *God has made humanity in such a way that they will even toil to find out what will happen* "without" "that" *they will not discover it.* How then should we read the negating particle ("without") and the conjunction ("that") so that together they connect sensibly the two parts of 3:11? Now the conjunction "that" can

---

140. Schoors, *Preacher*, 175–76.
141. Waltke and O'Connor, *Syntax*, §30.4b; cf. §31.3e.
142. Cf. Schoors, *Preacher*, 175.
143. Cf. Isaksson, *Language of Qoheleth*, 181.

mean "so that."[144] Then reading the negating particle as "but" or "yet," we have "yet so that," which fits the context perfectly.[145] No wonder this is the interpretation taken by a number of Bible translations.

Moving on to the phrase "to do good" (3:12), unfortunately most commentators do not understand it according to its plain sense and normal meaning—to do what is morally good. They highlight that the phrase is in the immediate context of enjoyment—"there is nothing good for them except to have enjoyment" (3:12)—and that it seems to parallel "sees good (has enjoyment) in all his toil" (3:13). So based on a similar Greek phrase, they argue that "to do good" must then mean something like "to experience good," and not to do what is morally good.[146] They do not see the relevance of the plain sense and normal meaning of the phrase here. Surely it is axiomatic that the plain sense and normal meaning of a word or phrase is to be given priority unless it does not make sense in its context. In the larger context of the theme of enjoyment, the combination of "there is nothing good . . . except"; "eat and drink"; "see good (have enjoyment) in his labor"; and "it is from the hand of God [a gift]" in 2:24–26 is repeated in 3:12–13. The only difference is that, instead of "those good in his (God's) sight" (in contrast to sinners) in 2:26, here we have "to do good in their lifetime" (3:12), which we saw above is rephrased as "fear God" in 3:14.

In view of the similarities between 2:24–26 and 3:12–13 and that both are presented as the proper response to vanity, it is obvious that 3:12–13 builds on 2:24–26. This is part of Qoheleth's cyclical development of his overall argument (see "Introduction to Ecclesiastes" under "Coherent Message"). And since Qoheleth says that *only* the one who is "good in his (God's) sight" (2:26) can "see good (have enjoyment) in his labor" (2:24) and thus "can have enjoyment" (2:25), "to do good in their lifetime" (3:12) must be clarifying what it means to be "good in his (God's) sight." Otherwise there is no development in the argument (note that every other time when the admonition to have enjoyment is repeated, something new is added). After all, how can one be good in the sight of a God who "will judge the righteous and the wicked" (3:17; cf. 11:9; 12:14) without being morally good? Also, the phrase "to do good" is embedded here in the immediate context of explaining why in view of vanity we should "fear God" (3:14), which is another way of saying, "do (moral) good" (cf. 8:11–13; 12:13).

In fact, if "to do good" does not mean "to do (moral) good," there is no adequate flow of thought in 3:10–14. In 3:10–11 Qoheleth stresses the futility of the preoccupation to discover the future in response to vanity. So this preoccupation is not an appropriate response to vanity. In 3:12–13 he repeats the sensible response to vanity already introduced in 2:24–26—to have enjoyment as a gift from the hand of God. But since to have enjoyment one must be good in God's sight, Qoheleth now adds to the admonition to have enjoyment the admonition "to do good" in one's lifetime.

---

144. Waltke and O'Connor, *Syntax*, §38.3.
145. Cf. Schoors, *Preacher*, 147.
146. Schoors, *Preacher II*, 37–38.

Then 3:14a reiterates the futility to discover the future by stressing that the future cannot be changed, which means even if one could discover the future, it would still be futile because one could do nothing about it. Thus Qoheleth reaffirms that the preoccupation to discover the future is not an appropriate response to vanity and thus indirectly admonishes again his audience to have enjoyment instead, and so they are "to do good" in their lifetime. Then 3:14b spells out that God so works in this world—including evoking the sense of vanity so that people want to discover and change the future—that they *should* fear him (so that they could have enjoyment). This means to be good in God's sight, "to do good," and to fear God mean the same thing. Otherwise 3:14 does not follow from 3:10–13.

Therefore it is rather tenuous and clearly unwarranted to read "to do good" as other than "to do (moral) good." Daniel Fredericks puts it forcefully: "The moral caveat to enjoyment is found later too in 11:[9], where youth are encouraged to enjoy life but to remember that God will bring them to judgment for all their actions. The same phrase ʽāśāh ṭôb (do good) is the uncontested meaning in 7:20 . . . . The antonymous grammatical and lexical phrase 'do evil' is used freely by Qoheleth (4:3; 5:1; 8:1–12). Only a rigid stripping of all conventional wisdom from Ecclesiastes would lead to eliminating this otherwise clear injunction to righteousness."[147]

Finally, the Hebrew of the last part of 3:15—"for God seeks *what has gone by*"—is obscure. What is it that God seeks? According to Crenshaw, "Several answers have been offered: (1) the persecuted; (2) the events of the past; (3) the same; and (4) what God sought previously."[148] On the basis that 3:15 "repeats ideas expressed in 1:9," Crenshaw infers: "There is nothing new. Why? Because God ensures that events which have just transpired do not vanish into thin air. God brings them back once more, so that the past circles into the present."[149] Of course this is not to be understood literally, that the exact past events—"what has gone by"—repeat themselves in the present and then in the future. As stressed in our exposition of 1:9, "there is nothing new" applies only in the limited sense that basic realities in the natural and human world do not change (see Excursus to 1:4–11).

Since 3:15 reiterates 1:9, it confirms that within the death-birth cycle ("a generation goes and a generation comes," that is, "a time to be born, and a time to die"), the claim that "there is nothing new" in 1:9 is limited to what humans basically experience ("a time to weep, and a time to laugh"), and in how and why they typically act or react ("a time to love, and a time to hate"). In the context of the poem in 1:4–11, the focus is that because basic realities do not change, there is (ultimately) no net gain or profit and thus all is vanity. In the context here, the focus is that the reality depicted in the second poem, which results in no (ultimate) profit to human toil (3:1–9), will not

---

147. Fredericks, *Ecclesiastes*, 118.
148. Crenshaw, *Ecclesiastes*, 100.
149. Crenshaw *Ecclesiastes*, 100; followed by Fox, *Time*, 213–14; cf. Holmstedt et al., *Qoheleth*, 135.

change and thus all the more we need to fear God so as to come to terms with this reality.

Observation to Reinforce Sense of Vanity (3:16–21)

> *3:16 Furthermore, I saw under the sun that in the place of justice, wickedness was there, and in the place of righteousness, wickedness was there. 3:17 I said to myself, God will judge the righteous and the wicked even though there is a time for every matter and for every deed there. 3:18 I said to myself concerning the children of man that God is testing them so that they see that they are but animals. 3:19 For the fate of the children of man and the fate of animals are one and the same. As one dies, so dies the other. In fact they both have the same breath, and man has no advantage over the animal, for both are fleeting. 3:20 Both go to one place. Both are from dust, and both return to dust. 3:21 Who knows as for the breath of man, whether it goes up and for the breath of the animal, whether it goes down into the earth?*

The word "furthermore" indicates that this passage builds on what precedes. What precedes is about the uncertainties of life. Now Qoheleth highlights that even in the courts of law, the very place where righteousness and justice are supposed to be guaranteed, wickedness and injustice may be present. There is no certainty even there. This means "there is a time for every matter" (3:1; 3:17b), which refers to the uncertainties of life as outlined in the poem, applies also to judgments meted out in the courts of law.

Thus he is going further to create a deeper and more graphic impression of the uncertainties of life. He is not saying there is no justice in the courts of law; we must not impose undue pessimism on him. He is simply saying he has seen unrighteousness and injustice even in the courts of law. In fact most people have also seen miscarriage of justice in the courts of law. So there is no certainty that if we live a righteous life, we will not suffer the fate of a criminal, and lose everything we have. This is simply realism. The purpose of reporting this observation at this point of the speech is then to reinforce the sense of vanity evoked through the poem above. This explains the apparent pessimism in the reflection that follows.

In response to this troubling observation, Qoheleth affirms that God will judge both the righteous and the wicked at the appropriate time, evidently to mete out the correct judgment. In other words, "*even though* [Qoheleth observes that] there is a time for every matter [uncertainties of life as outlined in the poem] and for the deed (done) there [miscarriage of justice even in the courts of law]," Qoheleth still believes that God will one day make things right.[150]

---

150. See below (Excursus to 3:16–21) for the exegetical basis for translating the conjunction as "even though" instead of "for."

Even Tremper Longman, who considers Qoheleth unorthodox, has to admit that in this text, (at the least) Qoheleth "addressed the injustice found in the human law courts.... He reminds himself of what he was surely taught..., namely that, though human justice is a rare and fleeting quality, God will set things right.... The innocent and the guilty would get what they deserve from the hand of God."[151] How God is going to do this, Qoheleth does not yet explain here; it could be within or beyond this life (see exposition of 8:11–13 and 12:14).

It is only after having reminded himself, and reassuring us, of God's own righteous judgment to make things right eventually that Qoheleth goes on to explain why God allows injustice even in the courts of law. Otherwise we will likely misinterpret his explanation as expressing pessimism. For he goes on to remind himself, and explain to us, that God is (only) "testing" humans to make them "see" for themselves that they are (in some ways) no different from animals.[152] The Hebrew word translated "testing" basically means "to separate," and can hence be translated, "choose, select, purify, [or] test,"[153] depending on the context. In this context, "the word says something about God testing people."[154] Evidently, the purpose of this testing is to purify character. In Daniel 11:35, this same word is used in the context, "to refine, *purge*, and make pure" a group of Jews whom God allowed to suffer persecution. How then does injustice in the courts of law cause people to see that they are like animals? And how does this relate to testing them in order to refine or purify them?

When a judge, sworn to uphold justice, perverts justice, especially when his inhuman treatment of an obviously innocent person brings about much suffering, he is not only treating his victim as sub-human, he himself is behaving like an animal without a conscience. In fact when someone behaves inhumanly toward others, we say, "You are an animal!" And we know that, given the right set of conditions, anyone is capable of such behavior. So when faced with this testing or trial—through experiencing or observing injustice in a court of law—we are inclined to see that human beings are like animals. This is because ("For"), after all, we do have the same "fate" (final outcome) as animals—return to dust (3:18–20).

In other words, occurrences of miscarriage of justice in the courts of law—judges behaving like animals as though they have no conscience—serve the purpose of showing us that we are indeed like animals since we die just like animals. Qoheleth highlights this purpose to great effect. His comparison of humans with animals may sound unduly negative. But even Longman affirms that "he is not making a blanket

---

151. Longman, *Ecclesiastes*, 127.

152. The grammatical form of the words translated "is testing them" and "they see" is unexpected in the context of this verse (see Schoors, *Preacher*, 180–81; Schoors, *Preacher II*, 74). However the meaning of the verse is clear—God allows injustice even in the courts of law so that humans recognize to their benefit that in some ways they are like animals.

153. Crenshaw, *Ecclesiastes*, 103.

154. Crenshaw, *Ecclesiastes*, 103.

comparison; he specifies one area of commonality—death."¹⁵⁵ Whybray says the first word, "For," in 3:19 "makes it clear . . . that he is comparing man with the animals only in one aspect: their mortality."¹⁵⁶ Since 3:19–20 is about the mortality of both humans and animals, "for all is *hebel* (vapor)" at the end of 3:19 means "for all is *fleeting*." Actually, translating it literally as "for all is vapor (transitory)" captures the mortality of both humans and animals more graphically—they are both (transient) like vapor.

Thus the statement, "man has no advantage over the animal," must not be taken beyond this point of comparison and so misunderstand Qoheleth as unorthodox. In fact, the basis for this statement is given: "They both have the same (kind of) breath." As noted by Whybray, "the view implied here, that God gives life to both men and animals by putting breath in them, and that when this breath is withdrawn, they die is the common biblical understanding of the matter."¹⁵⁷ For instance, referring to both humans and animals, Ps 104:29 says that when God "takes away their breath, they die and return to their dust." Later, Qoheleth himself spells out that when we die, "the dust returns to the earth as it was, and the breath returns to God who gave it" (12:7). And he would have said the same about animals. For obviously, "the breath returns to God who gave it" is another way of saying "God takes away (takes back) their breath," which applies to both humans and animals (cf. Job 34:14–15).¹⁵⁸

Furthermore, the reason humans have no advantage over animals is also spelled out: "All go to one place. All are from dust, and all return to dust" (3:20). That means, there is no advantage for humans only because there is no ultimate profit even to humans, as they also die like animals. It is like Qoheleth's comparison between a wise man and a fool (2:13–16), where it is clear that though he affirms ultimate vanity for both because both will die, he does not deny that the wise man has advantage over the fool. As a wise man, Qoheleth felt a deep sense of vanity when he realized that

155. Longman, *Ecclesiastes*, 128.
156. Whybray, *Ecclesiastes*, 79.
157. Whybray, *Ecclesiastes*, 79.

158. The Hebrew word translated "breath" (*rûaḥ*) in 3:19, 21 occurs in Ecclesiastes twenty-four times; ten times it refers to human or animal *rûaḥ* and in fourteen cases to the wind (we exclude the two cases in 8:8 as "wind"). In 7:8–9 and 10:4 it clearly means "spirit," which is the most common meaning outside of Ecclesiastes. Not surprisingly most Bible translations render the word in 3:19, 21 and 12:7 as "spirit." The NASB also renders it as "spirit" in 3:19, 21 though in the earlier versions it is rendered "breath" (NASB 77, NASB 95). We have rendered it here in 3:19, 21 as well as in 12:7 as "breath" because it refers to the life-breath (*něšāmâ*) that God put into Adam so that he "became a living being" (Gen 2:7). Surprisingly, all the translations that render *rûaḥ* in 12:7 (as in 3:19, 21) as "spirit" render it in Ps 104:29 as "breath" though both verses are about the body returning to dust and the *rûaḥ* being taken away by God or returning to God. And Job 34:14–15, which is also about the body returning to dust and God taking back the life-force, uses *rûaḥ* and *něšāmâ* interchangeably (cf. Job 27:3). No wonder Schoors, who still wants to retain "spirit" in his translation of *rûaḥ* in 3:19, 21, says that the Hebrew word "undoubtedly refers to the life spirit" (Schoors, *Preacher II*, 164). By this he means, "these verses and 12:7 suggest that it is . . . an impersonal principle of life," that is, *rûaḥ* in these verses has the same meaning as *něšāmâ*, which he considers the "older word for this reality" (Schoors, *Preacher II*, 164). Hence our translation of *rûaḥ* as "breath" in 3:19, 21 and 12:7 has sound exegetical basis.

ultimately, he had no advantage over the fool because he had to leave behind whatever he gained through his wisdom. Similarly, we would feel a deep sense of vanity when we realize that ultimately, we have no advantage over even animals. The seemingly pessimistic tone is to help recreate this feeling.

Hence, Qoheleth uses the observation of injustice in the courts of law to illustrate graphically the reality of not only the uncertainties of life but also the certainty of death to reinforce the sense of vanity. And he has said nothing unorthodox. However, some people think Qoheleth is skeptical that there is life after death. We will not dispute that he seems skeptical of the view that at death, "the breath of man goes up" while "the breath of the animal goes down" (3:21). But we must not assume that the phrase "the breath of man goes up" refers to life after death, and so conclude that Qoheleth is skeptical about the next life. It is unwise to make this conclusion based on a verse we do not really understand.

For even if we (wrongly) associate this phrase with Qoheleth's later affirmation that "the breath (of man) returns to God who gave it" (12:7), 3:21 is still not about whether humans have an afterlife (and animals do not). As just pointed out, the phrase in 12:7 simply means, at death, God takes back the (life) breath, which also applies to animals. We would only be (needlessly) accusing Qoheleth of inconsistency—here being skeptical that the breath goes up, then later affirming it. We should give him the benefit of the doubt, as is expected in a court of law, lest we ourselves become guilty of injustice.

Norbert Lohfink wisely says, "Verse 21 expresses skepticism concerning an otherwise unknown theory about the difference between human and animal death."[159] Roland Murphy adds, "It is useless to try and determine from this . . . his specific view on Sheol [the netherworld] and the next life."[160] It is all the more useless when we recognize that in this context Qoheleth has no need to say anything about the next life. When he affirms that humans have no ultimate advantage over animals because both will die, he is only saying that when we die, we cannot bring anything with us. Whether there is an afterlife is irrelevant since either way we leave everything behind; there is still no advantage in this sense.

Summing up, through the observation of injustice in the courts of law and his reflection on human beings being no different from animals, Qoheleth is actually continuing the discussion on how God uses the sense of eternity coupled with the sense of vanity to lead people to fear him. In this light, he is saying that God is testing people to make them see that they are like animals so as to evoke in them a deep sense of vanity in order to prod them to acknowledge him. We have already discussed how "God so works" in appointing events in this world so as to evoke the sense of vanity "that men should fear him" (3:14). But how does this testing result in purifying character?

---

159. Lohfink, *Qoheleth*, 67.
160. Murphy, *Ecclesiastes*, 37.

Learning to acknowledge and hence fear God is by definition becoming conscientious and thus seeking to be righteous. In other words, character is being refined.

When we experience or witness injustice even in the courts of law, we may become disillusioned with human institutions. We can actually become cynical about people. Qoheleth is implying that when we realize we cannot trust in people or human institutions, we should turn to God. In a premodern world this would be a natural response. But today, this may no longer be the case. Qoheleth's observation that in the very place where righteousness and justice are expected there may be wickedness and injustice can also be applied to organized religion. For injustice has been blatantly perpetrated in the name of God by some religious groups. Many people have thus become cynical about religion, if not about God.

One reason injustice is not only blatantly but also widely perpetrated in the name of religion is because God no longer feels real. Even people who are outwardly "religious" may be inwardly lacking the fear of God. Craig Gay has a book subtitled, "Why It's Tempting to Live As If God Doesn't Exist." In the chapter "The Irrelevance of God in the Technological Society" he says, "it is not difficult to see why science and technology have had a secularizing effect on modern culture. Scientific explanations of the world have eliminated the instrumental value of their religious alternatives. We no longer need religion to explain such things as disease or natural calamities."[161] And Gay concludes, "the impact of science and technology upon the modern imagination is such that it has effectively stripped us of the ability to apprehend the reality of any other meaning and any other purpose in the world save those which we managed to 'engineer' for ourselves."[162]

To a large extent, Gay's conclusions about science and technology having replaced religion to explain and experience reality are correct. But in our exposition of the previous passage (3:10–15) we showed that science and technology and the "progress" they bring fail to help people come to terms with the certainty of death and the uncertainties of life and hence make sense of the totality of human experience. We still need to turn to God. Gay's conclusions on how modern people view this world may be final only if they do not come face to face with the somber reality concerning life and death embodied in the poem, elaborated and reflected on in this passage (3:16–21). And if they would hear Qoheleth out, they could have an existential encounter with this sobering reality. They may then rediscover the ability to apprehend this world from a very different perspective.

Excursus to 3:16–21: Qoheleth on the Reality of God's Judgment

Our translation of 3:17—"I said to myself, God will judge the righteous and the wicked *even though* there is a time for every matter and for every deed there"—especially

---

161. Gay, *Way of the (Modern) World*, 102.
162. Gay, *Way of the (Modern) World*, 100.

in rendering the conjunction *kî* as "even though" is unique. Since *kî* carries different nuances in different contexts, to determine the nuance in this context, we need to first interpret the two halves of the sentence that it connects. The first half, "God will judge the righteous and the wicked," is clear. The second half, "there is a time for every matter and for every deed *there*," is problematic mainly because of the final Hebrew word (*šām*) translated "there" (in italics). Virtually every commentator has problems with it to the extent that some emend it to a different word. We will here make sense of the Hebrew text as it stands in the context of 3:1–15 since 3:16–22 flows from it.

The phrase "there is a time for every matter" is a repetition from 3:1 and thus "indicates how this section is related to the context. It reminds us that the poem in verses 1–8 serves as the background against which the various issues of this chapter should be interpreted."[163] And the poem depicts the certainty of death and the uncertainties of life. The phrase "and (also) for the deed (done) *there*" then specifies that Qoheleth is talking about the uncertainties that happen "there." In the context of 3:16, it is obviously referring to the uncertainties that happen *there* in the courts of law, where the innocent may be convicted and the guilty acquitted. The preposition (*'al*) translated "for (every deed there)" is the preposition that usually means "on" but can have the nuance "concerning," which fits the context here.[164] However, in Ecclesiastes it can also be synonymous with the earlier preposition (*lĕ*) translated "for (every matter)" and thus can likewise be translated as "for" in this verse.[165] In fact this is how most Bible translations render it. Whether we translate "concerning" or "for," it does not affect the meaning of the verse. We prefer "for" because it makes the connection clearer: "there is a time *for* every matter, and *for* every deed there."

So we have: God will judge the righteous and the wicked [correct the miscarriage of justice in the courts of law] *kî* there are uncertainties also for every deed done there [miscarriage of justice happens even in the courts of law]. What then is the nuance of *kî* that best fits its context? A possible fit would be "because": because there is miscarriage of justice in the courts of law, God will one day "judge" and thus correct it. However, this gives the impression that God will judge only because there is miscarriage of justice in the courts of law. This is not true even in the context of Ecclesiastes (see 8:11–13; 11:9; 12:14).

The conjunction can also mean "even though" as in, "He will accept no compensation; he will not be appeased *even though* you give many gifts" (Prov 6:35).[166] This nuance fits perfectly. It does not give that wrong impression and it captures the situation of Qoheleth contrasting his observation with his belief: even though he *observes* that there is miscarriage of justice in the courts of law (God allows it as "He makes

---

163. Ogden and Zogbo, *Handbook*, 112.
164. Crenshaw, *Ecclesiastes*, 101.
165. Fredericks, *Qoheleth's Language*, 151–52; Schoors, *Preacher*, 200–201.
166. Joüon and Muraoka, *Grammar*, §171b.

everything appropriate in its time"), he still *believes* that God will one day judge the righteous and the wicked and thus make things right (cf. 8:11–13).

Now one need not accept our specific interpretation of the second half of 3:17 to see that the first half is about what Qoheleth believes—God will make right the wrong that he observes in 3:16. Longman's conclusion cited in the exposition above is based on understanding *kî* as causal and rereading *šām* as "also, too" instead of "there" (this follows the suggestion of Whitney)[167]—"I said to myself, 'God will judge the righteous and the unjust, for there is a time for every activity and for every deed too.'"[168] He understands "that there is a *time for every activity and for every deed . . .* alludes to 3:1 and is here applied to the time of fair judgment."[169] In other words, despite what is observed in the courts of law, God will eventually make things right *because there is a time for fair judgment too*. Ogden and Zogbo, who also understand *kî* as causal but accept emending the adverb *šām* to the verb *śām* "put, place" and thus "appoint," conclude that "Because God has appointed a time for every matter, we can be certain that he will restore justice."[170] By making sense of the second half without emending *šām* and accepting its usual meaning ("there"), our interpretation makes the contrast between what Qoheleth observes and what he believes explicit.

ADMONITION TO CAREFREENESS IN LIGHT OF VANITY (3:22)

> 3:22 So I saw that there is nothing good except that man should have enjoyment in (the fruit of) his labors, for that is his lot. For who can bring him to see what will be after him?

This is the third time Qoheleth admonishes his audience to have enjoyment, and he will repeat it a few more times. Though it is always given in response to the vanity of life, each time the admonition occurs it is in a slightly different context and with something added. This enables us to have a more nuanced understanding of how enjoyment fits into the purpose or meaning of life. This time, the admonition is still in the larger context of God using the somber reality painted in the poem (the uncertainties of life and the certainty of death) to prod us to fear him (3:10–15). But its immediate context is that of recognizing that ultimately we do not even have advantage over animals (3:16–21). And it is in this context that Qoheleth introduces the idea that enjoyment is actually our "lot" in life. We will take a close look at this idea and then its implications in its immediate context here as well as in the larger context of 3:1–22.

The Hebrew word translated "lot" occurs eight times in Ecclesiastes (2:10, 21; 3:22; 5:18, 19; 9:6, 9; 11:2). It refers to what is allotted or apportioned by someone

---

167. Whitney, *Koheleth*, 34–36.
168. Longman, *Ecclesiastes*, 125.
169. Longman, *Ecclesiastes*, 127.
170. Ogden and Zogbo, *Handbook*, 112.

or to someone (except in 9:6 and 11:2, where it means "share" and "portion" respectively). But the exact nuance of the word and specifically what the allotment consists of depend on the context. We must be careful not to assume that the same word always means the same thing in different contexts. Also, note that the idea of a "lot" implies that what is allotted to us is all that we get. For instance, when receiving an inheritance, if one is told, "This is your lot (from your father's estate)," it implies, "This is all you get (from your father's estate)."

The first time the word occurs in Ecclesiastes (2:10), it is in the context of Qoheleth's pursuit of pleasure to see what was "good . . . to do." Pleasure then was his "lot" from all his labors, that is, pleasure (without satisfaction) was all that he got. He found the pleasure profitless as it did not satisfy him. So when he considered all his labors, he lamented that "all is vanity and a pursuit after wind" (2:11).

The second time the word occurs (2:21), it refers to a man's "estate" which would be allotted to his heir as an inheritance. Qoheleth also found this—allotting his estate to an heir—to be vanity: he had to leave behind everything he labored for with wisdom to one who may not have what it takes to make good use of it. These experiences led him to admonish us that there is nothing good except to have enjoyment, and not just raw pleasure.

The third occurrence is in the verse here. It refers to what is allotted to humanity. This meaning recurs three more times (5:18, 19; 9:9), all in the context of the admonition to enjoy life. To better understand Qoheleth's admonition, we need to give adequate attention to the concept of "lot" as first introduced in this verse. Qoheleth's idea that enjoyment is our "lot" is here presented in the context that humans have no advantage over animals because in the end they die and leave this world empty-handed just like animals (3:18–21). But animals never owned anything! So in the light of death, it is as if we had owned nothing. Since we have no say over whether we could take with us what we have when we die, which can happen at any time and without prior notice, how can we say that we own the things we work for? We do not even own our very life! They are not allotted to us as such. What is allotted is only the enjoyment these things can give us while we still have ("own") them.

To appreciate this reality, we need to view this world the way a child views a child-care center full of toys. What is "allotted" to him is the enjoyment of whatever toys he gets to "own" while he is there, but he cannot take any of them with him when he leaves. It would be foolish of the child to spend the few hours he has at the center busy looking out for and gathering his favorite toys, and then guarding them, as if he could bring them home, and in the process miss the opportunity to enjoy any of them.

For this very reason Qoheleth has been admonishing us that there is nothing good except to enjoy what we get to "own." He will soon be talking about those who have the ability to enjoy their wealth (5:18–20). So he is not speaking against *having* wealth but against *pursuing* after it as a goal in life, and in the process one is not able to enjoy what one already has. Qoheleth points out that enjoyment is actually our "lot" to help us see more clearly that besides enjoyment, there is indeed *nothing* good. For the implication is clear. If one does not enjoy life, he has not received what is allotted to him (6:1–9), and he is thus left with *nothing* good.

And as if to further drive home this point, Qoheleth asks, "For who can bring him to see what will be [in this world] after him?" Since "after him" means after his death (cf. 2:12; 6:12; 7:14; 10:14),[171] the rhetorical question affirms two things: our life in this world will end, and since we do not know the future, we do not know what will happen in this world after that. So we do not know whether what we have or do now in retrospect will be good in the long run, except to have enjoyment, which is not affected by what will happen in the future (this idea is repeated in 6:12 from a different angle and we will elaborate on it in our exposition there).

We must be reminded, in this context, that Qoheleth is not saying that enjoyment, let alone raw pleasure, is the goal of life. Enjoyment is not the highest, and certainly not the only, good in this life. Since this admonition is always given in response to the vanity of life, and the word "lot" when it refers to enjoyment, is always in relation to labor, the affirmation that there is "nothing good" except have enjoyment must be understood in terms of what we can expect from the things that we work for under the sun.

In fact, there is a higher good such as joy, a sublime form of good feeling which can be experienced apart from material things (Prov 21:15). It comes with a God-fearing disposition and way-of-life, which according to Qoheleth is also the prerequisite for the enjoyment of material things (see exposition on 5:18–20). So in practice when there is real enjoyment, there is also joy, making the enjoyment blissful and more meaningful. Perhaps this explains why when Qoheleth gave his admonition for the first time, he could say: "For who can eat or who can have *enjoyment* apart from him? For to a man who is good in his sight he has given wisdom, knowledge and *joy*" (2:25–26).

In Qoheleth's thinking, the goal of life and the highest good is then the fear of God, and what this means in practical terms. He goes so far as to say that in everything God does in this world, "God so works that men should fear him" (3:14). This then brings us to look at the idea of enjoyment as our "lot" in the larger context of 3:1–22, especially with respect to God using the somber reality embodied in the poem of 3:1–8 to goad us to fear him.

A major barrier to fearing God and living an upright life is the grip that temporal things have on the human heart. It is impractical to attempt to live a God-fearing and righteous life if we are still very much covetous at heart. It is in fact widely recognized that "the love of money is a root of all kinds of evil" (1 Tim 6:10). How then can we overcome this grip of temporal things on our heart? This is where Qoheleth's admonition to enjoyment, which teaches a realistic response to the vanity of life, comes in.

---

171. Seow, *Ecclesiastes*, 168.

As we just saw, the idea of enjoyment as our lot teaches us to view this world the way a child views a child-care center full of toys. This view enables us to look at temporal things, including what we already "own," with a degree of detachment. The greater the degree of our detachment from temporal things, the more prepared we are to let go of them and thus loosen the grip they have on us. In the process, we are learning to overcome a major barrier that keeps people from acknowledging God and fearing him. And this means the degree of our detachment from temporal things can be an indication of how much we really fear God.

Consider the biblical Job, who feared God greatly and lived an exceptionally upright life. He was certainly at peace with letting go of temporal things and thus with the somber reality that while death is certain, life is uncertain. For this was what he said when he lost not only all his wealth but also all his children: "Naked I came from my mother's womb, and naked I shall return there. The LORD gave and the LORD has taken away; blessed be the name of the LORD" (Job 1:21). Qoheleth will soon describe the vanity of a man's life in this way: "As he came from his mother's womb, naked he will depart as he came. And he will take nothing in (exchange for) his toil that he may carry away in his hand" (5:15). Hence the God-fearing Job was at peace with the reality that "All is vanity."

OBSERVATIONS TO SUSTAIN SENSE OF VANITY (4:1–5:17)

Qoheleth began his speech proper with recounting his past experiences to illustrate the reality that "All is vanity," and to admonish that the sensible response is to have enjoyment of life (1:12–2:26). His personal experiences do strike a responsive chord in the hearts of his audience. But they may not be able to identify fully with him. For no one was as wise, rich or powerful as he was, let alone had that many wives and concubines. The sharing of his own experiences was crucial to establishing his credibility to address convincingly the subject of vanity and his authority to admonish persuasively how then to respond. But to help his audience better identify with him he had to recount observations of vanity as experienced by the people. This is what he does in 4:1–5:17. Like his previous discussions on the vanity of life under the sun, this extended passage is followed by the admonition to enjoy life (5:18–6:9).

Oppressions in General (4:1–3)

> 4:1 And again I saw all the oppressions that are done under the sun. And look! The tears of the oppressed—but there is no one to comfort them. And power from the hand of their oppressors—but there is no one to comfort them. 4:2 So I consider the dead, who are already dead, more fortunate than the living, who are still alive. 4:3 But better than both of them is one who has not yet existed, who has not seen the evil activity that is done under the sun.

Qoheleth begins his series of observations with oppressions in general. The connective phrase "And again" signals some form of continuity with what precedes.[172] In 4:1–5:17 he is moving beyond discussing the vanity of life as pictured in the poem of 3:1–8. He is going to consider specific observations of vanity. But he is still building on the effects of the poem. For we saw that in 3:16–21 he used injustice in the courts of law, which is oppression through the abuse of judicial power, to reinforce the feeling of the uncertainties of life that the poem evokes. And so by returning to the subject of oppression he is in effect sustaining the sense of vanity built up there. This enables his audience to see more clearly that the futile pursuits he will soon recount are indeed vanity.

Obviously, when he says, "I saw *all* the oppressions that are done under the sun" (4:1), we are not to take it literally. For it is impossible that he could have seen every act of oppression in this world. The meaning of the hyperbolic expression is that he has seen "the full extent" of oppressions in this world.[173] This implies that he is aware of the sad reality that oppression is prevalent—the powerful are prone to oppress the powerless—and how bad the situation is. The phrase "power from the hands of their oppressors" is a literal translation from the Hebrew. It has been translated more idiomatically as "power was in the hand of their oppressors" or "power was on the side of their oppressors" (most Bible translations). However translated, the idea is that oppression is injustice perpetrated through the use (read: abuse) of some form of power, such as the case of miscarriage of justice in the courts of law.

When people (the powerless) are oppressed and "there is no one to comfort them," it is often because no one would help them due to fear, or everyone would side with the oppressor (the powerful) out of greed, or both. Oppression can occur anywhere. It happens not only in a concentration camp, where victims can expect to be mistreated, but also in a court of law, where justice is expected to be upheld. And people in power may even oppress in the name of religion.

---

172. Commentators are divided over whether the first word of 4:1 should be translated "And again" (literally, "And I returned") though most Bible translations translate it as such. The differing translations do not change the basic meaning of this and two other sections where it occurs (4:7 and 9:11, where it occurs without "And" and is better translated "Further"). However, translating it as "And again" (or "Further") alerts us to see that what is about to be said in the new section introduced by the word relates in some way to what has just been said in the previous section. Thus it helps us see coherence in the speech and understand it better. Fox rejects this translation because, "prior to 4:1 Qohelet did not 'see' oppressions" (Fox, *Time*, 219). This is being too rigid. Since Qoheleth spells out that the "oppressions" he sees in 4:1–3 are due to the abuse of power, is miscarriage of justice (abuse of judicial power) in the courts of law (3:16–21) not oppression? Must oppression be labelled as "oppression" or be in the exact same form as those labelled as such before it is oppression? Longman does not deny that prior to 4:1, Qoheleth had seen something that could be considered oppression though not labelled as such. His objection is that "Qohelet does not earlier deal with oppression as such [not labelled as oppression?]" (Longman, *Ecclesiastes*, 133). However, the question is whether prior to 4:1 Qoheleth had seen oppression in any form, and the answer is clearly yes.

173. Krüger, *Qoheleth*, 80.

Qoheleth's interjection, "And look!" transports us into the world of the oppressed to join him in looking at their plight so that we can identify with them. The terse descriptions, "tears of the oppressed" and "power from the hands of their oppressors," together with the sympathetic repetition, "there is no one to comfort them (the oppressed)," impress upon us the evil of oppression. While still immersed in this pathetic world of the most unfortunate, Qoheleth makes a comment that the dead, who are already dead, are better off than the living, who are still alive; and even better off than both of them are those not yet existed or born, who have not seen "the evil activity that is done under the sun," that is, oppression (4:2–3).

It is important to note that he did not merely say that the dead are better off than the living. He qualifies that the dead are already dead, and the living are still alive. Are these qualifications redundant? Of course the dead are already dead and the living are still alive. What is the point? To avoid the apparent redundancy, Fox renders the qualifications respectively as, "since they are already dead" and "since they are still alive," instead of "who are already dead" and "who are still alive."[174] The Hebrew conjunction can indeed be translated "since" ("because") or "who."[175]

We follow most Bible translations and retain the "who" meaning (in 4:2 and also in 4:3b). However, even then, the qualifications still have the "because" connotation. For "It is the fact that they have *already* died (and not some other conceivable quality) that makes those who are dead better off than the living, who are unfortunately . . . *not yet* dead."[176] In other words, the dead are better off than the living specifically because they are no longer alive. Similarly, those not yet born are even better off than both of them specifically because they have not even "*seen* the evil activity"—"have not experienced human oppression themselves, nor have they had to witness it."[177]

Now in what sense are those *already* dead better off than those *still* alive (4:2)? The qualifications are made following the observation that powerless people are being helplessly oppressed by powerful people (4:1). And those not yet born are said to be better off than both the dead and the living specifically because they have neither witnessed nor experienced oppression at all (4:3). So it is clear that the comment in 4:2 is made specifically in reference to life (*still*) under oppression—those "who are *already* dead" are more fortunate than those "who are *still* alive" because "death [is] the only escape from oppression."[178] The idea is that to be dead—having escaped from the oppression—is better off than *still* having to live under the oppression. This is how one would feel when oppressed to the point of tears with no one to turn to. Surely then, in this sense those who are not yet born, "who have not seen the evil activity," are even more fortunate than those who have died.

174. Fox, *Time*, 218.
175. Schoors, *Preacher*, 140.
176. Holmstedt et al., *Qoheleth*, 146.
177. Ogden and Zogbo, *Handbook*, 127; cf. Schoors, *Preacher II*, 62.
178. Ogden and Zogbo, *Handbook*, 127.

When oppression is prevalent, we can become oblivious to its horror. Qoheleth's comment is meant to sensitize us to what it is like to be oppressed to the point of tears, and have no one to turn to. Evidently Qoheleth wants us to feel how horrible the experience can be. People actually commit suicide to escape the oppression when they can no longer endure it. So there is no better way for him to evoke that feeling of horror than to make the shocking comment that it is more fortunate to be dead than to remain alive under oppression, and better still not to have been born and hence never see oppression at all.

Why then does he want us to see the evil, and feel the horror, of oppression? He is persuading us toward fearing God, and how we treat others is a reliable indication of how much we really fear God. To see the terror of oppression is thus to feel the horror of not fearing God. It is tempting to think that Qoheleth only complains about oppression but does nothing about it. If we make the effort to understand him on his terms, we can see that not only in this passage, but throughout his speech, he is making a passionate plea to turn away from doing evil, and here he calls oppression "the evil activity that is done under the sun." Krüger puts it eloquently when he says that, "Verse [4:]1 is often claimed as a testimony to the 'pessimism of Qoheleth': in contrast to the prophetic protest against injustice and oppression, he learns to live with present conditions in the world in 'resigned' (if not 'cynical') fashion. In the clarity with which oppression and its consequences are named, the text is in no way inferior to comparable statements in the prophetic writings."[179]

In 4:1–3 Qoheleth "protests" against injustice and oppression by recreating the experience of the victims so that we see oppression for what it is from their perspective and thus turn against oppression. For injustice and what it is like are most obvious from the perspective of those on the receiving end; they are in fact least if at all obvious from the perspective of those at the giving end.

Hence Qoheleth is not making a blanket statement that just because oppression exists in this world, it is better to be dead than alive and better still not even to be born. His comment applies specifically in the context of people *still* being oppressed to the point of tears, and is made to serve a rhetorical purpose. In fact, in a different context, he says it is definitely better to be alive than dead (9:3–6). He even affirms that it is good to be alive, with the qualification that only if we are able to enjoy life (11:7–8). It is therefore unfair to take his comment here out of context and conclude that he is expressing a pessimistic view of life. We must remember that he is giving a speech to persuade his audience, and not writing a treatise to present his views. He seeks to move our feeling and change our thinking so that we would fear God and keep his commandments, and not primarily to inform us of what he believes.

---

179. Krüger, *Qoheleth*, 95.

Competition for Advancement (4:4–6)

> *4:4 Then I saw that every toil and every skillful work is due to a man's rivalry with his neighbor. This also is vanity and a pursuit after wind. 4:5 The fool folds his hands and consumes his own flesh. 4:6 Better is a handful with rest than two handfuls with toil and a pursuit after wind.*

Qoheleth moves on to an observation of vanity which may appear to be totally unrelated to the previous observation on power and oppression. People are driven to work hard ("toil") and smart ("skillful work") out of rivalry with their neighbors. It is about pursuing socio-economic power and it explains why today competition is such a powerful motivating force that makes capitalism work so well. In fact, it works too well that it threatens the collapse of capitalism itself.

At the heart of the problem is that we do not want to feel inferior to others. Unless tempered by the fear of God, we not only want to feel superior to others, we also want them to feel inferior to us. Given the opportunity, we may even do something to make them feel this way. This partly explains the tendency of people to oppress or mistreat those they have power over even when there is no obvious personal gain involved. If the basic motivation behind our working hard and smart is to advance in society in terms of temporal things so that we feel superior to others, it is indeed vanity and a pursuit after wind. For it serves no useful purpose and there is no end to it.

In fact, it would be self-destructive, whether at the individual, national or even global level. According to the foremost Sumerologist Samuel Kramer, "one of the major motivating forces of Sumerian behavior [was] the drive for superiority and pre-eminence with its great stress on competition and success."[180] The Sumerian civilization flourished more than four thousand years ago. And just like today, "It is thus fairly obvious that the drive for superiority and prestige deeply colored the Sumerian outlook on life and played an important role in their education, politics and economics."[181] In the case of the Sumerians, "Sad to say, the passion for competition and superiority carried within it the seed of self-destruction and helped to trigger the bloody and disastrous wars between the city-states and to impede the unification of the country as a whole, thus exposing Sumer to the external attacks which finally overwhelmed it. All of which provides us with but another historic example of the poignant irony inherent in man and his fate."[182]

At the other extreme is one who is not motivated to work at all. Qoheleth calls him "the fool [who] folds his hands," a proverbial expression symbolizing idleness or laziness (Prov 6:10). As a result, "he consumes his own flesh," that is, destroys himself through poverty (Prov 6:11). Qoheleth advocates work, with "rest," that is, without

---

180. Kramer, *Sumerians*, 249.
181. Kramer, *Sumerians*, 267.
182. Kramer, *Sumerians*, 268.

rivalry or strife even if it means getting only "one handful" instead of "two handfuls," and thus having less than our peers.

This expresses the balance between the two extremes of indulging in complacency and pursuing after supremacy. It is unfortunate that without an adequate fear of God, most people are not motivated to work hard and smart when there is no competition. In light of the admonition to find satisfaction in our labor and the condition that only the God-fearing or the righteous person can have enjoyment, two other proverbs are instructive: "Better is a little with righteousness than a large income with injustice" (Prov 16:8); "Better is little with the fear of the LORD than great treasure and turmoil with it" (Prov 15:16).

Addiction to Advancement (4:7–8)

> 4:7 And again, I saw a (case of) vanity under the sun: 4:8 there is a man who is all alone by himself; he does not even have a son or brother. But there is no end to all his toil, and his eyes are not satisfied with riches. "For whom am I toiling and depriving myself of pleasure?" This also is vanity (absurd) and a grievous business.

Qoheleth goes on to recount an observation about a rich man who had more money than he could ever use and had no one to share or inherit his wealth. Yet he kept toiling to the point of depriving himself of pleasure. As indicated by the connecting phrase, "And again," this is an extreme example of self-destructive behavior driven by the competitive spirit highlighted in the previous passage. What seemed exceptional in Qoheleth's day is becoming common today.

Note that Qoheleth suddenly introduces a question in the first person: "For whom am I toiling and depriving myself of pleasure?" Some Bible translations add the phrase, "And he never asks," while others add, "And he asks," before the question. Did he ask or did he not? We tend to think that he did not ask because most people in a similar situation would not stop and ask themselves that question. This is pathetic.

But in general, when a first person discourse suddenly interrupts a third person narration, as is the case here, the assumption is that it is uttered by the character just referred to. This is how we read a narrative. If the man did indeed ask, but kept on doing what he was doing, it is even more pathetic. He was clearly addicted to the pursuit of wealth. So whether he asked or did not ask, "this also is vanity and a grievous business."

Note that "a grievous business" describes the experience of the participant of vanity and not that of Qoheleth the observer and speaker. In this particular context the idea of vanity carries the added nuance (connotation) of "absurdity." For this particular case of vanity is so absurd in the eyes of any sane observer that we can imagine Qoheleth the speaker actually thinking, "This (case of vanity) is indeed absurd!" (see further "Teaching of Ecclesiastes" under "The Pragmatics of Vanity"). Perhaps, the man did not actually ask the question himself. But he should have, and so Qoheleth puts the question into his mouth to express how absurd it is.[183]

Since this man could not spend all his money and there was no one to share or inherit it, was he then really pursuing after riches itself? The connective phrase, "And again" (4:7), indicates that this passage relates to that preceding it (4:4–6), which is about the drive to work hard and smart out of rivalry. In other words, "There is no end to all his toil, and his eyes are not satisfied with riches" because there is no end to his rivalry with his neighbors. For even when one is already at the top, one still needs to strive to remain at the top. This observation then is an illustration of what can happen when people are driven by the quest for superiority. Since material wealth and the social status that it brings often enable one to get what one wants, when people pursue after riches, it is often socio-economic power that they are really after.

However, like the pursuit of pleasure, this pursuit of power is just another expression of the God-given task of seeking after the meaning of life (1:13; 3:10). Psychiatrist Frankl would agree. Having affirmed that the search for meaning is the primary motivation in humans he said, "That is why I speak of a *will to meaning* in contrast to the pleasure principle (or, as we could also term it, the *will to pleasure*) on which Freudian psychoanalysis is centered, as well as in contrast to the *will to power* on which Adlerian psychology, using the term 'striving for superiority,' is focused."[184]

There is no question that people do pursue after pleasure (so observed Freud) or power (Adler), or even both. But according to Frankl, they do it in order to find the meaning of life. And according to Qoheleth, they will not succeed. Hence, just as Qoheleth observed, it is not surprising that the man was not satisfied with his wealth (and the socio-economic power that it brought). When what you have does not satisfy your real need, you are not satisfied with what you have no matter how much you have. So you are driven to pursue after more and more and thus become addicted to it.

Admonition on Cooperation (4:9–12)

> *4:9 Two are better than one, because they have a good return for their efforts. 4:10 For if either of them falls, one will lift up his companion. But woe to the one who falls and there is not another to lift him up! 4:11 Also, if two lie together, they keep warm, but how can one keep warm alone? 4:12 And if one can overpower him who is alone, two can withstand him—a threefold cord is not easily broken.*

Whybray captures the theme of this passage very well: "it is dangerous and unwise for the individual to attempt to face life alone, and simple common sense to seek the co-operation of others in all that one does (v. 9)."[185] When two people cooperate and

---

183. Cf. Whybray, *Ecclesiastes*, 86.
184. Frankl, *Man's Search for Meaning*, 121.
185. Whybray, *Ecclesiastes*, 86.

work together, their return is better than the sum of each working separately. This is because they can complement, not just supplement, each other's abilities. Three specific examples are used to illustrate this principle. When one person falls, especially if he injures himself and there is no one to help, it is indeed "woe to him." In ancient times, one effective way of keeping warm on a cold winter night is to lie together. This is not limited to husband and wife but can also refer to two male travelers. And finally, it is common experience that when one has a companion, one is less likely to be a victim of crime. So "two are better than one."

There is no need to read any significance into the unexpected occurrence of the number "three" (instead of "two") in the proverbial saying, "a threefold cord is not easily broken" as there is probably no such thing as a twofold cord. The meaning is clear: pluri-unity is strength. This nicely summarizes the theme of cooperation in this passage. It has wide applications, and in this context, it is the antidote to the vanity of rivalry.

The man addicted to the pursuit of wealth is an extreme example of someone working hard and smart, driven by rivalry in pursuit of self-advancement. The drive to compete with others is often fueled by the need to feel superior to them. But Qoheleth admonishes that it is better to cooperate with others so that we could bless them and be blessed in return. We can then prosper together with them. In our capitalistic culture of socio-economic rivalry, we may have to compete even when we are not seeking self-advancement. But we can still cooperate with others, especially those who share our goals.

If one is driven to pursue socio-economic power for self-advancement, one is less likely to use it to bless others. More likely, one will abuse it to oppress others in one way or another. For what is the use of the hard-gained power if you cannot display it? Those who oppress others alienate not just their victims but also some of their friends. And people who still side with them may be doing so only out of fear or greed, or both. So oppressors may not be able to tell who their real friends are, if they still have any. When trouble strikes, they may find themselves very much alone. So they need to fear God and heed Qoheleth's admonition on cooperation. In light of the uncertainties of life, they will never know when they will lose their wealth, status and power and come face to face with their greatest fear: they lack genuine friends when they desperately need them.

Vanity of Power and Popularity (4:13–16)

> *4:13 Better is a poor and wise youth than an old and foolish king who no longer knows how to take advice, 4:14 for he went from prison to the throne even though he had been born poor in his kingdom. 4:15 I saw all the living, those who walk under the sun, with the second youth who replaced him. 4:16 There was no*

end to all the people, to all before whom he appeared. Yet those who come later will not rejoice in him. Surely this also is vanity and a pursuit after wind.

We cannot be certain of the details of this story, but the overall message is clear: the vanity of power and popularity. In light of the foregoing discussion on rivalry and socio-economic advancement, this observation on political power is timely here. The thread of power runs through this chapter, beginning with oppression and the abuse of power, to competition and the pursuit of socio-economic power, and ending here with the delusion of the passing popularity that comes with political power.

Some translators remove the Hebrew word translated "the second" in 4:15 and read the phrase as, "with the youth who replaced him (the old and foolish king)." This would mean there are only two characters and not three in this story. But since the text as it stands makes adequate sense, there is no need to tamper with it.[186] In any case the message remains basically the same. For even if there is no mention that the wise young king who replaced the foolish old one is replaced by a second youth, "those who come later will not rejoice in him [the wise young king]" after he himself is later replaced—the vanity of power and popularity.

The focus of the text is on the transitoriness of the popularity of the wise young king. Being young was not a disadvantage because he was wise. His wisdom was first demonstrated in his ability to rise from prison to the throne even though he was born poor in the land he eventually ruled. So he was better than the former king, who though he had the advantage of age, he no longer knew how to take advice.[187]

This young king was an unlikely candidate to become king. For in premodern times the social status one was born with usually determined how far one could rise in the social ladder. And kingship is usually passed from father to son; an heir to the throne would not be born poor let alone be sent to prison. So the young king would be admired. And when he also proved to be wise in ruling the people in contrast to his foolish predecessor, he was bound to be very popular. Thus he was a positive example of power and popularity. This aptly concludes this thread of discussion on the pursuit and use of power. For to be king is to be at the pinnacle of social advancement, and the positive example here would show us whether power is worth pursuing. The lesson here applies to all pursuits for self-advancement.

Qoheleth observed that when this shining example of power and popularity was replaced, the people were with the next (youthful) king. The phrase translated, "to all before whom he appeared" (4:16), in the Hebrew text reads literally, "to all who he [= youth] was before them."[188] The idea is that the wise young king was so popular that there was "no end" to the people before whom he appeared "to acknowledge their

---

186. In fact, "it is difficult to see why anyone would add the word that has caused so much anguish for interpreters. All textual witnesses support its authenticity" (Seow, *Ecclesiastes*, 185).

187. Cf. Whybray, *Ecclesiastes*, 89.

188. Holmstedt et al., *Qoheleth*, 161.

allegiance."[189] The NLT captures the scenario vividly: "Endless crowds stand around him." But when even he, who had such an inspiring success story behind him, was replaced, the people throng to the next king. Not only that. The future generations ("those who come later") would not remember or celebrate his former greatness ("will not rejoice in him"). Past political leaders would understand what Qoheleth is saying here better than the rest of us.

All power and popularity are transitory. When pursued for the fleeting glory associated with them as a means to find the meaning of life, they will disappoint. Though it is not spelled out in the text, when a king, or anyone in power, heeds Qoheleth's admonition on cooperation, his power and popularity could be used to serve others, and he would then find satisfaction and thus meaning in his work.

Admonition to Fear God (5:1–7)

> *5:1 Watch your steps when you go to the house of God: draw near to listen rather than to offer the sacrifice of fools, for they do not know that they are doing evil. 5:2 Do not be rash with your mouth, and let not your heart be hasty to utter a word before God, for God is in heaven and you are on earth. Therefore let your words be few. 5:3 For as a dream comes with much preoccupation, so the voice of a fool with many words. 5:4 When you make a vow to God, do not delay fulfilling it, for he has no delight in fools. Fulfill what you vow. 5:5 It is better that you do not vow than that you do vow and not fulfill it. 5:6 Do not let your mouth cause you to commit sin, and do not say before the messenger that it was a mistake. Why should God be angry with your words and destroy the work of your hands? 5:7 For in many dreams and (thus) many words there is vanity. Rather fear God.*

Qoheleth's speech has so far been about the vanity of life with respect to temporal things. So this passage on a specific religious practice seems to be a digression, especially since in the passage that follows and in the rest of the speech, the subject matter returns to temporal things. This digression is only apparent, and it actually alerts us to the meaning of the text.

For this passage is not out of place if we recognize what it is really about. Though Qoheleth seems to have used far too many words, what he really wants to say is, "Fear God!" (5:7b). This admonition to fear God is in fact expressed right at the very beginning: "Watch your steps" (5:1), that is, proceed carefully with what you are going to do or say in the temple. If we have been following the preceding flow of thought, we can understand why he admonishes his audience to fear God. For he has been arguing that in light of the vanity of life the proper thing to do is to fear God so that we can have enjoyment. So it is a matter of time before he appeals to his audience to fear God. But if he does this only at the end of the speech, which he does in 12:13, his audience may not be prepared to respond. And this passage is an appropriate place to

---

189. Seow, *Ecclesiastes*, 185. Unlike NLT, most Bible translations fail to capture this scenario.

give a preliminary appeal as he has by now touched his audience emotionally as well as explained sensibly why they need to fear God. But why then all this talk about "the sacrifice of fools" and "fulfill what you vow"?

This is the first time Qoheleth directly admonishes his audience to fear God. When he talked about the need to fear God earlier, his audience may be smugly thinking that they already feared God. So they would take it as a tacit encouragement rather than an implicit admonishment. For his original audience, like all ancient peoples, was basically religious. And religious people, if they faithfully observe their prescribed religious practices, usually assume that they are already God-fearing. In fact, in some contexts such as Isa 29:13 and 2 Kgs 17:25–28, "fear of God means religious practices, or religion in general."[190] So if Qoheleth instructs religious people to fear God without also helping them see (in a non-offensive way) that they may not have been God-fearing at all, they will be taken aback and may even be offended: "Are we not God-fearers already?!"

Evidently Qoheleth had in mind an audience that was quick to make vows but slow to fulfill them. They did not even realize that this was evil, a clear sign that they were not really God-fearing. This explains why Qoheleth used the context of making vows to admonish them to fear God. Vows were voluntary and were usually made out of a psychological need in times of crisis. It was an attempt to "bribe" God to answer a desperate prayer. So what was vowed was usually very costly. Because of this, when the crisis was over, what was promised in the heat of the moment would likely be withheld. Since the vow was entirely between God and the person who made the vow, no one else knew about it unless the person shared it with others. Even then they could not hold him accountable as it was purely between him and God. Hence only a genuine God-fearer would be conscientious enough to fulfill it.

Put in general terms beyond the context of making vows, an excellent way for a person to know if he truly fears God is how readily he would avoid doing what is wrong and seek to do what is right when no one, except God, is watching or is holding him accountable. This is what it means to fear God. It usually works through the conscience (Rom 2:14–16) and a God-fearing person, whether he professes to believe in God or not, is thus an exceptionally conscientious person. For such a person would do what is right and not what is wrong (according to his conscience) even when no one (except God) is watching or holding him accountable.

This understanding of the fear of God is evident also in the New Testament. Christian slaves are commanded "to obey your earthly masters in everything, not with eye-service [when they are watching you] as men-pleasers, but in sincerity of heart, fearing the Lord" (Col 3:22). And Christian masters are commanded to "treat your slaves justly and fairly, knowing that you also have a Master in heaven" (Col 4:1), which implies that God is also watching and holding them accountable (cf. 1 Pet 2:17). This teaching is today applicable to employer-employee relationships; when

---

190. Sarna, *Songs of the Heart*, 87–88.

both parties fear God, there will be harmony in everything. In a parallel passage, Christians are commanded to "submit yourselves to one another in the fear of Christ" (Eph 5:21) as a consequence of being "filled with the Spirit" (Eph 5:18; cf. Acts 9:31). And because Christians "are the temple of the living God" (2 Cor 6:16), they are to "cleanse ourselves from every defilement of body and spirit, perfecting holiness in the fear of God" (2 Cor 7:1). So the fear of God is a key teaching of the New Testament too and is not to be taken lightly.

Hence the making and keeping of vows (promises to God), which is a "litmus test" of whether one truly fears God, is a serious matter. Qoheleth admonished his audience to "watch your steps" when they went to the temple. They should be careful with what they would say to God. To avoid making rash vows, it was better to go to the temple to listen than to speak. For just as preoccupation with the crisis one is facing results in dreams during sleep, speaking too many words in the temple results in saying foolish things before God (5:3).[191] This caution was applied particularly to people who went to the temple with a heavy heart. Perhaps the phrase "in many dreams" in 5:7 refers to the mental state of the worshipper at the temple: he was still preoccupied with the crisis he had been facing, and had thus been experiencing many dreams lately. People in such a condition were thus prone to make hasty vows, saying "many [profitless] words" before God and thus "there is vanity" even in coming before God in the temple. The command to fear God is thus most appropriate in this context.[192]

191. We have translated 5:3 as "For *as* a dream comes with much preoccupation, *so* the voice of a fool with many words" to make explicit the connection between the two halves of the verse (a proverbial saying). The word "as" is not in the text and the word translated "so" is the usual conjunction "and." Murphy points out that in this context—"The two lines of the saying are joined by 'and'"— the conjunction "can be rendered as 'so'" (Murphy, *Ecclesiastes*, 46, note 2a; cf. Kautzsch, *Grammar*, §161a). "The saying itself belongs to a type found in Proverbs (e.g. Prov. 11:16; 25:23; 26:20; 27:17) in which the truth of the second half is supported by an analogy, the two being linked not, as in many such sayings, by a comparative particle such as 'like' or 'as' but merely by *and*" (Whybray, *Ecclesiastes*, 94). We have seen in our exposition of 1:13 that the word translated "preoccupation" in 5:3 basically means "task, business, affair." However, translating 5:3a as, "For a dream comes with much business" (ESV), while technically correct, does not help us to understanding what it means in reality. What kind of "business" results in dreams? Since it is in the context of making rash vows, which happens during times of crisis, the "business" is preoccupation with the crisis. Hence rendering the word as "preoccupation" here as in 1:13 points the reader to what preoccupies a person who makes rash vows—the crisis he is going through. Some Bible translations even make it explicit by paraphrasing the word: "A dream comes when there are many cares" (NIV); and "Just as dreams come with much brooding" (NJPS).

192. The Hebrew of 5:7 is problematic. It reads literally: "For in many dreams and vanities and many words but fear God." What is certain is that the admonition "(but) fear God" contrasts the command in 5:6 not to make empty vows and the "many words" refers to the making of such vows. So no matter how we understand "in many dreams and vanities and many words," it does not affect the overall meaning of this passage—warning against making rash vows. What we need to do is make sense of this problematic string of words in a way that fits the context of making rash vows. Our rendering—"in many dreams and (*thus*) many words there is vanity"—takes the cue from 5:3a, which relates "a dream" as the result of "much preoccupation" to a crisis, which causes one to make a vow. It is similar to that of most Bible translations except that they do not show the connection (if any) between "many words" and "many dreams."

Therefore we must not take Qoheleth's admonishment about going to the temple to listen rather than to speak out of its context of making vows. As Fox notes, "the central theme [of the whole passage] is vows . . . [Even] the remarks about sacrifices and speech are subordinate to this theme and allude to the circumstances of vows."[193] Qoheleth was thus neither discouraging prayers at the temple nor advocating a very austere form of religion. As Whybray puts it, "these verses should not be taken as expressing the whole of his views about worship: he is concerned here only with one particular aspect of it."[194] Addressing this particular religious practice gave Qoheleth an appropriate context to ensure his religious audience understood what he meant by fearing God. As we will now see, it would also help promote a God-fearing way of life.

In the Old Testament God did not forbid, only regulated, vows: those who made vows must make sure they fulfilled it without delay (Deut 23:21–23). Qoheleth was simply reiterating this teaching. Since it was not required of them, it was better that they did not vow than to vow and not fulfill it. He likened a vow made impulsively in the presence of God to "the sacrifice of fools," a sacrifice that did not please but instead offended God. It was a foolish act. Making a costly promise in haste without first giving it adequate thought usually led to regret when it was time to fulfill it.

This would then lead to making an excuse before "the messenger," probably "the priest who officiates at the temple to which people come to confess that they have erred."[195] This lax attitude disregarded that "God is in heaven and you are on earth," amounting to not recognizing his majesty or even reality. It expressed, and would further cultivate, a lack of the fear of God, and would thus hasten a deeper decline in conscientious living.

Hence this religious laxness has social consequences. And it also has personal consequences. Qoheleth warned his audience that not fulfilling their vows was sin and they would not get away with it. God "has no delight in fools," meaning he is displeased by their foolishness. He would "be angry with your words" and would even "destroy the work of your hands." This statement must be understood in the context of the speech. In our exposition on 3:10–15 we explained that when Qoheleth refers to something as God's doing, he may not be talking about a supernatural involvement, but simply a naturally experienced or observed phenomenon. This is because he considers whatever happens as God's doing since it is either directed or permitted by God.

How then would vow-breakers experience this "destruction" of the work of their hands? Beginning with 2:24–26 Qoheleth has been saying that in order to have the ability to enjoy the fruit of one's labor, that is, "the work of your hands," one needs to please or fear God. And here, the statement that God would "destroy the work of your hands" is made in the context of not pleasing or fearing God. So the "destruction"

---

193. Fox, *Time*, 229.
194. Whybray, *Ecclesiastes*, 91.
195. Seow, *Ecclesiastes*, 201.

simply means that vow-breakers would not have the ability to enjoy the fruit of their labor.

This inability is not so much the direct consequence of breaking the vow. Note that the admonition, "(Rather) fear God," is given as the alternative to making empty vows and "God be angry with your words." It is also the antidote to "and destroy the work of your hands." That means, the actual reason behind the lack of enjoyment is the lack of the fear of God, of which the failure to honor vows is only a definite expression.

Qoheleth has yet to explain why the lack of the fear of God leads to the inability to enjoy life. But as already alluded to in one way or another in the course of our exposition of the preceding chapters, it is unlikely that people who do not fear God, such as those who are greedy and are dishonest in their dealings with others, can find satisfaction in life and enjoy the fruit of their labor. The lack of the fear of God expresses itself in more than one way. Some expressions (like greed and dishonesty) reveal more clearly than others (like the making of empty vows) why people who do not fear God cannot be happy. And of course, the fear of God or the lack of it actually falls on a spectrum. It is a matter of degrees and not a clear-cut dichotomy, as are the consequences.

As for Qoheleth's original audience, the making of empty vows to God was a clear indication that they were not really God-fearing. For us today, it may be the making of empty promises to fellow mortal beings. We can no longer do business with just a handshake. We need legally binding contracts before we have some assurance that people would honor their promises. Hence when promises are made without such contracts, they are usually not seen as binding. So those who make the promises may not consider themselves accountable to anyone. In such a culture, only those who are adequately God-fearing or conscientious would consistently honor their promises.

Oppression in High Places (5:8–9)

> *5:8 If you see the oppression of the poor and the violation of justice and righteousness in a province, do not be astonished at the matter, for an official is watched over by a higher one, and there are yet higher ones (watching) over them. 5:9 On the whole there is profit for the country when there is a king over cultivated field.*

Having "digressed" so that he could make a direct appeal to fear God (5:1–7), Qoheleth now returns to the subject of oppression. In chapter 4 he used this subject to open up a discussion on the futility of pursuing after power. Now he uses the subject to open up a discussion on the futility of pursuing after money (5:10–17). The reason for using oppression in each case is apparently to link his reflections on power and money to the poem of 3:1–8. For following a reflection on the poem (3:10–15) he had used oppression (3:16–22) to reinforce the sense of vanity evoked by the uncertainties of life that the poem expresses.

This present observation about oppression, more specifically about corruption in the government, would then also be intended to sustain the sense of vanity evoked through the poem. He tells his audience not to be astonished when they see corruption practiced rampantly and openly. This is because a corrupt official is "watched over," or protected by those more powerful than him.[196] It has been reported that in one country corrupt officials would "actually give you a receipt for your bribes."[197] And so blatant corruption is something to be "expected"—nothing to be astonished about! Qoheleth presents the sordid observation in this "sarcastic" way to make a stronger impact on the audience.

Qoheleth reminds his audience that despite a corrupt government, on the whole it is profitable to have "a king over cultivated field," that is, "for the sake of agriculture."[198] In other words, it is still better to have a corrupt government than to have no government. Otherwise there will be anarchy from within and without and agriculture (economic production) will not be possible. He is not condoning corruption. Later, he warns against doing evil even when evil deeds seem to go unpunished (8:11–13). By expressing apparent acceptance of the status quo, Qoheleth conveys a feeling of helplessness that sustains the sense of vanity. It also suggests the need to look to God, who in his own way and in his own time "will judge the righteous and the wicked (accordingly)" (3:17).

Addiction to Money (5:10–14)

Repetition of Theme: "What Profit is There?" (5:15–17)

> 5:10 *One who loves money will not be satisfied with money, nor one who loves wealth with income; this also is vanity.* 5:11 *When affluence increases, those who consume it increase. So what is the advantage to its possessor except to see it with his eyes?* 5:12 *Sweet is the sleep of the worker, whether he eats little or*

---

196. The second half of 5:8 is difficult and the Hebrew reads literally: "for a high/arrogant (one) over a high/arrogant (one) is watching and high/arrogant (ones) are over them." Since the verse as a whole is about rampant oppression and injustice in a political unit ("province") and is followed by a verse mentioning the king, it has to refer to the political system. And since 5:8–9 is followed by a discussion warning against the love of money (5:10–17), 5:8 is about greed in the political system—corruption (cf. Fox, *Time*, 233–34; Bartholomew, *Ecclesiastes*, 216–17). And this is something that can be observed even in "democratic" countries today. So it makes sense to interpret the high/arrogant ones as (corrupt) government officials and then translate the verse accordingly. This is the interpretation taken by most commentators and virtually all Bible translations.

197. Friedman, *Lexus and Olive Tree*, 148.

198. Garrett, *Proverbs, Ecclesiastes, Song of Songs*, 312. This is a valid interpretation of this difficult verse (cf. ESV, NJPS, NRSV). For a detailed discussion of the options, see the translator's notes to this verse in the *NET Bible*. Whichever interpretation is adopted (cf. HCSB, NASB, NIV, NKJV, NLT), 5:8–9 is about blatant corruption in government and one's helplessness to do anything about it. Since corruption is about the love of money, it sets the stage for 5:10–17. This is what matters in understanding the role of 5:8–9 in Qoheleth's rhetoric.

> *much. But the full stomach of the rich does not allow him to sleep. 5:13 There is a grievous affliction that I have seen under the sun: riches were hoarded by its possessor to his own hurt. 5:14 That is, those riches were lost in a bad investment and he fathered a son and had nothing in his hand. 5:15 As he came from his mother's womb, he will return naked—go as he came. So he will take nothing in (exchange for) his toil that he may carry away in his hand. 5:16 This is also a grievous affliction: just as he came, thus will he go. So what is the profit to him who toils for the wind? 5:17 Even all his days he eats in darkness with much vexation, sickness and anger.*

We noted above that Qoheleth uses the subject of corruption in the previous passage to introduce the observation on the love of money in this passage. There is a logical reason for him to do so. Corruption not only exposes the human predisposition toward greed but also demonstrates its inhumane ugliness. What Qoheleth just said about corruption, and the feeling of helplessness conveyed, should evoke a sense of outrage against greed. And the love of money is also about greed. So in terms of the art of persuasion, we cannot think of a better way for him to prepare his audience to see the evil of greed and of the love of money.

He declares without apology that he who loves money will not be satisfied with riches. Thus riches not only will be ultimately profitless as the possessor has to leave it behind when he dies, but it is also immediately profitless to him who loves money in the sense that it does not satisfy the possessor's actual needs.

This immediate vanity is experienced in two ways. Firstly, when "affluence (income) increases, those who consume it (expenditure) increase." We should not limit "those who consume it increase" to the involuntary increase in expenditure due to "parasitical friends and relations" and the "taxes and other expenses pertaining to a large fortune."[199] For human beings love riches because of the trappings of wealth. And this usually means not just the luxuries but also the glamor that riches bring. For what is the point of wealth if you cannot show it off? In fact, a good way to find out whether a high official is corrupt is to investigate whether he is living beyond his (legal) means.

So having more money to spend will often result in splurging on the family as well as on friends and relatives. And to support this lavish lifestyle, there will be more expenses on servants too. But neither wealth nor its trappings satisfy. So what is the advantage to the rich man except to see with his eyes lots of money coming in and going out, a privilege and pleasure the poor man does not share? But even this "advantage" comes with a price. The poor worker sleeps soundly, whether he eats much or little, but not so the rich person with his full stomach.

We must be reminded that Qoheleth is not commenting on wealth itself but on the love of money. For a wealthy person who loves riches is anxious not only to make more money, but also to keep making more money. And in a world full of uncertainties,

---

199. Whybray, *Ecclesiastes*, 99.

when you have the compulsion to protect a glamorous lifestyle and project a fabulous image, how well can you sleep?

Not every rich person treats his wealth and experiences its immediate vanity in the same way. For secondly, at the other extreme is the miser who hoards his money. Perhaps he cannot bear to see with his eyes so much money coming in and going out. He wants money to come in and stay. He derives his sense of being glamorous and fabulous from how much he is "worth," measured by the amount of wealth accumulated. But this is also harmful. For since he who loves money will not be satisfied with riches, he who hoards it will keep on investing it. Like the gambler at the casino who does not know when and how to stop even after a winning streak, he may invest compulsively even when prudence dictates otherwise. For to him, getting more is more important than having much.

His investments may not be as risky as gambling in a casino, but for one who loves and so hoards money, the risk of losing everything through a bad investment is there. "There is a time to make lots of money (laugh) and there is a time to lose them all (weep)," echoes the poem. In the specific case that Qoheleth observed, the miser did lose everything. And then, he fathered a son. What was supposed to be a source of joy became a cause for pain, for he had thought that his son would be the proud heir to a large fortune. But as neither he nor his son now has anything left, he feels the pain of loss not only for himself but also for his son. No wonder Qoheleth calls the hoarding of money, especially in this particular case, a "grievous affliction" as the man indeed hoarded money "to his own hurt."[200]

People who lose their wealth suddenly are known to be prime candidates for suicide. But even if one were to be so fortunate that he would never lose a lot of money in an investment, the stress that comes with investing a lot of money for quick gain is harmful enough. The difficulty in sleeping applies to him more than to his counterpart who spends lavishly. And even if he keeps winning without any setback, since he will die, sooner or later he will lose them all.

Qoheleth could not have stated it better: "As he came from his mother's womb, he will return naked—go as he came. So he will take nothing in (exchange for) his toil that he may carry away in his hand." The miser who loved and hoarded money to his own hurt through losing it all should have recognized this reality. If he did, his greed for more and more money could have been tempered and he may have avoided the painful eventuality. In light of this reality, what he did with his money does not make sense at all. So by highlighting this reality right after describing the misfortune of this rich miser, Qoheleth seeks to evoke the sense that the "affliction" of his hoarding

---

200. Unlike most Bible translations, we interpret the "and" at the very beginning of 5:14 as explicative (Kautzsch, *Grammar*, §154a.1b)—"It introduces the clarification of the previous verse" (Seow, *Ecclesiastes*, 206). We follow Seow in translating it as "That is." This makes the best sense of 5:13–14. In other words, 5:14 explains what Qoheleth says in 5:13, that is, it spells out how the miser hoarded money "to his own hurt" and why it was a "grievous affliction"—his compulsion to hoard money caused him to make that fateful investment which resulted in him losing all his wealth.

money was not only "grievous" but also meaningless. It does not make sense to hoard anything at all when one has to die and leave everything behind. It is all the more meaningless when one does so to one's own hurt.

He then adds that this reality, which he rephrased as "just as he came, so will he go," is also a grievous affliction (5:16). But we must not take what Qoheleth says out of context. This reality does imply that everyone "toils for the wind" as it means there is no ultimate profit to human labor. But in and by itself, it need not be a grievous affliction. In this context, Qoheleth is saying that this reality is a grievous affliction to a person like this miser, who would hoard money to his own hurt.

His comment, "Even all his days he eats in darkness," further clarifies why it would be a grievous affliction to him. Whatever the imagery "eats in darkness" means specifically, it gives the impression that when he eats, he is full of unhappiness because he eats "with much vexation, sickness and anger." Since he is a miser, this misery is most likely due to his compulsion to hoard money and thus his revulsion to spending it even on food. James Kugel even rereads the Hebrew word as "restraint" instead of "darkness"; thus the miser eats "in restraint," that is, eats sparingly—he is a miser!—instead of the enigmatic "in darkness."[201] A person like him will not be able to come to terms with the reality that, in the end, he will not be able to take his unspent money with him. It will afflict and grieve him.

This example is an extreme case of hoarding money. Most rich people who love money will fall somewhere in between the two extremes of spending and hoarding that Qoheleth discusses here. They will then experience to varying degrees a combination of the consequences of loving money expressed through splurging as well as hoarding. But it is possible to be rich and avoid these consequences. To this Qoheleth turns next.

Elaboration on Carefreeness (5:18–6:9)

Enjoyment of Prosperity (5:18–20)

> 5:18 Look! What I have seen is good, what is fitting, is to eat and drink and to see good (have enjoyment) in all of one's labor in which he toils under the sun the few days of his life that God has given him, for this is his lot. 5:19 In fact, (in the case of) every man to whom God gives wealth and possessions and (also) empowers him to partake of them and thus receive his lot and have enjoyment in his labor—this is a gift of God. 5:20 For he will not often remember the days of his life because God keeps him occupied with the gladness of his heart.

With the interjection "Look!" Qoheleth redirects our attention to what he has seen to be "good" and "fitting." Instead of being trapped in the grievousness of loving money (5:10–17), he admonishes us to enjoy our eating and drinking and so find satisfaction

---

201. Kugel, "Qohelet and Money," 38–40.

and thus have enjoyment ("see good") in all of our toils. He has already said three times there is "nothing good" except to have enjoyment (2:24; 3:12, 22) in response to the indirect question asked in his experiment with pleasure—"What is good ... to do" (2:3). Now he reiterates the answer here—What is good is to have enjoyment—in response to the issue raised in the previous section on the love of money. He also reiterates the reason why this is so: "for this is his lot" (cf. 3:22). Without repeating the discussion in our exposition of 3:22, this phrase means that the only good we can expect from the things we work for in this life is to find enjoyment in and through them. For only this and nothing else is what is allotted to us.

Here, Qoheleth adds that enjoyment is not only the only good but it is also "fitting" (5:18). The Hebrew word for "fitting" was earlier used in 3:11 in the statement that God "makes everything *appropriate* in its time." There it is used to express the idea that the events represented in the poem of 3:1–8 happen in this world in a way that is appropriate to, or is fitting in light of, an overall purpose. Here it expresses the idea that the enjoyment of the fruit of our labor "is fitting," or makes sense, in light of the brevity ("few days") of life under the sun. As can be seen in our exposition of 2:24–26, this idea was already implied when Qoheleth first presented enjoyment as the sensible response to the vanity of life.

In repeating the sub-theme of enjoyment here, Qoheleth also adds that even for one who has wealth and possessions, he is able to "receive his lot and have enjoyment" *only* if and when God "empowers him to partake of them"—as reflected in our translation of 5:19, it is implied that not everyone who has wealth and possessions is empowered to do so.[202] What does it mean? Earlier Qoheleth already spelled out that the ability to have enjoyment and thus receive one's "lot" is "a gift of God" received from the hand of God (3:13). And only those who are "good in his (God's) sight" (2:24), that is, those who are God-fearing and thus do what is (morally) good, get to receive this gift (3:12–14). What then does fearing God have to do with it?

Note that in the context here in 5:18–20, Qoheleth is talking about the enjoyment of wealth and prosperity. This passage is a response, and provides the solution, to the problem presented in the previous passage: the grievous afflictions that plague

---

202. Cf. Ogden and Zogbo, *Handbook*, 187. The Hebrew of 5:19 (5:18 in the Hebrew text) reads literally, "Also every man who God gives to him wealth and possessions and empowers him to eat from it, and to receive his lot and to have enjoyment in his labor, this is a gift of God." Besides adding "also (empowers him)," like with 3:13, we have also added "in the case of (every man)" to our rendering of this verse to make clear the implication that not everyone—not even everyone who has wealth—receives the "gift of God," that is, has the ability to have enjoyment of life even though this is his "lot" in this life. It matters that this implication is made clear because, in a deliberate contrast, 6:2 highlights the case of a man who has wealth but not the ability to have enjoyment of life. NJPS does it by adding "whenever" and "also": "whenever a man is given riches and property by God, and is also permitted by Him to enjoy them ... that is a gift of God" (NIV adds only "when"). NRSV does it by repeating "whom": "all to whom God gives wealth and possessions and whom he enables to enjoy them ... this is the gift of God." Most other translations do not make the implication clear. HCSB's rendering—"God has given riches and wealth to every man, and He has allowed him to enjoy them"—contradicts reality and even its own rendering of 6:2.

wealthy people who love money. It also confirms that Qoheleth was not speaking against wealth, but only against the love of money. Although this passage addresses enjoyment of prosperity and not enjoyment of life in general, it is clear that what it teaches about enjoyment is also applicable to it.

Qoheleth here explains that one who has received his lot as a gift from God is he to whom God has "*empowered . . . to partake of*"—to have the *ability* to enjoy—what God has given him.[203] To do this, "God keeps him occupied with the gladness of his heart" so that "he will not often remember the days of his life."[204] That means he is hardly bothered by the cares of this life. When we are burdened by cares, our days pass by slowly. But when we are occupied with gladness, we hardly "remember" or take notice of our days passing by. Recall how Jacob felt in anticipation of marrying Rachel: "So Jacob *served seven years* for Rachel but they *seemed a few days* to him because of his love for her" (Gen 29:20). Qoheleth is not saying, "he will *never* remember the days of his life." He recognizes that even a carefree person will face problems and experience sorrows and even have anxious moments (7:14). He is talking about a disposition that is basically carefree, a carefreeness that makes it actually possible even for a wealthy person to enjoy his prosperity.[205] In light of what Qoheleth has just said about the cares and miseries often associated with wealth, this comes as a breath of fresh air.

This elaboration on what it means to have enjoyment as a gift from the hand of God then clarifies the kind of enjoyment Qoheleth has in mind all along (2:24–26; 3:12–13, 22): experiencing pleasure and satisfaction out of a carefree disposition. And since not many people have such a disposition, the kind of enjoyment that Qoheleth has been referring to is not common. The experience we call "enjoyment" is very subjective. Anyone can say, "I am enjoying life." But unless one has a relatively carefree disposition, he has not known the blissful enjoyment Qoheleth is talking about. With this in mind, we are now ready to consider the fear of God in relation to the ability to have enjoyment.

---

203. We have taken for granted all along that the "gift of God" (3:13) is the *ability* to have enjoyment because when the sub-theme of enjoyment is first introduced, it is spelled out that enjoyment is "from the hand of God. For who can have enjoyment apart from him?" (2:24–25). So, though having pleasure is within our control, having enjoyment (pleasure that satisfies) is not (see exposition of 2:1–11 and Excursus to 2:1–11). We need to be given the ability (by God) to do so. And it is only here in 5:19 and 6:2 that Qoheleth spells out that we need God to "empower" us to have enjoyment. The verb literally means "cause to rule (have control)"—hence "empower" (Crenshaw, *Ecclesiastes*, 125). This is the meaning given in two of the three standard Hebrew dictionaries (Brown et. al., *Lexicon*, 1020; Clines, *Dictionary* VIII, 391). The other dictionary paraphrases it to "grant someone the opportunity to do something" (Koehler et al, *Lexicon*, 1522; Holmstedt et al., *Qoheleth*, 182, rejects this paraphrase because "the more literal rendering retains the basic idea of power or ability to do something"). This paraphrase implies that humanity on their own have the power or ability to have enjoyment; they only need to be "given . . . the opportunity" (NASB), "allowed" (HCSB), or "permitted" (NJPS) to do so. This misrepresents Qoheleth's teaching.

204. Cf. Holmstedt et al., *Qoheleth*, 183.

205. Cf. Whybray, *Ecclesiastes*, 103.

It may not be obvious to a contemporary reader that in this passage Qoheleth has actually begun to explain why only God-fearing people can enjoy life. But to his original audience, to fear God is to keep his commandments (12:13; cf. Deut 10:12–13). And they would have known the Ten Commandments by heart (Exod 20:1–17; Deut 5:6–21). When Qoheleth was describing the grievousness of loving money, they would have understood it as the consequence of violating the tenth commandment: "You shall not covet." In case any of them failed to do so, Qoheleth will soon make it clear enough that covetousness was indeed the problem (6:7–9).

And the love of money is a basic expression of covetousness. As "the love of money is a root of all kinds of evil" (1 Tim 6:10), covetousness is often the cause behind the breaking of the other nine commandments. So the tenth commandment forbids all forms of covetousness. It is not just against coveting one's neighbor's field (greed) but also his wife (lust) and "anything that belongs to him" (which includes envy and selfish ambition). Each of these negative feelings, in and by itself, already robs us of the gladness of our heart. What more when it leads to the actual violation of the other commandments. The possibility for carefreeness is then virtually ruled out. Consider the commandments against murder, theft, adultery, and perjury. Can anyone who commits, or is covetous enough that he is inclined to commit, any of these be carefree?

Since covetousness is in one's heart and no one else sees it except God, only the conscientious will be able to overcome it. A truly God-fearing person, whether rich or poor, will thus be relatively free from the love of money and the self-imposed cares and miseries that come with it. This will enable him to enjoy what God has given him. It is now obvious why a God-fearing heart is necessary to cultivating the carefree disposition needed to enjoy life.

Now if it is one's fear of God that gives him the ability to enjoy the fruit of his labor, how then can Qoheleth say that it is God who "empowers him to . . . have enjoyment" and that it is God who "keeps him occupied with the gladness of his heart"? We have been reminding ourselves that, since Qoheleth considers whatever happens as ultimately either directed or permitted by God, he attributes whatever we have or experience to the hand of God. In fact in this very passage, he considers even one's wealth as "given" by God (cf. 6:2). So to say that God has empowered one to have enjoyment means one has the ability to have enjoyment. But since God does not empower everyone, not everyone has the ability to do so. And since we do know the immediate cause behind one's ability to enjoy life, we can explore more specifically why not everyone has the ability to do so. We then will see in what ways we cannot have enjoyment apart from God (2:25).

First of all, God has created human beings with the predisposition not only to be aware of him (Ps 19:1–6; Rom 1:20) but also to fear him through their conscience by putting an awareness of his commandments in their hearts (Deut 30:11–14; Rom 2:14–16). This explains why people who have never heard of the Ten Commandments and may not even profess belief in God know it is wrong to commit murder, theft, adultery and perjury. And some of them may even be by nature conscientious enough that they would not consider committing any of these wrongs. In this sense they are innately prepared by God to be carefree. But of course not everyone is by nature conscientious enough.

In Old Testament wisdom thinking, God has created, and has been sustaining, the world in such a way that those who do not fear him and so violate his commandments will suffer the consequences (Prov 8:12–14, 22–36; 9:10). Qoheleth just highlighted one such consequence, namely, the inability to enjoy the fruit of their labor. His description of the misery of loving money illustrates this reality. The painful consequences of not keeping God's commandments are intended to goad us into fearing him, "for God so works that men should fear him" (3:14). When we take this somber reality to heart, we can see that coveting after what we do not have, and especially since it burdens us with cares and deprives us of the enjoyment of what we do have, is utterly meaningless. This realization can thus set us free from covetousness as well as set us free to keep God's other commandments. Since it is God who so works that we are prodded to fear him, ultimately it is God who keeps our hearts from the cares and miseries associated with not keeping his commandments. Certainly, not everyone is willing to yield to God's prodding to fear him and keep his commandments. This is the concern of the next passage (6:1–9).

A question now arises: Can one who lives a conscientious life but does not acknowledge God be "occupied with the gladness of his heart"? As we saw in our exposition of 3:10–15, when we are faced with the reality of the certainty of death and the uncertainties of life, it evokes in us a deep-seated sense of insecurity. This is true whether we are conscientious or not and is intended to make us feel the need to turn to the God who is just and is in control of whatever happens in this world. This then prods us to acknowledge and fear him by living our life on his terms through keeping his commandments.

By thus recognizing God's providence, we are enabled to cultivate a deep sense of security. People who do not acknowledge God may be conscientious enough to be free from the negative emotions associated with covetousness. They are certainly more carefree than those under the grip of covetousness. But they cannot be truly carefree unless they are also able to come to terms *emotionally* with the certainty of death and the uncertainties of life. Since according to Qoheleth, this somber reality is intended to prod us to acknowledge God, he would not think one who does not do so could be truly carefree.

Non-Enjoyment of Prosperity (6:1–9)

> *6:1 There is a grievous thing that I have seen under the sun, and it is prevalent among men: 6:2 a man to whom God gives riches, possessions, and honor so that his soul lacks nothing of all that he desires, yet God does not empower him to*

> *partake of them, but a stranger will partake of them. This is vanity and it is a grievous affliction.*

Qoheleth now deliberately contrasts the carefree person in the previous passage with one who is not able to enjoy the riches, possessions and even honor (evidently as a result of the wealth and not of righteousness) that God has given him. For unlike the carefree person, "God does not (also) empower him to partake of them," that is, to "receive his lot and have enjoyment" (5:19). He is like the sinner whom God "has given the business of gathering and collecting in order to give to one who pleases God" (2:26). Here Qoheleth calls the one who pleases God "a stranger." As we saw in the exposition of 2:24–26, what he means is that the wealth would only benefit some others who are able to enjoy it because they please God. Like in 2:26, Qoheleth says, "this is vanity." When wealth does not profit its possessor, it fails to fulfill even the immediate purpose why the wealth was pursued: satisfaction and enjoyment.

Qoheleth observed that one could have everything one ever wanted ("his soul lacks nothing of all that he desires") and yet finds no satisfaction. He himself had a similar experience (2:1–11). This observation of vanity reminds us that the ability to enjoy life is beyond self-determination; it is the side-effect of fearing God. Qoheleth introduces this observation with, "there is a grievous thing," and concludes with, "it is a grievous affliction." That is, to have wealth and cannot enjoy it is a painful experience. But because the non-enjoyment of prosperity is "prevalent among men," the experience of that rich man may not seem grievous. What is prevalent soon becomes the "norm" (average experience) and feels "normal" even though it is not what it should be.

Actually, the word translated "prevalent" can mean "much, many or great" and is most often translated "weighs heavily (on men)." We have preferred "prevalent"[206] because as pointed out above, Qoheleth already spells out *twice* that what is observed here is a "grievous" experience, so there is no reason to highlight that it "weighs heavily on men." Also, unless we assume that most people who had wealth then had enjoyment of life (which would mean they were God-fearing but Qoheleth did not seem to think so), what was observed would indeed be prevalent. However in the ancient world it was not as prevalent as today for there were fewer people with wealth then. Hence perhaps the painful experience was not felt to be "normal" like today. So in today's context, "prevalent" seems more appropriate even if Qoheleth had intended it to mean "weighs heavily."

> *6:3 If a man fathers a hundred children and lives many years, however many the days of his years may be, but his soul is not satisfied with good things, I say, even though it has no (proper) grave, the stillborn child is better off than he. 6:4 For it came in vain and goes in darkness, and in darkness its name is covered.*

---

206. Cf. NASB. This is also the option taken by Bartholomew, *Ecclesiastes*, 234; Longman, *Ecclesiastes*, 169; Ogden, *Qoheleth*, 96.

> *6:5 Even though it has not seen the sun or known anything, it has more rest than he. 6:6 Even if he had lived a thousand years twice over, yet does not enjoy good things—do not both go to one place?*

To help us feel the grievousness of the non-enjoyment of prosperity, Qoheleth compares the case of one who is not only wealthy but has many children and a very long life, with that of a stillborn child. In the ancient biblical world, "wealth, progeny, and longevity are the items that humans, even kings, most commonly requested from the deity."[207] In contrast, a stillborn child comes into this world "in vain" ("in *hebel*") as its birth amounts to nothing. To "see the sun" is to be alive in this world (7:11; 11:7; see Ps 58:8)[208] just as "under the sun" is the realm of the living. The stillborn "goes in darkness" because it goes to the netherworld without having "seen the sun" at all.

That means it never had the chance to taste even fleetingly what this life is like and hence "has not known anything" about it. It does not even have a grave to indicate that it ever existed as "stillbirths were cast into pits or hidden in the ground in no recognizable graves" (NJPS footnote to 6:3).[209] Since its "name" (memory) is thus "covered in darkness," it is considered to have never existed. As Robert Gordis aptly puts it, "the lot of the still-born was regarded with a particular horror precisely because both avenues of life, directly or vicariously, was denied to it, since it neither experienced life nor left any offspring or memory behind."[210]

As horrid as the case of the stillborn may be, Qoheleth tells us that it is better off than the one who has wealth, progeny and longevity but does not enjoy the good things he is blessed with. This is because "it has more rest" than the rich man. To appreciate this comparison, we need to recall what Qoheleth has just said about the consequences of loving money (5:10–17), that is, covetousness, which is the basic reason why a rich person could not enjoy his wealth (this is confirmed in 6:7–9). For his covetousness not only robs him of the gladness of his heart but also plagues him

---

207. Seow, *Ecclesiastes*, 225.

208. Cf. Seow, *Ecclesiastes*, 212.

209. Most Bible translations associate the clause in 6:3, "and also there is no burial (place) to him" (literal translation), with the rich man and not the stillborn child. The particle rendered "also" (usual meaning) in the literal translation can also mean "though" (Schoors, *Preacher*, 129), making it possible to associate the clause with the stillborn child. Thus, "I say: The stillbirth, though it was not accorded a burial, is more fortunate than he" (NJPS; the NJPS footnote to 6:3 on stillbirths having no recognizable graves relates to this translation of 6:3). This alternative, which we have adopted, makes better sense (also Crenshaw, *Ecclesiastes*, 126–27; Garrett, *Proverbs, Ecclesiastes, Song of Songs*, 315; Murphy, *Ecclesiastes*, 48). Seow, who associates the clause with the rich man, argues that the Hebrew word mostly translated as "burial," "in this instance does not refer to the act of burial . . . but the place of burial (Deut 34:6; Gen 35:20; 1 Sam 10:2; etc.)" (Seow, *Ecclesiastes*, 211). Again, this makes better sense. Though NJPS translates it as "(no) burial," its footnote says the stillborn has "no recognizable grave." Whichever is the correct interpretation does not affect the message. If the lack of a (proper) burial place refers to the rich man, it shows all the more the stillborn is better off than he. If it refers to the stillborn, it shows even then the stillborn is better off than he. Either way it shows the life of the rich man is not worth living.

210. Gordis, *Koheleth*, 259.

with cares and miseries. On the other hand, specifically because the stillborn never had a chance to know what it is like under the sun, it has never experienced unrest whatsoever. Thus Qoheleth "could not emphasize the rich man's plight more strongly than by this comparison. The stillborn lies at rest while the rich man continues in frustration."[211]

The only "advantage" the rich man has is the chance to experience life and even accumulate wealth under the sun. But what is the whole point of this "advantage" if his life lacks enjoyment since he must ultimately die and "go to the same place" as the stillborn? Compared to such a life, what does the stillborn really miss by taking a "short-cut" straight to the hereafter? Nothing, but the toils and sorrows that we must all bear in this life. So unless these inevitable experiences are adequately compensated for by an overall sense of carefreeness and satisfaction, life is not worth living. Many people are simply enduring such a meaningless existence. The stillborn is better off than them. Qoheleth affirms that this is still the case, "however many the days of his years may be," and even if he lives "a thousand years twice over," but is not satisfied with and thus does not enjoy the "good things" he has.

When life is worth living, longevity is a blessing. When it is not, it is a curse, a curse worse than the fate of the stillborn. By emphasizing the longevity to the point of fantasy, Qoheleth makes sure we do not miss the meaninglessness of an existence such as that of the rich man described here.

> *6:7 All the toil of man is for his mouth, and yet his appetite is not satisfied. 6:8 Indeed what advantage has the wise man over the fool? What is there for the poor by knowing how to conduct himself before the living? 6:9 What the eyes see is better than what the soul desires. This also is vanity and a pursuit after wind.*

Having considered the grievousness of the non-enjoyment of prosperity, Qoheleth states the cause: one who craves after prosperity cannot be satisfied by it. He has earlier made a similar statement that he who loves money will not be satisfied with it (5:10). Now he goes on to explain why.

He uses the universal human experience of eating to illustrate that our craving for more is insatiable. Similarly, when speaking to the Samaritan woman, Jesus used the experience of drinking to illustrate the same thing (John 4:13). For just as the food or the water that we put into our mouth will not remove our hunger or thirst once and for all, there is no end to our appetite for the other things that we toil for. We cannot deny our biological craving for food or thirst for water. But Qoheleth is calling us to deny our psychological craving or thirst for prosperity. The proverbial statement, "What the eyes see is better than what the soul desires [literally, 'wandering of the soul or desire']," is comparable to, "One bird in the hands is better than two in the bushes." One Bible translation captures the meaning well: "It is better to be satisfied with what

---

211. Crenshaw, *Ecclesiastes*, 127.

you have than to be always wanting something else" (GNB). Otherwise we will not be able to enjoy what we have, no matter how much we already have.

And when prosperity cannot be enjoyed, then "the wise man" who knows how to make wealth has no real advantage over "the fool." To further drive home the point, Qoheleth adds that there is then also no use for the poor to become rich through "knowing how to conduct himself (live wisely) before the living." In other words, "The poor . . . have no advantage in utilizing wisdom, which would teach them how to behave in order to get ahead in the world, to find satisfaction in wealth. Perhaps wisdom could make them rich, but it cannot satisfy their desires."[212] They are only graduating from one form of misery to another.

Qoheleth's concluding statement, "this also is vanity and a pursuit after wind," does not refer to the comparison—"what the eyes see is better than what the soul desires"—itself. It refers to the tendency implied in 6:7—attempting to satisfy our psychological "appetite" (same Hebrew word as soul) by means of the things we toil for in this world. And this is vanity (futility) in light of what is assumed in the comparison: the insatiability of "what the soul desires." But how do we overcome the craving of the soul? In the immediate context the answer is to be satisfied with what we already have ("what the eye sees"). This can happen through a heartfelt recognition that everything is ultimately profitless. This is partly why Qoheleth seeks to create, amplify and reinforce the sense of vanity in our heart.

But there is more to it. We have seen that Qoheleth wants us to feel deeply the reality that all is vanity so as to prod us into recognizing our accountability to God, to fear him and keep his commandments (3:14; 12:13). And another name for the craving of the soul is covetousness. We have also seen that it takes the fear of God to overcome covetousness. For one who truly fears God is aware that God knows what he is harboring in his heart and his God-given conscience restrains him from doing evil and constrains him to do good. He will not be perfect in keeping God's commandments. But his fear of God keeps him repentant, enabling him to progress in living a conscientious life. As a covetous person is "not satisfied with what he has but always wanting something else," he is by definition not a carefree person. So Qoheleth's teaching that the fear of God is basic to carefreeness and enjoyment of life is built on solid ground.

The soul, presented here as the seat of desire, is insatiable when one yields to its covetousness. But one could and should "let his soul see good (have enjoyment) in his labor" (2:24). We saw in the exposition of 2:24 that this refers to the soul finding *satisfaction* in and through one's labor and thus have *enjoyment* of its fruit. The idea that enjoyment is a function of satisfaction is only implicit in 2:24. It is now explicit in 6:1–6. For he whose "soul is not *satisfied* with good things" (6:3) is he who "does not *enjoy* ('see') good things" (6:6). And by now it is redundant to add that the prerequisite is a carefree disposition cultivated through a God-fearing way of thinking and living.

---

212. Longman, *Ecclesiastes*, 174.

To avoid misunderstanding, we must add that the word "carefree" as used throughout this exposition of Ecclesiastes does not imply being careless or complacent. Qoheleth will soon admonish us to be "careful" in light of the uncertainties of life (9:10–11:6).

Recapitulation of Theme and Sub-themes (6:10–12)

> 6:10 Whatever comes to be has already been called by name, and it is known that he is man—he is not able to dispute with one stronger than he is. 6:11 For (when) there are many words, they increase vanity. What is the profit to man? 6:12 For who knows what is good for man in his lifetime, the few days of his fleeting life, which he spends like a shadow? For who can tell man what will come to be after him under the sun?

This passage is exceptionally compact. Here Qoheleth pulls together the theme and the sub-themes and show in a direct and concise manner how they relate to one another. So to unpack the ideas we must interpret the passage in light of what he has said so far.

When Qoheleth first announced the theme of his speech, presented as, "Vanity of vanities; All is vanity (profitless)," as well as, "What profit is there?" (1:2–3), he recited a poem (1:4–8). The poem embodies the idea that, "whatever has come to be, that is what will come to be," which means, "there is nothing new under the sun" (1:9). It thus illustrates the idea of the theme: there is no net gain or profit in this world. But it also carries its own message: despite the cycles of one generation being replaced by another, basic realities about humanity remain unchanged (1:4).

When the theme is repeated for the first time, presented only as "What profit is there?" (3:9), it is expressed as a consequence to the reality captured in the second poem (3:1–8). This poem, which begins with "a time to die" (3:2), and ends with "a time for war" (3:8), embodies the reality that while death is certain, life is uncertain. In other words, there is no profit under the sun because we will one day lose everything we gain in this world, if not through a misfortune like war, then through death. In reference to the events represented in this poem, Qoheleth says: "Whatever comes to be, has already been; that which will come to be, already has been; for God seeks what has gone by" (3:15). This is a reiteration of 1:9, which carries the message that basic realities presented in the first poem have not changed. That means, the reality presented in the second poem—the certainty of death and the uncertainties of life—has not changed.

When Qoheleth's audience now hear him say "Whatever comes to be has already been called by name" (6:10), they will recognize that this statement is also another reiteration of 1:9. For when something has been "called by name" it is already known,[213]

---

213. Fox, *Time*, 248.

Our Reason for Being

and so it is already in existence[214] and its character has been determined.[215] Therefore it amounts to saying that whatever comes to be, whether a thing or an event, it is not something new. This statement is thus making a quick reference to the message embodied in the two poems: basic realities, including the unpleasant reality that death is certain and life is uncertain, have not changed.

Qoheleth's manner of reiterating 1:9 and thus 3:15 in this passage enables him to remind his audience of this unpleasant reality and in the same breath, highlight another unchanging reality about humanity: "it is known that he is man[216]—he is not able to dispute with one stronger than he is." This means it is known that being human, man is not able to dispute with God.[217] What is happening is this. Qoheleth confronts his audience with the unpleasant reality, which he told them was ordained by God and which they would want changed if they could (3:1, 11-15). He then says that it is useless to dispute with God to change it. For if a man is foolish enough to do that, no matter how many words he uses to present his case, his words will fail to impress God. The situation becomes one in which "(when) there are many words, they increase vanity (futility)" (6:11). In fact Qoheleth has already said earlier that there could be no change, for "everything God does cannot be changed; nothing can be added to it, nor anything taken from it" (3:14a).

Hence the rhetorical question that follows—"What is the profit to man?"—is asked in the context of two things: the reality presented in the second poem will not change; and any attempt to try and change it is futile, that is, it is unchangeable. Like the same question asked just after the second poem (3:9), it is a repetition of the theme. However, there is a difference. The question in 3:9 was asked in light of the unpleasant reality presented in that poem, which renders everything we gain in this world transitory and thus ultimately profitless. Here Qoheleth is asking whether there can be any profit at all when this reality not only will not change but is also unchangeable. This rhetorical question, here asked for the last time in the speech, has never been asked in light of a situation this desperate. Hence this recapitulation of the theme and sub-themes enables Qoheleth to reiterate the theme in a more forceful way.

In the very next breath, Qoheleth further explains why this unchangeable reality—the certainty of death and the uncertainties of life—results in no profit under the sun. Everything is vanity because no one "knows what is good in his lifetime, the

---

214. Crenshaw, *Ecclesiastes*, 130.

215. Whybray, *Ecclesiastes*, 110.

216. This is a literal rendering of the Hebrew text (cf. Holmstedt et al., *Qoheleth*, 192-93). Most Bible translations render it more idiomatically as "it is known what man is (like)." In terms of grammar this idiomatic rendering is off the mark (Seow, *Ecclesiastes*, 230-31), but in terms of meaning it is not, for the rest of the verse is about what it means to be human—not being able to dispute with God.

217. "The 'one who is stronger' is an oblique reference to the deity. One is reminded of Job's admission that no one can contend with the deity because 'he (the deity) is wise of heart and mighty in power' (Job 9:4-5)" (Seow, *Ecclesiastes*, 233). That the phrase is indeed an "oblique reference" to God is made clear in our exposition of 6:10 in light of 3:1-15.

few days of his fleeting life, which he spends like a shadow" (6:12). And this in turn is because no one knows "what will come to be after him under the sun," that is, no one knows what will happen under the sun (in this temporal world) "after him" (after his leaving this world).

In recapitulating the theme (and sub-themes) here, Qoheleth goes beyond merely reiterating the theme: All is vanity because when we die, we have to leave behind everything we have gained within our lifetime. For something that we do within our lifetime, including the pursuit of temporal things, though we have to leave them behind eventually, could benefit the people we leave behind in a meaningful way. Then what we do in our lifetime can be considered profitable and thus "good" and not vanity. But Qoheleth warns that we do not know if this would be the case because we could not know what would happen in this world after we die.

Why is it then that because we do not know what will happen in this world after we die, we do not know what is good in our lifetime? As Franz Delitzsch puts it, "The author means to say, that a man can say, neither to himself nor to another, what in definite cases is the real advantage [or good]; because, in order to say this, he must look far into the future beyond the limits of the individual life of man, which is only a small member of a great whole."[218] In other words, to know whether something is good in our lifetime we must look into the future beyond our lifetime to see whether it is indeed good in retrospect. For, in view of the uncertainties of life, even what seems to be undeniably "good" within our lifetime may result in disaster beyond our lifetime. And since we do not know what happens after we die, we cannot rule out that this might indeed be the case.

The need to look beyond one's lifetime in order to know what is good within one's lifetime explains why there is such an unusual emphasis here on the brevity of life: "few days," "fleeting life," and "spends like a shadow." The imagery of a shadow here gives a concrete sense of how brief human life is compared to human history. For just as a shadow lasts a fraction of the lifespan of the observer, so his lifetime is a fraction of the span of human history. That means, the reason there is no profit under the sun is not just because we have to leave this world (the certainty of death), but it is also because we do not know what will happen in this world after we have left (the uncertainties of life), and we thus do not know what is good. Hence this recapitulation of the theme and sub-themes also enables us to understand "What profit is there?" more clearly.

Actually Qoheleth is here speaking from experience. Recall that in light of the certainty of death, he had himself lamented the fact that he had to leave behind the fruit of his labor to his heir (2:18). He considered this vanity as well because, in light of the uncertainties of life, he would not know if his heir could make good use of it (2:19, 21). If Qoheleth were able to know the ultimate outcome of all that he labored

---

218. Delitzsch, *Song of Songs and Ecclesiastes*, 312.

for, and that in light of that outcome, his labor could be considered good, he would have found meaning in it.

Note that the rhetorical question "For who can tell man what will come to be after him under the sun?" (6:12) is essentially saying the same thing as "For who can bring him to see what will be after him?" (3:22). In 3:22 the question explains why "there is nothing good except that man should have enjoyment," which is the response to "What profit has the worker? [No profit]" (3:9). Here in 6:12 the question explains why no one "knows what is good for man in his lifetime," which is the reason for saying "What is the profit for man? [No profit]" (6:11).

This means, "(no one) knows what is good" (6:12) is in some way logically connected to "there is nothing good except... have enjoyment" (3:22). This seems contradictory. For if no one knows what is good, how can Qoheleth say there is nothing good except to have enjoyment, which means he knows there is something good, namely, enjoyment? The "(what is) *good*" in 6:12 refers to what is good in the long run (beyond one's lifetime). No one knows what is good in the long run because no one knows what will happen in the long run (after one's death). So the only good that one can know is a good that is not affected by what happens in the future. And there is only one such good—enjoyment of what we *now* have or do (3:22). Hence, leaving out spiritual realities taught in the New Testament, because "(no one) knows what is good (in the long run)," "there is nothing good except ... have enjoyment (now)."

Therefore 6:12 helps us better understand the sub-theme of enjoyment and in the process reinforces the admonition to have enjoyment. And since "who can have enjoyment apart from him" (2:25), this recapitulation of the sub-theme on enjoyment amounts to an indirect admonition to fear God.

This recapitulation is reiterating the basic message of Ecclesiastes in a more nuanced and penetrating way so as to continue preparing the heart and mind of his audience for the final exhortation: "The conclusion, when all has been heard: Fear God and keep his commandments" (12:13). As we shall see, before he makes that call to decision, having now recapitulated the theme and the sub-themes, in the next half of the speech he shifts his focus to deliberate on how to come to terms with the down-to-earth realities in this world in light of the uncertainties of life.

DELIBERATIONS ON LIFE IN LIGHT OF VANITY (7:1–11:6)

We do not know the future, whether the future within or beyond our own lifetime. As the previous section highlights, we therefore do not know what we decide or choose to do in our lifetime is in the long run good or otherwise. But even in the face of the uncertainties of the future, we still have to decide and choose what to do in our lifetime. How then do we decide? What then do we choose?

Qoheleth has actually answered this question. He has said that because human beings will not know the future, "there is nothing good for them except to have enjoyment *and to do (moral) good* in their lifetime" (3:11–12). In that context, "to do (moral) good" was presented as the prerequisite to enjoyment (cf. 2:24–26). Since enjoyment is good regardless of what happens in the future, "to do (moral) good" is therefore the basis for how we decide and for what we choose.

In that same context Qoheleth also said, "God so works," including making us face an uncertain future, "that men should fear him" (3:14b). This means, to fear God and thus do (moral) good is not merely so that we can enjoy life. As Qoheleth will further clarify at the end of the speech, this is the very purpose of life and so exhorts his audience to observe it (12:13–14).

For the next five chapters (7:1–11:6) he deliberates on how this purpose of life is to be lived out in light of vanity, in particular with respect to the uncertainties of life. He also deliberates on why it is the sensible way to live even in the face of the most baffling experiences in this world, such as when the righteous suffers while the wicked prospers. This will further prepare the hearts and minds of the audience to accept God's purpose for humanity to fear him and keep his commandments.

Proverbial Wisdom in Light of Uncertainties of Life (7:1–14)

Qoheleth begins his deliberations with an anthology of proverbs like those in the book of Proverbs. This is not surprising because no matter who actually wrote Ecclesiastes, Qoheleth takes on the persona of King Solomon (12:9), the author of most of the book of Proverbs. This means Qoheleth views this world and how it works, including the uncertainties of life expressed in the poem of 3:1–8, through the eyes of proverbial wisdom as taught in Proverbs. And this is particularly relevant to how we read 7:1–11:6.

According to Proverbs, when God created the world, he implanted an order to govern it (Prov 3:19–20; 8:22–31). Since this order is created (and sustained) by God, we call it the created order. It covers the physical, moral and social dimensions of life and governs the world according to the "You reap what you sow" principle (Prov 22:8; cf. 6:27–29). When we observe this order, we will experience pleasant consequences, but when we violate it, we will suffer painful consequences.[219] For instance, if we live as though gravity does not exist, sooner or later we will have to pay for it. Similarly, if we live as though greed is good or practice injustice, we will reap what we sow.

This "act-consequence relationship" is based on the "widely-spread concept of an effective power inherent both in good and in evil and subject to specific laws ... [that is,] by every evil deed or every good deed a momentum was released which sooner or later also had an effect on the author of the deed. To a great extent, therefore, it lay within his own power whether he exposed himself to the effects of disaster or of blessing."[220] It is significant that this relationship between how we act now and what

---

219. Cf. von Rad, *Wisdom in Israel*, 90–92, 124–29.
220. Von Rad, *Wisdom in Israel*, 128.

will happen later is described in terms of the agricultural imagery of sowing and reaping. Since it takes time before farmers can reap what they have sown, it implies that the consequences of our acts, whether painful or pleasant, take time to be effected except in cases (mainly in the physical realm) like defying gravity and jumping off a building.

Proverbial wisdom assumes this created order and guides us in navigating it so as to avoid the painful consequences of violating it. Since the consequences take time to be effected, the truthfulness of proverbial wisdom is not prescriptive but descriptive. Take for example the contemporary proverb, "Honesty is the best policy." It is "true" not in the sense that it *prescribes*, as though making a promise, that if we are honest, we will have no set-backs. But rather, it *describes* the usual outcome of a certain action under normal circumstances, especially in the long run. In this case, it means that it has been widely observed that honest people doing honest things, despite possible set-backs in the short term, usually prosper in the long run.

Hence, the "You reap what you sow" principle does not operate as an iron-clad formula. In other words, though God has implanted the created order to govern this world, bad things can happen to good people and good things can happen to bad people. And this gives rise to the uncertainties of life as expressed in the poem of 3:1–8. Though God works through an impersonal created order, it does not mean the act-consequence relationship is an impersonal one. For it is God who created and sustains this order and Qoheleth goes so far as to say that "everything" that happens, whether "good" or "bad," is appointed by God (3:1), who "makes everything appropriate in its time" (3:11). And even in Proverbs, the workings of the created order are attributed to God himself (Prov 10:2–5).[221]

Since life is full of uncertainties and we do not know the future, the wisest thing to do in making decisions and choices is to observe time-tested principles such as those embodied in sound proverbial wisdom. For at the least, proverbial wisdom "assures" us that in the long run, if not in the short term, we will reap what we sow. After all, "God so works [through the created order] that men should fear him" (3:14). And "the fear of the LORD is the beginning of wisdom" (Prov 9:10), which means God so works that we fear him and live according to proverbial wisdom. This explains why Qoheleth begins his deliberations on how one should live in light of the uncertainties of life with a series of proverbs.

> *7:1 A good name is better than good ointment,*
> *   And the day of one's death is better than the day of his birth.*
> *7:2 It is better to go to the house of mourning*
> *   Than to the house of feasting,*
> *   Because this is the end of every man,*
> *   And the living should take it to heart.*

---

221. Waltke, *Proverbs 1–15*, 75.

7:3 Sorrow is better than laughter,
  For when the face is sad, the heart may be glad.
7:4 The heart of the wise is in the house of mourning,
  While the heart of the fool is in the house of pleasure.

Qoheleth begins the series of proverbs saying, "A good name," that is, maintaining a good reputation, is better than "good ointment" (7:1a)—living in luxury. As Bartholomew comments, "According to Prov. 22:1, 'A good name is to be chosen rather than great riches, and grace is better than silver or gold.' Verse 1a sounds just like Proverbs—a good reputation is better than good ointment, an expensive and highly desirable item. . . . Fine ointment is listed among the treasures of King Hezekiah (2 Kgs 20:13) and was a highly desirable luxury item."[222]

Just before the recapitulation of the theme and sub-themes (6:10–12), Qoheleth was talking about the cares of loving money (5:10–17) and highlights a rich man who lived in luxury but could not enjoy his wealth because of covetousness—he did not fear God (6:1–9). This is in contrast to the rich man who could enjoy his wealth because of "the gladness of his heart," one that is free from the cares of covetousness (5:18–20). And Proverbs 22:1–5 associates "A good name" with "the fear of the LORD." All this is in line with the conclusion of Qoheleth's experiment with the pursuit of pleasure (luxury)—pleasure, when pursued cannot satisfy, and enjoyment is a by-product of a God-fearing life (2:1–11; 2:24–26; 3:12–14). So in light of biblical proverbial wisdom and what Qoheleth has been saying, 7:1a is saying that, if we have to choose between the two, it is better to live a God-fearing and thus blameless life and so maintain a "good name" than to live in luxury. He has shown that on the whole this is true even in the short term (5:10–6:9). Its truthfulness for the long run is widely attested even in our daily news today.

Why is it that "the day of one's death is better than the day of his birth" (7:1b) and what does it have to do with fearing God and maintaining a good reputation? This must be read in light of the next few verses (7:2–4), that is, in terms of the effects that lamentation ("house of mourning") as opposed to celebration ("house of feasting") has on people. In a funeral, they are graphically reminded of, and "should take it to heart,"[223] the inevitability of "the end of every man" and the unpredictability of when and how this happens. They are thus prodded to come to terms with their own mortality. And we have seen that the certainty of death and the uncertainties of life are designed to cause one to fear God (3:14). So lamentation instead of celebration empowers one to maintain a good reputation. And since the fear of God sets one free from the burdens that a covetous heart bears, "when the face is sad, the heart may be glad." This in turn empowers one to enjoy one's life.

---

222. Bartholomew, *Ecclesiastes*, 246.

223. Translating the verb as "should" and not "will" makes better sense here—one may not take it to heart (cf. HCSB, NIV, NJPS, NLT). The grammatical form can carry this modal sense (Waltke and O'Connor, *Syntax*, §31.4g).

So unlike the fool, the heart of the wise is in "the house of mourning" instead of in "the house of pleasure." It is one thing to go to the house of feasting once in a while, it is quite another for the heart to remain there. No wonder it is no longer "the house of *feasting*," but "the house of *pleasure*," signifying that the fool's heart is one that is given to the pursuit of pleasure, which is vanity (2:1–11). So we need to recognize that "Sorrow is better than laughter, for when the face is sad, the heart may be glad." As Crenshaw puts it eloquently,

> The reason for preferring grief to revelry resembles the thought in Ps 90:12 . . . . By pondering the implications of life's brevity and death's inevitability, we may acquire insight or even real wisdom. Qohelet advises one to face death squarely, without drowning awareness of mortality in endless drinking bouts and parties. . . . Since everyone eventually dies, a realist prepares for that moment. In considering that unwelcome event one encounters an astonishing paradox: suffering can instruct, purge the spirit, and offer increased learning. An astute observer of life makes a path for the house of mourning, anticipating an encounter with the essence of human existence. The fool takes up residence in the place of mirth.[224]

In fact, through confronting his audience repeatedly with the sense of vanity, Qoheleth has been goading his audience to come to terms with their own mortality up until the last passage (6:10–12). This set of proverbs in effect helps them to accept what he has been saying by graphically recreating the sense of their mortality and so prod them to fear God, which we have seen, equips them to face the uncertainties of life and an unknown future with proper confidence. And the effects of these proverbs will be reinforced when they heed the advice to actually give more attention to "the house of mourning" than to "the house of feasting." Hence the first four proverbs sum up and apply what Qoheleth has been saying so far.

> 7:5 *It is better to listen to the rebuke of the wise*
>   *Than for one to listen to the song of fools.*
> 7:6 *For as the crackling of thorns under a pot,*
>   *So is the laughter of the fool,*
>   *And this also is vanity.*

These two proverbs can be read as an application of the previous four. Just as the sorrowful experience of the death of a friend or family member is beneficial, so is the painful experience of being rebuked by the wise. For in light of the uncertainties of life we need the rebuke of the wise so that we would not stray from the path of wisdom. It is significant that Qoheleth here compares the rebuke of the wise with the song of the fools and not with the song of the wise. The focus of the comparison is not between rebuke and song, but between the respective *sources*—is it from a heart of wisdom or

---

224. Crenshaw, *Ecclesiastes*, 134–35.

a heart of folly? The song of the wise would also be better than the rebuke of the fools. For "the heart of the fool is in the house of pleasure" whereas "the heart of the wise is in the house of mourning" (7:4). We have already seen that going to "the house of mourning" is better than to "the house of feasting" (7:1) and that a heart that is in the house of pleasure is a heart of folly. So whatever comes from the heart of the wise, whether rebuke or song, will be better than that from the fools.

To better appreciate this comparison, consider Qoheleth's speech itself, which amounts to a rebuke of the wise about not fearing God. And within the speech, Qoheleth presents three somber poems highlighting the reality of death (1:4–11; 3:1–8; 12:2–7). Listening to them is like going to the house of mourning. And since songs are poetry set to music, these poems can be considered songs of the wise, which are used in the speech to move the audience emotionally to heed the rebuke about not fearing God. A fool, who by definition does not fear God and whose heart is in the house of pleasure, would not have presented poems that inspire us to fear God. So his song, no matter how pleasant to the ears, even when it brings laughter, would not be beneficial to the heart. And a fool's rebuke would also not be in sync with fearing God; in fact we may even be rebuked precisely because we fear God.

Qoheleth intends to say that the value (if any) of "the song of the fools" is reflected in the value of "the laughter of the fool," otherwise the "For," which conjoins 7:6 with 7:5, does not make sense. This is the case because both the song and the laughter come from a heart that is in the house of pleasure—a heart that pursues after pleasure, which we saw will not satisfy him (2:1–11). For his song and laughter come from an empty heart that cannot be satisfied because it does not fear God (6:1–9). Thus like the "crackling of thorns under the pot," the laughter of the fool is profitless ("vanity"). For its usefulness is like using thorns as fuel: "Thistles provide quick flames, little heat, and a lot of unpleasant noise."[225] In contrast, since the heart of the wise is in the house of mourning, though his face may be sad, his heart is glad. So his laughter is out of a heart full of gladness; it is an expression of his enjoyment of life (5:18–20). Hence Qoheleth is also implicitly comparing the laughter of the wise with that of the fool.

So we see 7:5–6 makes so much sense when read as an application of 7:1–4, which is itself a summing up and an application of what Qoheleth has said so far. Since Ecclesiastes itself amounts to a "rebuke of the wise," it means 7:1–6 is indirectly saying, in light of the uncertainties of life, we need to take seriously the "sorrowful" message of Qoheleth so that our heart may be filled with "gladness."

> 7:7 *Surely oppression makes the wise foolish,*
>   *And a bribe corrupts the heart.*
> 7:8 *The end of a matter is better than its beginning,*
>   *A patient spirit is better than a haughty spirit.*
> 7:9 *Do not be quick in your spirit to be angry,*

---

225. Crenshaw, *Ecclesiastes*, 135.

> *For anger resides in the bosom of fools.*
> *7:10 Do not say, "Why is it that the former days were better than these?"*
> *For it is not from wisdom that you ask about this.*

Having applied the first four proverbs, Qoheleth returns to the first proverb: "a good name"—a good reputation by living a God-fearing and blameless life—is better than "good ointment," that is, living in luxury without fearing God. For 7:7 is warning against oppression through corruption by accepting bribes[226] to live in luxury, which is precisely what 7:1—a good reputation is better than luxury—warns against. Even in the modern world with its "democracy," let alone in the ancient world of Qoheleth, it is not difficult to know which politician, official or judge has the reputation ("bad name") of being corrupt. It is often the case that a politician, official, or judge started off well—seen to be wise—but became corrupt and thus was made foolish when he failed to resist the temptation to accept a bribe due to the seemingly irresistible lure of the luxurious lifestyle.

Hence the warning here in 7:7 is a further application of 7:1. This is most apt in view of the observation that there is miscarriage of justice even in the courts of law (3:16)—evidently due to corruption—as well as the observation that oppression in general due to corruption may be blatant and rampant because corrupt officials are protected by those higher up (5:8–9). Qoheleth's warning here against oppression through corruption thus silences critics that he did nothing to what he observed in this regard.

Qoheleth then gives advice on making good decisions and choices that applies to everyone, but in this context it is particularly pertinent to those tempted to accept bribes. His advice is to look at "the end of a matter" and not "its beginning." For "there is a way which seems right to a man, but its end is the way of death" (Prov 14:12). In other words, consider the consequences of our decisions and actions. Is it a case of short-term gain but long-term loss? Are we willing to suffer short-term loss for long-term gain? If we have to violate sound proverbial wisdom, we can expect long-term loss, no matter how promising the short-term gain may seem to be. To do the wise thing often requires patience, which in this case is to endure the short-term loss. To do otherwise is in this sense "haughty," as it implies that one presumes one is able to go against the odds stacked against him and win.

An obvious but often ignored application of being patient is to avoid getting angry easily. Its foolishness is obvious to anyone when he is not angry. But too many people have suffered the consequences of reacting to the slightest provocation in anger, out

---

226. The word translated "oppression" (ESV, NASB, NKJV, NRSV) is also rendered "extortion" (HCSB, NIV, NLT) or "cheating" (NJPS). The same Hebrew word is used in 5:8, which is also in the context of corruption. When Ecclesiastes is read as a coherent speech, it is natural to read 7:7 as a critical response to—an admonition against—what is observed in 5:8 (and in 3:16). So since 5:8 is a follow-up on the observation in 4:1, where the word clearly means "oppression" and not "extortion," we have opted for oppression in 7:7 also.

of the "haughtiness" that they are able to get away with it. To help us cultivate the right spirit so that we react correctly to different kinds of unpleasant circumstances, Qoheleth says it is not wise to ask, "Why were the former days better than these?" For it reveals an impatient spirit and a habit of focusing on the current situation ("its beginning") instead of looking at the long term ("the end of a matter"). This predisposes us to act or react foolishly.

> *7:11 Wisdom is good like an inheritance,*
>   *And a profit to those who see the sun.*
> *7:12 For the protection of wisdom is the protection of money,*
>   *But the advantage of knowledge is that wisdom preserves the life of its*
>   *possessor.*

By reciting proverbs that are so similar to those in the wisdom book of Proverbs, Qoheleth is affirming the value of wisdom. He has shown that wisdom is vanity in light of the certainty of death and the uncertainties of life, in the sense that the things we gained through laboring with wisdom are transitory (2:12–17). And also, wisdom is not able to solve this basic problem of life (1:12–18)—the certainly of death and the uncertainties of life. But here he explicitly recognizes that, in a different sense, wisdom has profit in light of this very basic problem: its ability to protect against avoidable harm and loss, and even untimely death.

He compares wisdom with money because this is what people tend to trust in. Though money can offer protection, the love of it is a root of all sorts of evil, and leads to destruction. He has just reminded us of this in his warning concerning oppression through corruption. In this light 7:1–10 sets the stage for him to emphasize the value of wisdom with respect to money. Though most people do not have the opportunity of people in power to accept bribes, people in general tend to trust in money. So given the opportunity virtually anyone, no matter how "wise" one may have been, can be corrupted. Thus it is crucial for Qoheleth to highlight the advantage of wisdom over money.

In biblical proverbial wisdom, the reward of the fear of God, which is the beginning of wisdom, "are riches, honor ['a good name'] and life" (Prov 22:4; cf. Prov 3:13–18). For a God-fearing and thus wise person is trustworthy, hardworking, prudent with money, and avoids getting into legal, moral or social problems. Under normal circumstances he will usually do well materially ("riches"), be respected ("honor"), and is not likely to suffer an untimely death related to criminal or immoral activities ("life"). Since wisdom brings not just riches but also honor and life, it provides not just the kind of protection money offers, but also what money by itself cannot offer. Wisdom thus has a distinct advantage over money.

In broaching this subject by comparing wisdom with an inheritance, Qoheleth is indirectly addressing parents concerning what they would really want to leave behind for their children. He had himself done some serious thinking on this matter

(2:18–23). If more parents take this seriously, there would be more God-fearing people who would not be easily tempted to accept bribes and be corrupted.

In 7:12b knowledge is not to be understood as the same as wisdom. In biblical wisdom thinking, knowledge refers to the correct understanding of how the created order works in all its dimensions. Wisdom then is the correct application of this knowledge in daily living. Hence though knowledge and wisdom are not the same, they come in the same package. Confusion arises when people mistake information for knowledge. One may have gained information, but until and unless he has understood it adequately and so could use it profitably (wisdom), the information has not yet become knowledge.

> 7:13 Consider the work of God. For who is able to make straight what he has made crooked? 7:14 In the day of prosperity be glad, but in the day of adversity consider—indeed God makes the one as well as the other so that man will not find out anything after him.

Qoheleth now concludes what amounts to a series of proverbial admonitions with a call to "consider" or reflect on reality as ordained by God. The imagery of "what is made crooked cannot be straightened" was used earlier in the context of the inability of wisdom to solve the basic problem of life (1:14–15). Here he spells out that this "crooked" world is the result of "the work of God" as depicted in the poem that highlights the certainty of death and the uncertainties of life (3:1–8) and that God gives prosperity but also allows adversity. And just as we saw in the previous section, we cannot argue with God to straighten what is crooked. Qoheleth is thus reiterating and reinforcing what we saw in 6:10–12 and asking his audience to reflect on it.

He then gives an admonition on how to respond to this "crookedness": in times of prosperity be glad, for times of adversity will come; but in times of adversity "consider" or reflect on God's purpose in allowing adversity (in addition to prosperity), namely "so that man will not find out anything after him." In other words, God has ordained both times of prosperity as well as times of adversity, resulting in the uncertainties of life (3:1–8), in order that no one is able to know what will happen in this world after one's death. We just saw that this means no one "knows what is good for man (to do) in his lifetime" (6:12) except to have enjoyment (3:22), which cannot be had without pleasing God (2:24–26). Thus Qoheleth is reiterating and reinforcing the message that uncertainties of life are meant to prod people to acknowledge and fear God (3:14).

Actually the admonition here to consider the work of God, particularly why God allows adversity, takes this message further. Firstly, the series of proverbial admonitions are given as an application of this very message. Reiterating and reinforcing it here has the effect of persuading his audience to live by proverbial wisdom such as the admonitions just given. And since "the fear of God is the beginning of wisdom," this is an indirect call to fear God. Secondly, as a further application of the message, he admonishes his audience to reflect on it when they are actually experiencing adversity, when they are most receptive to the message—God is using their experience of adversity to prod them to fear him.

Admonitions in Light of Human Wickedness (7:15–8:15)

Through the series of proverbs, Qoheleth has just expressed the value of the fear of God and of wisdom in light of the uncertainties of life. But as we have seen, "You reap what you sow" is not an iron-clad formula that *always* works (especially) in the short term. This is how the created order that God has implanted into the world operates. Thus, by using the genre of proverbs to introduce his deliberations on how one should live in light of the uncertainties of life, Qoheleth has actually affirmed implicitly that the world as we know it is structured in such a way that the righteous may suffer and the wicked may prosper. And this has been widely observed to be indeed the case. Qoheleth now turns to address this problematic reality head-on.

The book of Proverbs itself does not address this problem though it recognizes that it exists[227]—the righteous may fall seven times, but rises again (Prov 24:16); and the wicked may succeed, but the heart aches (Prov 14:12–13). It is a matter of focus—Proverbs presents the reality of the created order and teaches how to navigate it by observing the "You reap what you sow" principle as expressed in proverbial wisdom. It is what can be considered "practical wisdom" as opposed to Ecclesiastes, which is "philosophical wisdom" designed specifically to make sense of life in all its complexities. After all, the complex problem of righteous suffering is the focus of the book of Job; and together with what we read in Ecclesiastes on this problem, the matter is adequately addressed in Scripture. Since the problem is already implied in proverbial wisdom as taught in Proverbs, neither Job nor Ecclesiastes contradicts, but they actually complement, Proverbs.

Even the book of Psalms, which like Proverbs, also teaches that "The fear of the LORD is the beginning of wisdom" (Ps 111:10) and has its own anthology of proverbs (Psalm 112), recognizes that the righteous may suffer and the wicked may prosper (Psalm 73). As a result, it even goes as far as Job to question God's justice (Psalm 44). Hence in recognizing this problematic reality Qoheleth is entirely consistent with the wisdom tradition of Israel. We should bear this in mind and thus benefit from his teaching on how to make sense of this enigmatic reality.

Fear God and Be Moderate (7:15–29)

> 7:15 *In my fleeting lifetime I have seen both: there is a righteous man who perishes in his righteousness, and there is a wicked man who prolongs his life in his wickedness.* 7:16 *Do not become overly righteous, and do not make yourself*

---

227. Cf. von Rad, *Wisdom in Israel*, 129–30.

> *excessively wise. Why should you ruin yourself? 7:17 Do not become overly wicked, neither become a fool. Why should you die before your time? 7:18 It is good that you grasp the one, and also not let go of the other; for he who fears God shall come forth with both of them. 7:19 Wisdom strengthens a wise man more than ten rulers who are in a city. 7:20 Surely there is not a righteous man on earth who (continually) does good and never sins. 7:21 Do not then take to heart all the things that people say, lest you hear your servant cursing you. 7:22 For you know too in your heart that many times you yourself have likewise cursed others.*

Qoheleth begins to address head-on the problematic reality that the righteous do suffer and the wicked do prosper by affirming that he himself has observed both. Now since the righteous do die young in their righteousness, they do not seem to prosper even in the long run. While this observation does not contradict what he has just expressed through proverbial wisdom, he still needs to address this enigmatic reality.

It is crucial to recognize that 7:16–17 is not about the *dispositions*, whether of the (overly) righteous/(excessively) wise or the (overly) wicked/foolish, but their *actions*.[228] Qoheleth is not saying that we should not be overly righteous in disposition. He is saying that, since there is no guarantee that righteous acts will be rewarded with temporal blessings, do not seek to act in a righteous way in order to attain prosperity and avoid adversity.[229] This will only drive one to behave in a way that is not a natural expression of one's actual disposition and thus become "overly righteous." And since righteousness is an expression of wisdom, when one is driven to act in a righteous way beyond what one really is in disposition, one is seeking to make oneself "excessively wise" by acting in a way that is "wiser" than one really is in disposition. Hence the warning against being "overly righteous" carries over to being "excessively wise."

One can be driven to become "overly righteous" and thus make oneself "excessively wise" because on the whole the righteous do prosper and the wicked do suffer.

---

228. The verb in 7:16a and 7:17a is rendered "become" and not "be" as in most Bible translations because the grammatical form of the verb ("jussive") is used "to express a more or less definite desire that something should or should not happen" (Kautzsch, *Grammar*, §109a). So it refers to something happening. Consider the same Hebrew word (*hāyāh*) in this grammatical form in this clause: "Let there be light" (Gen 1:3). The "be" is clearly about something happening. The expression "do not *become* overly righteous" then alerts us that Qoheleth is talking about disposition but action. Seow understands the clause to mean "do not show yourself to be [(overly)] righteous [through your actions]" (Seow, *Ecclesiastes*, 253). The understanding that the reference is to the action and not disposition is confirmed by the verb translated "(do not) make yourself (excessively) wise" (7:16). This verb in this form (here in the second person) occurs only one other time (in the first person—"let us") in the Hebrew Bible with the meaning: "Let us deal wisely (shrewdly)" (Ex 1:10), which unmistakably means, "[(let us)] behave wisely" (Seow, *Ecclesiastes*, 253). It refers to action not disposition. Similarly, our rendering of the verbs in 7:17a as "become (overly wicked)" and "become (a fool)" is to alert us that the verse is talking about wicked and thus foolish actions and not about disposition.

229. Actually "in his righteousness" and "in his wickedness" (7:15) can be translated as "in spite of his righteousness" and "in spite of his wickedness" (cf. HCSB, NJPS; see Gordis, *Koheleth*, 276–77; Koehler et al., *Lexicon*, 104, 7). Qoheleth will then be saying explicitly that righteousness may not be rewarded with temporal blessings.

When one is thus tempted, one would strive meticulously to avoid sinning and thus "ruin yourself"—wear oneself out.[230] For "Surely there is not a righteous man on earth who (continually) does good and never sins" (7:20). Qoheleth's comments about not taking seriously everything we hear because we and everyone have sinned with our lips (7:21–22) illustrate in a rather convicting way the truth that there is no one who never sins.

Qoheleth's warning on not becoming "overly wicked" (in action) is not implying that it is alright to become a little wicked. For since no one can avoid sinning altogether, we are already being a little wicked even when we seek to live conscientiously as an expression of our righteous disposition. The warning then is: do not "become a fool" by allowing our wickedness to go unchecked and thus "become overly wicked."

This warning is needed. For since even the righteous may suffer and the wicked may still prosper, one may conclude that there is no point in living righteously. However, wickedness on the whole does have painful consequences. Qoheleth's warning about dying before one's time if one does not heed this advice is a reaffirmation of sound proverbial wisdom: wisdom and righteousness do, on the whole, protect us from harm and even untimely death (7:11–12).

How then shall we live? Qoheleth admonishes that if we fear God and thus be wise, we will be moderate and "come forth with both of them,"[231] that is, on the one hand grasping the warning not to become overly righteous and thus make oneself excessively wise, and on the other hand not letting go of the other warning not to become foolish and thus overly wicked. So there is practical value in fearing God in light of even the enigmatic reality that the righteous do suffer and the wicked do prosper. Qoheleth goes so far as to say that wisdom, which is founded on the fear of God, is even stronger than the political strength of ten rulers put together.

It is obvious that fearing God helps us to keep our wickedness in check and so avoid becoming "overly wicked." But how does fearing God help us avoid becoming "overly righteous"? Qoheleth is implicitly saying that we should not seek to fear God and become righteous in order to receive (temporal) blessings from him. For this

---

230. The word translated "ruin yourself" has the root meaning "be desolated" or "be appalled." It occurs in this grammatical form only four other times in the Hebrew Bible (Ps 143:4; Isa 59:16; 63:5; Dan 8:27), where the meaning is in line with "be appalled." However virtually all Bible translations (except NJPS) translate the occurrence here in line with "be desolated" as it fits the context better. "Both the immediate context and the parallel phrase in vs. 17c ('Why should you die before your time?') show that here it must have the former ['be desolated'] meaning: it must refer to some undesirable consequence which will befall the person who ignores the foregoing admonitions" (Whybray, "Qoheleth," 197). There is no reason to conform the meaning here to the other four occurrences (cf. Brown et al., *Lexicon*, 1031; Koehler et al., *Lexicon*, 1566; Clines, *Dictionary* VIII, 446, accepts either option.) Either way, the basic meaning of this verse is not affected—it is a warning against being "overly righteous" and "overly wise."

231. In light of the first half of the verse, which is an admonition to heed both the warnings in the previous verse, this is the natural interpretation of the phrase (contra ESV, NIV, and NLT), and is adopted by most Bible translations (for a grammatical discussion supporting this interpretation, see Seow, *Ecclesiastes*, 255; cf. Schoors *Preacher II*, 235).

amounts to covetousness, from which the genuinely God-fearing (those with a God-fearing disposition) would repent. To fear God is then to fear him for who he is and not for what we can get out of him. What is implicit here is explicit in the book of Job—to truly fear God is to fear him "for nothing" (Job 1:9–10). Hence if we truly fear God, we will not become "overly righteous."

When Qoheleth admonishes us to fear God in order to avoid becoming either overly righteous or overly wicked, both of which have painful consequences, he is actually applying what he said before: "God so works [in this case, allows the righteous to suffer] that men should fear him" (3:14b). For we just saw that, in light of the baffling observation that the righteous do suffer, fearing God and so avoiding both these extremes is the sensible way to live. Since to truly fear God is to fear him *for nothing*, it means, God allows the righteous to suffer so that we would not fear him *for anything*. This then explains why the enigma of righteous suffering is necessary. Because human beings "have sought out many schemes" (7:29), if God guarantees that the righteous will never suffer, there would be few, if any, who would truly fear him. Because God is righteous, he created a world in which, on the whole, the righteous prosper and the wicked suffer. This should give us incentive to live righteously but it should not tempt us to "fear him" *for something*. Hence Qoheleth is teaching us how to live in such a world.

> *7:23 All this I have tested with wisdom. I said, "Let me become wise," but it was far from me. 7:24 That which comes to be is far off, and is very deep; who can discover it? 7:25 I turned my heart to know, to explore and to seek, wisdom and the sum (of things), to know (that) wickedness is folly and foolishness is stupidity. 7:26 And I discover more bitter than death the woman whose heart is snares and nets, whose hands are fetters. He who is good in God's sight will escape from her, but the sinner is captured by her. 7:27 Look! this is what I have discovered, says Qoheleth, (adding) one thing to another to find the sum—7:28 that which I have sought continually but have (still) not ascertained (is this): "One man among a thousand I found, but a woman among all these I have not found." 7:29 Look! only this I have ascertained, that God made man upright, but they have sought out many schemes.*

In light of what follows, "*all this* I have tested (examined) with wisdom" (7:23) refers to the two observations made above concerning righteous suffering (7:15) and inevitable wickedness (7:20). Qoheleth makes a quick comment on the outcome of his examination of righteous suffering and then elaborates on the outcome of his examination of inevitable wickedness.

He says he tried "to become wise," that is, sought the wisdom needed to accomplish something, but failed ("it was far from me"). And what he sought to accomplish is about "that which comes to be," which refers to whatever happens (1:9), including the observation that the righteous may suffer and the wicked may prosper (7:15). But after examining the matter even with his incomparable wisdom, he concedes that

"that which comes to be (whatever happens) is far off and very deep; who can discover it?" He is thus reaffirming the sub-theme that the uncertain future, even when it concerns the fate of the righteous and the wicked, cannot be known ahead of time (this is elaborated in 8:17–9:1).

Hence we have to accept the enigmatic reality that bad things can happen to even good people and live with not knowing if and when it will happen to us. Qoheleth is reiterating the uncertainties of life captured in the poem of 3:1–8. He has explained in that context that "God so works that men should fear him" (3:14). So by reaffirming the sub-theme of the uncertain future in this context, he is reminding his audience of the need to fear God, this time in light of the enigmatic reality. In other words, he is implicitly saying that his admonition above to fear God and thus be moderate, which is in line with God's purpose, is the outcome of having examined the matter with his wisdom. So what he says here has the effect of urging them further to heed his admonition to fear God and be moderate (7:16–18).

After recognizing that he could not become wise enough to discover the future, Qoheleth turned to examine with wisdom the observation concerning inevitable wickedness. So he set his heart to know—to explore and to seek—wisdom and thus the sum of things, that is, how things add up, in order "to know (that) wickedness is folly and foolishness is stupidity."[232] In other words, since wickedness is inevitable—even the righteous sins—and in view of the enigmatic reality that the righteous do suffer while the wicked do prosper, he wanted to understand the scheme of things regarding wickedness and righteousness in order to learn how ("know" that) wickedness is indeed stupidity.[233] In part he was also trying to "discover why, if God 'made everything fitting in its time' (3:11), human folly and wickedness should exist."[234] Evidently, on this matter he did accomplish what he set out to discover. For we have seen that in his speech he displays great wisdom when he admonishes his audience on how to live wisely even in light of the enigmatic reality (7:1–22). And his admonitions are clearly based on a profound understanding that, regardless of what we observe, wickedness is still stupidity.

In the process of exploring and seeking wisdom to understand "the sum of things," Qoheleth made three discoveries or findings concerning wickedness (7:26, 27–28, 29). The first discovery supports the conventional wisdom concerning "the immoral woman against whose temptations men are constantly warned in the ancient Near Eastern wisdom literature and specifically, in the Old Testament, in Prov.

---

232. The Hebrew reads literally "to know wickedness folly and foolishness stupidity." Since there is no evidence that the two pairs of juxtaposed nouns respectively mean "wickedness of folly" and "foolishness of stupidity," they are both read as verbless clauses: "wickedness is folly" and "foolishness is stupidity" (Ogden and Zogbo, *Handbook*, 267). And this reading makes good sense here: "to know (that) wickedness is folly and foolishness is stupidity," that is, to know that wickedness is stupidity (cf. HCSB, NIV, NLT).

233. Ogden and Zogbo, *Handbook*, 268.

234. Whybray, *Ecclesiastes*, 126.

2:16–19; 5:3–6; 6:24–26; 7:5–27."[235] Like the book of Proverbs, the implied audience of Ecclesiastes is male. It is an admonition to them to fear God and thus be "good in God's sight" so that, unlike the sinner, they will escape from the snares, nets and fetters of such a woman. Like the other teachings and admonitions in Ecclesiastes, this one can also be applied to a female audience. For a God-fearing woman would also escape from the seductions of an immoral man.

So this focus on the immoral woman is not to be understood as anti-women. In fact, the second discovery, as reflected in our translation of 7:27–28, can be interpreted as a defense of, rather than an attack on, women. Though this interpretation makes good sense of the text, most interpreters either ignore or are not even aware of it. This is probably because most interpreters see an unorthodox and inconsistent Qoheleth. But by interpreting Ecclesiastes as a persuasive speech and giving Qoheleth the benefit of the doubt whenever there is no valid reason not to, we have so far found him to be consistently orthodox. If this is the perception one has of him, this interpretation can readily be accepted. Even Murphy, who does not share this perception, presents and defends it.[236]

According to this interpretation, Qoheleth is not the one making the offensive claim, "One man among a thousand I found (righteous), but a woman among all these I have not found." Rather, in his second discovery, he found that though he has sought continually, he still could not ascertain the validity of this claim made by others. "Only this I have ascertained," he counter-claims emphatically, "that God made man upright but they have sought out many schemes." Men and women are equally guilty. This is his third discovery, which confirms the observation above that there is no one so righteous that he will never sin (7:20). Qoheleth cites the claim in order to counter it so as to qualify what he just said about evil women. Otherwise his audience may jump to the conclusion that he supports the claim.

Note that the offensive statement in 7:28 does not explicitly claim there is one *righteous* man out of a thousand and thus there is not even one righteous woman out of a thousand. This can be inferred from the context. Prior to this Qoheleth is warning about wicked women, and following it, Qoheleth makes the counter-claim that both men and women are wicked despite being made upright. Undoubtedly Qoheleth is here echoing the teaching of the book of Genesis on the origin of humanity (Genesis 1–2) and its wicked bent (Genesis 3–4). He affirms that though wickedness characterizes humanity, humanity was originally created "upright." It was humanity that chose to become wicked, explicitly affirming the freedom of choice in human behavior. Yes, God makes everything appropriate in its time (divine sovereignty), yet at the same time humans are free to carry out "many schemes" and thus human folly and wickedness still exist (human responsibility).

---

235. Whybray, *Ecclesiastes*, 125.

236. Murphy, *Ecclesiastes*, 74–78. For a defense of this interpretation, see below (Excursus to 7:15–29).

The Hebrew word translated "schemes" here shares the same root with that translated "thoughts" in: "Then the LORD saw that the wickedness of man was great on the earth, and every inclination of the thoughts of his heart was only evil continually" (Gen 6:5). The phrase "every inclination of the thoughts of the heart" can be more idiomatically translated as "every plan devised by the mind" (NJPS). The "schemes" are thus contrivances of the covetous heart bent on breaking God's commandments ("wickedness"). Only those who truly fear God have the inner strength to overcome this wicked bent to escape from the "foolishness" and the "stupidity," and even then not completely (7:20).

This discovery of Qoheleth has far reaching implications. We have noted that the world as we know it is structured in such a way that the righteous may suffer and the wicked may prosper. For the "You reap what you sow" principle, through which the created order governs the world, is not an iron-clad formula, thus giving rise to the uncertainties of life expressed in the poem of 3:1–8. Now the created order was implanted when God created the world (Prov 3:19–20; cf. Genesis 1). Does it then mean that the world God originally created was already one in which the righteous may suffer and the wicked may prosper?

No, it does not. Humanity was originally created "upright" and what we read in 3:1–8 describes the world after humanity "have sought out many schemes," that is, after sin has come into this world through the disobedience of Adam (Genesis 3). In fact, prior to that no one was "wicked" to begin with. It is only after that tragic turn that the "righteous" may suffer because of the reality of human wickedness—even those in power, called to uphold justice, may abuse their power and oppress others. And since "there is not a righteous man on earth who (continually) does good and never sins" (7:20; cf. Gen 4:7; Rom 5:12; 7:14–20), even the "righteous" may have caused others to suffer.

Further, since creation as a whole was declared to be "very good" (Gen 1:31), even suffering caused by natural disasters exists only because the good creation was corrupted after sin entered the world (Gen 3:17–18; Rom 8:20–21). In fact, the reality of death itself is a consequence of sin (Gen 2:17; 3:19). All this means that the certainty of death and the uncertainties of life that we read in the poem in 3:1–8 is a reality only because sin has entered this world.

Hence the world as structured at creation was such that the righteous may suffer and the wicked may prosper only *if and when* sin came into this world. In other words, God structured the world at creation through the created order in such a way that humanity should have feared him and not have sinned and "sought out many schemes" at all. Humanity has been reaping what it has sown ever since.

Excursus to 7:15–29: Qoheleth's View of Women

Since most commentators take for granted an anti-women sentiment in 7:28, we need to present adequate exegetical support for our interpretation and translation of 7:27–29. Firstly, the Hebrew word translated "sum (of things)" and "sum (conclusion)" respectively in 7:25 and 7:27 occurs in this form only in Ecclesiastes (7:25, 27 and 9:10); and in a different form only in 7:29 (translated "schemes") and 2 Chr 26:15, where it means "(invented) devices." The root meaning behind the word is "to think" and from the different contexts in which the word occurs, it can be inferred that the word refers to either an activity that involves thinking—devising or deducing something—or its outcome.[237] Since the word as used in 7:25 and 7:27 is referring to the outcome of the same kind of activity (that of deducing), and in 7:27 the activity is presented as "(adding) one thing to another," we have translated the outcome in terms of "sum." In the context of 9:10, the word refers to the activity itself and is translated there as "planning." As for the case in 7:29, corresponding to the meaning in 2 Chr 26:15—(material) outcome of devising—it means (mental) outcome of the devising and is translated as "schemes" with a negative connotation. It has a negative connotation because it is "in opposition to the 'right' state in which God made humanity."[238]

A more literal translation of 7:27–29 would then be: "Look! this *I have found*, says Qoheleth, (adding) one thing to another to find the sum which I have sought continually but *I have not found*. One man among a thousand *I have found*, but a woman among all these *I have not found*. Look! only this *I have found*, that God made man upright, but they have sought out many schemes." Obviously the key to the meaning of this text is to make coherent sense of the string of "I have found" (three times) and "I have not found" (two times). A sensible first step is to isolate the offensive statement—"One man among a thousand *I have found*, but a woman among all these *I have not found*"—and look at it in light of what precedes and what follows it. Then we need to make coherent sense only of the "I have found" and the "I have not found" that precede it as well as the "I have found" that follows it. What did Qoheleth find (two times) and what did he not find?

The meaning of the "I have found" that follows the offensive statement is clear—"God made man upright, but they have sought out many schemes." What about the "I have found" that precedes the offensive statement? Reading the text plainly, it has to do with Qoheleth's attempt in adding one thing to another to find the sum (conclusion), which he did not find despite seeking it continually. So what he *found* (discovered) is that despite seeking continually for the "sum" or conclusion, he has *not found*—could not ascertain—it. What then is this conclusion that he could not ascertain? It is the offensive statement. Instead, what he has *only found*—could only ascertain—is that God made man (both man and woman) upright, but they have both gone astray.

---

237. Cf. Schoors, *Preacher II*, 445–47; Ogden and Zogbo, *Handbook*, 266.
238. Schoors, *Preacher II*, 446.

Fear God and Be Carefree (8:1–15)

> 8:1 Who is like the wise? And who knows the interpretation of a matter? A man's wisdom makes his face shine, and the severity of his countenance is changed. 8:2 I say, Keep the king's command, because of the oath before God. 8:3 Do not be in a hurry to leave his presence. Do not take a stand in an evil matter, for he could do whatever he pleases. 8:4 For the word of the king is power, so who can say to him, "What are you doing?" 8:5 Whoever keeps a (royal) command will not experience anything harmful, and the wise heart will know the proper time and procedure. 8:6 For there is a proper time and procedure for every matter, though a man's misery is heavy upon him. 8:7 Since no one knows what will come to be, who can tell him what will come to be? 8:8 No man has power over the (life) breath, to retain the (life) breath, or power over the day of death; and there is no discharge from war, nor will evil deliver those who practice it. 8:9 All this I have seen while setting my heart on every deed that has been done under the sun, at the time when a man had power over (another) man to his hurt. 8:10 Thereupon I saw the wicked <brought> to the grave, and they proceeded from a holy place; and they were <praised> in the city where they had done such things. This also is vanity.

Qoheleth has affirmed the value of proverbial wisdom rooted in the fear of God even in the face of righteous suffering. He has also attested that humanity is characterized by wickedness. He now applies all this to the case of a despotic king who is causing his subjects to suffer, especially those who serve in his court. How should a court official respond to such a king? The answer is still to fear God and act wisely. For only then is he in the position to know the "interpretation of a matter," that is, understand the situation adequately to come up with a solution.

For in this particular case, firstly, the wise official will have the right outward appearance ("wisdom makes his face shine, and the severity of his countenance is changed"). To make "his face shine" is an idiom that means "to be gracious" or "to be pleasant,"[239] or both as in this context. Thus wisdom enables the wise official "to suppress an angry or defiant look before the king and show, instead, a pleasant countenance."[240]

Secondly, he will honor his oath of loyalty to the king made before God, and so continue to "keep the king's command" as well as not be "in a hurry to leave his presence." To "leave his presence" here means to desert the king and "take a stand in an evil matter" by joining in a rebellious conspiracy.[241] By doing so, in a world in which "the word of the king is power"[242] and thus cannot be questioned so that the king "could

---

239. Seow, *Ecclesiastes*, 277.
240. Seow, *Ecclesiastes*, 278.
241. Whybray, *Ecclesiastes*, 131.
242. Though a little awkward, this literal rendering of the Hebrew still communicates what it means. A more idiomatic rendering like "the word of the king has power/authority" weakens the

do whatever he pleases," the wise official will escape the harmful consequences of rebellion (cf. Prov 24:21–22). More than that, because of his continued access to the king coupled with his pleasant countenance before him, the official is in the best position to "interpret" the situation.

Qoheleth is certainly not advocating that we do nothing about the injustice perpetrated by people in power. He affirms that "there is a proper time and procedure for every matter." As in 3:1, the word translated "matter" in this context has the root meaning of "desire" and so refers to a "desired or purposed event." But unlike 3:1, the "matter" here refers to an event desired or purposed by a wise heart, who is supposed to know "the proper time and procedure"—what to do and when to do it.[243] Thus unlike 3:1, it is not about divine sovereignty but human responsibility to act appropriately at the appropriate time.

How then would a wise heart know the proper time and procedure for a particularly matter? Qoheleth does not give a "one size fits all" solution. But the wise official who fears God and so observes sound proverbial wisdom, "though his misery is heavy upon him," will have the needed composure (7:7–10) to be in the position to "interpret" the situation and discern the right opportunity and the best approach to address the problem (cf. 10:4).

In fact Qoheleth's reiteration of the sub-theme that "no one knows" and so no one can tell us "what will come to be" reaffirms the value of proverbial wisdom rooted in the fear of God (7:1–14). Since we do not know what our uncertain future holds, we had better live by principles that on the whole will deliver us from harm. Hence this reiteration of the sub-theme is to reinforce the proverbial admonition to court officials on how to respond to a despotic king.

He further reinforces this admonition through a graphic depiction of what it is really like to face an uncertain future in light of the certainty of death. He says we have no power over our life-breath, to stop it from leaving us, that is, we have no power to resist death when it happens (cf. 3:19; 12:7).[244] The imagery of having been drafted to fight in a war evokes the sense that death can happen anytime. And the idea that there is no discharge from the war captures the reality that we have no escape from facing such an uncertain future. Qoheleth spells out that even the manipulative scheme of

---

meaning; in the ancient world the king's word is literally power, for his word is absolute and cannot be questioned.

243. The adjective "proper (time)" is not in the Hebrew of 8:5, 6, but it is clearly implied. And the word "time" is known to carry the connotation of "appropriate/proper/right/suitable time" (Brown et al., *Lexicon*, 773, 2b; Clines, *Dictionary* VI, 626, 4a; Koehler et al., *Lexicon*, 900, 6).

244. The Bible translations prefer to render the two occurrences of *rûaḥ* in 8:8 as "wind" rather than "breath" or even "spirit" (see discussion of the meaning of *rûaḥ* in 3:19, 21). The meaning is ambiguous in this verse; we prefer (life) "breath" over "wind" because the verse is talking about humans having no power over death—to stop the life-breath from leaving the body. If we render it as "wind," it means, just as we have no power over the wind to restrain it, we have no power over death. Either way it does not really change the meaning of the text.

those "who practice it (evil)" will not succeed in delivering them from this reality; they can only make things worse (7:11–12).

What Qoheleth reports in 8:9—an observation he made as part of his investigation "at the time when a man had power over (another) man to his hurt"—indicates that the admonition on how a court official should respond to a despotic king is based on an observation on the use of power and its hurtful consequence. We have rendered the verb "had power" (ESV) rather than "exercised authority" (NASB) because "authority" is legitimate power, which means it is circumscribed and is not absolute. One who exercises authority can be held accountable if he abuses it. But this is not the case with kings or even warlords in the ancient world. And this verse follows a reference to a despotic king, whose word "is power" and what he does cannot be questioned. Even in the modern world, when a man in power "exercised authority" over another man "to his hurt," it usually means the one in power has abused his authority. Effectively he has gone beyond his authority (legitimate power) and thus "had (illegitimate) power" over an unfortunate man.

Whether in the ancient or modern world, the abuse of authority or the use of illegitimate power is a common cause of righteous suffering. Grammatically the phrase "to his hurt" is ambiguous as to whether it refers to the one in power or his subordinate. In terms of context, the most natural reference is to the subordinate. But in terms of real life experience, when this happens, the one in power is, in the long run at least, also hurting himself. Perhaps Qoheleth deliberately left it ambiguous to alert us to this implication.

As he observed and pondered over the grievous phenomenon of people in power oppressing their victims to their hurt, he noticed that such a perpetrator may *seem* to get away with their wickedness—get an honorable funeral ("brought to the grave . . . from a holy place") and are even praised in the very city they had committed their wicked deeds (8:10).[245] This reinforces that "the word of the king is power" and he "could do whatever he pleases" because an evil king will still likely be buried with honor and be praised despite his wickedness. He seems "untouchable," at least in this world. Such an enigmatic phenomenon can be observed even today. But to put it in perspective, it does not mean that such evil people did not suffer for their wickedness at all. At the least, they will not have peace in their heart to the day of their death (Isa 59:8). And there have been wicked dictators who paid for their crimes before, or in, death. But even if not, the honorable funeral and the exuberant eulogy, being undeserved, are to an observer meaningless. The people know it—it is all a show. This, Qoheleth says, is also vanity (profitless).

> *8:11 Because sentence against an evil deed is not executed quickly, therefore the heart of the children of man is fully set to do evil. 8:12 For a sinner does evil a*

---

245. For a discussion on the translation of this difficult verse and an exposition on its significance in Qoheleth's rhetoric, see below (Excursus to 8:1–15).

hundred times and may prolong his life—although I know that it will be well with the God-fearers because they fear him. 8:13 But it will not be well with the wicked, and he will not prolong his days like a shadow, because he does not fear God.

As translated, the meaning of 8:11–13 is clear. Stuart Weeks captures it well:

> In Ecclesiastes 8:12–13, Qohelet expresses with unusual clarity, by his standards, the opinion that things will work out well for those who fear God, but not for the wicked: whoever has no fear before God will fail to prolong his own life. This claim is sandwiched, however, between an acknowledgment that sinners may sometimes get away with it for a very long time (8:10–12), and an observation that what happens to the righteous and wicked seems sometimes to be the wrong way round, so that people do not always get what they deserve, or deserve what they get [8:14].[246]

And Weeks notes that "Qohelet observes that humans behave badly . . . because there is no swift and visible penalty for doing something wrong."[247] In other words, people do not fear God and are thus not afraid to do evil because evil doers seem to get away with it—a wicked person who "does evil a hundred times" may live long because "sentence against an evil deed is not executed quickly." So wicked people assume consciously or unconsciously that God either does not exist or does not care and so their heart is given to do evil. It is for this very reason that Qoheleth warns that it will be well eventually for God-fearers but not for wicked people. More specifically, Qoheleth warns that though wicked people may seem to get away with their evil deeds for even a long time, their evil deeds will certainly catch up with them eventually. Why is this so?

Recall that God has implanted the created order to govern this world (Prov 3:19–20; 8:22–31), and so humanity is subject to the "You reap what you sow" principle (Prov 6:27–29; 22:8). A wicked person may seem to get away with his wickedness only because the workings of the created order is such that *usually* the effects of "You reap what you sow" are manifested in the long run and not in the short term. Hence "sentence against an evil deed is not executed *quickly*." However, in affirming that the sentence is not executed "quickly," Qoheleth is also implicitly affirming that there is indeed sentence (punishment) against evil deeds and it will be executed *eventually* (cf. 3:17 and 12:14). And as noted earlier, though God works through an impersonal created order, the execution of the sentence is not impersonal as it is God who created and sustains this order. So one can be assured that eventually it will be well with God-fearers but not with the wicked.

It may seem redundant for Qoheleth to qualify that it will be well for God-fearers *because they fear God*, and it will not be well with the wicked *because they do not fear*

---

246. Weeks, "Divine Judgment and Reward," 155.
247. Weeks, "Divine Judgment and Reward," 161.

God. What is he trying to say? To fear God is to keep his commandments (12:13; Deut 10:12–13). So Qoheleth is emphasizing that it will be well with God-fearers (disposition) specifically because they keep God's commandments (actions), and it will not be well with the wicked (disposition) specifically because they violate God's commandments (actions). This passage is about (wicked) people given "to do evil" (not keeping God's commandments) because "an evil deed" (violation of God's commandments) is not punished immediately.

As we saw earlier, Qoheleth has implicitly explained why God cannot allow the righteous to always prosper. But the question arises as to why he does not always cause the wicked to suffer and so deprive them of their undeserved prosperity. Actually God has been doing that but not "quickly." This is because he has "delegated"[248] much of the execution of sentence against evil deeds to the created order that he implanted into this world. To enhance the efficacy of the created order God has also instituted government to punish evil and praise good (Gen 9:6; Rom 13:1–7). Though government is often corrupt and there is even miscarriage of justice in the courts of law, most criminals do get punished eventually. But until that happens, it seems that they are getting away. This is not to deny that there are wicked people who will "never get caught" and they really do seem to "get away" with their crimes.

God as Creator cannot be limited by what he has created and instituted. He could and would sometimes bypass the created order and execute the sentence directly and immediately. In the Bible, when this is recorded to have happened, the punishment was usually though not always immediate death, and it was executed either with or without human agency (Lev 10:1–3; Num 16:31–33; Josh 7:24–26; 1 Kgs 13:4; 2 Chr 26:19–20; Acts 5:5, 10; 12:21–23). Why then does God not always bypass the created order and punish wickedness directly and immediately so that no one will ever "get away" with his wickedness? There is no need for Qoheleth to spell out that humanity would be eradicated if God were to *always* punish evil deeds directly and immediately because "there is not a righteous man on earth who (continually) does good and never sins" (7:20). Since "God so works that men (people) should fear him" (3:14), there must be opportunities for everyone, including the very wicked, to turn to God. This is in fact confirmed in the New Testament: God's forbearance and patience is intended to lead people to repentance (Rom 2:4).

However, partly out of ignorance and partly out of stubbornness, like the despotic king, people take God's forbearance and patience as license to sin and set their heart on doing evil. This explains why wickedness may abound even though God is still in control. But Qoheleth warns that it will not be well with those whose heart are "fully set to do evil" (unrepentant) especially in the long run. To emphasize this, he points out that though a person who "does evil a hundred times" may prolong his life, he will not prolong it indefinitely like "a lengthening shadow as the sun goes

---

248. Von Rad, *Wisdom in Israel*, 92.

down"[249]—he will have to die eventually. Since sentence against evil deeds will be executed eventually, the implication is that his wickedness will catch up with him after death if not before that.

After death, it will then no longer be the created order or human government but the Creator himself that the wicked have to reckon with. Here Qoheleth only hints at a judgment after death; at the very end of the speech, he spells it out (see exposition of 12:14). This is Qoheleth's answer to the problematic observation above—a wicked person may be given a good funeral and praised in the very place he had committed evil (8:10). Hence Qoheleth's warning about God's righteous judgment here in 8:11–13 is part of a sub-theme that begins with 3:16–17 and ends with 12:14. He is preparing his audience to heed that final warning.

> 8:14 *There is a vanity (enigma) that takes place on earth, that there are righteous people to whom it happens according to the deeds of the wicked, and there are wicked people to whom it happens according to the deeds of the righteous. I said that this also is vanity (enigmatic). 8:15 So I commend enjoyment, for there is nothing good for a man under the sun except to eat and drink and have enjoyment, and this will accompany him in his toil all the days of his life which God has given him under the sun.*

Having explained that people are not afraid to do evil because evil-doers seem to get away with their wickedness and then warning that God will judge them eventually, Qoheleth now returns to the problematic observation he introduced in 7:15–18—God allows the righteous to suffer and the wicked to prosper. Qoheleth rephrases this observation bluntly: the righteous may get what the wicked deserve and vice-versa. He considers this vanity also. In light of his warning not to become "overly righteous" in order to obtain prosperity and avoid adversity, this "vanity" refers to the times when, contrary to expectations, the outcome of righteous living is not "profitable" in terms of temporal blessings—reaping the expected consequence of wicked living instead. To make matters worse, wicked living may in turn reap the expected consequence of righteous living. This irony is enigmatic and it is rather hard to understand and accept. Since this is also how Qoheleth the speaker feels about this vanity, the word "vanity" has the connotation "enigma" or "enigmatic" and in this specific context can be translated as such (for further discussion, see "Interpretation of Ecclesiastes" under "The Pragmatics of Vanity").

We saw that earlier, in response to this enigma, Qoheleth indirectly admonished his audience to fear God and thus be moderate. Here he commends enjoyment, for in light of the (possible) vanity of even righteousness, "there is nothing good except . . . have enjoyment" (8:15). By now it should be clear that this is again another indirect admonition to fear God. For we have seen repeatedly that to have enjoyment one must have a carefree disposition, which means one must fear God, repent from

---

249. Crenshaw, *Ecclesiastes*, 156.

covetousness and cultivate a healthy sense of detachment from temporal things and thus be (relatively) free from the cares of this world.

In fact Qoheleth's qualification here that the "enjoyment" he is talking about "will *accompany* him in his toil all the days of his life which God has given him under the sun" reinforces the teaching that "enjoyment" is a by-product of a God-fearing disposition (5:18–6:9). One who does not fear God may in certain isolated circumstances experience "enjoyment" in the narrow sense that they experience pleasure that "satisfies." But enjoyment as a by-product of a God-fearing disposition is independent of circumstances, as such a disposition is independent of circumstances. This is why Qoheleth says enjoyment "will accompany" such a person "all the days of his life." As a rule pleasure satisfies such a person because his heart is no longer covetous, for by definition a covetous heart cannot be satisfied.

The (indirect) admonition to fear God makes sense in this context because the fear of God enables us to come to terms with the enigma of righteous suffering. We noted in our exposition of 1:12–18 that to have a truly meaningful life we must not only have a worthwhile purpose to live for, but we must also be able to see how the different aspects of life, especially the painful ones, contribute to that overall purpose. Then we saw in our exposition of 7:15–22 that the fear of God enables us to see how even painful experiences such as righteous suffering is in line with Qoheleth's teaching that God so works (even allows righteous suffering) that we should fear him (for nothing). Hence the fear of God enables us to see how the enigma of righteous suffering contributes to God's (worthwhile) purpose for humanity (3:14b; 12:13) and thus helps us make sense of and come to terms with undeserved suffering (for further discussion, see "Teaching of Ecclesiastes" under "Perceiving Coherence in Life").

People who do not fear God or accept Qoheleth's teaching will have to look elsewhere to find meaning in undeserved suffering. Some may even use this apparent lack of meaning to argue for the non-existence of God. The irony is that, according to Qoheleth, the very purpose of painful experiences is to goad them to acknowledge who God is. Unless we submit to God's purpose—to fear him and be carefree—we do not have the disposition needed to appreciate and accept undeserved suffering and to experience the meaning of life as envisioned by Qoheleth.

Excursus to 8:1–15: Qoheleth on the Certainty of God's Judgment

We have translated 8:10 as, "Thereupon I saw the wicked <brought> to the grave, and they proceeded from a holy place; and they were <praised> in the city where they had done such things." However, as Crenshaw puts it, "Interpretations of [8:10] have one thing in common: tentativeness."[250] All interpretations and thus translations of 8:10 are tentative because not only is the interpretation of the verse uncertain, even the

---

250. Crenshaw, *Ecclesiastes*, 154.

Hebrew text as we have it is itself uncertain. Our translation indicates through the use of the angular brackets that it has adopted emendations proposed to the Hebrew text at these two places.[251] Ogden and Zogbo adopt this interpretation in their handbook for Bible translators. This is the translation they suggest: "Then I saw that wicked people were given public burial. They were taken from the holy place and buried, and they were honored by people in the city where their evil deeds were done."[252]

The verse has also been translated without accepting any emendation to the Hebrew text: "Then I observed the wicked *buried*. They used to go in and out of the holy place, but they were *forgotten* in the city in which they acted in this way."[253] In other words, though the wicked are "ripe for judgment," they seem to have escaped punishment for their wickedness—"Judgment never came while they were alive, and now they are forgotten, so that they will not even be remembered for what they were really like."[254] Again it is still about the wicked not getting what they deserve before and when they died, which is widely observed even today.

In other words, though both the text and its translation are uncertain, it is clear that the verse is talking about injustice perpetrated in this world not being corrected even when the person concerned has died. This explains Qoheleth's response to the observation—"This also is "vanity (enigmatic)." In fact this observation is expected here as the context is about one in power oppressing others (8:9) and evil deeds not being quickly punished (8:11)—the wicked seem to be getting away with their evil deeds. And since the broader context is about a despotic king perpetrating injustice (8:1–8), even the interpretation that the wicked are praised in the very place they had committed the evil deeds fits in here as this can be observed even today when a wicked politician dies.

This observation is not only enigmatic, but can be deeply troubling. For as Krüger comments, "Under the presupposition that death is the definitive end for a human

---

251. For the first emendation, see Seow, *Ecclesiastes*, 284; for the second emendation, see Barton, *Ecclesiastes*, 155. Both these emendations in 8:10a and 8:10b have textual support whereas the emendation of the text in 8:10a to "the wicked *approaching* . . . the holy place" (Crenshaw, *Ecclesiastes*, 154) is conjectural—without any textual support. This changes the meaning of the verse significantly as it is no longer about the (death and) burial of the wicked people. Since the verse makes good sense with the textually-supported emendations we have adopted, there is no good reason to consider this conjectural emendation.

252. Ogden and Zogbo, *Handbook*, 296.

253. Bartholomew, *Ecclesiastes*, 287 (italics added); cf. Fredericks, *Ecclesiastes*, 188. This is the interpretation taken by NASB and NKJV whereas ESV, HCSB, NIV, NLT, and NRSV adopt the emendation in 8:10b from "forgotten" to "praised"—with or without the emendation, the word is read as having passive and not reflexive sense (cf. Waltke and O'Connor, *Syntax*, §26.3a). Thus most Bible translations present a situation similar to that of the translation we have adopted—the wicked received a proper burial and were forgotten, if not praised, in the very place they had committed evil. The only difference is that it is not spelled out that the funeral proceeded from a holy place (highlighting the honorable burial), which can be assumed especially since it is said that they used to frequent the holy place (highlighting their hypocrisy).

254. Bartholomew, *Ecclesiastes*, 290.

being, the processes in v. 10 are finished and no longer correctable, the wicked have already gone to their grave with honor . . . ."[255] The question is whether the presupposition that "death is the definitive end for a human being" is true. The very last verse of Ecclesiastes (12:14), which talks about a judgment of everyone for every deed ever done in this world, implies that it is not. This means injustice in this world that is not corrected will be corrected eventually (see exposition of 12:14).

Now we saw that Qoheleth has earlier affirmed the reality that God will eventually judge both the righteous and the wicked to make things right (3:17). This means observations like what we read in 8:10 point to, and prepare the heart and mind of readers for, the teaching in 12:14—there is a final accounting of everything done in this world beyond death. We have chosen a translation that gives the maximum effect to this end. However even the translation without any emendation to the Hebrew text, which gives minimum effect, is good enough.[256]

The next few verses following 8:10 also needs to be read in light of both 3:17 and 12:14. The meaning of the Hebrew text of 8:11–13 depends on how we understand the conjunctions 'ăšer (first clause of 8:11 and 8:12 and the last clause of 8:12 and 8:13) and kî gam (second clause of 8:12). Our translation understands all four occurrences of 'ăšer as "because" or "for," which is clearly the case in 4:9 and 8:15[257] and kî gam as "although."[258] The result is that the meaning of the text is not only clear, it also presents a Qoheleth who is consistent in his view concerning God's judgment of wickedness despite the observation that evil-doers seem to get away with their wickedness (see exposition of 3:17).

Our translation of 8:11–13 is virtually the same as that of Murphy[259] and Longman[260] though the interpretations differ. A plain reading of the text as translated shows that Qoheleth believes in and thus warns of God's eventual judgment against wickedness. Longman,[261] however, reads into the text and follows the view of Gordis[262] that when Qoheleth says "(although) I *know* it will be well with God-fearers . . . ," he is only parroting a view—that of orthodox wisdom—which he himself does not accept. To indicate this interpretation, Gordis inserts (reads) into 8:12b a phrase that is neither present nor implied in the Hebrew text and treats the orthodox view that Qoheleth purportedly rejects as a quotation: "though I know *the answer* that 'it will be well in

---

255. Krüger, *Qoheleth*, 159.

256. Since we are aware that the wicked do get an honorable funeral and even a glorious eulogy regardless of whether this is the observation Qoheleth refers to in 8:10, our discussion (here and elsewhere) that assumes this observation does not depend on whether our translation of 8:10 is correct. Even if incorrect, it serves to remind us of a phenomenon pertinent to Qoheleth's rhetoric.

257. Schoors, *Preacher*, 140–43; cf. Joüon and Muraoka, *Grammar*, §170e.

258. Schoors, *Preacher*, 134–35; Seow, *Ecclesiastes*, 288.

259. Murphy, *Ecclesiastes*, 79.

260. Longman, *Ecclesiastes*, 216–17.

261. Longman, *Ecclesiastes*, 219.

262. Gordis, *Koheleth*, 297.

the end with those who revere [fear] God . . . .'"[263] Other than this, Gordis's translation of 8:11–13 is virtually the same as ours. Even Fox, who does not consider Qoheleth an orthodox sage, affirms "There is no sign that 8:12b–13 are the words or opinion of another person or party [other than that of Qoheleth]. . . . Although Qohelet 'knows' the principle of retribution and nowhere denies it, he *also* knows there are cases that violate the rule."[264]

Like Gordis, Longman supposes that the unusual form of the Hebrew word translated as "know"—a participle instead of a finite verb—"is a signal that he is stating an argument that is not his own,"[265] with the implication this principle of retribution that Qoheleth says he "knows" is not something that he himself accepts thus rendering him unorthodox. For support Longman cites Bo Isaksson that the use of the participle here indicates that "Qohelet is imparting 'the kind of knowledge that represented the *comme il faut* [conforming to accepted standards] teaching of the sages.'"[266] However, this only supports the supposition that Qoheleth "is stating an argument not his own," but not that he rejects it also. In fact, Isaksson himself says that though the participle indicates that it is not "a knowledge that Qoheleth has acquired by observation and experience," it is a "traditional wisdom" that Qoheleth has "simply taken over, as most people would have done."[267] Ogden and Zogbo go so far as to say, "a participle 'knowing' followed by an emphatic 'I,' demonstrates how certain Qoheleth claims to be of the truth he affirms."[268]

Though Murphy rejects Gordis's quotation theory, he is non-committal as to whether Qoheleth accepts the orthodox wisdom: "It is better to understand 'I know . . .' as introducing Qoheleth's awareness of [but not acceptance and belief in?] the orthodox claim concerning retribution."[269] Why hesitate to affirm what is plainly in the text (that Qoheleth believes in the orthodox view) when in 3:17, even Murphy himself admits that, "It can be said that he [Qoheleth] clings to the biblical belief that God is somehow just and that God does judge [both the righteous and the wicked], however contrary the evidence may appear to be"?[270]

Like in 3:17, we need to distinguish between what Qoheleth believes and what he observes, which may *seem* to contradict what he believes. Then there is no reason to doubt that Qoheleth accepts and believes in what he explicitly says *in Hebrew*, "I know." In Hebrew, "to know" (*yd'*) cannot mean merely "to be informed" even when it means "to be aware" as in "Do you [Gedaliah] not *know* that Baalis . . . has sent

---

263. Gordis, *Koheleth*, 184 (italics added, indicating the inserted phrase).
264. Fox, *Time*, 286.
265. Longman, *Ecclesiastes*, 219.
266. Longman, *Ecclesiastes*, 219; Isaksson, *Language of Qoheleth*, 67.
267. Isaksson, *Language of Qoheleth*, 67.
268. Ogden and Zogbo, *Handbook*, 300.
269. Murphy, *Ecclesiastes*, 85.
270. Murphy, *Ecclesiastes*, 36.

Ishmael . . . to kill you?" (Jer 40:14). The response was "Gedaliah . . . did not *believe* them." Obviously they did not mean to ask, "Are you not aware (informed but do not believe) that . . . ," but rather, "Are you not aware (informed and believe) that . . ." (cf. Exod 3:7; 1 Sam 20:39; Jer 44:15; 50:24).

Weeks, having recognized that Qoheleth affirms the reality of divine judgment in his speech, however claims that this sub-theme is "so alien to much else in his speech" that "it serves not as an idea that he wishes to promote, but as an assumption that he expects his readers to hold."[271] Thus "divine judgment . . . is not a conclusion towards which Qohelet is working."[272] These denials are not surprising given Weeks's doubts that 12:13-14 is intended "to summarize Qohelet's monologue [in 1:2-12:8] faithfully,"[273] let alone that it is actually part of Qoheleth's speech. In contrast, our exposition of Ecclesiastes *as a coherent speech* indicates that this sub-theme is not foreign to the rest of the speech, and that 1:2-12:8 flows naturally into 12:13-14 as Qoheleth's own conclusion to his speech (see exposition of 12:13-14).

There seems to be a persistent resistance among commentators to take Qoheleth seriously when he affirms the reality of God's judgment. In contrast to our exposition of 8:11-15, Belcher claims that, "Although Qohelet may make statements that affirm God's judgment (3:17) and the deed consequence relationship (8:12b-13), he does not allow those statements to solve the problems with which he is wrestling. Such statements stand side-by-side with the problems he observes in life. Instead of allowing the theological affirmations to explain the anomalies in life, the problems Qohelet observes take centre stage without a resolution to those problems."[274] Clearly, like Weeks, Belcher fails to see how 3:17 and 8:12b-13 are crucial parts of a sub-theme integral to Qoheleth's argument that begins with 1:2-3 and ends with 12:13-14. And this argument takes "center stage" in Ecclesiastes (see "Introduction to Ecclesiastes" under "Coherent Message").

Our translation of 8:11-13 is also virtually the same as that of ESV and HCSB except that, like most other Bible translations, they render the first two clauses of 8:12 as "Though (*'ăšer*) a sinner does evil . . . yet I know . . . ," instead of "For (because) a sinner does evil . . . although I know . . . ." However Gordis stresses that the conjunction *'ăšer* "cannot mean 'although,' for which there is no warrant here or elsewhere."[275] Since the accepted causal sense "because, for" makes such good sense in this context, one wonders why so many Bible translations opt for the questionable concessive sense. Nevertheless, it does not change the meaning of the passage as a whole. The difference is that the causal sense spells out that "a sinner does evil a hundred times

---

271. Weeks, "Divine Judgment and Reward," 156.
272. Weeks, "Divine Judgment and Reward," 165.
273. Weeks, "Fear God," 115.
274. Belcher, *Ecclesiastes*, 52.
275. Gordis, *Koheleth*, 296-97; cf. Longman, *Ecclesiastes*, 217.

and may *prolong his life*" is a specific reason why "the heart of the children of man is fully set to do evil."

This then makes it more obvious that the enigmatic observation in 7:14—"there is a righteous man who perishes in his righteousness, and there is a wicked man who *prolongs his life* in his wickedness"—is a reason why people do not fear God and thus do evil. And this enigmatic observation is rephased in 8:14 as "there are righteous people to whom it happens according to the deeds of the wicked, and there are wicked people to whom it happens according to the deeds of the righteous." So Qoheleth's statement of God's judgment in 8:12b–13 is to warn against using such observations as an excuse to avoid fearing God (see exposition of 8:11–15). This means our translation of 8:12 makes it more obvious that, contra Belcher, Qoheleth is using this statement of God's judgment to "solve the problems" of the enigmatic observations he presents in 7:15/8:14 and 8:10—the wicked may live long and even die with honor. Our exposition of 7:15–22 shows how the fear of God is Qoheleth's key to "explain the anomalies of life." As for how Qoheleth's statements of God's judgment contribute to the "resolution to those problems," it is discussed at the end of our exposition of 12:13–14 (and elaborated in "Teaching of Ecclesiastes" under "Experiencing a Sense of Closure to History").

Elaboration on Uncertainties of Life (8:16-9:6)

> 8:16 When I set my heart to know wisdom, and to consider the preoccupation that is done on earth—even though one's eyes should neither see sleep by day nor by night—8:17 I observed all the work of God, (and conclude) that man is not able to discover the work that is done under the sun. Therefore man may toil to seek, but he will not discover. And even if the wise attempts to know (it), he is not able to discover (it). 9:1 For all this I took to heart and examined it all (and recognized) that the righteous and the wise and their deeds are in the hand of God. People do not know whether it will be love or hate; both await them.

Earlier on Qoheleth shared that (because of the uncertainties of life) he had personally sought the wisdom that would enable him to discover what was to happen, but failed miserably (7:23–24). Now he elaborates on that quest. He says he was determined ("set his heart") to acquire ("know") that kind of wisdom. In doing this he was also "to consider," or evaluate, "the preoccupation that is done on earth." Since this preoccupation is the human drive to find out about the uncertain future in order to make sense of life (see exposition of 3:10–15), Qoheleth was then himself participating in this very preoccupation. His conclusion, as already affirmed repeatedly, is that this preoccupation will be futile (3:11; 6:12; 7:14, 23–24; and now 8:17). Here he stresses that neither determination, hard work ("one's eyes . . . neither see sleep by day nor by night") nor even wisdom[276] will make a difference. Though the meaning of the connective phrase in Hebrew translated "Therefore" (8:17b) is uncertain, and has also been translated as "Even though," or "Because however much," the meaning of 8:16–17 is clear—we will never discover the uncertain future no matter how hard we try.[277]

In his own quest, Qoheleth had "observed all the work of God." But what he observed concerns "the work that is done under the sun." Lohfink insightfully comments: "This verse is very important in understanding the whole book, because it makes the action of God equivalent to the activity 'that is carried on under the sun,' something that was to be surmised in any case from the use of passive formulations in many other texts. What is especially meant is all human activity. This then is at the same time always divine activity."[278] Therefore, "This verse explicitly equates God's work with activity on earth—elsewhere Qohelet only implies that whatever occurs is God's doing."[279] Qoheleth is thus reiterating God's sovereignty over human activity (see exposition of 3:1–15). In this exposition we have already taken this perspective into consideration, and have been (and will be) doing so consistently in interpreting Qoheleth's speech. Otherwise we would misunderstand him.

The conjunction "For" in 9:1 indicates that Qoheleth now explains how he came to the conclusion that no one, not even the wise, can discover the future. He said he

---

276. We have rendered the first clause of the last sentence of 8:17 as, "And even if the wise *attempts* to know (it)" (cf. NKJV), instead of "*claims* to know (it)" (most Bible translations) for reasons of grammar and meaning. In terms of grammar, the phrase—literally, "he says to know (it)"—is in the form "say + infinitive," which "normally indicates purpose or expectation (Exod 2:14; Josh 22:33; 1 Sam 30:6; 2 Sam 21:16; 1 Kgs 5:19)" (Seow, *Ecclesiastes*, 290). Thus in 2 Sam 21:16, "he said to kill David" means "he intended to kill David" (HCSB, NASB). Hence "he says to know (it)" means "he intends to know (it)." In the context of the conditional clause in 8:17, "attempts to know (it)" captures the nuance better. In terms of meaning, since "know (it)" means "discover (it)" (see footnote below), it fits the context perfectly: even if the wise attempts to discover it, he will not be able to discover it.

277. We noted in the footnote on our translation of 3:11 that though Krüger recognizes that the Hebrew word (*māṣā'*) translated "discover" in 3:11 literally means "find out," on the basis of 8:17 he translates it as "comprehend" instead of "find out" or "discover" (Krüger, *Qoheleth*, 80, 163). He draws our attention to the parallel between *yāda'* (literally, "know") and *māṣā'* (literally, "find out" or "discover") in the last sentence of 8:17. Instead of "And if the wise attempts to *know* (it), he is not able to *discover* (it)," Krüger renders it as, "And if the wise man claims to *understand* (it), he still cannot *comprehend* (it)" (Krüger, *Qoheleth*, 163; italics added). It is as though whenever Qoheleth uses the word "know," it has to mean something like "understand" or "comprehend" and never "find out" or "discover." This assumption is wrong (cf. Clines, *Dictionary* IV, 100, 7). In the very next verse, Qoheleth says, "People do not *know* whether it will be love or hate; both await them" (9:1b). The meaning of "know" (*yāda'*) clearly has to mean "discover" or "have discovered," and not "comprehend" or "understand," as it refers to humanity's inability to know ahead of time, that is, find out what "awaits them"—what might happen to them, which may be "love" or "hate." Here, even Krüger has to render it as "know" and not "understand" as it clearly does not fit the context (Krüger, *Qoheleth*, 166). But in both 8:17 and 9:1b, the same Hebrew word is referring to the same human inability, which is unmistakably to "know" or "discover" the future.

278. Lohfink, *Qoheleth*, 110–11.

279. Crenshaw, *Ecclesiastes*, 157.

had taken to heart and "examined" and thus "recognized"[280] that even "the righteous and wise and their deeds are in the hand of God." This means what happens to even the righteous and to their deeds are not only beyond their control but also subjected to the uncertainties depicted in the poem of 3:1–8. So even they do not know "whether it will be love or hate" (cf. 3:8a) that "awaits them."[281]

For this reason, Qoheleth will soon admonish his audience to be careful (9:10–11:6). This is another affirmation that proverbial wisdom does not teach that the righteous will *always* prosper and *never* suffer. So the wise, even though they understand proverbial wisdom and know what would normally happen to the righteous, cannot pinpoint ahead of time whether it will be love or hate that awaits them. If even they cannot discover the future, no one can.

> *9:2 It is the same for all; there is one fate for the righteous and the wicked; for the good (and the evil), the clean and the unclean; for him who sacrifices and him who does not sacrifice. As the good one is, so is the sinner; he who swears is as he who is afraid to swear. 9:3 This is a grievous thing in all that happens under the sun, that there is one fate for all. Therefore also, the hearts of the children of man are full of evil, and stupidity is in their hearts throughout their lives, and after that they go to the dead. 9:4 But whoever is joined with all the living, there is hope; for a living dog is better than a dead lion. 9:5 For the living know that they will die, but the dead do not know anything; and they have no more recompense, for the memory of them is forgotten. 9:6 Even their love, their hate and their envy have already perished; and forever they have no longer a share in all that is done under the sun.*

In this passage Qoheleth elaborates on what he says in 9:1, which is, the righteous and the wise and their deeds are in the hand of God and subjected to the reality expressed in the poem of 3:1–8 concerning the certainty of death and uncertainties of life. He begins by reaffirming that "it is the same [fate] for all," which is death (2:14; 3:2; 6:6). Here he spells out and elaborates in no uncertain terms that no one will escape this final outcome. For it does not matter whether one is righteous or wicked, good or evil, clean or unclean, *et cetera*. Then (in the next passage) Qoheleth goes on to help his audience see why fearing God is the sensible response to this reality.

To assure his audience that he has not been glib about this painful reality, he expresses that "This is a grievous thing." For besides the observation that "there is one fate for all," he also found something else grievous (painful to observe). We just saw that because God does not punish wickedness immediately and thus evil-doers may live long, people are not afraid to do evil (8:11–13). Here Qoheleth adds another reason why evil is prevalent. As reflected in our translation of 9:3, "Most commentators see a causal nexus between the two parts of the verse: 'A common fate comes to everyone

---

280. Schoors, *Preacher II*, 354.
281. Cf. Seow, *Ecclesiastes*, 298.

[whether righteous or wicked], *therefore also* the heart of man is full of evil.'"[282] This means, the reality that both the righteous and the wicked have to die is thus taken to mean that there is really no difference whether one is righteous or wicked, and so why fear God and be righteous? As a consequence, "stupidity [or folly] is in their hearts throughout their lives." One outcome is that, "instead of reckoning with the meaning of death, humans fill their lives with the distraction of a thousand passions and squander what little time they have to immediate but insignificant worries."[283] No conscientious person would deny that this is painful to observe.

To counter this tendency Qoheleth explains that, actually ("But"), "there is hope" for the living because, unlike the dead, they "know that they will die." This seems ironic, but it is not. For this "hope" is "the opportunity this present life affords to consider the fact of death, as the Preacher has been constantly urging, and to evaluate life accordingly."[284] In contrast "the dead do not know anything." The statement refers to the dead in relation to this world—they do not know what happens in this world—and not their condition in the hereafter (cf. Job 14:20–22). Why then is it important to take the opportunity to evaluate our life before we die?

"Love" and "hate" sum up how people relate to one another; "envy" or rivalry (4:4) sums up how people relate to their work. When Qoheleth says that all these perish when people die, he is describing in a graphic way that the dead forever have no more "share" (literally, "lot") in what happens in this world and in what it offers. Even the only possible "recompense" left, namely, the memory of them, will soon be lost. It emphasizes the lack of "hope," or second chance, after we die to do what we could and should have done before we die. This echoes "It is better to go to the house of mourning than to the house of feasting, because this is the end of every man, and the living should take it to heart" (7:2).

We should then consider the implication of not taking the opportunity to evaluate our life in light of the certainty of death and our inability to know when that will happen because of the uncertainties of life. Since "God so works that men should fear him" (3:14), this evaluation should lead us to fear God before it is too late—the "hope" is gone. In fact this is where Qoheleth's speech, which in itself is already guiding us through such an evaluation, is leading us (12:13). For if we do not act on this "hope" in time, we will forever lose the opportunity to leave this world as one who fears God, that is, "one who is good in God's sight" (2:26).

Since "God will bring every deed to judgment" (12:14), this cannot be taken lightly. No wonder Qoheleth says "a living dog is better than a dead lion." In other words, it is better to be alive than dead even if this means being despised like a lowly dog. For unlike the dead, even if they were admired like the mighty lion, the living still

---

282. Schoors, *Preacher*, 132.
283. Garrett, *Proverbs, Ecclesiastes, Song of Songs*, 331.
284. Eaton, *Ecclesiastes*, 126.

have the opportunity to make it right with their Maker before facing him after death (cf. 12:1–7).

Admonition to Carefreeness (9:7–9)

> 9:7 Go (then), eat your bread with enjoyment, and drink your wine with a glad heart, for God has already approved your actions. 9:8 Let your garments be white at all times, and let not oil be lacking on your head. 9:9 Enjoy life with a woman whom you love all the days of your fleeting life, which he has given you under the sun; for this is your lot in life and in (the fruit of) your toil for which you toil under the sun.

This admonition to enjoy life is in response to what has just been said: the uncertainties of life, the certainty of death, and the need to evaluate life in this light. Here Qoheleth specifically affirms that "God has already approved your actions," that is, our eating with enjoyment and drinking in gladness. Whybray is probably right: "this may mean the enjoyment of God's gifts is something which God has decreed from the beginning (cf. 5:18, 'for this is his lot')."[285] Wearing white garments and anointing the head with oil both "were signs of joy" as these "were practiced on festive occasions." And since Qoheleth admonishes wearing white "at all times" and not letting the oil "be lacking," he is commending "the enjoyment of life whenever possible."[286]

In this passage Qoheleth highlights for the first time the social dimension of enjoyment: "enjoy life with a woman whom you love." His choice of the phrase "a woman" instead of "the woman" does not mean he has in mind just any woman; he is still referring to one's wife.[287] This choice enables him to address men in general, whether married or not. For the admonition to enjoy life "with *a* woman whom you love" applies to those who already have such a woman (their wife), as well as those yet to have one; "with *the* woman whom you love" excludes unattached men. The admonition then also has the effect of encouraging single men to get married (cf. Prov 18:22). It implies that true enjoyment cannot be confined to the individual level. We shall soon see why.

It is significant that Qoheleth highlights enjoyment at the social level in response to the certainty of death as well as to the uncertainties of life. According to him, uncertainties in life are intended by God to prod us to fear him (3:10–15). Just as the pain from a shepherd's goading is relieved when the sheep turns and moves in the direction the shepherd wants it to go, the distress caused by the uncertainties of life is alleviated by fearing God and keeping his commandments. We now apply this teaching

---

285. Whybray, *Ecclesiastes*, 144.
286. Whybray, *Ecclesiastes*, 144.
287. Seow, *Ecclesiastes*, 301.

to enjoying life with one's spouse and see why and how this enjoyment relieves the discomfort of not knowing what awaits us.

Since the "enjoyment" Qoheleth has in mind is that which is experienced "with a glad heart" (9:7), that is, out of a carefree disposition (5:18–20), the very experience of enjoying life with one's spouse already means that uncertainties in life are no longer bothersome. So the admonition to enjoy life with one's spouse basically amounts to cultivating the disposition needed for this to happen. Given the human propensity toward selfishness, this requires one to fear God and keep the commandment "you shall love your neighbor as yourself" (Lev 19:18b), which sums up all the commandments (Gal 5:14; cf. Matt 7:12). This is in fact implied in the admonition to "enjoy life with a woman *whom you love*." Enjoying life *with* one's spouse involves enjoying one's spouse as well. This cannot happen without love.

The ability to love and enjoy one's spouse has far reaching implications. Since in this world we do not know whether it will be love or hate that awaits us, we will never experience the blessedness of a stable loving relationship unless we experience it with someone whose love we can always count on. And this is what a spouse is meant to be (Prov 31:10–12). It is a common experience that unless we cultivate at least one lifelong ("all the days of your fleeting life") relationship of such quality, the deepest longings of our heart will not be fulfilled; and it is then hard for life to make sense. Indeed, quality relationships constitute another crucial component to the meaning of life.[288]

The disposition that enables one to build a quality relationship with one's spouse will also enable one to do the same with others. And when life is meaningful and friends and family are helpful, we are more prepared to face adversities, and hence less bothered by uncertainties. Otherwise, we will be afflicted with the cares of this world, and no true enjoyment whatsoever is possible. Hence unless we have the disposition to enjoy life at the social level, we do not have what it takes to enjoy life at the individual level. This shows that if one does not observe the commandment to love one's neighbor as oneself, one will become vulnerable in a seemingly hostile world. Since this commandment sums up all the commandments, it sums up God's purpose for human life (12:13). If we do not observe it, we are out-of-sync with what we are and should be; life will not be peaceful and meaningful.

In our exposition of 3:22, we have already discussed the meaning and implication of enjoyment being one's "lot" in this world—enjoyment of life is all that is allotted us and if we do not receive it, we are left with "nothing good." When Qoheleth uses this word in his admonition to have enjoyment in life, he always uses it to refer to the enjoyment of the fruit of human labor except here in 9:9. Here, to "enjoy life with a woman whom you love" is said to be "your *lot* in life." So "lot (in life)" is not exactly enjoyment of the fruit of labor.

---

288. Cf. Baird, "Meaning in Life," 119–20.

However, this enjoyment is also said to be "your lot . . . in (the fruit of) your labor for which you toil."[289] So it is still somehow connected to the fruit of labor. The most obvious connection is that labor enables us to meet our material needs. Otherwise, lacking a proper shelter and without adequate food and clothing, it would be very difficult to have enjoyment of life with friends and family. That means the fruit of our labor is not only meant to be enjoyed in and of itself but also to meet our basic needs so that we are set free to enjoy life as a whole. This teaching is particularly crucial in the present time when people live to work, instead of work to live.

Admonition to Carefulness (9:10–11:6)

> 9:10 *Whatever your hand finds to do, do it with your might, for there is no work or planning or knowledge or wisdom in Sheol, where you are going.*

Because of the certainty of death and the uncertainties of life, we are not living sensibly if we do not make the most of the opportunities we still have in this world (8:16–9:6). Qoheleth's admonition to enjoy life with one's spouse was given in light of this (9:7–9). He now extends his admonishment to "whatever your hand finds to do." The phrase does not refer to whatever we happen to be doing.[290] It is an idiom that means doing what needs to be done that is within our capacity to do (1 Sam 10:6–7; 25:8; Lev 12:8; Judg 9:33). And we are to do it zealously ("with your might").

The admonition is about what we should and could be doing before we die. If we do not heed it, we would feel a deep sense of meaninglessness when on our deathbed and perhaps even before that, we consider how we have lived. This is particularly so with regards to our lifework or occupation, which occupies most of our waking hours.[291] In today's terms, we are here admonished to fulfill our "calling" or "vocation."

What then is a vocation? "If you have a *vocation*, you have a strong feeling that you are particularly suited to a particular job or role in life, especially one which involves serving other people."[292] When we view and so treat our occupation as our vocation, we zealously seek to serve humanity by meeting people's needs ("what needs to be done") according to our gifts and opportunities ("within our capacity to do"). This would require us to fear God and observe the commandment to love other people as ourselves.

Unfortunately, for some time now, it has been taken for granted that one's occupation is one's "career" rather than one's calling. When we view our occupation as a career, we treat it as "a course of professional life or employment . . . that offers

---

289. The Hebrew reads literally, "your lot . . . in your toil which you toil." As in 2:18, the first "toil" means the fruit of toil or labor. As discussed in Excursus to 2:1–11, the word "can designate both the *process* and the *result* of the work" (Krüger, *Qoheleth*, 58).

290. Fox, *Time*, 295.

291. Cf. Brown, *Ecclesiastes*, 95.

292. HarperCollins, *Cobuild English Dictionary*, 1747.

advancement or honor."²⁹³ This is because "work as career is motivated by the desire for success and recognition."²⁹⁴ This led many people to choose an occupation based on the money or the prestige, or both, that it offers, rather than on what they are gifted in and have a passion for. So instead of fulfilling their calling to serve humanity, they are pursuing their career for self-advancement and temporal success. Qoheleth has already warned that this is vanity and a grievous affliction (2:12–23; 4:4–8, 13–16; 5:10–17; 6:1–9). We will not find life (and work) fulfilling or meaningful (for empirical evidence that fulfilling our calling is the most meaningful way to live and work, see "Teaching of Ecclesiastes" under "Corroborating Empirical Evidence").

To increase the sense of urgency to make the most of our limited time in this world, Qoheleth reiterates that "there is no work or planning or knowledge or wisdom in Sheol, where you are going." As in 9:5, this statement describes the dead in relation to this world and not their condition in the hereafter. The opportunity for human activities in this world, such as working and planning, and using human abilities like knowledge and wisdom, no longer exists once we die. As Michael Eaton puts it, "The Preacher does not provide any positive description of Sheol. Negatively it is characterized by the absence of opportunity for earthly life; more than that he does not say."²⁹⁵ The message is that, "When this life is terminated, there is absolutely no opportunity of making up for the tasks left undone, no matter how many and varied our gifts may have been."²⁹⁶

In effect, this is an admonition to be *careful* in how we live (and work). And it qualifies and complements the oft-repeated admonition to be *carefree*. For to be carefree does not mean to be complacent and careless; we are to be careful. And to be careful does not mean to be full of cares; we are to be carefree. In the extended passage that follows, Qoheleth elaborates on what it means to be careful in the face of the uncertainties of life (9:11–11:6). And he pays attention to making the most of our occupation.

> 9:11 *Further, I saw that under the sun the race is not to the swift, and the battle is not to the valiant, and neither is bread to the wise, nor riches to the discerning, nor favor to those with knowledge; for time and chance befall them all. 9:12 For indeed man does not know his time: like fish caught in a dreadful net, and like birds caught in a snare, so the children of man are ensnared at a time of calamity, when it falls upon them suddenly.*

Qoheleth has previously made the observation that even the righteous and the wise cannot discover what will happen to them because they and their deeds are also "in the hand of God" (8:17–9:1). So they do not know "whether it will be love or hate;

---

293. Bellah et al., *Habits of the Heart*, 119.
294. Baumeister, *Meanings of Life*, 119.
295. Eaton, *Ecclesiastes*, 129.
296. Leupold, *Ecclesiastes*, 217.

both await them." The phrase "both await them" refers not only to what happens to them personally but also to the outcome of their deeds, whether they are successful (signified by "love") or otherwise ("hate").

The connecting word "Further" here in 9:11 indicates that Qoheleth is building on this observation. Obviously the verse is not saying, "the race is *(always) not* to the swift...," but rather, "the race is *not (always)* to the swift...." It elaborates graphically Qoheleth's observation that it is *possible* that those expected to be successful because of their abilities, *may* not succeed. This is because "time and chance befall them." In other words, an unexpected outcome ("hate" instead of "love") may be awaiting them.[297]

We experience unexpected outcomes because "man does not know his time." The word "time" here, and in "time and chance," refers to the time or occasion an event happens, as in "a time to love, and a time to hate" (3:8). So we may even encounter a calamity that befalls us suddenly. To recapture for us this sense of unexpectedness, Qoheleth uses the imageries of fish getting caught in a net and birds getting trapped in a snare. We should make the qualification that the phrase "time and chance befall them," which is the same as "both [whether love or hate] await them," may refer to a *positive* event ("love" instead of "hate"). Qoheleth uses negative imageries to illustrate it because he is now highlighting the possibility that those expected to win may actually lose. This is in line with his admonition to be careful.

This qualification reminds us that the phrase "time and chance" refers back to the set of opposite (positive and negative) events represented in the poem of 3:1–8. There we are told that the "times" are actually appointed by God (3:1, 11). Hence, though we may encounter an event as "chance" because we do not expect it, it is still "in the hand of God" (9:1). And though this means that what happens to us is beyond our control, it is within God's control. So those who acknowledge the sovereignty of God and his purpose in making "everything appropriate in its time ... [so] that men should fear him" (3:11, 14) are able to entrust their times to him and be carefree. In fact, because the God of the Bible is a personal Being, the psalmist could beseech him: "My times are in your hand; save me from the hand of my enemies and from my persecutors" (Ps 31:15).

> *9:13 I have also seen this (about) wisdom under the sun, and it is significant to me. 9:14 There was a small city with few men in it, and a great king came to it and surrounded it, and built huge siegeworks against it. 9:15 But there was found in it a poor wise man and he might have delivered the city by his wisdom. Yet no one considered that poor man. 9:16 So I said, "Wisdom is better than might." But the poor man's wisdom was despised and his words were not heard. 9:17 The words of the wise (spoken) in calmness are to be heard rather than the clamor of a ruler among fools. 9:18 Wisdom is better than weapons of war, but one sinner destroys much good.*

297. Cf. Schoors, *Preacher II*, 117, 205.

Qoheleth then recounts an observation "with regard to wisdom"[298] which made an impression on him: a wise man *might have delivered* a city from being captured by a powerful enemy but no one *considered* him (9:15). This was due to prejudice against him because he was poor, and so he and his wisdom were despised. They would rather suffer calamity than be delivered through a poor man's wisdom. This observation is an illustration of what is said in the previous passage—the best does not always win, specifically "favor [may not be] to those with knowledge" (9:11).[299] And it reflects a larger phenomenon that is seen even today. Often a nation or an organization is heading toward disaster because those in power do not operate by sound proverbial wisdom. And they despise those in their midst who are wise, because heeding their wisdom means going against their own personal agenda. So those in power would not even allow the words of the wise to be heard.

This particular observation demonstrated to Qoheleth that "Wisdom is better than might . . . and weapons of war." So he declares that the unassuming counsel of the wise is to be heard rather than the pretentious claims of even the best ("ruler") among the fools (cf. 7:5). But since the observation also illustrates what Qoheleth has just said earlier that "favor [may not be] to those with knowledge [and thus wise]," he qualifies that wisdom may fail to secure a favorable outcome: "one sinner destroys much good." A "sinner" is one who is not "good in God's sight" and hence lacks "wisdom, knowledge and joy" (2:26). In other words, it takes just one person who does not fear God to undo the wisdom of the wise and wreak havoc through his folly. This is particularly true if that foolish person happens to be the one in power. In the next passage Qoheleth counsels those who could avert this kind of unfortunate outcome.

> 10:1 *Dead flies make the perfumer's ointment give off a stench; a little folly outweighs wisdom and honor.* 10:2 *A wise man's heart is (inclined) to the right, but a fool's heart to the left.* 10:3 *Even when the fool walks on the road, his sense is*

---

298. The word "wisdom" in 9:13 is in the "accusative of limitation" (Joüon and Muraoka, *Grammar*, §126g; Waltke and O'Connor, *Syntax*, §10.2.2e); here it limits the scope or reference of "this" (Holmstedt et al., *Qoheleth*, 261; Seow, *Ecclesiastes*, 308–9). What Qoheleth observed is not "this wisdom," but "this (about) wisdom." And the "this" refers to what follows.

299. In most Bible translations the two verbs in 9:15 that we translate as "might have delivered" and "considered" are rendered as "delivered" and "remembered" respectively. In other words, the poor wise man did deliver the city but no one remembered him. However, the translation we have adopted fits the context better as this observation is an illustration of what was said in the previous passage that the best does not always win. Also, 9:16 says, "the poor man's wisdom was despised and his words were not heard." So they would not have considered him and thus the city would not, though it could, have been delivered. As for the verb translated "might have delivered," which is in the Hebrew perfect(ive), Seow says, "The perfect is used here to indicate a hypothetical situation (what might have happened)" (Seow, *Ecclesiastes*, 310; cf. Kautzsch, *Grammar*, §106p). This interpretation would not be possible if the verb translated "considered," which basically means "remember," could only mean recall something in the past. But as Crenshaw points out, the word in 12:1—"Therefore *remember* your Creator in the days of your youth"—must mean "give thought to" (Crenshaw, *Ecclesiastes*, 166). Thus "considered" is an apt translation in 9:15. So the poor wise man might have delivered the city if they had considered him. They did not. What a graphic illustration that the best does not always win.

> *lacking, and he says to everyone that he is a fool. 10:4 If the spirit (temper) of the ruler rises against you, do not leave your (official) position, for composure allays great offenses. 10:5 There is a misfortune that I have seen under the sun, an error indeed proceeds from the ruler: 10:6 folly is set in many high places, and the rich sit in humble places. 10:7 I have seen slaves on horses, and princes walking like slaves on the ground.*

He begins by reiterating that, just as a dead fly destroys a bowl of ointment, a little folly has a greater impact than ("outweighs") wisdom and the esteem ("honor") that comes with it. He then assures us that it is not difficult to detect folly (and be forewarned). For a fool's decision or action is conspicuously unwise as his heart is not inclined to the path of wisdom (not "to the right" but "to the left"). The contrast between "to the right" and "to the left" may just mean that the hearts of the wise and the fool are inclined toward opposite directions. More likely it also highlights the different destiny of each direction. "The right side is the side of prosperity and good fortune (cf. 'Benjamin,' Gen 48:14; Matt 25:33), and the left that of disaster and ill omen."[300] So "even when the fool walks on the road," signifying how he conducts himself in public, "his sense is lacking" and it is obvious to everyone except to himself that he is a fool since hardly anyone deliberately displays his folly publicly.

It is certainly true that we can recognize folly when we see it, and that we often fail to recognize it when we are the ones committing it. This means we need others, especially those who care about us, to alert us when we are being foolish. This is not to suggest we take seriously every criticism directed at us. But we need to take special note when someone points out that what we are doing actually violates what we ourselves accept as sound proverbial wisdom.

In 8:1–5 court officials are counseled on how to respond to a king who is acting unjustly. Since injustice (read: folly) is obvious to an observer and usually not so to the one perpetrating it, a court official is to respond carefully and wisely to the unjust king. He is not to desert the ruler quickly, but to maintain a composure that would enable him to know when and how to address the problem. Here in 10:4, Qoheleth gives a similar counsel. The court official is not to abandon his official position even when the ruler becomes angry with him. For his conciliating composure may enable him to influence the ruler so that he does not make a decision which is foolish and "an error *indeed* proceeds from the ruler"[301] that eventually brings about upheavals in society such as: "folly is set in many high places . . . and princes walking like slaves on the ground" (10:5–7). Qoheleth said he has seen such a misfortune actually happening. Indeed, if there were more aides who are God-fearing and truly wise to people in power, less misfortune would befall innocent people.

---

300. Murphy, *Ecclesiastes*, 101.
301. Cf. Gordis, *Koheleth*, 319; Longman, *Ecclesiastes*, 241.

> 10:8 *He who digs a pit may fall into it, and he who breaks through a wall—a snake may bite him. 10:9 He who quarries stones may be hurt by them, and he who splits logs may be endangered by them. 10:10 If the iron (tool) is blunt, and he does not sharpen the edge, he must exert more strength. But the advantage of wisdom is success. 10:11 If the snake bites before it is charmed, there is no advantage to the charmer.*

Having given counsel to court officials to make the most of their privileged position, Qoheleth applies it to occupations in general. He reminds us that in every line of work there are "occupational hazards" (10:8–9). Therefore we need to be careful at all times. Otherwise we may not be able to fulfill our vocation. Then he reaffirms that wisdom is better than might for "the advantage of wisdom is success"[302]—wisdom enables us to succeed in what we are called to do. He uses the illustration that if our tool is sharp (working wisely) we need less effort to do the work. But if we are complacent and careless, we may be like the snake charmer who got bitten by an uncharmed snake. His skills in snake-charming gave him no advantage over the rest of us who have no such skills. So we need to be careful—be prudent and discreet—in doing our work so as to decrease the possibility of tragedy and to increase the possibility of success. In doing this we are heeding the admonition to make the most of our abilities and the opportunities we still have (9:10).

Since Qoheleth is talking about carefulness in what we consider "non-moral" aspects of life, it may not be obvious that he is actually reaffirming the value of sound proverbial wisdom. Biblical proverbial wisdom, which is based on the Ten Commandments, enables us to avoid violating the created order, which affects not only the moral and social but also the physical dimensions of life (note the Sabbath commandment). This means biblical wisdom covers not only how we relate to one another but also how we relate to our occupation. For instance, in Proverbs, the shepherd is admonished to "know well the condition of your flocks, and pay attention to your herds" because "riches do not last forever" (Prov 27:23–24). In other words, if the shepherd is not careful in his work, his wealth will soon be depleted.

> 10:12 *The words of the mouth of the wise win him favor, but the lips of a fool devour him. 10:13 The beginning of the words of his mouth is folly, and the end of what he says is harmful stupidity. 10:14 Yet the fool multiplies words. No man knows what will come to be, so who can tell him what will come to be after him? 10:15 The toil of a fool wearies him, because he does not know the way to the city.*

In line with his reaffirmation of sound proverbial wisdom, Qoheleth now reassures us that words of wisdom do bring about a favorable outcome.[303] He did qualify that there

---

302. Longman, *Ecclesiastes*, 245.

303. Actually 10:12a says literally, "The words of the mouth of the wise (are) grace/favor" and the clause is most often translated "The words . . . are gracious." Taking this clause by itself, it is indeed "not obvious whether Qohelet means that the *words* . . . dispense favor or effect favor for the wise

are no guarantees (9:11–12). But he did also imply that with carefulness, unfavorable outcomes can be minimized (10:8–11). It simply means that we are to use, not worship, wisdom. To emphasize the usefulness of wisdom Qoheleth highlights the harmfulness of folly. The words of a fool are from beginning to end harmful and have an unfavorable effect on ("devour") him, yet he "multiplies words," apparently oblivious to the foolishness of his "*harmful* stupidity."[304]

In 10:14b Qoheleth reiterates the sub-theme that no one "knows what will come to be" in order to contend that the fool could not have known ("so who can tell him . . . ?"), because no one knows, "what will come to be [in this world] after him," that is, after one has left this world (cf. 6:12). For Qoheleth observes that the fool multiplies words as if he knew about the distant future! Qoheleth has warned that we do not really know what is indeed good for us to do in our lifetime since we do not know what is going to happen in this world after we are gone (6:12). It is foolish to talk as if we did. So perhaps the fool here keeps on asserting that what he is doing is good (even when it violates sound proverbial wisdom), as fools are wont to do.

As we saw in our exposition of 6:10–12, "God so works," which includes not letting us know about the future, whether within or beyond our lifetime, so "that men should fear him" (3:14). And 7:1–14 demonstrates the usefulness of sound proverbial wisdom in facing an unknown and uncertain future. But a fool, who by definition does not see the need to fear God and be careful to respect God's created order by observing sound proverbial wisdom, is prone to live as if he knew about the future. In fact some foolish people, especially those who happen to be in power, behave as if they were even in control of the future!

Because a fool cannot outsmart the created order, his toil "wearies him"—he toils long and hard but there is little result. He works with an "iron tool [that] is blunt" because he does not "sharpen the edge" (10:10). He does not even realize he is working with a blunt tool! Qoheleth likens him to a child, who "does not know the way to the city," which is an idiom for basic incompetence.[305] For a fool is basically incompetent when it comes to observing sound proverbial wisdom.

> 10:16 *Woe to you, O Land, whose king is a child, and whose princes feast in the morning! 10:17 Blessed are you, O Land, whose king is of nobility, and whose princes eat at the proper time—for strength, and not for drunkenness! 10:18 Through slothfulness the roof sags, and through slackness of hands the house leaks. 10:19 Food is prepared for merriment while wine cheers up life, and money*

---

person . . . , but the parallel with the second colon [10:12b], in which the fool's words harm him, shows that the latter sense is definitely intended" (Longman, *Ecclesiastes*, 247). Hence we translate "The words . . . win him favor" (ESV; cf. NLT).

304. The last phrase of 10:13 is literally "evil stupidity," but the Hebrew word for "evil" need not, and does not here, mean moral evil and the phrase has even been translated as "dangerous nonsense" (Murphy, *Ecclesiastes*, 97). As for our preference of "stupidity" over the usual "madness," see footnote to exposition of 1:17.

305. Seow, *Ecclesiastes*, 320.

answers to both. 10:20 Even in your thoughts, do not curse the king, nor in your bedroom curse the rich, for a bird of the air may carry your voice, or a winged creature may report the matter.

Qoheleth now looks at the economic consequence of an imprudent and incompetent government. To set the tone, he laments over ("woe to") a nation whose king is immature and incompetent ("a child") and whose princes lack discretion ("feast in the morning"); and congratulates ("blessed are") a nation whose king (or prime minister) is noble and whose princes (or cabinet ministers) are prudent. People who are not rich can expect economic hardship when the government is complacent and careless. Qoheleth uses the imageries of a sagging roof and a leaking house to recreate the irksome experience.

Money is needed to buy ("answers to") food and wine (10:19).[306] A lack of it means a lack of access to even the basic pleasures of life. It is natural then to "curse the king" out of anger for the misfortune he has caused or failed to avert, as well as to "curse the rich," perhaps for how they contributed to their misfortune or even out of envy for their continued access to much food and wine. Prudence and discretion dictate that we should be careful with our words even in the privacy of our homes, as we would say today, "Walls have ears." And to avoid inadvertently saying things that we may regret, we should also avoid entertaining them even in our thoughts.

> *11:1 Send forth your bread on the surface of the waters, for you will find it after many days. 11:2 Give a portion to seven, or even to eight, for you do not know what misfortune may come upon the land. 11:3 If the clouds are full, they pour rain on the earth; and whether a tree falls in the south or in the north, in the place where the tree falls, there it will be. 11:4 He who watches the wind will not sow, and he who looks at the clouds will not reap. 11:5 Just as you do not know the path of the wind or how bones develop in the womb of the pregnant woman, so you do not know the work of God, who does both things. 11:6 In the morning*

---

306. Unfortunately, most Bible translations render the Hebrew phrase *hakkol* "the all" in 10:19 as "everything" instead of "both" (food and wine), thus making the verse say: "money is the answer to everything." This gives the impression that Qoheleth is not quite orthodox. However, as in the case of 1:2, the phrase "the all" refers to a specific "all" to be determined from the context. In the context of 1:2 (also 1:14; 2:11, 17; 12:8), it refers to everything that human beings gained under the sun through human toil (for discussion, see "Interpretation of Ecclesiastes" under "The Transience of Vapor"). In the context of 3:11, it refers to all the 14 pairs of opposite things listed in the poem of 3:1–8. In the context of 9:2, it refers to all those listed, which represent all human beings. In the context of 12:13, it refers to "the all (that) has been heard"—the entire speech from 1:2–12:8. In the contexts of 2:16, 3:19–20, 6:6, 7:15, 9:1, and 11:5, as is the case here, "the all" refers to the two things under purview (cf. Schoors, *Preacher II*, 3–5; Crenshaw, *Ecclesiastes*, 104). In 2:16 the two things are the wise and the foolish ("both will have already been forgotten"); in 3:19–20 they are man and beast ("both have the same breath"); in 6:6 they are the rich man and the stillborn child ("both go to one place"); in 7:15 they are the two observations (the righteous may die young and the wicked may live long); in 9:1 they are love and hate ("both await them"); here in 10:19 they are food and wine ("money answers to both"); then finally in 11:5 they are the path of the wind and the development of bones in the womb (it is "God, who does both things").

sow your seed, and in the evening do not let your hand be idle, for you do not know which will succeed, this or that, or whether both of them are equally good.

Good and bad governments come and go, and there are also other causes of economic uncertainties. Hence Qoheleth admonishes economic prudence on the part of his audience. His advice on sending forth "bread" (perhaps, here means commodity) upon the waters probably refers to overseas investment. And since misfortune may happen, we had better factor it into our economic planning. The wisdom in dividing the portion "to seven, or even to eight" is similar to the contemporary saying, "Do not put all your eggs into the same basket."[307] This piece of advice has wider application today than in Qoheleth's day, especially within the economic realm (think of the different ways one can invest money today).

Whether these two verses actually refer to overseas investment or not, the basic message is that, in light of the uncertainties of life, we need to be prudent in planning for the future, and to minimize the risks involved. But unless one fears God and restrains one's greed, one may become so careless (read: foolish) that one loses all of one's savings (cf. 5:14).

And since we cannot avoid taking risks, Qoheleth illustrates the need to take risks through the use of imageries related to farming. When the clouds are full, the rain will fall; but we do not know when they will become full. And we do not know where a tree will fall until it has fallen, for we do not know which direction the blast of wind which uproots it will blow. So even when clouds that have become full are in sight, we cannot tell where the wind will blow them.[308] Therefore a farmer cannot determine the perfect time for sowing (when rain is needed) or reaping (when rain is to be avoided) by watching the wind or looking at the clouds. He who does this will neither sow nor reap (nor eat). We need to go ahead to do "what our hand finds to do" (9:10) even though we may not have the certainty that we will succeed. This should drive us to fear God and observe sound proverbial wisdom, which describes the most likely outcome of what we do or do not do, in all our endeavors.

Besides ignorance about the path of the wind, Qoheleth also uses ignorance about how bones develop in the womb to reiterate again the sub-theme that we "do not know the work of God," that is, we cannot discover what is going to happen (8:17).[309] So Qoheleth admonishes sowing seed "in the morning" and "in the evening," as one does not know which time of sowing will succeed. Since these words are used as imageries to convey how we are to work in general, a farmer is not to take them

---

307. Gordis, *Koheleth*, 330.

308. Cf. Seow, *Ecclesiastes*, 345.

309. To be consistent, we have translated the last clause of 11:5 as "who does both things" instead of "who does everything," which is also true of God. For the object is *hakkol* ("the all"), which refers to "all" the things that are specified in, and identifiable from, the context—in this case it refers to *both* the wind and the bones (see footnote above). Thus Qoheleth is saying, since his audience do not know the path of the wind and development of the bones, both of which are God's work, they do not know God's work in general.

literally. Qoheleth is basically saying, since we have to act without knowing what actually works, we need to be prudent and try different approaches, if not concurrently then consecutively.

It is significant that we are here called to exercise human responsibility ("Send forth your bread . . . sow your seed . . .") in the very context that explicitly affirms divine sovereignty (". . . God, who does both things"). Hence to Qoheleth, divine sovereignty and human responsibility are definitely not incompatible. In fact, they are inseparable in the experience of those who fear God, who are thus able to be carefree and careful at the same time. For in fearing God they acknowledge his sovereignty and become *carefree* through recognizing divine providence (see exposition of 3:10–15). And because they fear God, they exercise the responsibility to observe sound proverbial wisdom and so keep his commandments. In this way they are being *careful* through exercising human prudence in the face of the uncertainties of life.

By now it is clear that we need to be both carefree and careful to make the most of life and to live sensibly. This means, in order to adequately make sense of human experience, we need to accept Qoheleth's paradoxical assumption that God is sovereign over human actions and yet human beings are responsible for what they choose to do or not to do.

Admonition to Carefreeness in Light of Vanity (11:7–12:7)

> 11:7 Light is pleasant, and it is good for the eyes to see the sun. 11:8 Indeed, if a man lives many years, let him have enjoyment in them all, and let him remember the days of darkness, which may be many. All that comes is vanity. 11:9 Young man, have enjoyment in your youth, and let your heart make you glad in the days of your youth. So follow the impulses of your heart and the desire of your eyes. But know that for all these things God will bring you into judgment. 11:10 So remove vexation from your heart, and put away pain from your body, for youth and the prime of life are fleeting.

Qoheleth did say that a stillborn child who "never sees the sun" is better off than a rich man who could not enjoy his wealth, no matter how many children he may have and how many years he may live (6:1–7). Now, as he continues to speak about making the most of life, he clarifies that actually "light is pleasant" and it is "good for the eyes to see the sun," that is, to be alive in this world (cf. 9:3–6). And this is provided that no matter how many years one may live, "let him have enjoyment in them all" (we translate "have enjoyment" in 11:8–9 instead of "rejoice" as in most Bible translations because this passage is part of and concludes the sub-theme on enjoyment that begins in 2:24–26). Otherwise he is no better off than the stillborn child, as "all that comes," which means all that he gains under the sun, "is vanity."

Qoheleth then qualifies, "and let him remember the days of darkness." As "light" symbolizes life, the "days of darkness" refer to death and the days of physical frailty ("which may be many") preceding it (12:1–7). To "remember the days of darkness" is to recognize that when the body becomes increasingly frail, one begins to lose his ability to have enjoyment. So Qoheleth admonishes the "young man" to "have enjoyment in your youth" and so make the most of life before it is too late, "for youth and the prime of life are fleeting." In 5:18–20 he made it clear that real enjoyment is experienced out of a carefree disposition. There, emphasizing God's sovereignty, he said it is God who enables one to be carefree ("God keeps him occupied with the gladness of his heart"). Here, emphasizing human responsibility, he says one is to be carefree ("let your heart make you glad"). He then explains how we can enjoy life with a carefree disposition.

To enjoy life, one must be able to follow the "impulses of your heart and the desire of your eyes." This means we must be able to do what seems and feels good for us to do. Some people find this teaching out of place in the Bible. But imagine what it is like if we must *never* follow the impulses of our heart and the desire of our eyes. If we must not choose a line of work that seems and feels good for us to do, we must exclude any line of work which we are good at and enjoy doing, which by definition is our vocation. Or, if we must not follow our heart and our eyes in our choice of leisure, we must exclude any activity that seems and feels good for us to do, which is what leisure is supposed to be. Can we then enjoy life?

It is a common misconception that this teaching contradicts the prohibition in Num 15:39: "(do) not follow after your own heart and your own eyes." In that context, the people were being admonished to observe all the commandments of God. That prohibition is about not following after one's heart and one's eyes when doing so violates God's commandments. But there is adequate room to follow one's heart and one's eyes without violating any commandment.

In fact Qoheleth himself qualifies ("But know") that "for all these things," that is, how we follow after our heart and our eyes, "God will bring you into judgment." The "judgment" here is the same as that in 12:14, where it covers "every act . . . whether it is *good* or *evil*," which in this context means whether the act is consistent with keeping God's commandments or not (12:13). Hence the "judgment" need not be negative, as doing what seems and feels good to do is not necessarily evil. In other words, we are to follow the impulses of the heart and the desire of the eyes, "*but* know that one must not exceed the bounds of what God approves,"[310] that is, it must be within God's moral framework built on the Ten Commandments. The admonition to "follow the impulses of your heart" comes right after the admonition to "have enjoyment . . . and let your *heart* make you *glad*." This means the "impulses" Qoheleth has in mind are those of a carefree heart, which is a God-fearing heart inclined to obey God's commandments.

To ensure that one does have a carefree heart, Qoheleth adds, "So remove vexation from your heart, and put away pain from your body." And this requires one to fear God and keep his commandments. For consider the vexation of the heart that we

---

310. Seow, *Ecclesiastes*, 350.

have looked at: being burdened by the cares of this world (see exposition of 5:10–17). We saw how this relates to violating the moral dimension of the created order by breaking the tenth commandment: covetousness (see exposition of 5:18–6:9). And covetousness is basically about putting too much value on the transitory things of this world. The seventeenth-century theologian John Owen warned that "an overvaluation of temporal things" will only cause us to "spend our lives in fears, sorrows and distractions."[311]

Since "a joyful heart is good medicine, but a stricken spirit dries up the bones" (Prov 17:22), very often our physical pain is caused by vexation of the heart. Hence removing the vexation through observing God's commandments helps one to put away pain from the body. And physical affliction can also be directly caused by the violation of God's commandments. The Sabbath commandment shows that we are also to respect the physical dimension of the created order by having adequate rest. But covetousness often causes one to overwork to the detriment of one's health. Sheer complacency and carelessness about the way the physical world and our physical body is ordered can also damage our health. All this unnaturally hastens the coming of the "days of darkness." But one who fears God respects his created order in all its dimensions and thus cultivates a carefree disposition as well as minimizes physical affliction.

Therefore, not only is there adequate room within God's moral framework to enjoy life by doing what seems and feels good for us to do, outside of God's moral framework there is no room at all for real enjoyment.

> *12:1 Therefore remember your Creator in the days of your youth, before the days of trouble come and the years draw near of which you will say, "I have no delight in them"; 12:2 before the sun and the light, the moon and the stars are darkened, and the clouds return after the rain: 12:3 in the day when the keepers of the house tremble, and the strong men stoop, and the grinders become idle because they are few, and those who look through the windows grow dim, 12:4 and the doors on the street are shut, while the sound of the grinding is low, and one rises up at the sound of a bird, and all the daughters of song are brought low; 12:5 also they are afraid of heights and terrors on the road; the almond tree blossoms, the grasshopper drags itself along, and the caperberry fails, for man goes to his eternal home, and the mourners walk about in the street; 12:6 before the silver cord is broken, and the golden bowl is crushed, and the pitcher is shattered at the fountain, and the wheel is crushed at the cistern; 12:7 and the dust returns to the earth as it was, and the (life) breath returns to God who gave it.*

Qoheleth admonishes the "young man" to remove vexation from his heart and put away pain from his body because "youth and the prime of life are fleeting" (11:10). This is in order to make the most of life in light of the coming "days of darkness" (11:8). In this passage, Qoheleth captures vividly what these dark days entail using

---

311. Owen, *Glory of Christ*, 32.

high prose, or even poetry (though the parallelism characteristic of Hebrew poetry is not that prominent, the passage is practically a poem as it is relatively terse and full of imageries). He calls these dark days the "days of trouble," and when these troublesome "years draw near" one will say, "I have no delight in them," because one can no longer enjoy life. "Therefore," Qoheleth admonishes, "remember your Creator in the days of your youth" (in order to enjoy life), before the arrival of these unpleasant years. But what does remembering our Creator have to do with enjoying life?

The Hebrew word translated "remember," like its English counterpart, does not always mean to recall the past (cf. 5:20; 9:15; 11:8). To remember something can also mean to remember to do what one is supposed to do with respect to that something. To *remember* the Sabbath day (Exod 20:8) is to remember to *observe* it and keep it holy (Deut 5:12). Hence to remember our Creator is to remember our accountability to him as our Maker and thus obey him.[312] And this verse (12:1) is parallel in meaning to the one preceding (11:10). For the phrase "before the days of trouble [bodily frailty] come" is another way of saying "for youth and the prime of life are fleeting." So to "remove vexation from your heart and put away pain from your body" one must "remember [or obey] your Creator." We have already inferred this much above. Here Qoheleth makes it explicit that the fear of God is basic to the enjoyment of life. This anticipates the final exhortation to fear God and keep his commandments (12:13–14).

We are to remember our Maker "*before* the days of trouble . . ." (12:1); "*before* the sun and the light . . . are darkened . . ." (12:2–5); and "*before* the silver cord is broken . . ." (12:6–7). The often figurative descriptions in the second and third "before"-clauses elaborate on the "days of trouble" in the first. And these "days" begin to draw near after one reaches "the prime of life." Since the third "before"-clause is undoubtedly referring to death (see below), the second "before"-clause has to be about what precedes death. The most sensible interpretation is that it refers to infirmities in old age, the onset of what the first "before"-clause is about—"the days of trouble" when one would say "I have no delight in them."

The darkening of the sun, moon and stars and the returning of the clouds signal the dawn of the "days of darkness" (11:8), when "light" (or life) is disappearing (cf. 11:7). In due time the hands "tremble," the legs "stoop," the teeth "become few," the eyes "grow dim," and because the ears are failing, like "the doors on the street [that] are shut," they keep much of the sound out. Due to the lack of teeth, there is little chewing; they become idle and "the sound of grinding is low." And because the ears are failing, one is unable to appreciate music ("the daughters of song are brought low"). Though the hearing is bad, one is easily awakened because he does not sleep soundly ("one rises up at the sound of a bird"). As one advances in age, the hair grows white like an almond tree blossoming. When he begins to walk with difficulty, like a grasshopper dragging itself along, he is afraid of heights and feels terrified on the road. And the

---

312. Cf. Whybray, *Ecclesiastes*, 163.

caperberry, "reputed to have been stimulants for the appetite and thought to have worked as aphrodisiacs," also fails.[313] The time to enjoy life is over.

The degeneration of the body is part of the natural process in which one eventually dies and "goes to his eternal home," sent off in a funeral ("mourners walk about in the street"). The third "before"-clause is obviously describing death even though it is not clear how the images in 12:6 concerning "the silver cord," "the golden bowl," "the pitcher," and "the wheel" are references to death. For 12:7 "solidifies the[se] references to death by using two familiar biblical images: 'dust,' *'āpār*, and 'breath' or 'spirit,' *rûaḥ*. That the dust returns to the earth recalls both Gen 2:7 and 3:19; (cf. Eccl 3:20). In the Gen 3:19 [sic] it stands as the symbol of humanness: humans are made of dust and to dust they return."[314]

Qoheleth himself has earlier presented these expressions as depicting death: the life-breath returns to God and the body, made from dust, returns to dust (cf. exposition of 3:18–21). Since each of the items, whether the "golden bowl" or "the pitcher," is said to be damaged beyond repair (like a cord broken or a wheel crushed), perhaps these are ancient idioms about some vital organs failing beyond remedy.[315] This fits the context as Qoheleth is describing natural bodily degeneration that leads to death.

Encapsulation of Theme: "All is vanity" (12:8)

12:8 "Vanity of vanities," says Qoheleth. "All is vanity!"

With this statement, Qoheleth concludes his thesis. It is essentially an exact repetition of the statement he began his speech with (1:2). It thus encapsulates the contents of the speech, confirming that the theme of the speech is indeed "all is vanity." And "all is vanity" because "the dust returns to the earth as it was, and the breath returns to God who gave it" (12:7). In other words, there is ultimately no net gain. It confirms what we have inferred right from the beginning, that when Qoheleth first asserted that there is no profit under the sun (1:3), he was talking about ultimate profit. In light of death there is indeed none. Also, it is clear from his speech that he recognizes immediate profit under the sun.

So Qoheleth's theme is neither pessimistic nor unorthodox. There is then no reason to assign, as is often done, the positive and orthodox exhortation to "fear God and keep his commandments" (12:13–14) to someone other than Qoheleth. And we have been highlighting how, right from the beginning, Qoheleth prepares his audience intellectually, emotionally and volitionally for this exhortation, which draws the speech to a natural conclusion.

---

313. Seow, *Ecclesiastes*, 363.
314. Horne, *Proverbs-Ecclesiastes*, 537.
315. Cf. Kaiser, *Ecclesiastes*, 120–21.

Elaboration on Speaker and His Teaching (12:9–12)

> 12:9 And in addition, because Qoheleth was a wise man, he continually taught the people knowledge; and he pondered, explored and put together many proverbs. 12:10 Qoheleth sought to find words of delight and honest words of truth were written. 12:11 The words of wise men are like goads, and the collected sayings are like well-fixed nails; they are given by one Shepherd. 12:12 But beyond these, my son, beware. Of making many books there is no end, and much study is weariness to the body.

This passage elaborates on Qoheleth as the speaker and the nature of his teaching in the third person. Who wrote it? Obviously it is the same person who first introduced Qoheleth as the speaker (1:1), and who punctuated the speech with the three occurrences of "says Qoheleth" (1:2; 7:27; 12:8). It is often assumed that this person is someone who "frames" Qoheleth's speech and is thus called the "frame narrator." Even then, could the person who wrote the speech as Qoheleth be the same person who "framed" it? This amounts to asking, Could the person who wrote the speech *as* Qoheleth in the first person also wrote *about* Qoheleth in the third person?

The writer of this exposition, now writing in the third person, sees no reason why the author of Ecclesiastes could not have written both as Qoheleth and as the frame narrator. In fact, today the biodata that introduces the writer of an article in the third person is often written by the writer himself. And the writer of this exposition has good reason to believe that, in this context, if Qoheleth the persona would elaborate on himself and his teaching, he would do so in the third person. For Qoheleth makes much use of personal experiences and observations as a means to persuade his audience. And by presenting himself as a reliable teacher in the third, instead of the first, person he places himself "in the realm of history and sets a degree of objectivity and distance between the reader and the Teacher, a distance that would not exist if the entire book were written in the first person . . . [and] thus lifts the book above the level of personal reflection and presents the Teacher as an authority whose words ought to be heard."[316]

However, in our exposition so far we have not assumed that the person who wrote the speech (1:2—12:8) as Qoheleth also wrote 12:9–12. We will continue to take this neutral position for the rest of our exposition. As we now look at what 12:9–12 has to say about Qoheleth and his teaching, recall that the very first verse of Ecclesiastes has already introduced the speech as "the words of Qoheleth." So the three occurrences of the phrase "says Qoheleth" (1:2; 7:27; 12:8) are not really needed. Since the persona Qoheleth is identified with King Solomon, each of the occurrences then has the effect of giving extra weight to what is just said as coming from a speaker with the credibility to say it with authority. And taken together (one right at the beginning,

---

316. Garrett, *Proverbs, Ecclesiastes, Song of Songs*, 262.

one somewhere in the middle, and one toward the end) they also indicate explicitly that "the words of Qoheleth" extend from 1:2 up to at least 12:8.

The phrase "And in addition" (12:9) then connects 12:9–12 to "the words of Qoheleth" marked out by the three occurrences of "says Qoheleth." In other words, 12:9–12 tells us more about the work of Qoheleth "in addition" to this speech on the vanity of life under the sun. "These verses describe the work of Qoheleth out of which the present book arose."[317] And 12:9 conveys that Qoheleth was a wise man, and besides writing the speech in Ecclesiastes, he also taught the people knowledge as well as put together proverbs based on reflection ("pondered") and investigation ("explored").[318] This reminds us of Solomon: "He spoke three thousand proverbs" (1 Kgs 4:32). Thus Ecclesiastes begins with introducing Qoheleth as king over Israel (1:1) and ends with describing the king as a teacher of proverbial wisdom. In fact there is proverbial wisdom in the second half of Ecclesiastes (most distinctly in 7:1–14). Hence this confirms that Qoheleth is the persona of Solomon from beginning to end. The passage goes on to describe the nature, purpose and origin of Qoheleth's teaching. All this further establishes the credibility of the speaker in light of the somber and sobering message just heard.

Qoheleth is said to have made an effort ("sought") to compose "words of delight" and to have written "honest words of truth" (12:10).[319] As Crenshaw puts it, "The emphasis falls on elegance and truth: Qohelet devoted time and energy both to the aesthetic of his composition and to the reliability of what he said."[320] However, Crenshaw qualifies that "Many readers have not concurred in the statement that Qohelet's observations are both pleasing and trustworthy."[321] Thus "many readers" are claiming to have understood Qoheleth's speech better than whoever wrote 12:9–12.[322] Evidently, they do not read 1:2–12:8 as a coherent speech that is artistically composed to elaborate on the theme, "All is vanity," in such a way that it moves the audience intellectually, emotionally and volitionally to respond to the conclusion, "Fear God

---

317. Krüger, *Qoheleth*, 209.

318. Our translation, "And in addition, because Qoheleth was a wise man, he continually taught the people knowledge" (12:9a), differs from those of a number of Bible translations as in, "Besides being wise, the Preacher also taught the people knowledge" (ESV). Even if we accept these translations, 12:9 is still—though now not explicitly—about what Qoheleth did *besides* writing the speech in Ecclesiastes. Our translation is similar to those of NJPS, NKJV, and at least three commentaries (Bartholomew, *Ecclesiastes*; Fredericks, *Ecclesiastes*; Seow, *Ecclesiastes*). It is based on a straightforward reading of the Hebrew text which supposes that here the particle *še-* has the causal sense, "because" or "for," which is clearly the case in Song 1:6 and 5:2 (Seow, *Ecclesiastes*, 383; cf. Schoors *Preacher*, 140).

319. Note that 12:10 is a statement about the speech Qoheleth wrote in Ecclesiastes regardless of whether the verse itself is referring to everything Qoheleth wrote or to just the speech. Either way, what is affirmed in 12:10 applies to the speech. Evidently this is assumed by commentators.

320. Crenshaw, *Ecclesiastes*, 191.

321. Crenshaw, *Ecclesiastes*, 191.

322. See below (Excursus to 12:9–12) for an elaborate exegetical defense of our interpretation and translation of this passage.

Our Reason for Being

and keep his commandments" (see "Introduction to Ecclesiastes" under "Coherent Message"). Apparently it did not occur to them that they may have misread the profound speech—"commentator after commentator has agonized over the book [of Ecclesiastes] as if *it*, rather than *they*, had a problem."[323]

Qoheleth's "delightful" words of truth are meant to persuade the audience to make a decision or take a course of action, or both. For like goads made from nails fixed to sticks that shepherds use, Qoheleth's words and the "collected sayings" of wise men like him prod us to move in a certain direction.[324] If we are already moving in that direction, the prodding will hardly be painful. It simply nudges us to keep going in that direction. But if we are moving in the opposite direction, the prodding will be most painful. To avoid the pain, we need to yield to the goading. As for Qoheleth's words in Ecclesiastes, they goad us to fear God and keep his commandments (12:13).

To further assure us that Qoheleth's words are truthful, the claim is made that they are "given by one Shepherd." The most natural interpretation is that the "one Shepherd" is the God of the Old Testament, the Creator of the universe. It is so natural that "This is the opinion of the majority of commentators and translators."[325] Though Whybray recognizes that "God . . . is called shepherd elsewhere in the Old Testament," he has doubts about the identification of the "one shepherd" with God because he sees "no good reason why this epithet should be used of him in this context" and thinks that the "apparent assertion of the oneness of God also seems to be made with no obvious reason."[326] However, he admits that "no plausible alternative interpretation of the sentence has been offered."[327]

The "good reason" for the epithet "Shepherd" to be used here is that the text says the words of wise men like Qoheleth are like goads to prod their audience in the direction they want them to go, just like what shepherds would do with their goads to their flock. According to Bartholomew, "The idea of 'one shepherd' would make sense as indicating the unified source of the diverse words of the wise if it is understood as referring to God as the ultimate source of such wisdom. . . . Thus v. 11 not only positions Qohelet's teaching among the wise but also traces the origin of such wisdom to one shepherd, namely God."[328] In fact Gordis renders "given by one shepherd" as "coming from one Source."[329] Hence the "obvious reason" for using the word "one" is to make explicit that the "one Shepherd" referred to is God himself to avoid any ambiguity, because in the Old Testament a human king is also called a "shepherd." So the text is making it obvious it is referring to the King, the God, of Israel. After all, right after

---

323. Provan, *Ecclesiastes/Song of Songs*, 34 (italics added).
324. Cf. Whybray, *Ecclesiastes*, 172.
325. Whybray, *Ecclesiastes*, 172.
326. Whybray, *Ecclesiastes*, 172.
327. Whybray, *Ecclesiastes*, 172.
328. Bartholomew, *Ecclesiastes*, 368–69.
329. Gordis, *Koheleth*, 200.

the elaboration on the speaker (12:9–12) is the call to decision to make a commitment to fear God and keep his commandments (12:13). What better way to ensure that the audience would respond in obedience than to say that ultimately it is God who has been speaking to and prodding them?

We are not told exactly how Qoheleth's words of truth are given by God and thus are ultimately the words of God. But it means that the prodding effects of the words are ultimately the goading of God, the ultimate Shepherd. Qoheleth had actually made a parallel claim when he said, "God so works that men (people) should fear him" (3:14). The best way to test these claims is to compare Qoheleth's teaching on the meaning of life with one that denies God and see which teaching, when consistently lived out, gives the deepest sense of fulfillment (see "Teaching of Ecclesiastes" under "Corroborating Empirical Evidence"). A theory about the meaning of life that, when consistently lived out, brings despair is actually most harmful.

In light of competing teachings, the audience—addressed as "my son" as in the wisdom literature of the ancient biblical world[330]—is warned to be careful of books that are "beyond these," that is, books other than the writings "of wise men" like Qoheleth that are "words of truth ... given by one Shepherd." For there will be "no end" to human speculations, and hence to "the making of many books" about the meaning of life and other truths essential to living life to the fullest. Studying them wearies the body. Understood in context, the warning here is not against the writing and reading of books. It is a warning to be careful when it comes to books other than those "given by one Shepherd," that is, Scripture inspired by God. On the one hand, "it is an affirmation of the completeness and sufficiency of the text [of Scripture]"[331] and so there is no need to go beyond it. On the other hand, "The reader is warned against poring over unsuitable literature, which will only weary him and do him harm."[332]

Excursus to 12:9–12: Canonicity of the Book of Ecclesiastes

We saw that Crenshaw, having affirmed that 12:10 attests to the elegance and truthfulness of Qoheleth's speech, qualifies that "Many readers have not concurred in the statement that Qohelet's observations are both pleasing and trustworthy."[333] This means that they consider not only 1:2–12:8 but also 12:9–12 as unreliable. Then the entire book of Ecclesiastes is considered an unreliable piece of literature with respect to truthfulness. They do not concur in 12:10 because its positive and supportive evaluation of Qoheleth contradicts their supposition that Qoheleth is inconsistent and unorthodox. It seems they would rather question the evaluation of Scripture than their own supposition. This is a drastic decision. Those who would neither question

---

330. Cf. Seow, *Ecclesiastes*, 388–89.
331. Seow, *Ecclesiastes*, 388.
332. Whybray, *Ecclesiastes*, 173.
333. Crenshaw, *Ecclesiastes*, 191.

Our Reason for Being

the evaluation of Scripture nor their own supposition are caught in a dilemma. Their option is to question the interpretation of 12:10—does it really give a positive and supportive evaluation of Qoheleth? They will then have to read against the grain of 12:9–12 to conclude that 12:10 is neither positive nor supportive of Qoheleth. We will now take a close look at how this actually happens, for it has far-reaching implications.

The Hebrew word (passive form) translated "were written" in 12:10b is often considered awkward in this context and so re-pointed to mean "wrote" (ESV, NJPS) or "to write" (NASB, HCSB). Without repointing the word, it can be understood as "(the thing that was) written."[334] Then we would translate 12:10b as, "and what was written is honest truth" (cf. "and *what was* written *was* upright—words of truth" NKJV). However, as noted by Martin Shields, the exact form of the word in a similar construction occurs in Ezekiel 2:10 and it is not awkward there:[335] "[and] words of lamentation, mourning, and woe *were written* on it" (HCSB; italics added). So we have adopted this reading—"and honest words of truth were written." An alternative would be "words of truth were honestly written." What difference does all the different readings, with or without repointing the word, make to the evaluation of Qoheleth? Actually not much; they all indicate that 12:10b is positive and supportive of Qoheleth.

Longman, who sees inconsistency and unorthodoxy in 1:2–12:8, argues that though 12:10 says "Qohelet *sought* to find words of delight and *to write* honestly words of truth,"[336] it "falls far short of commending either Qohelet's literary skills or his truthfulness."[337] In other words, "the frame narrator . . . chooses words that cast doubt on Qohelet's success,"[338] that is, Qoheleth sought to write words of truth but may not have succeeded. However, the previous verse commends that "Qoheleth was a wise man [who] also taught the people knowledge"[339] and "comment[s] respectfully on Qohelet's diligence."[340] So Longman recognizes that 12:9 is complimenting Qoheleth but, without any indication from the text, downplays it, saying "it is somewhat complimentary [of Qohelet] but very reserved."[341]

Now the verb "sought," which governs "to find" in 12:10a, "clearly has the connotation of an effort to realize a purpose."[342] In other words, having "commented respectfully on Qoheleth's diligence,"[343] the "frame narrator" chooses words to commend the effort Qoheleth put in. Following Longman's own translation of 12:10, this is how the

---

334. Holmstedt et al., *Qoheleth*, 305.
335. Shields, *End of Wisdom*, 67.
336. Longman, *Ecclesiastes*, 275 (italics added).
337. Longman, *Ecclesiastes*, 278.
338. Longman, *Ecclesiastes*, 278.
339. Longman, *Ecclesiastes*, 275.
340. Longman, *Ecclesiastes*, 278.
341. Longman, *Ecclesiastes*, 277.
342. Schoors, *Preacher II*, 211.
343. Longman, *Ecclesiastes*, 278.

text flows: Qoheleth was a wise man who taught the people knowledge and he was *diligent* in compiling many proverbs (12:9); he *sought—made an effort*—to find delightful words and *to write* honestly words of truth (12:10). Why then read "cast doubt on Qohelet's success" into the text when Qoheleth is said to be a wise man who taught (*succeeded* in teaching) the people knowledge (of truth)? Longman is clearly reading against the grain of 12:9–10 even based on his own translation.

Fox, who also sees inconsistency and unorthodoxy in 1:2–12:8, once held that "The frame-narrator certainly does not deny that Qohelet succeeded in his attempt . . . to write the truth, but neither does he commit himself as to the success of this attempt."[344] Apparently Fox has since come around and reads along the grain and so translates 12:10b as, "and *wrote* the most honest words of truth."[345] He even spells it out that "The epilogist . . . testifies that Qohelet was indeed a sage with praiseworthy goals and spoke honest words of truth."[346] As for Longman, in his more recent commentary he qualifies: "Even if . . . the NIV [translation of 12:10b] is correct, it does not radically affect my overall understanding of Qoheleth. . . . I will argue that in a limited sense Qoheleth does write the truth when he says, 'Life is hard and then you die.'"[347] Now the NIV translates 12:10b as, "and what he [Qoheleth] wrote was upright and true." But Longman's "overall understanding of Qoheleth" includes Qoheleth "reflecting the skeptical point of view of a confused wisdom teacher"![348]

The truthfulness of Qoheleth's words is clearly affirmed in the very next verse—they are "given by one Shepherd" (12:11). Fox, though he also recognizes that the "one shepherd" is "almost always thought to be God," rejects this traditional and most natural interpretation.[349] In a more recent and much shorter commentary, Fox reiterates that, "The difficulty with the traditional understanding of 'by one Shepherd' is that the metaphor of shepherd for God refers to his role protecting and providing for people—a role that is not relevant here. A shepherd does not 'give' words or commands. Nor, unlike law and prophecy, are the words of the wise ever considered to be given by God."[350] However, David says "the LORD is my Shepherd . . . . He leads me in *paths of righteousness*" (Ps 23: 1, 3). As our exposition shows, this is precisely the purpose of the words of the wise given by one Shepherd—to goad us to fear God and keep his commandments. So the role of God as Shepherd is certainly relevant here. A shepherd does speak to his sheep in a "language" the sheep can understand. This is why Jesus, using this very metaphor can say: "My sheep hear my voice . . . and they

---

344. Fox, "Frame-narrative in Qohelet," 101.
345. Fox, *Time*, 349 (italics added).
346. Fox, *Time*, 371.
347. Longman, "Ecclesiastes," 330.
348. Longman, "Ecclesiastes," 301.
349. Fox, *Time*, 355–56.
350. Fox, *Ecclesiastes*, 84.

follow me" (John 10:27). Who are we to say that the "one Shepherd" could not speak to his sheep through the words he "gives" to wise men?

Fox has assumed that words "given by God" can only mean the kind of revelation in law and prophecy. So when 12:11 says the words of the wise men are "given by one Shepherd," he rules out that it can mean the words are "given by God" (we will soon see that otherwise, his reading of 12:11 will be inconsistent with not only that of 12:12 but also 1:2–12:8). And in saying that the words of the wise are never considered to be "given by God," Fox also assumes the wise men of Israel were never said to be given God's word in the sense of prophecy. However Fox himself recognizes that the words of the *wise man* Agur in Proverbs 30 are said to be an "oracle" like those of David (2 Sam 23:1) and Balaam (Num 24:15), which are said to be based on "what God spoke to him" (David) and "what God told him" (Balaam).[351] Hence these words are said to be "given by God" in the narrow sense of prophecy though as Fox points out they are mostly not direct quotes from God.

In view of 12:12, a natural interpretation of "given by one Shepherd" is that the words of the wise men are canonical. Commenting on "Beyond them, . . . beware" in 12:12, Seow says, "The warning is simply not to go *beyond* the words of the wise, in this case, the words of Qohelet. . . ; it is an affirmation of the[ir] completeness and sufficiency."[352] "The intent of the warning is the same as the so-called [do not add/subtract] 'canonical formula' found in Deut 4:2; 13:1 (Eng 12:32); Sir 42:21; Rev 22:18–19. It serves to establish the complete reliability of the text in question."[353] Seow includes Sirach 42:21 as an example of the canonical formula, but the "formula" in Sir 42:21 (like in Eccl 3:14) is phrased as "nothing can be added/subtracted" (indicative), not "do not add/subtract" (imperative). And it is about the immutability of God's works,[354] not the canonicity of the text in question. Yet Seow leaves out Prov 30:6 as an example, which strengthens his reading of 12:12 as having the same intent as the canonical formula. For unlike the examples in Deuteronomy (law) and Revelation (prophecy), Proverbs 30:6 is an unmistakable example within wisdom literature. Even Fox recognizes that Prov 30:6 "echoes" the two examples in Deuteronomy.[355] The canonical formula in Prov 30:6 associates a piece of wisdom writing that is "given by God" (the "oracle" of Agur) with being canonical.[356]

Therefore 12:12 is "warning against an open attitude toward the canon."[357] In an Israelite context, this warning makes sense only if the words of the wise in 12:11, though neither law nor prophecy, are considered given by the God of Israel—the "one

---

351. Fox, *Proverbs 10–31*, 852–53.
352. Seow, *Ecclesiastes*, 388.
353. Seow, *Ecclesiastes*, 394.
354. Fox, *Proverbs 10–31*, 859.
355. Fox, *Proverbs 10–31*, 858.
356. Cf. Waltke, *Proverbs 15–30*, 477.
357. Crenshaw, *Ecclesiastes*, 191.

Shepherd." This then explains why the historical books of Joshua, Judges, Samuel, and Kings, known as the "Former *Prophets*," though neither law nor prophecy, are canonical (considered "given by God"). And the wisdom books are classified together with the book of Daniel, a book of prophecy, in the "Writings." There is no basis to limit words "given by God" to only law and prophecy. There is really no reason to reject the traditional and most natural interpretation that "one Shepherd" refers to the God of Israel.[358]

Now our translation "beyond these (*yōtēr min*-these) . . . beware" (12:12), as assumed above, is the same as that of most Bible translations and commentators.[359] In spite of this strong support, there are influential works that argue otherwise and promote a negative view of Ecclesiastes, whereas this widely accepted translation promotes a positive view of Ecclesiastes—it is inspired by God. So we need to establish this translation exegetically.

The Hebrew word *yōtēr*, like *yitrôn* ("profit" or "advantage" depending on context), has the root meaning "excess over." In the Hebrew Bible *yōtēr/yôtēr* occurs seven times in Ecclesiastes (2:15; 6:8, 11; 7:11, 16; 12:9, 12) and twice outside of Ecclesiastes (1 Sam 15:15 and Esth 6:6). In Ecclesiastes twice it means "excessively" (2:15; 7:16); thrice it is synonymous with *yitrôn* (6:8, 11; 7:11); this leaves the occurrences in 12:9 and 12:12. In 12:9 (and-*yōtēr*) it means "(and) in addition."[360] Seow says the "and" conjunction here "does not necessarily link this verse to the preceding; it introduces a new subject matter."[361] Though he prefers the "new subject matter" alternative, he does not rule out the "link to the preceding" alternative taken in the exposition above. Actually it does not matter as both alternatives end up saying, either explicitly or implicitly, that 12:9 describes what Qoheleth did *besides* writing Ecclesiastes.

As for 12:12 (*yōtēr min*-these) it is crucial to also compare the use of *yōtēr* in the two occurrences outside Ecclesiastes. In 1 Sam 15:15 (the-*yôtēr*), it means "(the) rest"—what is *beyond* "the best." And in Esth 6:6 (*yôtēr min*-me), where it occurs in the same grammatical form (*yôtēr min-*) as in 12:12, the phrase clearly means "other than or *beyond* (me)." And this meaning is attested even in postbiblical Hebrew.[362] Hence grammatically the most natural translation of 12:12a is, "But beyond these, . . . beware." Also, this translation fits the context perfectly. The previous verse says the words of the wise men are given by "one Shepherd," so this verse warns, "beyond these" words, be careful!

---

358. Cf. DeRouchie, "Shepherding Wind and One Shepherd," 12–15.

359. E.g., Bartholomew, *Ecclesiastes*; Crenshaw, *Ecclesiastes*; Enns, *Ecclesiastes*; Ginsburg, *Coheleth*; Krüger, *Qoheleth*; Murphy, *Ecclesiastes*; Seow, *Ecclesiastes*.

360. Cf. Seow, *Ecclesiastes*, 383.

361. Seow, *Ecclesiastes*, 383.

362. See Ginsburg, *Coheleth*, 476; Seow, *Ecclesiastes*, 383.

Our Reason for Being

Fox recognizes that "these," refers to "the subject of the preceding sentence, the words of the sages/proverb collections."[363] And in his more recent commentary, he spells out that "the words of the wise ... [refer] not only to unorthodox writings like Ecclesiastes ... but to wisdom books generally."[364] Likewise Longman affirms that "*these* would comprise of all the wisdom writings, including Qohelet's."[365] However, both of them translate the Hebrew phrase *yōtēr min*-these in 12:12 as "Furthermore, of these ... (beware)" instead of "beyond these, ... (beware)." This makes 12:12 a warning against "these" rather than what is "beyond these." Longman goes so far as to affirm that 12:12 is saying: "Qohelet's thinking is dangerous material—be careful."[366] If Qoheleth's thinking is dangerous material, so are "all the wisdom writings." Longman does not qualify whether "these" wisdom writings exclude the book of Proverbs.

Why would Fox and Longman go so far as to say 12:12 is warning against not only Qoheleth's speech but also "wisdom books in general"? It is one thing to say Qoheleth questions the wisdom tradition of Israel, it is quite another to say the same of even the supposed "frame narrator." Evidently it is because to them, Qoheleth cannot be anything but inconsistent and unorthodox; since "these" in 12:12 lumps the words of Qoheleth together with those of wise men in general, the verse has to be read as a warning against all "these," thus implicating not only Qoheleth, but also wise men in general. (The following critique of Fox's interpretation of 12:11–12 applies also to Longman, who follows Fox in his reading of these two verses).

Now if 12:12 warns against the words of the sages/proverb collections in 12:11, there must be something about them that deserves the warning. They are said to be like goads and nails (12:11a). Fox reads 12:11a in such a way that they are harmful in some ways. He recognizes that "Commentators have invariably considered the tenor of the comparison between goads and words of sages to be the fact that both spur people to better behavior," but he qualifies: "A goad prods one on to thought and better behavior, but it also hurts. . . . The words of the sages, in other words, can be uncomfortable, even dangerous."[367] And he spells out that, "While evincing respect and appreciation for Qohelet, the epilogist sets a certain distance between himself and the words of Qohelet—and of other sages as well. . . . This must be stressed: the epilogue's circumspection is directed not toward Qohelet's words in particular, but toward wisdom as such, of which Qohelet's teaching is a part."[368]

And since the words of the sages can be dangerous, they cannot be given by God. So Fox reads 12:11 in such a way that what is "given by one shepherd" are the goads and

---

363. Fox, *Time*, 356.
364. Fox, *Ecclesiastes*, 84.
365. Longman, *Ecclesiastes*, 281.
366. Longman, *Ecclesiastes*, 281.
367. Fox, *Time*, 354–55.
368. Fox, *Time*, 371–72.

the nails, and not the words of the sages.[369] To make it fit, he reads the Hebrew word for "give" as "set or stuck" and the Hebrew word for "one" as an indefinite article. So he translates 12:11 as: "The words of the sages are like goads, and the [words of] masters of collections are like implanted nails set by a shepherd."[370] Fox claims his reading of 12:11 is "more natural" because "the words of the sages" is "in the distant" from the verb "given/set" whereas the goads and the nails are "immediately preceding nouns."[371] Thus "given/set by one/a shepherd" (12:11b) qualifies the goads and the nails and not the words of the sages. But this reading is unnatural because 12:11b—now interpreted as a relative clause, "[that are] given/set by one/a shepherd"—qualifies only the nails and not the goads. Actually, in the Hebrew text, the noun that immediately precedes the supposed relative clause is not even "implanted nails" but "the [words of] masters of collections." So according to this interpretation, it is the proverb collections that are "given by one Shepherd"! To avoid this problem, even Longman translates 12:11b simply as "They are given by a shepherd."[372] But contra Longman,[373] "They" refers most naturally to the words of sages/proverb collections (subjects of the respective clauses) and not the goads and the nails (predicates of the respective clauses).

We can now confirm which reading is more natural based on the flow of the text of 12:9–12. As shown above, a plain reading of 12:9–10 shows that, regardless of which translation of 12:10b is adopted, it commends Qoheleth as a sage who had carefully or honestly written "delightful" (not dangerous) "words of truth." Now words of sages not given by God need not be dangerous and so need not be warned against. Hence, even granted Fox's reading of 12:11—it is the goads/nails and not the words of the sages that are "given by God"—there is no need to tamper with the most natural reading of 12:12—"Beyond these [words of sages], . . . beware"—and make it to read as, "Furthermore, of these [words of sages] . . . beware." Thus though Seow accepts Fox's reading that the words of the sages are not given by one Shepherd, he rejects Fox's reading of 12:12 as a warning against the words of the sages.[374] It is Fox's presupposed reading of 12:12 as a warning against the words of the sages like Qoheleth that requires him to see the words of the sages as useful but dangerous and so cannot be given by God (12:11).

And as we have seen, like most commentators, Seow recognizes that the warning is simply not to go *beyond* the words of the sages, and even comments that the intent of the warning is similar to the so-called "canonical-formula" found in the Bible. This means the words of the sages are considered canonical in Israel, which then means they have to be, as Gordis renders it, "coming from one Source"—the God of Israel.

369. Fox, *Time*, 355–56.
370. Fox, *Time*, 349.
371. Fox, *Time*, 349.
372. Longman, *Ecclesiastes*, 276.
373. Longman, *Ecclesiastes*, 279.
374. Seow, *Ecclesiastes*, 386–88.

Seow's comment is fully in line with, and gives the fullest support to, the reading that the words of the sages, including those of Qoheleth, are "given by one Shepherd" thus making them canonical. This may well be the reason Ecclesiastes was canonized. All this means, Fox's "more natural" reading of 12:11, so as to be consistent with the presupposition that Qoheleth is both inconsistent and unorthodox, is actually going against the grain of 12:9–12.

Fox warns interpreters that, "Koheleth has some unusual things to say, and his views should not be forced to fit presuppositions of what a biblical book *must* say. One need not grant the truth of all his opinions; the other biblical authors would not have."[375] This dictum presupposes that "Koheleth *has* some unusual [read: unorthodox] things to say," and effectively it is intended to force one's view of Qoheleth to fit the presupposition that Qoheleth must be unorthodox. Now Fox himself recognizes that 12:10b says Qoheleth "wrote the most honest words of truth."[376] How then can Qoheleth be saying unorthodox things? Longman is more consistent in continuing to read 12:10b as saying Qoheleth only "sought . . . to write honestly words of truth,"[377] but may not have succeeded.[378] However, as we have seen, Longman has to read 12:10b against the grain of 12:9–10, let alone 12:9–12. So Longman's reading of 12:10b is forced to fit his and Fox's presupposition.

This discussion of the views of Longman and Fox on 12:10 and 12:12 shows that, if we do not read 12:9–12 as positive and supportive of Qoheleth as a wise and reliable teacher *whose words we must take heed*, we are reading against the grain (or the goads) of the text. So interpreters who see inconsistency and unorthodoxy in Qoheleth's speech (1:2–12:8) will face knotty exegetical problems in reading 12:9–12 unless, like the "many readers" who do not concur in the positive and supportive evaluation of 12:10, the interpreter comes to the drastic conclusion that even 12:9–12 is unreliable.

All this points to the question: Why did the author of Ecclesiastes even bother to make the statement that Qoheleth sought—made an effort—to write "words of delight" and that what he had thus written are "honest words of truth"? Why did he assure readers—in effect decide for them—that Qoheleth's words are truthful? It is as though he wants to preempt any reading of Qoheleth's speech that makes Qoheleth inconsistent and unorthodox. And why did the author spell out that Qoheleth's "words of truth" were deliberately written artistically unless it matters that we seek—make an effort—to read Qoheleth's speech as artistically written, or else we will not understand it? This means, insofar as "words of truth" are "words that contain the truth,"[379] the statement cautions that to see the truth that Qoheleth's speech presents, one needs to

---

375. Fox, *Ecclesiastes*, ix.
376. Fox, *Time*, 349; cf. Fox, *Ecclesiastes*, 83.
377. Longman, *Ecclesiastes*, 275.
378. Longman, *Ecclesiastes*, 278.
379. Ogden and Zogbo, *Handbook*, 437; cf. Prov 22:21.

recognize the unusual artistry in his rhetoric (this is demonstrated in "Introduction to Ecclesiastes" under "Coherent Message").

CONCLUSION AND CALL TO DECISION (12:13–14)

12:13 The end (conclusion) of the matter, (when) all has been heard: fear God and keep his commandments, for this is (the essence of) every man. 12:14 For God will bring every deed into judgment, including every hidden thing, whether good or evil.

Our translation of 12:13a spells out that when "all has been heard" (what has been said in 1:2—12:8), the "conclusion of the matter" is what we read in 12:13b–14. It is similar to most Bible translations (e.g., NASB, NIV, NJPS). The most natural reading is that 12:13–14 are the concluding words of Qoheleth. Even though Murphy says 12:13a "clearly introduces a significant conclusion of the epilogist,"[380] and not that of Qoheleth, his translation of 12:13 is virtually the same as ours: "The end of the matter, when all is heard: fear God and keep his commandments, for this is (the duty of) everyone."[381] (For an elaborate discussion on our translation and how it affects the reading of Ecclesiastes as a whole, see "Interpretation of Ecclesiastes" under "The Rhetoric of Ecclesiastes").

For our purpose, it does not really matter whether the third-person statements in 12:9–12 are written by the same person who wrote the speech as Qoheleth. Even if they are not, we could still and should in fact read 12:13–14 as part of Qoheleth's speech that begins in 1:2. For if the speech ends abruptly with the encapsulation of the theme in 12:8, the audience would ask, "All is vanity... So what?" Though, as our exposition has shown, the answer—to fear God and keep his commandments—has already been given implicitly as part of Qoheleth's rhetoric to prepare the audience for the final exhortation to do just that, it still has to be given explicitly. For without a concluding exhortation in direct response to the theme of the speech, the speech is incomplete.

As a matter of fact, if Qoheleth were presenting the speech orally, the next thing he would have said following 12:8 would essentially be what we read in these two verses. But since this is a written speech, the author of Ecclesiastes makes full use of the written medium to strengthen his case through a third-person elaboration on Qoheleth and his teaching, before making the final appeal to the audience to do what he has been implicitly prodding them to do. This author, whether he is Solomon or a "ghost writer" impersonating Solomon, is indeed a master in the art of persuasion. This person, if he is not Solomon, has a wisdom that may be comparable to that of Solomon's.

---

380. Murphy, *Ecclesiastes*, 126.
381. Murphy, *Ecclesiastes*, 123.

The conclusion, says Qoheleth, in light of "all (that) has been heard" in the speech (1:2–12:8), which is summed up in the theme "All is vanity" (1:2; 12:8), is indeed what has been anticipated all along: "fear God and keep his commandments." We recognize that actually in 1:2–12:8, Qoheleth does not *explicitly* associate the fear of God with keeping his commandments. And we have indicated in the exposition that he does so implicitly throughout his speech when he refers to fearing God whether directly or indirectly. But why not explicitly?

Qoheleth's persuasive speech is effectively a sermon as its purpose and goal are spiritual. We can look at the conclusion of his speech like the conclusion of a sermon (on comparing Qoheleth's speech to a sermon, see further "Introduction to Ecclesiastes" under "Coherent Message"). According to John Broadus, who was not only a great preacher himself but also a great educator of preachers, "Rhetorically, psychologically, and spiritually the conclusion is a most vital part of the sermon. It is not an addition to the sermon but an organic part of it, necessary to its completeness of form and effect. It gathers up the various ideas and impressions of the message for one final impact upon the minds and hearts of the hearers. . . . In most cases it is the place of the sermon's climax—or anticlimax."[382]

Now when Qoheleth was talking about fearing God throughout his speech, his Old Testament audience would have in their own minds associated it with keeping God's commandments. The most effective way for a preacher to persuade his audience is to let them say to themselves what he wants them to hear. Imagine then the "one final impact" on their "minds and hearts" when Qoheleth finally at the "climax" of the speech says explicitly ". . . and keep his commandments" thus nailing into their hearts what is already on their minds. If Qoheleth had earlier spelled it out explicitly, his conclusion would in fact become an "anticlimax." Hence Qoheleth here confirms the intuition of preachers who when appropriate would reserve something to be spelled out explicitly only at the very end to give the conclusion the "punch" needed to make it impactful and memorable.

Qoheleth has been preparing his audience intellectually, emotionally and volitionally for this conclusion; by now there is no need to defend it. He goes on to spell out that "this is every man" (literal translation of the Hebrew clause), which is not idiomatic English. This non-idiomatic translation is presented here to highlight that there is much more to what the Hebrew text is saying than what we read in the Bible translations. What then does the text really mean?

The construction of the Hebrew clause is similar to that of "I am prayer" (Ps 109:4). According to Fox, "The effect of this construction seems to be an intensification of the equation: Not only am I prayerful, I am prayer itself."[383] We would call

---

382. Broadus, *Preparation and Delivery of Sermons*, 109.

383. Fox, *Time*, 362. Fox's interpretation of "I am prayer," and thus of "this is every man," is in accordance with established Hebrew grammar. Such clauses are called nominal (or verbless) clauses. In these two cases the predicate ("prayer" or "every man") is also a noun. "The predicate in such nominal

someone who regularly prays like this Mr. Prayer, just as we would call someone who has so completely given himself to the cause of the environment, Mr. Environment ("He is environment"). Similarly, "this is every man" means that "*this*—the fear of God and obedience to his commandments—is the substance . . . of every person."[384] In other words, this is what being human is all about. It is the very essence or purpose of human existence. No wonder when a human being violates God's commandments and commits something unconscionable, we would say, "He is not a human being!"

It is important to recognize that this teaching is also implicit in 1:2–12:8. For central to Qoheleth's argument is that "God so works that men (people) should fear him" (3:14), even through painful adversities as captured in the poem of 3:1–8. Why would God do that unless it is essential for humanity to fear God (and keep his commandments)? Again we see Qoheleth spelling out explicitly in his conclusion what has already been implicit in the speech leading up to the conclusion.

Christians may wonder whether this Old Testament teaching on the purpose of humanity has been revised if not replaced in the New Testament. The answer is most clearly spelled out in what is known as the Great Commission, where Christ himself commands that his disciples (Christians) are to be taught to observe everything he has commanded them, even to the end of the world (Matt 28:18–20). What he has commanded them is the same as what God has commanded in the Old Testament—love God with all their heart and love their neighbors as themselves (Matt 22:37–40; Lev 19:18; Deut 6:5; cf. Rom 13:8–10). Hence the purpose of life for Christians is the same as that for humanity as a whole—to fear God and keep his commandments (for an elaboration on this, see "Teaching of Ecclesiastes," especially under "Experiencing the Meaning of History").

Therefore "God so works that men should fear him" (3:14) applies even till the end of the world. And life will not really make sense until and unless we live according to this purpose. In our exposition we have already discussed how the fear of God contributes in different ways to the meaning of life. What needs to be stressed here is that the fear of God provides a transcendent purpose for living under the sun. A transcendent purpose is certainly more worthwhile and meaningful than one which is not. And human beings do express the need for such a purpose. As sociologist Peter Berger puts it, "The religious impulse, the quest for meaning that transcends the restricted space of empirical existence in this world, has been a perennial feature of

---

predications can have a variety of functions. It can designate the material from which something is made ['the altar was (of) wood' (Ezek 41:22)], . . . the abstract quality, [or] a concrete particularity ['all her paths are peace(ful)' (Prov 3:17)]" (Fox, *Time*, 362; drawing on Joüon and Muraoka, *Grammar*, §154e, which includes Ps 109:4 as an example for the predicate expressing "the abstract quality, or a concrete particularity").

384. Fox, *Time*, 362. For our purpose, it does not really matter whether Fox's interpretation of 12:13b is correct. One just need to consider how Bible translations render this clause—the most common of which is "this is the whole *duty* of man"—and see that though watered-down, these translations already indicate that 12:13b teaches that fearing God and keeping his commandments is the purpose of human life, the observance of which every human being is accountable to God (12:14; see later).

humanity. (This is not a theological statement but an anthropological one—an agnostic or even an atheist philosopher may well agree with it.) It would require something close to a mutation of the species to extinguish this impulse for good."[385]

Theologian Alister McGrath confirms that even prominent atheists like Sigmund Freud and Karl Marx do not deny the fact that human beings do seek for transcendent meaning; they simply sought to explain away this human desire as "nothing more than a coping mechanism thrown up by the human mind to shield us from the unbearable pain of knowing [from their atheist point of view] that life is pointless."[386] Even if it is indeed purely a "coping mechanism," being able to cope with reality is still better than bearing the "unbearable pain" of meaninglessness. And what if Qoheleth is correct, that this "coping mechanism" is not just an invention of the human mind but also an intention of the divine will?

If Qoheleth is correct, "God will bring every deed into judgment, including every hidden thing, whether good or evil" (12:14). This judgment is here given as the reason ("For") to heed his exhortation to fear God and keep his commandments, which is the basis for his judgment because it is God's purpose for humanity. This judgment is comprehensive, especially since even "every hidden thing" (cf. Rom 2:16) that is "good" (cf. 2 Cor 5:10) is included. And it is declared after a poem on impending death (12:2–7). So naturally it refers at least partly, if not solely, to a judgment after death. For as Ginsburg argues,

> The declaration that *every deed* will be brought into judgment, which cannot possibly refer to an earthly tribunal (comp. v. 7), and the fact that this judgment is to be over *every secret thing*, i.e., is to extend over every action of ours, which is concealed from our fellow-creatures, and can therefore not take place in ordinary courts of justice, shew incontestably that Coheleth speaks of a future judgment, when God, the righteous Judge, shall reward every man according to his deeds, whether they be good or evil. So plain and convincing are the words of the text, that even Knobel, who labours to prove that Coheleth denies the immortality of the soul, is constrained to say, *if one considers this passage impartially, he must admit that it speaks of a formal judgment, which, as is believed, will take place after death.*[387]

In fact, Knobel "considers this so plain and certain as a result of the language, that he denies the genuineness of the verse, because, as he says, Coheleth had no knowledge of such a judgment, or belief in it."[388]

Actually the conclusion that 12:14 is talking about a formal judgment after death is not only "plain and certain" from its language. Taking Ecclesiastes as a coherent

---

385. Berger, "Desecularization of the World," 13.
386. McGrath, *Glimpsing the Face of God*, 11–12.
387. Ginsburg, *Coheleth*, 478.
388. Stuart, *Ecclesiastes*, 287.

speech, this has to be the case. For in response to the observation that there is miscarriage of justice even in the courts of law, Qoheleth has assured the audience that God will one day judge both the righteous and the wicked to make things right (3:17). However, it is observed that often things are not made right in this world—the righteous may be oppressed and die young (7:15) while the wicked may die at a ripe old age and then be given an honorable burial and praised in the very place they had oppressed the righteous (8:10). This is indeed an enigmatic observation.

In response Qoheleth explains why people are not afraid to commit evil—the sentence against evil deeds is not executed *quickly*, implying that it will be *eventually* (8:11). So he is warning that even such an enigmatic observation—some people seem to be completely getting away with committing evil—is no excuse to commit evil. He then underscores that it will be well with God-fearers but not so with those who do not fear God, specifying that though the wicked may prolong their life, they will not do so indefinitely—they will have to die eventually (8:12–13). This comment on the certainty of judgment and of death made in response to the enigmatic observation—some wicked people seem so powerful that they are untouchable in this world—implies that they will be "touched" in the next world. In view of this train of thought, the judgment at the end of Qoheleth's speech has to be a formal judgment after death. Otherwise his exhortation to fear God lacks what it takes to move the audience's conscience to take God and his commandments seriously.

Also, on the part of the audience, in view of the observation that things are often not made right in this world, their own heart cries out for a final accounting of all that is done under the sun. For as human beings, we have a deep-seated sense of justice. And to make sense of evil left unpunished in this world and soothe our violated sense of justice, our conscience cries out, "There must be punishment of evil beyond death!" Now if and when our very own conscience tells us that this must be the case, whether we believe in God or not, we need to come to terms with the message of Ecclesiastes. This again illustrates how "God so works," such as even allowing evil to go unpunished in this world, "that men should fear him" (3:14). This then explains why Qoheleth relentlessly recounts enigmatic and painful realities in his speech—to prepare us to respond to his call to fear God and keep his commandments.

All this means Qoheleth's conclusion would be an anticlimax if the judgment at the end of his speech is not the final judgment. And it shows that the final judgment in 12:14 is already anticipated in 1:2–12:8. Thus Qoheleth is here again making explicit what has already been implicit throughout the speech. Hence in his conclusion he sums up and spells out what he has been getting at throughout his speech. This illustrates how Qoheleth the preacher *par excellence* "gathers up the various ideas and impressions of the message for one final impact upon the minds and hearts of the hearers"—what a potent climax to a powerful speech!

However, since "Surely there is not a righteous man on earth who does good and never sins" (7:20), who then can pass the stringent judgment after death? Thus

Our Reason for Being

Ecclesiastes ends with pointing us to a crucial teaching of the Bible—we need to repent and turn to God for the forgiveness of sin. To explore and appreciate how crucial the final judgment and its outcome is to the meaning of life, we turn next to a "systematic" exposition of the teaching of Ecclesiastes on the meaning of life.

Teaching of Ecclesiastes

Ecclesiastes is a persuasive speech. The implied, even if not the actual, speaker is King Solomon (1:1, 12), who has the "credentials" to say with authority all that is said in the speech. The expressed purpose of the speech is to persuade the audience to "fear God and keep his commandments" (12:13a). Hence it aims at instilling the fear of God and thus promoting a God-fearing way of life as taught in not only Ecclesiastes, but also the rest of the Bible. Since the speech has a spiritual purpose and goal, it is a sermon and we can thus call the speaker the Preacher.

The speech is the product of an investigation into human life based on the Preacher's personal experiences (2:1–23) and personal observations (3:16–8:15). This is the nature of wisdom literature in general. However, no one interprets one's experience or observation in a vacuum. It is always informed and shaped by one's presuppositions concerning the nature of this world.

In the case of the book of Proverbs, which is canonized as Scripture inspired by God, monotheistic revelation would have informed and shaped the interpretation of the experiences and observations upon which the individual proverbs are based, as well as supplemented the composition of the book as a whole. For the book itself claims that "the fear of the LORD [the God of biblical monotheism] is the beginning [foundation] of knowledge [such as what is presented in the book]" (Prov 1:7). Also, numerous proverbs—like "The eyes of the LORD are in every place, watching the evil and the good" (Prov 15:3)—could not have been based on experience or observation alone. Clearly monotheistic revelation has supplemented experience and observation here.

Ecclesiastes itself claims that the words of the Preacher are "given by one Shepherd." The most natural interpretation is that this "one Shepherd" is God himself. In fact, "This is the opinion of the majority of commentators and translators [and] no plausible alternative interpretation . . . has been offered."[1] Since Ecclesiastes is indeed canonized as Scripture inspired by God, we can assume that monotheistic revelation would also have informed and shaped the interpretation of the experiences and observations, as well as supplemented the composition of the speech.

---

1. Whybray, *Ecclesiastes*, 172.

This assumption is corroborated when we see how the profound insights of this speech uncannily address the question of not only the meaning of life but also the meaning of history in the most satisfying way. For this reason, the claim that wisdom teaching like this speech is "given by one Shepherd" all the more can only mean that its ultimate source is the God of Israel.

We will begin our study of the teaching of Ecclesiastes with an exposition of the basic argument of this profound speech and then consider how it addresses the question of the meaning of life, which is the key teaching of the book. (Except for the inclusion of materials from medical sociology, the following section is mostly a summary of the Preacher's argument as presented in the "Exposition of Ecclesiastes." Besides providing the base material for an exposition of the teaching of Ecclesiastes on the meaning of life, it also serves as a *thematic* summary of Ecclesiastes that complements the *linear* summary presented in the "Introduction to Ecclesiastes.")

ENCOUNTERING THE REALITIES OF LIFE

The speech proper, which takes up almost the entire twelve chapters of the book, begins and ends with the somber declaration, "Vanity of vanities, all is vanity!" (1:2; 12:8). This is the theme of the speech. The speech argues that in light of this theme, "The end [conclusion] of the matter, (when) all has been heard, is fear God and keep his commandments, for this is (the essence of) every man (person)" (12:13).

Why is it that because "all is vanity" (theme), we are to "fear God and keep his commandments" (conclusion)? Ecclesiastes is a speech, not a treatise; the logical flow of the argument is thus not necessarily presented linearly. When this is recognized, the logical connections between "All is vanity" and "Fear God" can be readily discerned.

The Hebrew word translated "vanity" literally means "breath" (Isa 57:13) or "vapor," that is, breath condensed in cold air (Prov 21:6). Just as condensed breath is transitory, the word is often used figuratively to refer to something fleeting, which is the case in a number of contexts in Ecclesiastes (3:19; 6:12; 7:15; 9:9; 11:10).

However, in the context of the theme of the speech, the figurative meaning takes on the further nuance of "vanity" (for an elaborate defence of this interpretation and translation, see "Interpretation of Ecclesiastes" under "The Meaning of *Hebel*"). For the theme is also expressed as, "What profit is there?" (1:3; 3:9; 5:16; 6:11). In fact the opening declaration—literally, "Vapor of vapors, all is vapor!" (1:2)—is the expected answer to the rhetorical question, "What profit is there? [No profit!]" (1:3). Hence "All is vapor (transitory)" in this context means "All is vanity (profitless)." As James Crenshaw puts it, "This unforgettable refrain unifies the entire book: from first to last nothing profits those who walk under the sun."[2]

---

2. Crenshaw, *Ecclesiastes*, 35.

The Certainty of Death

"All is vanity" means there is no profit under the sun because the theme is about the worth of temporal things in light of the certainty of death. For the opening declaration, "All is vapor" (1:2), is followed by a poem which makes vivid the idea that though "one generation goes [death] and one generation comes [birth] . . . there is nothing new [no net gain or profit] under the sun" (1:4–9). And the closing declaration (12:8) that "All is vapor" follows a poem which makes vivid the reality of old age leading to death (12:2–7). Since we can take nothing with us when we die, everything we work for in this world is transitory like vapor, and thus ultimately profitless or worthless to us (see 5:15–16; cf. 2:13–16). In fact life itself is transitory like vapor to begin with (6:12; cf. Ps 144:4). In other words, in view of death, "all is vanity and a pursuit after wind, and there is no profit under the sun" (2:11; cf. 1:3).

The phrase "under the sun," used twenty-nine times in Ecclesiastes and nowhere else in the Bible, refers to this temporal world as opposed to the netherworld (see especially 4:15, where "the living" are described as "those who walk under the sun"; and 9:5–6, where "the dead" are said to "have no longer a share in all that is done under the sun"[3] (for further discussion, see "Interpretation of Ecclesiastes" under "The Meaning of 'Under the Sun'"). Hence there is no (ultimate) profit in this (temporal) world. It is thus futile for people to pursue temporal things as though the reality were otherwise.

Therefore in view of the reality that "all is vanity," it does not make sense (is meaningless) to pursue the things of this world and in the process fail to enjoy what we already have (4:4–8). Hence the most sensible (meaningful) thing to do is to have enjoyment in our life (2:24–26; 3:12–13; 5:18–20; 6:6; 7:14; 8:15; 9:9; 11:7–10). In fact, based on an elaborate experiment to find out "what is good . . . to do" (2:3), the Preacher concludes that "there is nothing good" apart from or except having enjoyment (2:24; 3:12, 22; 8:15). But to truly have enjoyment of life, we must avoid not only physical pain but also emotional anguish (11:10) so as to have a relatively carefree disposition (5:20). For how can we have enjoyment when we are full of cares?

Now even covetousness—violation of the last of the Ten Commandments—in and by itself already robs us of the carefreeness needed to have enjoyment (5:10; 6:7, 9). For a covetous heart is a restless heart. How much more when it also leads to cheating, stealing, adultery or even murder? In other words, because "all is vanity," the most meaningful thing to do in life is to fear God and keep his commandments. Hence the realization that "all is vanity" goads (12:11) us to "fear God and keep his commandments."

However, to be carefree does not mean to be careless. Because life is uncertain (see below)—even bad things can happen to good people (7:15–8:15)—we need to be careful and live by proverbial wisdom (7:1–14), which is not the same as being full of cares (9:10–11:6). It also does not mean we are to be complacent. Because death is

---

3. Cf. Seow, *Ecclesiastes*, 104–6.

certain, no matter how wise or righteous we are (9:1–3), we need to be proactive in doing what we have been called to do (9:10). And of course, what we are called to do has to be in line with "fear God and keep his commandments" (12:13), which we shall see is God's purpose for humanity, and he will judge everyone on this basis (12:14).

The Uncertainties of Life

When the theme expressed as "What profit is there?" is repeated for the first time (3:9), it sums up a poem with fourteen pairs of opposites which highlight not only the certainty of death but also the uncertainties of life: "There is . . . a time to be born, and a time to die . . . a time to weep, and a time to laugh . . . a time for war, and a time for peace" (3:1–8). The pairs of opposites show that what we gain in a positive experience ("a time for peace") may be lost in a negative experience ("a time for war"). And life is so uncertain that we may even lose everything we have before we die, and we may even die before we grow old. Thus "all is vanity" is to be viewed in light of not only the certainty of death but also the uncertainties of life. So this somber reality is relevant to even a young person in good health.

Since death and uncertainties are sovereignly appointed by God (3:1, 11a), there is another logical connection between "all is vanity" and "fear God and keep his commandments," and it also involves carefreeness and thus enjoyment of life (3:12–13). For "God so works that men (people) should fear him" (3:14b). This means, the certainty of death and the uncertainties of life, which result in "all is vanity" (1:2; 12:8), are designed by God to goad us to fear him and keep his commandments (12:13). Fearing God involves keeping his commandments because to fear God is to do what is right and not what is wrong (according to his commandments) even when no one, except God, is watching or holding us accountable to what we do or fail to do (see "Exposition of Ecclesiastes" on 5:1–7).

We saw how the realization that "all is vanity" goads us to fear God because in view of vanity, the sensible thing to do is to have enjoyment, which pre-requires a carefreeness that only the fear of God can bring. The realization of the certainty of death and especially the uncertainties of life itself, also goads us to fear God for a different reason—it burdens us with a sense of insecurity about the future. Unlike animals, "God has put eternity" in human hearts so that they can think about the past and the future. Their ability to think about the past causes them to recognize that the certainty of death and the uncertainties of life as depicted in the poem are both true. So their ability to think about the future causes them to feel insecure about the future.

In the ancient world people practised divination (to find out their future) and magic (to change their future if necessary) to feel secure. But one can neither find out nor change one's future (3:11b; 3:14a). Divination and magic gave them a false sense of security. Today, we seek to overcome this sense of insecurity by doing what is within our control such as buying insurance and having adequate savings for the "rainy days." But much is beyond our control. And so a gnawing sense of insecurity about the future persists and it creates chronic stress, which is not good for our health.

Medical sociologist Aaron Antonovsky propounded an approach to health known as *salutogenesis* (origins of health) to explain how and why certain people stay healthy. According to him and his followers, an important contributing factor to health is the ability to see this world as coherent and not chaotic and thus have "a strong sense of coherence [which] involves a perception of one's environment, inner and outer, as *predictable and comprehensible*."[4] However in reality, as highlighted in the poem, death is certain and life is uncertain regardless of whether one is righteous or wicked (this is graphically elaborated in 8:16–9:6). Thus good things can happen unexpectedly to bad people and bad things can happen unexpectedly to good people, including dying young and tragically (7:15–8:15). Even believers of God find this enigmatic. How then can one have the perception that one's inner and outer world is "predictable and comprehensible"?

According to Antonovsky, this "perception" is not primarily cognitive (based on reason) but rather affective (based on feeling). Thus even "frustration, failure, and pain [are] tolerable without vitiating a strong sense of coherence" if we somehow have "a sense [feeling] of control."[5] And to feel this way one need not be able to say, "I am in control" as long as one can say "things are under control."[6] For "The important thing is that one has a sense of confidence, of faith, that, by and large, things will work out well . . . as can reasonably be expected."[7] The control may be "located in a deity or in the hands of powerful others [like the government]."[8]

In other words, to "perceive" coherence in life, one need not be able to cognitively (logically) see that one's world is predictable and comprehensible as long as one is able to affectively (emotionally) feel a sense of security about the uncertain future because of "a sense of confidence, of faith" that "things are under control" and thus "things will work out well." This means we need to be able to feel as though we could see the world as predictable and comprehensible. How then do we cultivate this sense of confidence or faith?

Ecclesiastes presents the existence of a God who not only is all-powerful and is thus in control of everything that happens, whether good or bad (3:1, 11a), but is also just and fair and thus will not pervert justice (3:17; 8:11–13; 12:14). And our sense of insecurity about the future can only be adequately relieved by believing that this God is watching over us. For only then can we have the assurance that no bad things can happen to us unless God allows it. And when God allows it, we have the assurance that it is for a good (and thus meaningful) purpose because he is just and fair.

4. Antonovsky, *Health, Stress, and Coping*, 125 (italics added).
5. Antonovsky, *Health, Stress, and Coping*, 127.
6. Antonovsky, *Health, Stress, and Coping*, 155.
7. Antonovsky, *Health, Stress, and Coping*, 127.
8. Antonovsky, *Health, Stress, and Coping*, 155.

The New Testament even assures believers that "all things work together for good to those who love God, who are called according to his purpose" (Rom 8:28). Also in all circumstances God's grace is sufficient for them (2 Cor 12:9) so that they can bear with whatever that might happen to them (Phil 4:13). Hence one can feel secure about the uncertain future and thus be carefree and have enjoyment. This means to be truly carefree, it is not enough just to be not covetous. We need to actively believe in such a God and trust in him to watch over us; thus being not covetous has to be a by-product of this faith in God.

However, to be able to believe that such a God is *watching over us* (Ps 34:15; 1 Pet 3:12), we must first wholeheartedly believe that he exists and is *watching us* (Heb 11:6; Prov 15:3). And when we wholeheartedly believe in the existence of a God who is all-powerful and will not pervert justice, and that he is *watching us*, we will fear him—keep his commandments even when no one (except him) is watching us or holding us accountable (cf. Job 37:23–24). Otherwise we are living as though God does not even exist; how then can we believe in him and feel secure? Thus the uncertain future goads us to acknowledge God and to fear him. Hence this further explains how "God so works that men should fear him." But why has God designed the world and why does he work in this manner? Why is it necessary to "fear God and keep his commandments"?

The Certainty of Judgment

Two reasons are given in the speech. Firstly, "this is every man" (literal translation of 12:13b). The "this" refers to "fear God and keep his commandments" (12:13a). But "this is every man" makes no sense in English. The construction of this expression is similar to that of "I am [in] prayer" (Ps 109:4). According to Michael Fox, "The effect of this construction seems to be an intensification of the equation: Not only am I prayerful, I am prayer itself."[9] Similarly, "this is every man" means that "*this*—the fear of God and obedience to his commandments—is the substance . . . of every person."[10]

So "this"—fear God and keep his commandments—is the essence of humanity, the reason for human existence and thus the purpose of human life. In any case the most common translation of 12:13b, "this is the whole *duty* of man," though watered-down, already teaches that fearing God and keeping his commandments is the purpose of life, the observance of which every human being is accountable to God. This leads to the second reason why we need to fear God and keep his commandments: "For God will bring every deed into judgment, including every hidden thing, whether good or evil" (12:14). This judgment, based on how well we fulfill God's purpose for humanity by fearing him and keeping his commandments, covers "every deed" ever done, even "every hidden thing" (cf. Rom 2:16) that is "good" (cf. 2 Cor 5:10). And it is

9. Fox, *Time*, 362; cf. Goldingay, *Psalms 90–150*, 279.
10. Fox *Time*, 362.

declared after a poem on impending death (12:2–7). It has to refer at least partly, if not solely, to "a judgment after death"[11] (for an elaboration on this point, see "Exposition of Ecclesiastes" on 12:14).

Hence it will involve the final judgment at the end of history first revealed in the book of Daniel: "Many of those who sleep in the dust of the earth (the dead) shall awake (be resurrected), some [the wise and righteous] to everlasting life, while others to shame and everlasting contempt" (12:2; cf. Isa 66:22–24; Rev 20:11–21:8). Therefore *the end of life in this world is not the end of the whole story*.

However, "Surely there is not a righteous man on earth who does good and never sins" (7:20). Who then can pass such a stringent judgment at the end of the story and thus "awake . . . to everlasting life"? The Preacher did not seem concerned. Neither would his Old Testament audience unless they refused to repent of their sin and trust in God. For under the Mosaic covenant in the Old Testament, a sacrificial system was available specifically because it was (and still is) impossible for imperfect human beings to keep God's commandments perfectly. Those who sincerely feared God and repented of their sin and thus lived a reasonably righteous life would confess their sins and receive forgiveness through faith in God by offering the appropriate sacrifices (Num 5:5–10; cf. Ps 51:15–19). In this way, their overall righteous life, though not sinless, would pass the judgment. This means, though good deeds will characterize those who eventually pass the judgment, no one, no matter how sincere, can pass by doing good works.

Experiencing the Meaning of Life

Turning now to the question of the meaning of life, recall that the Preacher's speech is the product of an investigation into human life based on his personal experiences and observations. The investigation itself is "to inquire and to explore by wisdom everything that has been done under the heavens" (1:12). It is thus a comprehensive philosophical investigation to understand what human life everywhere in this world is all about.

In other words it is a quest for the meaning of life. And this quest is "a grievous preoccupation that God has given to the children of man with which to be preoccupied" (1:13; cf. 3:10). Since not all "children of man," but only some philosophers, would be preoccupied with such an investigation, it is actually an expression of a more basic God-given preoccupation that affects all humanity: the "relentless quest for meaning" propelled by the innate drive to "make sense of our world."[12]

The quest for the meaning of life is "a grievous preoccupation" because people are looking for the answer in the wrong places; a comprehensive philosophical investigation to find it will only end in "much grief" and "increasing pain" (1:12–18). The

11. Ginsburg, *Coheleth*, 478.
12. McGrath, *Glimpsing the Face of God*, 11, 13.

most common way people express, usually unconsciously, the grievous preoccupation is through the pursuit of pleasure and leisure (2:1–11), or of wealth and success (2:12–23), which may include power and popularity (4:13–16), or a combination of these. All these laborious pursuits are found to be futile in terms of finding the meaning of life. No matter how one expresses the preoccupation, sooner or later one realizes the grievous reality about human existence and earthly experience. And one will then have to come to terms with the inevitability of vanity in this world.

What then is the meaning of life according to Ecclesiastes, and how does one experience it? We will begin by answering the second part of the question first. For the thrust of Ecclesiastes is to teach us how to meet the two key conditions for experiencing the meaning of life.

Fulfilling the Purpose of Life

When the question "What is the meaning of life?" is asked, it usually means, "What is the purpose of life?" For it is a common human experience that our temporal life makes sense (has meaning) only if and when there is a worthwhile purpose to live for. One need not believe in God to recognize that this is a key condition for experiencing the meaning of life.

Atheist philosopher Paul Edwards in his classic essay on the meaning and value of human life argues that if we ask "whether life has any meaning" in terms of "whether there is a superhuman intelligence [read: God] that fashioned human beings along with other objects in the world to serve some end [a God-given purpose]," the answer is "negative." However if "we ask whether a particular person's life has or had any meaning" in terms of "whether certain purposes are to be found in his life" that he considered worthwhile, "most of us would say without hesitation that a person's life had meaning if we knew that he devoted himself to a cause (such as the spread of Christianity or communism or the reform of mental institutions)."[13]

In other words, though Edwards denies that there is such a thing as a God-given purpose of human life, he recognizes that one's life has meaning only when one has a worthwhile purpose and thus goal to live for. And to him one's goal can be considered "worth pursuing independently of any divine commandments."[14] However this means, "As long as I was a convinced Nazi (or communist or Christian or whatever) my life had meaning [even when] most of my actions were extremely harmful."[15] Consider "someone like [the Nazi] Adolf Eichmann—'While he was carrying out the extermination program, his life *seemed* worthwhile [and *was* thus meaningful] to him, but since his goal was so horrible, his life *was not* worthwhile.'"[16]

---

13. Edwards, "Meaning of Life," 351.
14. Edwards, "Meaning of Life," 352.
15. Edwards, "Meaning of Life," 352.
16. Edwards, "Meaning of Life," 353.

Edwards is arguing against fellow unbelieving philosophers: "Having rejected the claims of religion, they therefore conclude that life is not worthwhile and that it is devoid of meaning."[17] So he seeks to demonstrate that, even given the assumption that God and his purpose for humanity are neither relevant nor real, a human life can still be both meaningful and worthwhile. Yet he comes to the surprising conclusion that, like in the case of Eichmann, a life that is meaningful need not be a life that is worthwhile. This conclusion is consistent with the teaching of Ecclesiastes—indeed one's life can have meaning and yet is not worth living, and we will see that such a life is actually a direct consequence of living according to the assumption that there is no God.

Ecclesiastes teaches that we need *the*, not just *any*, worthwhile purpose to live for—fear God and keep his commandments. It is *the* purpose of life because we have seen that it is God's purpose for humanity, and that one day, God will judge humanity on that basis. It is the most *worthwhile* purpose because of the eternal consequences of that judgment. It has been found that though people living according to *any* "worthwhile" purpose that is short of *the* worthwhile purpose may indeed experience *a* meaning *in* life, it is far less meaningful than *the* meaning *of* life (see below under "Corroborating Empirical Evidence"). And as philosopher Keith Ward points out, "A human life can have meaning without an objective purpose, value, or pattern. We can construct our own values and purposes in a [supposedly] morally patternless world. . . . But if a set of religious beliefs is true, those who do not accept it, however meaningful their lives may seem to be, will indeed have missed the meaning of life."[18]

Even in temporal and material terms, fearing God and keeping his commandments matters as it enables us to be carefree and enjoy life and thus come to terms with the reality that "all is vanity." Consider what happens when we fail to come to terms with this reality. Fox explains why he translates the theme of Ecclesiastes as, "Everything is absurd": "In other words, 'toil' may be futile, but *the fact that* toil is futile is absurd."[19] So he recognizes that the Hebrew word he translates as "absurd" (when applied to toil) in and of itself does not mean "absurd," but rather "futile." However *the fact that* toil is futile evokes the reaction that it is absurd.

Why is there such a reaction? The reality that (in view of inevitable death) toil is futile is not acceptable to people who put their hopes in this world, which means most people living in the modern world. They thus have such a pessimistic reaction to the reality that "all is vanity" because they are unable to come to terms with it. Sooner or later they will realize that their life is not worth living. People living in the modern world, especially in somber moments, do find life meaningless if not absurd and thus not worth living. In fact, translating the theme as "Everything is meaningless" strikes a responsive chord in the heart of most people.

---

17. Edwards, "Meaning of Life," 346.
18. Ward, "Religion and Meaning," 29–30.
19. Fox, *Qohelet*, 31 (italics his).

Ecclesiastes goes so far as to teach that life is not worth living unless we have enjoyment through living a carefree life. For the Preacher repeatedly says that "there is nothing good" except to have enjoyment (2:24; 3:12; 3:22; 8:15). The reason is that we do not know what will happen in this world after we have died and therefore do not know what is good to do before we die except to have enjoyment (3:22; 6:12). For to know what is good or worthwhile to do in our lifetime, we need to know its final outcome in the long run, even long after our death.

It is not difficult to think of examples where in retrospect a supposed "bad thing" turns out to be a blessing in disguise, and a supposed "good thing" turns out to be a curse in disguise. We have seen enough of such examples that it should cause us to realize that what we think is a good thing for now may turn out to be a tragic thing, especially after we have died. In case we forget, the poem on the certainty of death and the uncertainties of life (3:1–8) should remind us.

Even then, what turns out to be a blessing in disguise in the "long run" may in the still longer run turn out to be otherwise. It is only in the "final run," which will be way beyond our death, that we will know whether it is truly a blessing in disguise. What then is good or worthwhile to do in our lifetime? To have enjoyment in what we do and what we have. There is nothing like having enjoyment. For regardless of what happens in the near or distant future, it is good—in light of "all is vanity," it is the meaningful or good thing to do and it gives us a good time.

However, though there is nothing good except to have enjoyment, it does not mean having enjoyment in itself is what makes life really worth living. For we saw that to have enjoyment in what we have and what we do, we need to first be carefree by fearing God and keeping his commandments. So having enjoyment is only an expression of a God-fearing life. When we fulfill God's purpose for humanity through such a life, it also gives us a sense of purpose and meaning that helps us cope with not only the uncertainties but also the difficulties of life.

Psychiatrist Viktor Frankl, who survived four German concentration camps, including Auschwitz, is fond of quoting Nietzsche: "He who has a *why* to live for can bear almost any *how*."[20] What more when the "why to live for" is God's very own purpose for humanity? Thus fearing God and keeping his commandments helps to make life worth living even in the face of adversities and hardship. Since this comes together with having enjoyment, it is another reason having enjoyment is good.

Actually we cannot depend on human perspectives to decide whether one's life is worth living. As we saw above, even an atheist philosopher like Edwards recognizes that the life of Adolf Eichmann "*was not* worthwhile" though it "*seemed* worthwhile to him." Edwards explains:

> One might perhaps distinguish between a "subjective" and an "objective" sense of "worthwhile." In the subjective sense, saying that a person's life is

---

20. Frankl, *Man's Search for Meaning*, 79.

worthwhile simply means that he is attached to some goals that he does not consider trivial and that these goals are attainable for him. In declaring that somebody's life is worthwhile in the objective sense, one is saying that he is attached to certain goals which are both attainable and of positive value [note: if God does not exist, who then decides what is "of positive value" based on objective—true for *everyone*—standards?].[21]

Thus a dictator who squanders his country's wealth through a life of extreme luxuries and wanton pleasures may, for these reasons, consider his life worth living. But even if his instruction for an exceptionally grand state funeral is followed through after he died (cf. 8:10), his subjective perspective that his life is worth living can be considered valid only if the end of his life is the end of the whole story. Ecclesiastes teaches that there is an objective criterion—what happens in the "final run" at the end of the whole story—to decide whether his life is indeed worth living. This criterion is God's final judgment of our life on the basis of how well we have fulfilled God's purpose for humanity in this world.

Evidently this criterion is applied in the case of the rich man who cannot enjoy even his wealth because of covetousness (6:1–9). His life is clearly one that does not please God, which results in him not having enjoyment in spite of his wealth. According to the perspectives of at least some people, his life on this account alone is already considered not worth living. But since we cannot judge based on subjective human perspectives, this cannot justify the Preacher saying that the rich man's life is not worth living to the extent that even if he fathers many children and lives for many years, the stillborn child is better off than he (6:1–3).

However, since in the Preacher's biblical view of the grand scheme of things there will be a final judgment and one in which the covetous rich man will not fare well, he can objectively say this man's life is not worth living—it is not good for one like him even to have been alive at all. This is significant, for it means that not being able to have enjoyment is a symptom that this man's life is not worth living. No wonder there is nothing good except to have enjoyment.

Hence whether life is worth living ultimately depends on how well one lives according to the one truly worthwhile purpose—fear God and keep his commandments. For in this scheme of things there is not only the most worthwhile *purpose* to fulfill but also the most worthwhile *goal* to achieve—to fare well in the final judgment and thus reap the eternal reward. Hence there is not only the purpose but also the goal of life to live for.

A superficial reading of this text (6:1–3) can make one think that the Preacher is not only pessimistic but also self-contradictory as he later says it is good to be alive (11:7–10). We have already resolved the apparent contradiction (see "Introduction to Ecclesiastes" under "Apparent Contradictions"). Now that we have taken a deeper and

---

21. Edwards, "Meaning of Life," 353.

more coherent look at the issue, we can see that he is clearly neither pessimistic nor self-contradictory.

This example serves to illustrate an important point. Given that Ecclesiastes is canonized as Scripture like Proverbs, we must not jump to conclusion that it is pessimistic and contradictory based on a superficial or incoherent reading of the speech. We need to adopt the humble attitude that if a text seems pessimistic or contradictory, it means we have not really understood it. Iain Provan, whose interpretation of Ecclesiastes is consistent with Ecclesiastes as Scripture, has cautioned that Ecclesiastes "is a book that grapples with reality, and reality is complex. Should the words of a wise man about reality not be difficult to simplify? . . . Yet commentator after commentator has agonized over the book as if *it*, rather than *they*, had a problem, because it is resistant to linear, systematic treatment."[22]

Perceiving Coherence in Life

Besides having a worthwhile purpose, there is another key condition for experiencing the meaning of life. As Ward puts it, "When people complain that life is meaningless, they often mean that they cannot see how the events that happen to them fit into any overall pattern. To see the meaning of a human life would be to see how its various elements fit into a unique, complex, and integrated pattern."[23] For "how people make sense of each other and the world they live in [involves] the activity of fitting something puzzling into a coherent pattern of mental representations that include concepts, beliefs, goals, and actions."[24] Ecclesiastes (1:12–18) confirms that even a comprehensive philosophical investigation *in and by itself* will not find "the key that will unify the whole of life."[25]

In other words, to experience the meaning of life not only must we have a truly worthwhile purpose to live for, but we must also be able to perceive how the different aspects of life, including the painful ones, cohere with one another and with that overall purpose of life. And Ecclesiastes (together with Job)—informed, shaped and supplemented by monotheistic revelation "given by one Shepherd"—offers the most satisfying teaching on how to meet this condition of perceiving coherence in life.

Every experience in temporal life, whether positive or negative, is represented in the poem that highlights the certainty of death and the uncertainties of life (3:1–8). For what is named in each of the fourteen pairs of opposites represents a range of events. For example, "a time to weep" refers not only to weeping itself, but also to the different painful events that make us cry. And "a time to laugh" includes not just laughing, but also all sorts of events that cause us to rejoice. Also, as already noted, the

---

22. Provan, *Ecclesiastes/Song of Songs*, 33–34 (italics added).
23. Ward, "Religion and Meaning," 22.
24. Thagard, *Coherence in Thought and Action*, xi.
25. Wright, "Interpretation of Ecclesiastes," 149.

poem shows that what is gained in a positive experience can be lost in a corresponding negative experience. Even if not, everything gained since birth will be eventually lost in death. Hence everything is ultimately profitless (3:9).

Thus every aspect of life coheres with one another resulting in "all is vanity." Ecclesiastes teaches that the sensible (consistent and thus coherent) response to "all is vanity" (theme of the speech) in light of the certainty of death is to have enjoyment through cultivating a carefree disposition by fearing God and keeping his commandments (conclusion of the speech). And being carefree is not being careless and complacent. For it also teaches that in response to "all is vanity," in light of the uncertainties of life we need to be careful in living a God-fearing life and be proactive in doing what we are called to do. Therefore (contra Wright)[26] God has already provided the key to perceive how every aspect of life coheres with one another as well as with the worthwhile purpose of life: fear God and keep his commandments.

Furthermore, Ecclesiastes also addresses head-on the thorny issue of undeserved suffering. Life is so uncertain that the widely observed principle "You reap what you sow" may seem to have failed, for even the righteous may suffer the consequences of the wicked (7:15; 8:14; cf. Job 1–2). This principle is not an iron-clad formula; it only *describes* the observed consequences, and not *prescribes* the deserved consequences, of how we live—it is observed the righteous will *likely* (but not always) prosper and wicked will *likely* (but not always) suffer. Now on our own it is indeed difficult, if at all possible, to perceive how undeserved suffering coheres with any worthwhile purpose of life. The teaching that "God so works that men (people) should fear him" (3:14b) does apply specifically to undeserved suffering. For God allows undeserved suffering so that humanity would (truly) fear him. Thus undeserved suffering does cohere with God's purpose for humanity. Why then is the reality of undeserved suffering needed so that people would truly fear God? We need to first understand what it means to truly fear God.

In the prologue of the book of Job, we read about Satan's rhetorical question in response to God praising how righteous Job was: "Does Job fear God for nothing?" (Job 1:9). Thus Satan was making the accusation that Job or any human being would fear God only because of what God gives ("for something"), and not because of who God is ("for nothing"). God then allowed Job to experience undeserved suffering to demonstrate that Job did indeed fear God for nothing, which means it is possible for a human being to fear God solely for who God is and not for what God gives.

This helps us perceive how undeserved suffering coheres with God's purpose for humanity. For Satan's accusation and Job's experience show that to truly fear God one has to fear God for nothing. Imagine what happens if God guarantees that everyone who fears him will always be blessed in temporal and material terms. Given fallen human nature there will then be few, if any, who truly fear God. For when people "fear" God for something, it is no longer the fear of God. So God has to do the wise though

---

26. Wright, "Interpretation of Ecclesiastes," 140.

painful thing of allowing the righteous to suffer and the wicked to prosper to avoid tempting people to "fear" God for temporal and material gains. Ecclesiastes 3:14b should therefore be understood as, "God so works that men (people) should fear him *for nothing.*"

Hence Job's undeserved suffering fits coherently into God's purpose for humanity: Fear God (for nothing) and keep his commandments. However God did not explain to Job himself the reason he suffered. What God did in response to Job's persistent challenge for an answer, besides affirming his justice, was to overwhelm Job with a deep sense that God is all-wise and all-powerful. This was all Job needed to hear. For if God is all-powerful, he can stop the suffering if he wants to; and if God is all-wise, he knows what he is doing in allowing and not stopping the suffering. Since God is just, it is for a good purpose. One like Job, who believes in the existence of such a God, should be able to have the assurance that eventually everything will turn out well and thus have the strength to bear with the suffering. Job was indeed satisfied with God's "answer" and was able to accept his tragic experience of undeserved suffering.

Job's experience provides an important lesson with respect to perceiving coherence in life. No doubt as we recall, Antonovsky says "a strong sense of coherence involves a perception of one's environment, inner and outer, as predictable and comprehensible." However, he then qualifies that one need not be able to logically see this coherence (a tacit admission that no one can) as long as one can emotionally sense that "things are under control" and that "things will work out well" and so feels secure about the future as though one could see it logically. In accepting God's "answer," Job was certainly assured that things were under control and would work out well and thus emotionally he had a sense of coherence though he could not comprehend logically why he suffered.

This means what really matters is not the logical but the emotional perception of coherence. This explains why neither Ecclesiastes nor Job on its own spells out how to perceive the coherence logically. We have to look at both books together to piece it together. They help us to see logically that unpredictability (uncertainties of life) and even undeserved suffering fit into a coherent whole with God's purpose for humanity. Thus Ecclesiastes together with Job enable us to see logically the world as coherent in terms of comprehensibility though not in terms of predictability itself, for while death is certain, life is uncertain or unpredictable.

No doubt it is helpful to be able to comprehend logically that the world is coherent. At least, when we are not suffering, it gives us the intellectual satisfaction that despite appearance, life is coherent and thus meaningful, and so enables us to give an intellectual answer to skeptics who argue that God does not exist because of the existence of suffering. However, when we are suffering, like in Job's case, what we really need is to be able to perceive (sense) coherence in life emotionally through submission to God and his purpose. To be able to see coherence in life logically only will not enable us to accept undeserved suffering when we are going through it.

In fact "God so works [at all times] that men should fear him." And when we yield to God's prodding to fear him, we can experience emotionally a sense of coherence and feel secure about the future, even if we are not yet able to see logically the coherence, by believing that God is both watching us and watching over us. We are then able to feel the coherence as though we can see it logically. This prepares us for undeserved suffering that may come our way. Of course, now that Ecclesiastes and Job have enabled us to perceive even logically that the world is indeed coherent, together with the emotional perception (sense) of coherence, we can experience the meaning of life even better.

Since what really matters is not the logical but emotional perception of coherence through living a life consistent with God's purpose, Ecclesiastes elaborates on how to respond sensibly to the uncertainties of life, including undeserved suffering, through living such a life. Midway through the speech, after summarizing the theme and sub-themes (6:10–12), the Preacher begins the next half on how one should live in response to the uncertainties of life with an anthology of relevant proverbs (7:1–14). He is indirectly saying that in view of inevitable uncertainties, we need to live by proverbial wisdom, which describes the *likely* consequences to our chosen way of life—"You (will likely) reap what you sow." And since "the fear of the LORD is the beginning of wisdom" (Prov 9:10), to live by proverbial wisdom one needs to fear God. This is the most sensible or consistent response. For if bad things can already happen to us no matter how we live, we will increase the likelihood of painful experiences if our chosen way of life by itself will *likely* bring painful consequences. The speech then moves on to focus on undeserved suffering (7:15–8:17), which is most often the consequence of human wickedness inherent in fallen humanity (7:29), before addressing how to thus live prudently in the social, political as well as economic contexts (9:1–11:6).

This means the first half of the speech focuses on being carefree by recognizing *divine sovereignty*. But, as already pointed out, being carefree does not mean being careless, for bad things can happen to even good people. So the second half focuses on being careful (but not full of cares) by exercising *human prudence* (7:11–12; 8:5–6; 9:10–11:6). Hence Ecclesiastes even teaches how to live with the biblical paradox of divine sovereignty (the focus of 3:1–15) and human responsibility (the focus of 9:10–11:6). Thus together with Job, Ecclesiastes has no rival when it comes to helping us perceive and experience coherence in life.

Coming back to undeserved suffering, since "You reap what you sow" is not an ironclad formula, the Preacher warns that it is not wise to go to the extreme of strenuously trying to become (outwardly) "righteous" to attain prosperity and avoid adversity (7:15–16), which is to "fear" God for "something," and in the process fail to enjoy our life (8:14–15). On the other hand, it is also not wise to go to the other extreme of allowing our inherent wickedness (7:20) to be unrestrained and thus increase the likelihood of disaster (7:17). Living by proverbial wisdom out of a genuine fear of God will help to avoid either extreme (7:18). Thus the teaching on how to respond to the uncertainties of life in general—living by proverbial wisdom—applies specifically to undeserved suffering as well.

We have so far considered why God allows undeserved suffering and how this fits coherently with God's purpose for humanity—to fear him and keep his commandments. But the uncertainties of life are such that not only the righteous may suffer, but also the wicked may prosper. How does undeserved prosperity fit into God's plan? Again, "God so works that men should fear him (for nothing)" (3:14b). When the wicked are seen to prosper and do not receive what their wickedness deserves, especially even by the time they die (8:10), our hearts cry out for a final accounting after their death (12:14; see below under "Experiencing a Sense of Closure to History"). This means that there must also be a final accounting for our own sins. Then our hearts should also cry out against our sins and drive us to fear God and keep his commandments. So even undeserved prosperity fits coherently with God's purpose for humanity.

To sum up, Ecclesiastes teaches us how to live sensibly and consistently, and thus coherently, in (realistic) response to "All is vanity," and so experience the meaning of life.

Corroborating Empirical Evidence

A dissertation by S. G. Tan accepted by the University of Bangor put the teaching of Ecclesiastes on the meaning of life to the test by seeking to find out whether it can be corroborated by actual human experience.[27] Extensive empirical data were collected from intensive interviews with people (referred to as "research participants" or RPs) who thought they had found the meaning of life.

Since suffering and wealth are crucial issues in Ecclesiastes, qualified RPs must also have had experienced significant suffering in their life and were financially independent (no longer need to work for the necessities of life). To limit the number of variables, potential RPs were confined to ethnic Chinese Malaysian businesspeople who were married. From a shortlist of twenty-seven potential RPs, thirteen accepted the invitation to be interviewed.[28]

In accepting to be a RP, one needed to complete the Meaning in Life Questionnaire (MLQ), copyrighted by the University of Minnesota. A high MLQ score may indicate that a person has indeed found the meaning of life and serves as an initial screening process to identify people who are likely to have found the meaning of life. The need to complete this questionnaire may be one reason why the other fourteen potential RPs declined the invitation, for in completing the MLQ one could already anticipate a low score and thus this may have helped to filter out those who did not

27. Tan, "Empirically Corroborated Theology."
28. Tan, "Empirically Corroborated Theology," 173.

qualify. Of the thirteen, eleven had high scores while the other two technically did not qualify but were interviewed nonetheless. Among the eleven with high scores, there were seven Christians (two females), two Buddhists and two with no religion (all male). Of the two with low scores, one was a Christian (male) and the other Buddhist (female).

For the purpose of this research, the teaching of Ecclesiastes was translated into categories that are applicable to people of a different or no religion. Most significant is what it means to "(fear God and) keep his commandments," which is the purpose of life. The Bible itself summarizes the commandments of God into loving God and loving one's neighbor as oneself (Lev 19:18; Deut 6:5; Matt 22:37–40), which are in turn summarized into the golden rule (Matt 7:12; cf. Rom 13:8–10; Gal 5:14)—do to others what you want others do to you.

The golden rule, especially the negative version—do not do to others what you do not want others do to you—is taught in virtually every religion[29] and accepted by even atheists.[30] When put into practice as the purpose of life, the golden rule as taught in the Bible and assumed in Ecclesiastes is about living a life to serve humanity in fulfilling a calling and not pursuing a career (see "Exposition of Ecclesiastes" on 9:10). So a crucial criterion in deciding whether one has found the meaning of life is whether one has given one's life to serve others. This is the criterion used in the dissertation.[31]

The collected data show that the eleven with high MLQ scores have indeed found the meaning of life based on adequate observance of the golden rule as the purpose of their life. And based on this criterion the two with low MLQ scores indeed have not found the meaning of life though they think they have.

All the eleven with high MLQ scores experienced a transition from living according to "*a* purpose *in* life" (which varies among them but are all self-centered) to living according to "*the* purpose *of* life" (which is based on the golden rule and is thus others-centered). They all now live a life that they find highly meaningful.

Among the seven Christians there are two categories. The first category consisting of four of them consider their life prior to the transition meaningless—three make this assessment only in retrospect (they thought it was meaningful then but changed their view in light of their new found experience of true meaningfulness).

In contrast, the other three in the second category still consider their previous experience of life as meaningful but since the transition, they find their life much more meaningful.[32] The earlier experiences were, and still are, considered meaningful because they were purposeful though self-centered (a man pursuing happiness as a reaction to childhood poverty and hardship), or not exactly others-centered (a man seeking to be successful so as to give a better life to his mother, a widow who had

29. Neusner and Chilton, *Golden Rule*.
30. Epstein, *Good Without God*.
31. Tan, "Empirically Corroborated Theology," 252.
32. Tan, "Empirically Corroborated Theology," 204–8.

raised him and his siblings through hardship). These purposes can be experienced as meaningful but fall short of the purpose of life—to live for others unconditionally. In the case of these Christian RPs the transition involved turning from living for self to living for God and thus for others.

We surmise that in most cases, Christians who have found the meaning of life are like the four who can only testify that before they began to live according to the purpose of life, their life was meaningless. We cannot compare a person who lives for "a purpose in life" with another who lives for "the purpose of life" and then evaluate whether the latter is more meaningful than the former; comparing the experiences of different people is too subjective. But the empirical data in this research are able to compare the experience of the same person, who can testify that based on his own experience, living according to the purpose of life is found to be far superior in meaningfulness than living according to a purpose in life that falls short of the purpose of life.

A similar pattern is also found in the case of the two Buddhists and one of the two non-religious RPs who had high MLQ scores.[33] Hence the empirical data find six who can testify that living according to the purpose of life is significantly more meaningful than living according to any other purpose. The crucial difference is that in the cases of the Christian RPs the transition from "a purpose in life" to "the purpose of life" was triggered by a crisis of some sort that resulted in them no longer living for self but instead for God and thus for others. Their experiences illustrate more explicitly the teaching that "God so works that men should fear him."

As for the two Buddhists the transition was a result of gradually embracing a way of life that is consistent with the Buddhist teaching of *Dharma*, in particular the law of *Karma*, which is the Buddhist expression of the "You reap what you sow" principle. Similarly, the two non-religious RPs experienced the transition through gradually embracing a way of life that is consistent with the "You reap what you sow" principle. The experiences of these four illustrate implicitly that "God so works that men should fear him" because, according to the book of Proverbs, it was God who implanted the "You reap what you sow" principle into the world when he created it. All this means human experience testifies to the reality of *the* purpose and thus *the* meaning *of* life.

The dissertation also considers the impact of living according to the purpose of life on one's view of suffering and one's experience of work. Based on the data collected, it is found that almost all RPs had painful experiences both before and after their transition from "a purpose in life" to "the purpose of life." They were able to cope better after the transition because they could find meaning in their suffering by drawing lessons from it as well as giving a reason for it (the Christians) or at least interpreting it (the non-Christians).

Interestingly the Christians give virtually the same reason for their suffering before and after the transition because they are able to view even their past suffering

---

33. Tan, "Empirically Corroborated Theology," 220–23, 229–31.

in light of their new purpose for living. This means in retrospect they can see meaning even in their previous suffering. And all of them, Christians and non-Christians, also find work more meaningful and thus more satisfying and enjoyable as it is now about fulfilling a calling consistent with the purpose of life. Hence they not only have found the purpose of life, but have also experienced a sense of coherence in life.[34] No wonder even those who had previously experienced meaning in life have found life to be significantly more meaningful than before.

In contrast to the RPs who had high MLQ scores and are confirmed to have found the meaning of life, it turns out that the two with low scores (a Christian and a Buddhist) indeed did not experience a transition from "a purpose in life" to "the purpose of life" and have not experienced a significant increase in meaningfulness to their life. And there is no corresponding change in their view of suffering and their experience of work.

Tan attributes the impact of the change from "a purpose in life" to "the purpose of life" on one's view of suffering and experience of work to the corresponding change in their view of life, which "represents what is most important about life, undergirded by a certain worldview about life and existence."[35] For the Christian and Buddhist RPs who have found the meaning of life, their view of life is changed to one that is consistent with their respective religions. For the two RPs with no religious beliefs, there is also a change in their view of life. In one case the change is expressed through taking seriously the "You reap what you sow" principle, which resulted in him wanting to live an ethical life through helping others. In the other case it is a change from a self-centered to an others-centered view of life, which is actually another expression of taking seriously the "You reap what you sow" principle.

Based on the experience of Job discussed above, the RPs who found the meaning of life when they changed their view of life experienced a sense of coherence not necessarily because they could cognitively (logically) see how their suffering fits into a coherent whole. It depends on whether their respective religions have the resources to enable them to see it. Even Job, who did not have the resources we now have in the Bible, could not see it.

The Christians RPs could give a reason for their suffering but not the one we have derived from Ecclesiastes and Job, which is, so that we should fear God for nothing. Their reasons are in line with that given by Job's fourth friend (Elihu), which is, to discipline Job to prevent him from committing a sin so serious that it might bring a consequence as severe as premature death (Job 33:12–22). This reason for undeserved suffering—to save us from experiencing a more severe (deserved) suffering—is a sensible answer to the question of undeserved suffering and helps us see how it fits into God's purpose for humanity. And it is taught in the New Testament (see Heb 5:8; 12:4–11).

---

34. Tan, "Empirically Corroborated Theology," 263–65.
35. Tan, "Empirically Corroborated Theology," 254.

There is no indication that the non-Christian RPs who found the meaning of life gave this or an equivalent reason for their suffering. Thus it confirms that one need not be able to logically see coherence to have a sense of coherence as long as they have a change in their view of life that resulted in a change from "a purpose in life" to "the purpose of life."

According to Tan, the need for a change in one's view of life in order to find the meaning of life is confirmed by the fact that in most of the cases, the transition from "a purpose in life" to "the purpose of life" happened long after the RPs concerned had "converted" to their respective religions. And the case of the Christian and the Buddhist who have not found the meaning of life confirms that merely adhering to a religion without a change in one's view of life to one consistent with the religion will not result in the crucial change in one's purpose for living and thus way of life.

The question then arises: Why would one not truly hold—and not just profess—a view of life consistent with one's religion? The obvious answer is that one cannot truly change one's view of life without changing one's way of life, and vice-versa. So the basic problem is the lack of commitment to live a life consistent with the teachings of one's religion (or conscience, in the case of non-religious people).

In the case of the Christian RPs, the change in their view and way of life came as a result of a crisis in life. This explains why the Preacher in Ecclesiastes uses the vanity of life (as a result of the certainty of death and uncertainties of life, including the reality of undeserved suffering) to persuade his religious audience to commit themselves to fear God and keep his commandments. He goes so far as to explain that "God so works that men should fear him," that is, God has in fact been using the vanity of life, especially during times of crisis, to prod them to live a life consistent with what they profess to know about God.

To sum up, Tan's dissertation has corroborated, albeit based on a limited scale of empirical evidence, the teaching of Ecclesiastes on the meaning of life, especially with respect to the purpose of life (for details, including the testimonies of the RPs in their own words, see Tan's dissertation).[36] For Bible believers who accept Ecclesiastes as Scripture inspired by God, there is really no need for corroborating empirical evidence to help them believe that Ecclesiastes is indeed teaching the truth. However, the real-life testimonies of people who live out the truth taught in Ecclesiastes serve as heart-warming illustrations to help them better appreciate the authoritative truth of Scripture.

Perhaps we should reflect on how surprisingly relevant Ecclesiastes is to the modern world. In fact the very theme of Ecclesiastes—"All is vanity"—as applied to the pursuit of the things of this world in search for the meaning of life is particularly modern. In the ancient world, it was directly relevant to only the Preacher's target audience, who consisted of the elites like powerful court officials (8:1–7; 10:4–7). They

---

36. Tan, "Empirically Corroborated Theology," 196–271; an electronic copy of the entire dissertation is available online (http://e.bangor.ac.uk/9822).

were the socio-economic equivalent to the modern "middle class," who treat their occupation as a "career"—a means to pursue socio-economic advancement. The very concept of a "career" is exclusively modern. It is as though the Preacher anticipated the modern way of life.

Excursus: Secular Psychology on the Meaning of Life

Before moving on we take note that "two recent works in the field of psychology have categorized research about the meaning of life into a threefold scheme comprised of 'coherence,' 'purpose,' and 'significance.'"[37] According to this scheme, "'Coherence' refers to the human's cognitive comprehension of life, as life 'makes sense' because predictable and recognizable patterns [of cause and effect] are discernable within it";[38] "significance in life . . . refers to its worth or value, answering the question, 'Is life worth living?'";[39] and as for "'purpose,' [it] arises when life has a future, overarching goal. This goal gives direction to life and bears significance for present activities, so that to say 'my life has purpose' amounts to saying 'my life has meaning.'"[40]

These works corroborate to some extent our interpretation of Ecclesiastes with respect to its teaching on the meaning of life. It shows that recent research in psychology on the meaning of life is moving toward the teaching of Ecclesiastes on this subject. As we have seen, "purpose," "coherence" and "significance" (whether life is worth living) are also categories that we have used to explore what Ecclesiastes has to say about the meaning of life. The question then is how these categories are defined and applied.

The definition of "purpose" in terms of a future goal that "bears significance for present activities" is generic and cannot be disputed. However, to experience meaning that is significant, the goal and thus the purpose must be "worthwhile." We have shown that Ecclesiastes teaches that there is only one truly worthwhile purpose and goal, which involves fearing God and keeping his commandments. Since our concern is the teaching of Ecclesiastes on the meaning of life, we will not get into a debate with philosophers and psychologists who insist that there is no such thing as "*the* worthwhile purpose" and hence "*the* meaning *of* life" (see above on empirical evidence that corroborates this teaching of Ecclesiastes).

The psychological definition of "coherence" in terms of "predictable and recognizable patterns" as presented by Keefer overlaps with but differs from that of Ward cited above: "To see the meaning of a human life would be to see how its various elements fit into a unique, complex, and integrated pattern." It overlaps in terms of

---

37. Keefer, "Meaning of Life," 450; referring to Martela and Steger, "Meaning in Life"; George and Park, "Meaning in Life."
38. Keefer, "Meaning of Life," 450.
39. Keefer, "Meaning of Life," 455.
40. Keefer, "Meaning of Life," 450.

seeing "recognizable patterns" compared with Ward's "integrated pattern." It differs in terms of "patterns" (plural) versus "pattern" (singular). If we can only see "patterns" and not a "pattern," we still do not see life as an integrated whole. The coherence is thus limited.

And it differs more significantly with Ward's definition in that it requires the pattern(s) to be "predictable," which requires life to be predictable. We have seen that Ward's definition of coherence is consistent with the teaching of Ecclesiastes. If coherence is defined in terms of predictability, Ecclesiastes is saying life is not coherent and thus not meaningful because it stresses the uncertainties or unpredictability of life.[41] It will then imply that Ecclesiastes is pessimistic.

However, uncertainties or unpredictability of life is an observed reality. So even if we define coherence in terms of predictability, the view that life lacks coherence (predictability) and thus lacks meaning is still realistic, and not pessimistic as it is consistent with observed reality. But human beings have difficulties accepting this reality because an unpredictable world will be seen as a chaotic and not coherent world. No one is at peace with a chaotic world. Apparently the psychologists define "coherence" in terms of "predictability" because human beings do have a need to see cognitively (logically) the world as predictable and thus not chaotic to make sense of life. But since this is not possible, many find life meaningless for this reason.

Since "God so works that men should fear him" (3:14b), the unfulfilled need to see logically the world as predictable is meant to prod us to acknowledge and fear God. For the world is unpredictable only to us, certainly not to God, who holds the future. So when we fear and trust in God, who watches over us, we can live as though the world is predictable. We can then experience a sense of coherence and thus meaning despite the unpredictability of life.

Furthermore, we have also seen that Ecclesiastes together with Job show how the uncertainties of life, even undeserved suffering, fit coherently and thus comprehensibly into one "integrated pattern" with God's purpose for humanity. Since this (logical) coherence incorporates the uncertainties of life, we can still logically see the world as coherent and comprehensible despite the unpredictability of life. This then soothes even our apparent need to see logically this world as predictable because what we actually need to see is not that this world is predictable, but that it is coherent and comprehensible.

As for the meaning of "significance" in life, defined in terms of whether life is worth living, we saw that it correlates with the purpose of life and is hence relevant to experiencing the meaning of life. But it has been argued that, since "'significance' refers to life's value or worthwhileness, wherein factors past, present, or future generate a life that 'matters,'"[42] it is distinct from though it overlaps with purpose. Thus, "significance evaluates life as a whole—past, present, and future—while purpose

41. Cf. Keefer, "Meaning of Life," 449, 452–55.
42. Keefer, "Meaning of Life," 450.

focuses on the future alone and serves as a motivation for life."[43] So then, even without a present worthwhile purpose, one can still have significance based on one's past. This means who we are or what we have accomplished, like having won the Nobel Prize, can independently make life worth living regardless of our current purpose for living.

However we saw that, since we do not know what will happen in this world after we have died, we do not actually know what is really good or worthwhile in our lifetime, including winning the Nobel Prize. Also we saw that in light of the final judgment, life is not worth living unless we live according to God's purpose for humanity, which is the most, and only, worthwhile purpose to live for. This is true regardless of whatever "factors past, present or future" that may seem to "generate a life that 'matters.'"

Hence significance is not independent of purpose and is thus not a separate condition for experiencing the meaning of life. In fact separating significance from purpose can mislead us into thinking that a life that is not consistent with God's purpose can still be worthwhile. So defining and applying "significance" as a condition separate from purpose can have far-reaching consequences.

Experiencing the Meaning of History

We have so far only considered the two key conditions—having a worthwhile purpose of life and perceiving coherence in life—for experiencing the meaning of life and how both are met in "fear God and keep his commandments." But we have not actually answered the question, "What is the meaning of life?" that is, What is life really all about? And this involves making sense of our life taken as a whole, from birth to death, not just making sense of it in terms of the different aspects of life, which is what we have done so far. Is "fear God and keep his commandments" still the answer?

Our life taken as a whole, as expressed in the first poem (1:4–8) and echoed in the second poem (3:1–8), is one extended story-shaped event that is part of a very much larger story we call history: "A generation goes [death, end of a life story] and a generation comes [birth, beginning of a life story], yet the world remains as ever [history goes on as before]" (1:4; 3:2). History will go on as before because it will in one sense repeat itself: "Whatever has happened, that is what will happen; whatever has been done, that is what will be done; there is nothing new under the sun" (1:9). This sub-theme, introduced in reference to the first poem, is reiterated in reference to the second poem as "Whatever comes to be, has already been; that which will come to be, already has been; for God seeks what has gone by" (3:15).

In the context of the first poem, the focus is that in spite of the repeated cycles of one generation being replaced by another, "there is nothing new" in the sense that there is no net gain (or profit) because basic realities in the natural and human world

---

43. Keefer, "Meaning of Life," 451.

remain as ever. The second poem is about the certainty of death and the uncertainties of life: "A time to be born, and a time to die . . . A time to love, and a time to hate; a time for war, and a time for peace" (3:2–8). In other words, the reality of the certainty of death and the uncertainties of life as depicted in this poem will repeat itself and thus narrows down in what sense history repeats itself.

In other words, the Preacher affirms that "there is nothing new" and thus "history repeats itself" based on the observation that through the ages, humanity and how they respond to circumstances (whether with love or hate) remain essentially the same. In fact the circumstances themselves (whether it is a war fought with arrows, swords or guns) remain essentially the same. The specific form of the circumstances and the corresponding responses may be different, but they are all expressions of the same essence. It is in this sense that history will go on as before, repeating itself.

Now, if history keeps going on like this without end, it will have serious implications on the meaning of life. So we need a proper interpretation of the Preacher's conclusion that "there is nothing new under the sun." According to Crenshaw, the Preacher contradicts the prophets of Israel "who envisioned things wholly new."[44] The prophets indeed envisioned new things: the establishment of the new covenant, which assumed a new heart (Jer 31:31–34); the promise of a new heart as well as a new spirit (Ezek 36:26); the new exodus (Isa 11:11–16); and at the end of history, the new Jerusalem and the new heavens and the new earth (Isa 65:17–25). These are all about a new work of God to redeem humanity.

However the Preacher is only saying that, *based on observation*, in spite of the repeated replacement of one generation by a "new" generation, natural phenomena *as God created it* and human phenomena *as we know it* have not changed essentially, which implies that human nature has not changed—it is covetous as ever. The Preacher does teach that natural and human phenomena cannot be changed *by humans* (6:10). He never says that God the Creator cannot change them. Why would anyone assume that the God who is powerful enough to create all things is not powerful enough to change what he has created? Thus Ecclesiastes does not exclude the possibility of God himself doing something really new to his creation.

In fact it is precisely because humanity and how humans behave have not changed, and cannot be changed apart from God's intervention, that the prophets envisioned God himself doing something new, even creating a new humanity in a new world through a new work. Hence Ecclesiastes is in effect demonstrating why what the prophets envisioned is necessary. Thus, though history repeats itself, it will not go on *forever*, but is moving toward a goal at the end of history as envisioned by the prophets. And we saw that in the last verse of Ecclesiastes the Preacher himself highlights the final judgment as envisioned by the prophet Daniel. In other words, the Preacher affirms the Old Testament's linear-cyclical view of history—it is flowing in a cyclical

---

44. Crenshaw, *Qoheleth*, 6; cf. Krüger, *Qoheleth*, 25–26.

manner toward an ultimate goal (see "Exposition of Ecclesiastes" under "Excursus to 1:4–11"). What then are the implications on the meaning of life?

Returning now to answer the above questions—What is the meaning of life? What is life really all about?—we need to consider the meaning or significance of our individual life story (from birth to death) taken as a whole as an (extended) event. And "To ask about the meaning or significance of an event is to ask how it contributed to the conclusion of the episode [or story, of which the event is a part]."[45] We need to consider the conclusion or end of the story because, "The ending is a necessary part of the story, notwithstanding its open-endedness; it is not a dispensable part. It affects proleptically every part of the story; no part can be considered apart from it. . . . Regardless of how unexpected or incongruent the end of a story is, it is decisive for the story's meaning."[46]

This is why the meaning or significance (if any) of a scene in a movie depends on how the movie ends. In fact the focus of Ecclesiastes is on the meaning or significance of events in our life in view of how our life ends in this world. The answer turns out to be, "all is vanity." But since death in this world is not the end of the whole story, death is not the goal of life and thus "all is vanity" is not the final verdict on the meaning of one's life; for that we need to wait till the end of history.

Contributing to the Purpose and Goal of History

In other words, the meaning of life is found in how our individual life story contributes to the purpose as well as to the goal of human history. And needless to add, as far as Ecclesiastes is concerned, "human history" is the history of the world as presented in the Bible—from the very beginning, the creation of the present universe (Genesis 1–2), to the goal of the (re)creation of the new heavens and the new earth at the end (Isa 65:17–25; Revelation 21–22).

In fact the Preacher assumes this history as a backdrop to his speech. For he alludes to the *beginning* of the world—the Creation and Fall of humanity as taught in Genesis 1–3: "God made (hu)man(ity) upright, but they have sought out many schemes" (7:29). And we saw that he also alludes to God's final judgment of humanity at the *end* of history as revealed in Daniel 12, which is related to the creation of the new heavens and the new earth. He even uses this judgment as a reason for exhorting his audience to "fear God and keep his commandments" (12:13b–14).

Since Ecclesiastes teaches that "God so works [in history] that men (people) should fear him" (3:14b), the *purpose* of history is so that people of all nations would fear him and keep his commandments (cf. Matt 28:18–20). And the Bible, of which Ecclesiastes is a part, reveals how this purpose has been and will be worked out in

---

45. Polkinghorne, *Narrative Knowing*, 6.

46. Mostert, "Theodicy and Eschatology," 106; cited in Seachris, "Proleptic Power of Narrative Ending," 146–47.

history through God fulfilling his promises (see Leong).[47] So by fearing God and keeping his commandments, our life story coheres with and thus contributes *passively* to the purpose of history in the sense that the purpose is being fulfilled *in* us. And if we seek to help others to also fear God and keep his commandments, our life story contributes *actively* to the purpose of history in the sense that the purpose is being fulfilled in others *through* us.

We have also noted that the *goal* of history is the establishment of the new heavens and the new earth, "in which righteousness dwells" (2 Pet 3:13; cf. Rev 21:27). This means, when the goal of history is reached, God's purpose for humanity to fear him and thus become righteous through keeping his commandments will be perfectly accomplished. Therefore by fearing God and keeping his commandments, our life story also contributes *passively* to the goal of history in the sense that the goal will be fulfilled *in* us. And our life story likewise contributes *actively* to the goal of history if we seek to help others to also fear God and keep his commandments in the sense that this goal will be fulfilled in others *through* us.

Hence, the admonition "fear God and keep his commandments" is the key to how our life story contributes, whether actively or passively, to both the purpose as well as the goal of history. Obviously a life story that contributes not only passively but also actively to the purpose and goal of history is more meaningful than one that contributes only passively. And one that does not even contribute passively (does not fear God and keep his commandments) not only will suffer temporal consequences due to the "You reap what you sow" principle, but is also out-of-sync with the purpose and goal of history and so suffer eternal consequences.

Hence it does not make sense (is meaningless) for a life story to disregard this admonition. We have seen earlier that the purpose of humanity is to observe this admonition. Since the goal of history is that this purpose be perfectly accomplished in humanity, we now see that the goal of history is also the goal of humanity. So to fear God and keep his commandments is the purpose of human life in this world which leads to the goal of human life beyond this world. The purpose and goal of human life then answers the questions, What is life really all about? and What is the meaning of life? Therefore the admonition is not just about how to experience the meaning of life; it also expresses the very meaning of life itself. No wonder, to "fear God and keep his commandments" is the essence of every human being (12:13b).

Now the purpose and the goal of history together answer the question, What is history all about? just as the purpose and goal of human life answer the question, What is life all about? Thus the purpose and goal of history constitute the meaning of history. "It is not by chance that we use the words 'meaning' and 'purpose' interchangeably, for it is mainly purpose which constitutes meaning for us. . . . History . . . is meaningful only by indicating some transcendent purpose beyond the actual

---

47. Leong, *Our Reason for Hope*.

facts. But since history is a movement in time, the purpose is a goal."⁴⁸ Put differently, "In order for history to have significance, it must have a goal. Without a purpose or goal, neither history nor individual human lives can have significance."⁴⁹ This means the meaning of life is interwoven with the meaning of history as the purpose and goal of life are the same as the purpose and goal of history. And to "fear God and keep his commandments" is indispensable to experiencing not only the meaning of life but also the meaning of history.

Even secular philosophy of history pays attention to the meaning of history in terms of the purpose and goal of history. For "Philosophers have raised questions about the meaning and structure of the totality of human history. Some philosophers have sought to discover a large organizing theme, meaning, or *direction* [implying goal] in human history.... The ambition in each case is to demonstrate that the apparent contingency and arbitrariness of historical events can be related to a more fundamental underlying *purpose* or order."⁵⁰

Such philosophers are labelled "speculative philosophers" and their theories of history are evaluated as "speculative philosophies." As W. H. Walsh puts it, though they

> claimed that their conclusions rest on fact..., it is all too clear that their reading of fact is by no means compulsive. The charge that they pick their facts to suit their thesis is hard to avoid: in their work we are apt to find tremendous emphasis laid on certain happenings which fit in conveniently with their theory, whilst others which are less convenient go unmentioned.... The sea of fact is apparently so vast that it is always possible to fish up some fact or other to support no matter how extravagant a view.⁵¹

Hence, "No matter how much data Hegel, Marx, Spengler, Toynbee, and the rest may appeal to, in the final analysis, their theories are *imposed upon* history, not *derived from* it."⁵² This has to be the case—the Preacher disclaims that one can discover the purpose and goal of history by merely observing history (1:13; 3:10–11; 6:12; 7:14). They would, and in fact have, come up with conflicting and confusing opinions (Nash

---

48. Löwith, *Meaning in History*, 5.

49. Nash, *Meaning of History*, 38.

50. Little, "Philosophy of History" (italics added). Jörn Stückrath has shown that "the modern expression 'meaning *(Sinn)* of history' (in the sense of 'purpose,' 'goal,' 'value' of history)" has a relatively recent origin; it "can barely be traced back in the German language further than the mid nineteenth century" (Stückrath, "Meaning of History," 65, 72). Though the expression "meaning of history" itself is recent, the concept of the purpose/goal/value of history is ancient; historians have rightly applied the expression to the historical thought of even Augustine. We do not include "value" in our conception of the "meaning of history" because it is subsumed in the "purpose" and "goal." For the purpose and goal of history that we have in mind are worthwhile, thus giving "value" to history.

51. Walsh, "Meaning in History," 305.

52. Nash, *Meaning of History*, 59.

shows how Toynbee, in the course of writing his twelve-volume study of history, changed his view on the meaning of history twice).[53]

The purpose and goal of history, if they exist, have to be revealed by the Creator, the God of history. For to speculate on the goal of history even based on (selected) historical facts necessarily means that the final end of history is merely a projection into a future that is still within this world. Such a goal cannot stand scrutiny. This is particularly the case of speculative theories of history promoting the secular doctrine of "progress."[54] This belief is "a secularization of the Christian view of history," a belief that "eventually, according to many versions, man would attain a state of unparalleled happiness [in] a form of utopia at the climax of history."[55] Though the belief in "progress" is now discredited and discarded,[56] we do well to consider its implication for our personal experience of the meaning of history so that we may appreciate the necessity of a goal of history based on revelation.

For even if history does eventually "progress" to the secular utopia envisioned, only that future generation of humanity gets to share in the blessing. And "there is a serious moral objection to the whole notion of progress.... Individuals at the earlier stages are treated not as ends in themselves, but as means to the end of human improvement.... Even when it manages to generate hope, the idea of progress confines the realization of hope to others [a future generation]."[57] "Thus the religion of progress regards all the generations and epochs that have been as devoid of intrinsic value, purpose or significance, as the mere means and instruments to the ultimate goal."[58] "However, as long as men live, justice will demand that those of every generation shall be able to fulfill their historic destiny and share in the meaning of history. To satisfy the cravings of the human soul, the consummation of history must lie beyond history in the new heaven and the new earth, so that those of all ages may share in its glory."[59]

The Preacher claims that what he teaches, which we saw includes the creation of the world and the final judgment of humanity, is "given by one Shepherd," that is, the Creator God—his teaching is based on revelation. So unlike speculative philosophies, the Preacher did not come up with his teaching on the purpose and goal of history by analysing historical data; as just pointed out, he even disclaims it can be done. And

---

53. Nash, *Meaning of History*, 138–39.

54. According to Stückrath, "it was Herman Lotze who introduced the expression 'meaning *(Sinn)* of history' into the philosophical discourse." And the expression "enters the philosophical discourse within the critique of knowledge ... in the skeptical remark that 'God alone understands the meaning *(Sinn)* of history.'... The emergence of the metaphysical term *Sinn*, then, is [a] critique of a philosophy of history that attempts to determine it metaphysically with the aid of the idea of progress" (Stückrath, "Meaning of History," 75, 79).

55. Bebbington, *Patterns in History*, 68, 69.

56. Nash, *Meaning of History*, 85, 87.

57. Bebbington, *Patterns in History*, 91.

58. Berdyaev, *Meaning of History*, 189.

59. Newport, *Life's Ultimate Questions*, 60; cited in Nash, *Meaning of History*, 82.

as already noted, we can test whether the Preacher's claim to revelation is credible by considering how satisfying his profound teaching on the meaning of life is to the human heart compared to its ancient religious or modern secular counterparts. Thus it is a category mistake for Walsh to associate "The Christian conception of history as a drama proceeding from the Creation through the Incarnation to the Last Judgment"[60] with the speculative philosophies of history.

Daniel Little in his overview of philosophy of history in *The Stanford Encyclopedia of Philosophy* has a more balanced evaluation:

> A legitimate criticism of many efforts to offer an interpretation of the sweep of history is the view that it looks for meaning where none can exist. Interpretation of individual actions and life histories is intelligible, because we can ground our attributions of meaning in a theory of the individual person as possessing and creating meanings. But there is no super-agent lying behind historical events . . . and so it is a metaphysical mistake to attempt to find the meaning of the features of the event[s] . . . . The theological approach purports to evade this criticism by attributing agency to God as the author of history, but the assumption that there is a divine author of history takes the making of history out of the hands of humanity.[61]

Based on the assumption that there is "no super-agent [read: God] lying behind historical events," Little's comment that speculative philosophers look "for meaning where none can exist" is appropriate. Unlike Walsh, Little does not associate the Christian conception of history with speculative theories. And he allows the "theological approach" (such as that of Augustine) to hold the assumption that God is the author of history. (As indicated above, which approach is not based on assumption?) However, Little is misinformed that the "theological approach . . . takes the making of history out of the hand of humanity." For as we have seen, Ecclesiastes teaches not only divine sovereignty over whatever happens in history but also human responsibility over whatever humanity does or fails to do in history. A key verse we have been repeating says: "God so works [in history] that men should fear him [and live accordingly *in history*]." And as we have highlighted above, by fearing God and keeping his commandments, an individual life story can contribute at least passively if not also actively to both the purpose and goal of history. Hence philosophers of history have much to learn from Ecclesiastes, the most philosophical book of the Bible.

All this means, if our world is not created by God with a purpose and goal for human life, history has no purpose and no goal and thus there is no such thing as "*the meaning of history*." And if God the Creator does not reveal the purpose and goal of history, we will not find out and will not experience the meaning of history. Thus our experience of the meaning of life will be limited. But can we really live without a sense

---

60. Walsh, "Meaning in History," 304.
61. Little, "Philosophy of History."

of our place in the flow of human history? Drawing on insights from empirically-based studies, personality psychologist Robert Emmons writes:

> Although historical generalizations can be risky, it appears that more than at any previous time in history, people are concerned with determining their place within an evolving universe.[62] Embedding one's finite life within a grander all-encompassing narrative appears to be a universal human need, as the inability to do so leads to despair and self-destructive behavior.[63] . . . Various fields of psychology, in particular the more applied areas of clinical, counseling, health, and rehabilitative psychology, are becoming increasingly aware of and impressed by the centrality of religious and spiritual concerns in people's lives.[64]

And as noted above, the Bible claims that God not only has revealed the purpose and goal of history but has in fact been working toward fulfilling them. And Ecclesiastes teaches that God so works that we should do our part in fulfilling them in and through our life.

Experiencing a Sense of Closure to History

We have assumed that human life and human history take the form of a story-shaped narrative. Actually this is something we recognize intuitively, for just as an artist paints based on what he sees in the natural and human world, a novelist writes based on what he observes about human life in this world. Thus "Narrative imitates life . . . just as art imitates life."[65] And most significantly the Bible itself presents human life and human history in the form of a story-shaped narrative.

In a stimulating essay literary scholar Meir Sternberg not only defends that biblical narrative is historical narrative and not fictional narrative (that is, as far as the biblical narrators are concerned, they are writing history and not fiction),[66] but also argues that "this art of narrative has no parallel in ancient times" with features that are "landmark[s] in the development of history writing."[67] And he demonstrates that "one simply cannot tell fictional from historical narrative,"[68] which means fiction imitates history. Sternberg's "miniature illustration" from 2 Samuel 12 on "the Robbing of the Poor Man's Ewe-Lamb" (the parable used by the prophet Nathan to indict David of his adultery with Bathsheba) is rather compelling:

---

62. Ramachandran and Blakeslee, *Phantoms in the Brain*.
63. Singer, *Message in a Bottle*.
64. Emmons, *Psychology of Ultimate Concerns*, 5.
65. Bruner, "Life as Narrative," 692.
66. Sternberg, *Poetics of Biblical Narrative*, 23–41.
67. Sternberg, *Poetics of Biblical Narrative*, 31.
68. Sternberg, *Poetics of Biblical Narrative*, 29.

> After the Bathsheba affair, Nathan recounts the tale to David and David fulminates against the rich man's rapacity, whereupon Nathan springs on him the proverbial "You are the man!" Accordingly, as one purpose gives way to another—seeking redress for an anonymous sufferer to passing sentence on the king—the tale transforms from the history of an injustice [what David did to Bathsheba's husband] to a fictional parable of injustice [what the rich man did to the anonymous poor man].[69]

Hence human life and human history share the same literary features as fiction, and they thus take the form of a story-shaped narrative. This has significant implications for the meaning of human history and thus of human life. For "the *ending* of a narrative, or the presence of *closure*, is especially important to [the understanding] of the narrative *as a whole*. . . . [However a] narrative can end without closure. Perhaps it ends in a way that is unsatisfying, and thus the sense of closure we seek fails to obtain."[70] This means, to be meaningful, history not only must have an ending, but the ending must also bring a satisfying or meaningful closure to human life in this world.

What then is "closure" to a narrative and why is it important to the meaning of the story? H. Porter Abbott in a classic textbook on narrative explains:

> The term "closure" can refer to more than the resolution of a story's central conflict. It has to do with a broad range of expectations and uncertainties that arise during the course of a narrative and that part of us, at least, hopes to resolve, or close. . . . What we can say is that closure is something we tend to look for in narratives. We look for it in the same way that we look for answers to questions or fulfillment to expectations. This would appear to be a natural human inclination. For this reason, the promise of closure has great rhetorical power in narrative. Closure brings satisfaction to desire, relief to suspense, and clarity to confusion. It normalizes. It confirms the masterplot.[71]

Since history takes the form of narrative, we can apply Abbott's insights on closure to history. Thus the "the broad range of expectations and uncertainties" arising from the "central conflict" during the course of history tend to create the desire for a satisfactory *resolution* in terms of a meaningful *closure* to relieve the suspense of the uncertainties and thus clarify the *confusion* as well as fulfill the *expectations*.

What then is the "central conflict" of history? It is a two-fold conflict. Firstly, it is the observed incongruity arising from the certainty of death—both the righteous and the wicked alike have to die, sometimes even tragically (9:1–3). There seems to be no justice and this needs *resolution* after death.

Secondly, it is the observed incongruity due to the uncertainties of life—there is miscarriage of justice even in the very place where justice is supposed to be guaranteed:

---

69. Sternberg, *Poetics of Biblical Narrative*, 30.
70. Seachris, "Meaning of Life as Narrative," 11, 22.
71. Abbott, *Cambridge Introduction to Narrative*, 57, 64.

the courts of law, the last bastion of justice (3:16). And "Because the sentence against an evil deed is not executed quickly, therefore the heart of the children of man is fully set to do evil" (8:11). And worst of all, "there are righteous people to whom it happens according to the deeds of the wicked, and there are wicked people to whom it happens according to the deeds of the righteous" (8:14; cf. 7:15). This enigma gives rise to the *confusion* that awaits clarity.

In response to the miscarriage of justice in the courts of law, the Preacher affirms that one day God will make things right again by judging both the righteous to vindicate them as well as the wicked to incriminate them (3:17). This is his expectation, which represents our expectation as it resonates within our conscience. And the Preacher warns that for those who are "fully set to do evil" because they seem to get away with it due to delayed judgment, it will not be well with them (8:13). Again this resonates within our conscience giving rise to further expectation that the wicked will get their just deserts. These and other similar *expectations* await fulfillment.

The Preacher is evidently responding to the need of the human heart to see justice done with respect to both the righteous and the wicked—the need for a satisfactory resolution and a meaningful closure. In fact by highlighting these issues, his speech has the power of a narrative in provoking the conscience of his audience to activate their "natural human inclination" and thus evoke in their heart a deep desire to actively seek a satisfactory resolution to the central conflict of history in the form of a meaningful *closure*.

However the observation is that even blatant injustice perpetrated by the wicked may not seem to be corrected at the ending of their life in this world: "Thereupon I saw the wicked brought to the grave, and they proceeded from a holy place; and they were praised in the city where they had done such [unjust] things" (8:10). So if death in this world is the end of the whole story, then human life in this world lacks closure. This then gives rise to uncertainties as to whether the confusion will be clarified and the expectations fulfilled.

Thus the human heart cries out for a final accounting, a resolution and closure, beyond this world for all that is done in this world. What kind of ending to history then will bring the most meaningful closure to how human beings treat or mistreat one another, other than that taught in the Bible? Unless in the end righteousness is vindicated and wickedness incriminated, our God-given sense of justice is violated. If history is like a movie that ends with the villain vanquishing the hero, or even with the hero perishing together with the villain, life does not make sense.

This need of the human heart for a meaningful closure to human life in this world is unwittingly expressed through the works of speculative philosophers of history. For why would they speculate on the meaning of history specifically in terms of its purpose and goal? According to Walsh, "these speculations . . . had a theological origin and a recognized place in Christian apologetics."[72] He adds that these phi-

---

72. Walsh, *Philosophy of History*, 121; cf. Nash, *Meaning of History*, 78–79.

losophers "too were attempting to trace a pattern in the course of historical change; they too . . . were convinced that history was going somewhere. And despite their many differences from the theologically minded, they felt the same need on being confronted with the spectacle of human history, the need to show that the miseries men experienced were not in vain, but were rather inevitable stages on the way to a morally satisfactory goal."[73] In other words, "History will make sense . . . only if it can be seen as a drama which is morally satisfying. The impetus to think in this way comes from reflection on the miseries and evils of which so much of history appears on the surface to consist: it is felt that these cannot be 'pointless,' but must serve some good purpose."[74]

Hence the impetus behind speculative philosophies of history is to see history as a morally satisfying drama with a *morally satisfactory goal (closure)* to make sense of it in view of the miseries and evils observed in this world. We have seen that the only morally satisfying closure is that taught in the Bible. However, unlike the premodern mind, the modern mind finds the teaching of a final judgment incredulous and even modern people who profess belief in God may find it embarrassing. In retrospect it is providential that Ecclesiastes is what it is. The Preacher confronts his audience with a graphic reflection on the miseries and evils observed in this world so that their heart cries out for a closure to history and thus comes to appreciate his conception of history as a drama beginning with the creation of the world and ending with the final judgment of humanity. And he claims that all this is in fact given by God the Shepherd as goads to prod humanity in the way they should go. It is his modern audience that needs it more than his ancient audience; it is as though he anticipated the modern mind.

We have sought to recreate the force of the Preacher's rhetoric in bringing us to recognize that it is only with an assurance of a final and just accounting *beyond this world* as taught in the Bible that we can have the assurance that every individual life story will eventually find a closure after death that is the most satisfying morally and thus most meaningful existentially. Only then do we know the true significance or meaning of what we do, or fail to do, in this temporal world. Just as "the promise of closure has great rhetorical power in narrative," the biblical promise of a closure that is most satisfying and meaningful has great "rhetorical power" in creating in us a deep sense of meaning even in the face of the certainty of death and the uncertainties of life.

---

73. Walsh, *Philosophy of History*, 121.

74. Walsh, "Meaning in History," 304. Thus "The question of the 'meaning *(Sinn)* of history' is also aimed at the problem of whether and how the costs of history—devastation and destruction, misfortune and suffering—can be justified theologically or philosophically" (Stückrath, "Meaning of History," 69). This explains why besides "purpose" and "goal," "value" is included as a component of "meaning of history." For in view of the "costs of history," history lacks meaning unless it has "value." As indicated earlier, the question really is whether the purpose and goal of history are worthwhile even in the face of the "costs."

Coming now to the end of our exploration of the teaching of Ecclesiastes on the meaning of life, we conclude that the meaning of history and of life taught in the Old Testament is the most satisfying morally to the human heart. However, since no one can perfectly fear God and keep his commandments, as "there is not a righteous man on earth who (continually) does good and never sins" (7:20), no "righteous person" can have the hope that he "shall awake" at the end of history "to everlasting life" in the new heavens and the new earth unless he has the assurance of God's forgiveness of his sins. The New Testament not only teaches that this forgiveness is now provided for through Jesus Christ under the new covenant, but also explains what it means to "awake . . . to everlasting life" as revealed in Daniel.

Presupposing the reality of the vanity of temporal life, the New Testament presents with unwavering optimism a glorious hope in relation to it. For "the creation [like humanity] was subjected to vanity . . . in the hope that the creation itself will also [along with humanity] be set free from its bondage to corruption into the freedom of the glory of the children of God" (Rom 8:20–21). The "glory of the children of God" refers to "the redemption of our bodies" (Rom 8:23), which means "the children of God" will eventually be redeemed with bodies that are no longer subject to corruption (death) and hence be completely freed from vanity. With his hope, one can say, "I consider that the sufferings of this present time are not worthy to be compared with the glory that is going to be revealed to us" (Rom 8:18).

Without this glorious hope, even a God-fearing person has no assurance that his own individual life story will eventually find a closure after death, let alone one that is the most satisfying and meaningful. So no matter how much he seeks to fear God and keep his commandments and help others do the same, without this hope his experience of the meaning of life is incomplete and thus is still not as satisfying and meaningful as it could and should be.

Interpretation of Ecclesiastes

Ecclesiastes has a powerful message for today. Unfortunately, it is also the most difficult biblical book to interpret coherently. Most interpreters do not even think it can be done. And most commentaries render almost the entire book useless in terms of authoritative teaching. In view of the intricate issues involved, this essay undertakes elaborate spadework on the book to break new grounds in order to present and defend an interpretation that recovers the coherent message of Ecclesiastes and affirms the book in its entirety as authoritative Scripture.

Ecclesiastes is the only book of the Bible where how we understand a key word in the book determines how we understand the whole book. Thus how the word is translated is crucial to how we interpret the book. To translate it correctly we need to determine what Qoheleth the author means when he uses the word.

That key word is *hebel*, which occurs seventy-three times in the Hebrew Bible, thirty-eight times of which are in Ecclesiastes. It is "the key word *par excellence* . . . because it is found at strategic points of the exposition and embodies the thinking and mood that pervades this sapiential book."[1] It has been traditionally translated into English as "vanity," a "rendering [that] has dominated the modern translations for generations, up to the present time. However, according to more recent critical study of [Ecclesiastes], this translation is no longer valid."[2] But why not? We will here reconceive this traditional translation and explain why it remains the best translation. In the process we present and defend the interpretation adopted in our exposition of Ecclesiastes.

Graham Ogden, who rejects this widely accepted translation, complains that "The real difficulty with retaining the traditional term 'vanity' is not only the fact that it is ambiguous, referring to an individual's excessive pride or arrogance, as well as that which is vain in the sense of worthless. The more troubling fact is that both meanings represent a negative set of values and so give an overall cast to the book that is

---

1. Schoors, *Preacher II*, 119.
2. Schoors, *Preacher II*, 119–20.

misleading."³ To him, "The notion that *hebel* equals 'vanity' and that it is a catchword for a pessimistic view of the world is a long way from the truth as we have seen it."⁴

Properly understood "vanity" is neither a catchword for a pessimistic view of the world nor is it ambiguous—whether it means worthless or excessive pride—in the context of Ecclesiastes. We shall see that it is a catchword needed to adequately capture the various nuances of *hebel* to present a realistic view of the world.

The Meaning of *Hebel*

Hebel as Vapor

It is generally accepted that the literal meaning of *hebel* is "breath" (Isa 57:13) or "vapor"—breath condensed (fleetingly) in cold air (Prov 21:6)—and that with its (material) sense as vapor the word can be used as a metaphor to make references to things that are like vapor in some way. For instance, "Surely every man is [short-lived like] vapor (*hebel*)" (Ps 39:11; cf. 144:4). According to Douglas Miller, "A number of different [metaphoric] references may be discerned for *hebel* in Ecclesiastes, each of which finds connection with some aspect of *hebel*'s material sense [as vapor]: its insubstantiality, transience, or foulness."⁵ This view has been gaining acceptance.⁶

We concur that insofar as "vapor" is both transient and lacks substance, it can be used as a metaphor to refer to different things that are transient or insubstantial, or even both. It is like the word "lion," which can refer to the animal lion (material sense) as the "king" (of the jungle) or as a "predator" (in the jungle)—two aspects of its material sense—and thus can be used as a metaphor to refer to Jesus Christ as King (Rev 5:5; cf. Gen 49:10) as well as to Satan as predator (1 Pet 5:8). Thus a single metaphor can have different references in different contexts.

As to Miller's claim that the material sense of *hebel* as vapor also includes "foulness" as one of its aspects, even his own mentor C. L. Seow argues that "foulness is not really a trait of *hebel*. Whereas *hebel* is always transient and always insubstantial, it is not always foul."⁷ In fact if *hebel* has the material sense of "bad air [or vapor] . . . which is putrid and brings illness,"⁸ it cannot at the same time be "insubstantial" and "transient" as well. For "bad air [or vapor]" manifests "foulness" (it is offensive) precisely because the air or vapor is substantial and not transient ("is putrid and brings illness"). As we shall see, there is a need for *hebel* to have "transience" and "insubstantiality," but

---

3. Ogden, *Qoheleth*, 32.
4. Ogden, *Qoheleth*, 224.
5. Miller, *Symbol and Rhetoric*, 15.
6. E.g., Bundvad, *Time in Ecclesiastes*, 76–78; Caneday, "Everything Is Vapor," 33–34; Frydrych, *Living under the Sun*, 45; Fuhr, *Inter-dependency within Qohelet*, 42–44; Salyer, *Private Insight and Public Debate*, 255–56.
7. Seow, "Beyond Mortal Grasp," 13.
8. Miller, *Symbol and Rhetoric*, 97.

not "foulness," as aspects of its material sense for it to be used as a metaphor that can adequately account for all its nuances in Ecclesiastes.

The Transience of Vapor

Since "vapor" is transient, *hebel* can be used as a metaphor based on this aspect of its material sense to describe something that is transient and thus transitory. Hence in some contexts *hebel* means "fleeting" and should be translated as such (3:19; 6:12; 7:15; 9:9; 11:10). The clearest examples are: "all the days of your *fleeting* life" (9:9) and "the prime of life is *fleeting*" (11:10). The *hebel* (brevity) of the prime of life or of life itself is presented realistically as a matter of fact. The message is clear: make the most of life, especially the prime of life, because it will soon be gone. All the other examples are like 9:9, describing human life as fleeting. This is realism and not pessimism.

In the context of 1:2–3, the assertion "all is *hebel* (vapor)" (1:2) answers the rhetorical question, "What profit does man have in all his toil? [No profit]" (1:3).[9] Hence "all is vapor" means "all" that is gained through "his toil" is profitless. So in this context (the theme of Ecclesiastes; cf. 12:8), "vapor" has the nuance of "profitless." Thus *hebel* is here clearly used as a metaphor to refer to something that is profitless. But what is the connection between vapor—something transient or transitory—and something profitless?

In this context, the Hebrew word translated "profit" (*yitrôn*) refers to a specific kind of profit. The noun *yitrôn* has the root meaning "remain over or exceed."[10] Later in the speech when commenting on a man who loved money, Qoheleth says, "just as he came [naked from his mother's womb], thus will he go [with no *net gain*]; so what *yitrôn* ["remain over"] to him who toils for the wind? [None]" (5:15–16). Hence *yitrôn* in the rhetorical question here means "remain over" in the sense of net gain over a period of time—one's life as a whole from birth to death. Since this rhetorical question is essentially the same as that in 1:3, "all is vapor" in 1:2 means, in view of death, there is *eventually* no net gain or profit to our life as a whole.

Commenting on 1:2–3, James Crenshaw says, "the author must imply something in these two verses that will come to explicit expression later: the finality of death. Implicit within the word *hebel* is the sense of transience. Perhaps the word *yitrôn* points to this direction, for one cannot calculate the profit or loss of individual activity until it ceases. Prior to this final closure all judgments of expenditures and receipts are necessarily provisional."[11] In other words, as Peter Enns puts it, "according to Qohelet, . . . since death levels the playing field for all, and since you cannot take it with you, it is the inevitability of death that ensures that no human activity will provide

---

9. Cf. Horne, *Proverbs-Ecclesiastes*, 383.
10. Schoors, *Preacher II*, 423.
11. Crenshaw, *Ecclesiastes*, 60.

anyone with any profit or surplus (e.g., 3:19–22). This is what renders life 'under the sun' *hebel*."[12]

Paraphrasing 5:15–16, when we finally close our accounts at our death, what will be the "remain over" or net gain from all our toil since the day of our birth? Zero. This means 1:2 is saying, "*All* (that we gain through our toil is profitless because it) *is* (transitory like) *vapor*"—it does not remain (over) with us beyond our fleeting life in this world. So by qualifying "All is *hebel* (vapor)" in 1:2 with "What *yitrôn* (profit) does man have in all his toil?" in 1:3, Qoheleth is saying that he is talking about profitlessness as in 5:15–16—we leave this world with no net gain. This is again realism and not pessimism.

In other words, Qoheleth is not saying that there is no profit whatsoever to human toil. There is immediate (transitory) profit; otherwise we have no reason to toil at all. But in light of death there is no *ultimate* (eternal) profit. For instance, he acknowledges the value of wisdom and the advantage of toiling with wisdom; a wise man will do better in life than a foolish one (2:13–14). But the wise man must die like the fool and leave behind all the fruit of his toil to an heir, who may squander them (2:18–23). So he declares that even wisdom and the success it brings are in this sense *hebel* ("vapor"), that is, (ultimately) profitless (2:15, 17, 19, 21, 23). In case we think that we will lose everything we have gained only when we die, the poem in 3:1–9 shows that we may lose them even before we die and we may die young because the reality as presented in the poem is that while death is certain, life is uncertain.

As indicated above, in the context of 1:2–3, "*all* is vapor" in the sense that everything is (ultimately) profitless, refers to all that is gained through human toil. It does not refer to everything that exists or happens in this world—this would indeed be pessimism. The Hebrew text actually says "*hakkol* (the all) is *hebel* (vapor)." And "the all" refers to "everything" that is "specific and identifiable," which in this case "strictly refers to everything that was within Qoheleth's purview during his investigation, although it might also be taken as a logical extrapolation that Qoheleth makes based on what he has observed."[13] And "the all" that Qoheleth investigated and observed is about temporal and material things, which in reality are ultimately profitless.

Therefore the theme of Ecclesiastes—"(the) all is vapor"—is also realism, not pessimism. We will now survey the other nuances of *hebel* in Ecclesiastes to see if this word ever expresses pessimism.

The Insubstantiality of Vapor

Since "vapor" is also insubstantial, *hebel* can also be used as a metaphor to refer to something that lacks substance, that is, "something of no consequence, perhaps

---

12. Enns, *Ecclesiastes*, 9.
13. Holmstedt et al., *Qoheleth*, 51

similar to the current [English idiom] 'hot air.'"[14] It can refer to something that is intrinsically insubstantial and hence is *intrinsically* profitless or useless, such as empty or futile words uttered to God (5:7; 6:11) or "the laughter of the fool" (7:6).

It can also be used to refer to something not intrinsically profitless but which lacks substance and is thus useless (only) when used for a purpose it cannot fulfill. For instance, wealth in itself is not intrinsically profitless, but when it is pursued or used to find satisfaction in life, it lacks substance and is thus useless for this purpose (5:10). This metaphoric use of *hebel* (based on the insubstantiality of vapor) is common outside of Ecclesiastes. Tremper Longman observes that "In thirteen passages [such as Deut 32:21 and Jonah 2:8] the word characterizes idols. It is absolutely certain that these passages are attributing uselessness or meaninglessness to the idols, not transitoriness."[15] From the perspective of orthodox Old Testament faith, idols are certainly "useless" or profitless, because by definition they are used for worship, and as objects of worship they lack substance as real gods (Jer 16:19–20).

The idols referred to are in the form of statues (Jer 10:8, 14–15). So when a statue is worshipped as a god (used as an idol), it is useless. But when a statue as a work of art is used for pleasure, it is not useless. In fact some of the very statues once used as idols are today on display in museums, serving a useful purpose beyond pleasure—education. This illustrates how something (a statue) not intrinsically profitless can become useless when used for the wrong purpose (as an idol, an object of worship). Hence Longman is correct that when *hebel* is used metaphorically to refer to idols, it carries the nuance of "uselessness."

However the nuance of "meaninglessness" that Longman also attributes to *hebel* is not inherent to this metaphoric use of *hebel*. Something insubstantial is useless, but it need not be meaningless. This nuance, if it can be discerned in a particular context, is only a connotation that comes from the "meaninglessness" of doing something futile—in this case, the senseless act of worshipping "useless" idols (see below for discussion on connotations of *hebel* in Ecclesiastes).

We now return to the metaphoric use of *hebel* as insubstantial vapor in Ecclesiastes. In the context of 1:12–18, wisdom is "*hebel* (profitless)" because it is used in vain to solve the basic problem of life—the ultimate profitlessness of temporal things in 1:2–3. In this context, though wisdom is not intrinsically profitless, it does not even have immediate profit because it is used to do something it cannot do—it lacks substance for this purpose. Otherwise, as we saw above, wisdom does have immediate though not ultimate profits (2:12–17).

In the context of 2:1–11, which is Qoheleth's experiment with the pursuit of pleasure, pleasure is found to be *hebel* or profitless (2:1) for a similar reason. Like wisdom, pleasure is not intrinsically profitless and does have immediate though not ultimate profit. And like wisdom, when pleasure is used for a purpose or pursued for a profit

14. Pinker, "Doings of the Wicked," 16.
15. Longman, *Ecclesiastes*, 63.

that it lacks substance for, such as to fill the emptiness of one's heart, it is in this sense *hebel* ("profitless"). For "When he comes to assess the results of this [experiment] in 2.11, however, he finds that it too is vapour, which has failed to grant him the sort of profit that he really wants."[16] Thus the vanity of material or temporal things is now extended to include *immediate* profitlessness (2:11). This is possible because transient vapor is also insubstantial.

In the context of 7:15–8:15 (under the sun the righteous may suffer while the wicked may prosper), though righteousness is not intrinsically profitless, it is *hebel* (profitless) because it lacks substance when it is used or pursued as though it can guarantee material and temporal profits. The observation that the righteous may suffer while the wicked may prosper does evoke a negative ("foul") reaction from even Qoheleth the speaker, but as we shall see, it does not require *hebel* to have "foulness" as an aspect of its material sense to account for this "foul" reaction to *hebel*. For as we will see, even in this case of immediate profitlessness, let alone in the above two cases (wisdom and pleasure), *hebel* is expressing realism and not pessimism.

Daniel Fredericks argues that *hebel* be consistently translated with a word that means "transience" throughout the book.[17] But "there are *hebel*-texts [4:7–8; 5:7; 6:11; 7:6] for which 'transience' will not work."[18] Consider Fredericks's translation of 7:6, which is about "the laughter of the fool": "Really, as the crackling of thorns under a pot, is the fool's laughter. Also this is temporary."[19] Assuming that *hebel* must be translated with a word that means "transience" (here "temporary"), he says the fool's laughter is *hebel* because it "is as short-lived as the thin dried thorns in fire. Nothing could be cooked over such a *useless* fire, and *nothing can be gained* from the fools' shallow laughter."[20]

So he still has to introduce the nuance of (intrinsic) profitlessness demanded by the context. It may be argued that the fire is useless because it is "short-lived," but even then it cannot be assumed that similarly the fool's laughter is useless because it is "short-lived." Does lengthening the laughter make it useful? The obvious similarity between the fire and the laughter expressed here is that both are useless, not that they are transient. The most sensible interpretation is that the "fools' *shallow* laughter" is (intrinsically) profitless because it lacks quality (insubstantial), not quantity (transient). Evidently Fredericks is trying to remove the supposed pessimism in Ecclesiastes. But, as we shall see, there is actually no pessimism on the part of Qoheleth as the speaker. Thus there is really no need to resort to such a tenuous interpretation of *hebel* to demonstrate that Qoheleth is not pessimistic.

---

16. Weeks, *Ecclesiastes 1–5*, 15.
17. Fredericks, *Coping with Transience*; Fredericks, *Ecclesiastes*.
18. Miller, *Symbol and Rhetoric*, 14.
19. Fredericks, *Ecclesiastes*, 158.
20. Fredericks, *Ecclesiastes*, 169 (italics added).

Knut Heim, based on the material sense of *hebel* as vapor, claims that "The majority of the occurrences of the word *hebel* in the Old Testament carry the meaning 'mirage', referring either to an optical illusion or to an illusion in general. In Ecclesiastes, all occurrences of the word *hebel* refer to an illusion."[21] Insofar as vapor is both transient and insubstantial, the idea of "mirage" or "illusion" is not too far off and would fit a number of contexts. But what is problematic is the claim that *all* cases in Ecclesiastes carry this nuance. In cases where *hebel* obviously means fleeting, it will render Ecclesiastes unnecessarily pessimistic.

For instance, Heim translates the *hebel*-clause in 11:10 as "for youth and black hair are a mirage!"[22] To say that just being youthful is an illusion is surely pessimistic. To avoid this sense Heim argues that "The nouns *youth* and *black hair* are metaphors for youthful arrogance and naïve overconfidence. Qoheleth declares them a mirage not only because they are transient, but also because they can create a self-image of invincibility which may draw young hotheads into violent conflicts with the occupying power."[23] Heim still has to bring in the sense of transience, which is required by the context, but the added nuances of arrogance, naivety and self-image of invincibility are foreign to the flow of the text even granted the supposed historical context ("the occupying power") that Heim assumes and imposes on the text (see below on Heim's view on "under the sun").

Qoheleth says, because "youth and black hair (prime of life) are *hebel*" (11:10b), "Therefore remember your Creator in the days of your youth, before the days of trouble come and the years draw near" (12:1)—referring to the onset of old age leading to death (12:2–7). Obviously "the days of your youth"—the days before the onset of old age—refers back to "youth and prime of life are *hebel*." Hence, though "black hair" is a metaphor for youthfulness ("prime of life"), "youth" itself is not a metaphor at all.

What then does *hebel* here mean and is there a place for arrogance, naivety and self-image of invincibility regardless of any historical context assumed? Krüger, who assumes the very same historical context,[24] rightly translates the clause (11:10b) as "For youth and black hair are fleeting"[25] and comments that "With its reference to the transitoriness of youth, v. 10b underlines the call to the young man to enjoy life . . . in the present (v. 7) and not to postpone pleasure and enjoyment until an uncertain future," and nothing more than this.[26]

To sum up, *hebel* in Ecclesiastes can mean "fleeting," or one of the nuances of "profitlessness": ultimate profitlessness because it is transient; immediate profitlessness

---

21. Heim, *Ecclesiastes*, 7.
22. Heim, *Ecclesiastes*, 191.
23. Heim, *Ecclesiastes*, 191.
24. Krüger, *Qoheleth*, 19–21.
25. Krüger, *Qoheleth*, 190.
26. Krüger, *Qoheleth*, 197.

because it is insubstantial for the purpose it is used or pursued; intrinsic profitlessness because it is intrinsically insubstantial, that is, it is of no consequence whatsoever.

The Semantics of Vanity

Having considered (temporal and material) things gained or pursued through toil, we now look at the human effort of toiling itself. In 1:2–3, we know *hebel* in 1:2 refers to the (ultimate) *profitlessness* of all that is gained through human effort because 1:3 asserts the (ultimate) *futility* of all human toil (it fails to produce profit). The two ideas are inseparable, one implying the other. If the fruit is profitless, the toil is futile, and vice-versa.

So it is not surprising that *hebel* can be extended to refer to the futility of an activity which pursues or gains something that is profitless. Thus in 4:8, "*This* also is *hebel*" refers to the futility of the miserable workaholic's *pursuit* of wealth (also 4:7). Similarly in Ps 94:11: "they (the thought-plans of man) are *hebel* (futile)." Hence *hebel* (vapor) can mean "profitless" when referring to an object of pursuit or "futile" when referring to the activity (toil) of pursuing it.

There is even a case in Ecclesiastes where *hebel* refers to the futility of an activity which does not involve an object of pursuit. Qoheleth says a stillborn child "comes" into this world "in *hebel*" and leaves "in darkness" because it does not "see the sun" at all, and "in darkness its name is covered [it is buried without a name]" (6:4–5). Since to "see the sun" is to be alive in this world (7:11; 11:7),[27] Qoheleth is saying, as Robert Gordis puts it, the stillborn child "comes in vain into the world, since it does not see the light of day [born dead] and leaves no name behind."[28]

The alternative interpretation that it comes "in brevity" does not do justice to the text because a stillborn child, unlike a child who dies in infancy, does not even have a brief moment of existence in this world and (in their context) it does not even leave behind a name. Thus it comes into this world "in *hebel* (futility)" (6:4); it comes for nothing (in vain). Similarly in Ps 78:33: "So he ended their days in *hebel*," that is, their days ended "in *hebel* (vain)." Also, when *hebel* describes an activity involving an object of pursuit, *hebel* by itself can mean "in vain." Thus, "I labor *hebel* (in vain)" (Job 9:29); "they busy themselves *hebel* (in vain)" (Ps 39:6 [Heb. v. 7]); "they shall help *hebel* (in vain)" (Isa 30:7); "we watched *hebel* (in vain) for help" (Lam 4:17); "they comfort *hebel* (in vain)" (Zech 10:2). In fact it is more idiomatic in English to translate 6:4 as "(it comes) in vain"[29] instead of "(it comes) in futility."[30]

Now that *hebel* as "vapor" can refer to the futility of an activity or the profitlessness of an object of pursuit, what is the best English word to translate it when it does

27. Cf. Seow, *Ecclesiastes*, 212.
28. Gordis, *Koheleth*, 259.
29. Gordis *Koheleth*, 170.
30. Crenshaw, *Ecclesiastes*, 120.

not mean "fleeting"? The more idiomatic translation of 6:4, "it comes in *hebel* (vain)," points the way. The word "vanity," which is associated with the word "vain," has been defined as "The quality of being worthless or futile."[31] Apparently "vanity" can mean "worthless (profitless or useless)" or "futile" because it embodies the quality of "being *vain* (worthless)" as well as "being *in vain* (futile)."

Hence "vanity" is best suited to translate *hebel*. But since *hebel* has nuances in Ecclesiastes that cannot all be translated with the same English word, we need to use different words: "fleeting" when this is the meaning of *hebel* in the text; "vanity" when it does not mean "fleeting"; and "(it comes in) vain" in 6:4 as it is more idiomatic than "(it comes in) vanity."[32]

Does it then make sense to use different English words to translate the same Hebrew word? Consider this English sentence: "When he looked into the *empty* sky, his heart felt *empty* and he cried out 'everything is *empty*!'" The English word "empty" in this sentence has three different nuances. This writer has experimented with at least seven seminary students, each with a different native language, to translate that sentence into their native language. When asked whether they could use the same word to translate all three occurrences of the word "empty," all of them said "No."

This experiment demonstrates two things. Firstly, the same word ("empty" in English or "*hebel*" in Hebrew) can have different nuances even in the same sentence. And if the reader or listener has adequate competence in the respective language, it is usually clear from the context which nuance is intended. One who has adequate competence in English can discern immediately the different nuances of "empty." Similarly the original audience of Ecclesiastes could discern immediately the various nuances of "*hebel*." Just as in the English example, "Given the wide range of possible meanings [of *hebel*] that can be attached to such a metaphor, it seems likely that the original audience would have to have been guided to Qohelet's intended sense by their understanding of the contexts in which he uses it."[33] Today we need linguistic analysis to discern them because we do not have the native competence of the original audience.

Secondly, when translating into another language, we may have to use different words in the target language to express the different nuances of the word evident in the original language. However as far as possible, we should limit the number of words used so that the reader in the target language can have a sense of the original. So we have chosen "vanity" to translate *hebel* in most of the contexts because like *hebel*, vanity can refer to either a "profitless" object or a "futile" activity.

We can now see why "vanity" remains the best translation for *hebel* when it does not mean "fleeting." The question of "ambiguity" in the meaning of the English word "vanity"—worthless or excessive pride—raised by Ogden (and others) is a non-issue. We have just seen that in Ecclesiastes *hebel* itself already has different

---

31. *Lexico.com*, "Vanity," s.v.
32. Seow, *Ecclesiastes*, 202.
33. Weeks, *Ecclesiastes 1–5*, 22.

nuances—"fleeting" and the various nuances of "profitlessness" and "futility" that only "vanity" can handle. Hence "ambiguity" cannot be avoided. And we are not aware of any context in Ecclesiastes where there is an ambiguity when *hebel* is translated as "vanity," whether it may refer to excessive pride or otherwise.

We have seen that in 1:2–3 "all is *hebel* (vanity)" (cf. 12:8), which expresses the theme of Ecclesiastes, expresses realism and not pessimism. Why then do scholars read pessimism into it and translate it as "everything is meaningless" or even "everything is absurd"? It is instructive to consider Michael Fox's own explanation as to why and how he derives the pessimistic sense of absurdity from the reality of the (ultimate) futility of human toil:

> The quality of absurdity does not inhere in a being, act, or event in and of itself . . . , but rather in the tension between a certain reality and a framework of expectations. . . . "Futile" is properly predicated of an intentional action and refers to its failure to achieve its goal. "Absurd" can be applied at a higher level of abstraction. In other words, "toil" may be futile [a reality], but *the fact that* toil is futile is absurd [a reaction to the reality].[34]

When Fox says, "*the fact that* toil is futile is absurd," he is not supposing that toil is intrinsically or immediately futile. For he later says, "Though youth is precious [not intrinsically worthless], it is rendered absurd, like life itself, by its brevity. Like toil its significance is inevitably undone."[35] This means, toil is "futile" (*hebel*) because of the brevity of life due to the inevitability of death (as noted earlier, Enns, who follows Fox in translating *hebel* as "absurd," spells out that "it is the inevitability of death that . . . renders life 'under the sun' *hebel*"). Hence Fox implicitly agrees with us that when Qoheleth says "all is *hebel*" (1:2), he is actually saying toil is ultimately futile (1:3), and that this is an *objective* reality (a "fact"). However, Fox asserts that this "fact" is absurd—this is a *subjective* reaction to the reality. Thus Fox is not translating the meaning of *hebel* but a reaction ("absurd") to the meaning ("futile").

In other words, Fox equates the reality of the vanity or (ultimate) futility of toil with absurdity because he has assumed that everyone has the same "framework of expectations" and will thus react the same way to this reality. Only people who for some reason cannot accept the reality of the vanity of toil and whose "framework of expectations" is seriously violated would react *pessimistically*: "This (futility of toil) is absurd."

However it is possible to have a different "framework of expectations" so as to react *realistically* to the vanity of toil, which is the teaching of Ecclesiastes: enjoy what you have; it does not make sense (it is meaningless or even absurd) to pursue more of what is vanity (that which you cannot take with you when you die) and in the process

---

34. Fox, *Qohelet*, 31 (italics his): cf. Fox, *Time*, 31.
35. Fox, *Qohelet*, 42–43; cf. Fox, *Time*, 39–40

cannot enjoy what you already have (2:24–26; see below on how this teaching fits into the rhetoric of Ecclesiastes).

Besides Fox's "absurd," recent translations of *hebel* as other than "vanity" or "futility" include "meaningless,"[36] "enigmatic" or "incomprehensible,"[37] and "ironic."[38] Since all these interpreters accept the root meaning of *hebel* as breath or vapor, like Fox each of them is also (implicitly or explicitly) making the assumption that because temporal profit is vapor ("vanity"), it necessarily evokes a negative reaction.

Consider Timothy Polk's own explanation why *hebel* means irony or the ironic. He acknowledges that "Time and again in the book *hebel* occurs in the closest conjunction with the concept of 'toil' (*'āmāl*) in order to emphasize the consistent failure of human efforts to result in 'gain' (*yitrôn*) or to effect advantageous change of any sort."[39] Then he clarifies:

> Primarily, irony is a unique mode of perception and manner of expression. It involves, as Good says, "the perception of the distance between pretense and reality,"[40] between what is and what ought to be, or perhaps, as in the case of Qohelet, between what one *thinks* ought to be and what ought to be in fact. In short it involves the perception of incongruities. . . . That work ["toil"] does *not* yield wealth ["gain" or profit], this is the *hebel*! In the context of wisdom's standard expectations, that is incongruity, i.e., an irony.[41]

One cannot help but see the similarity in argument, even in vocabulary, between Polk and Fox. Instead of Fox's "framework of expectations," which cannot be assumed to be the same for every person, and which may or may not be violated by the (ultimate) futility of human toil, Polk applies an impersonal "wisdom's standard expectations" against the reality of futility.

We cannot deny that "wisdom's standard expectations" will be violated if indeed toil does not yield any profit at all (unlike Fox, Polk is thinking of the immediate, not ultimate, futility of toil to "yield wealth"). But Qoheleth is not saying that. All he is saying is that in light of death, there is no *ultimate* profit. Anyone or any standard that expects otherwise lacks wisdom. Thus "all is vanity (profitless)" is congruent with "wisdom's standard expectations" and there is no irony. Again, we see that a proper understanding of "all is *hebel*" invalidates attempts to derive a further meaning for *hebel* (as in "all is *hebel*") beyond "vanity" (ultimate profitlessness or futility).

The ironic is the incongruous, that is, that which goes against expectations. Ogden views the enigmatic (his primary meaning for *hebel*) as "the ironic dimension of

36. Longman, *Ecclesiastes*.
37. Ogden and Zogbo, *Handbook*; Bartholomew, *Ecclesiastes*.
38. Polk, "Wisdom of Irony," following Good, *Irony in the Old Testament*, 176-83; Ogden, *Qoheleth*, 17.
39. Polk, "Wisdom of Irony," 6.
40. Good, *Irony in the Old Testament*, 14.
41. Polk, "Wisdom of Irony," 7.

human experience."[42] In other words, interpreting *hebel* as "enigma" is simply specifying in what way one considers the futility of toil ironic. Toil should not (is not expected to) be futile, even ultimately, according to the assumed "framework of expectations." When toil is futile, it is thus ironic and incomprehensible or enigmatic.

This is actually a calmer reaction to the supposed irony. A stronger reaction would be "This is meaningless" or even "This is absurd" because one cannot accept it. In an extreme case the reaction may be worse: "This is tragic!" because this is how one feels about the futility of toil. Is *hebel* then to be understood as tragedy or the tragic? All this means we cannot take a subjective reaction to the objective reality of vanity as the meaning of *hebel*.

The Pragmatics of Vanity

This is not to say that subjective reactions to the objective realities captured by the word *hebel* ("vanity") have no place in understanding or even translating Ecclesiastes. To appreciate the different types of subjective reactions to *hebel*, we need to first differentiate the different points of view in Ecclesiastes: that of the *speaker* (Qoheleth when he gave his speech), the *observer* (Qoheleth when he observed realities and people who participated in vanities under the sun), and the *participant* (Qoheleth himself when he participated in vanities as part of his experiment, as well as the people he observed).

Even Fox, whose overall interpretation of Ecclesiastes differs from what is presented here, has observed that Qoheleth's speech encompasses two time-frames with two corresponding "levels of perspective": "Qohelet-the-reporter, the narrating 'I,' who speaks from the vantage point of old age and looks back on . . . Qohelet-the-observer, the experiencing 'I,' who undertook the investigation that the book reports."[43] This means we can differentiate how he viewed vanity when he gave the speech from how he reacted to vanity when he undertook the investigation. Every speaker who recounts his past experience to make a point in his speech can affirm this.

Consider then the situations where Qoheleth uses the following expressions: *ʿinyan rāʿ* (1:13; 4:8), which means "grievous business"; *rāʿāh ḥôlāh* or *ḥŏlî rāʿ* (5:13, 16; 6:2), which means "grievous affliction"; *rāʿāh* (2:21; 6:1; 9:3; 10:5), which means "grievous thing." For convenience we will use the phrase "grievous experience" to represent all the above four Hebrew expressions.

There are three categories of situations, which may or may not be *hebel* (vanity) situations, where Qoheleth uses these expressions: (1) Qoheleth is the *observer* of a vanity situation and the grievous experience is that of the *participant* (4:7–8; 5:13–16; 6:1–2); (2) Qoheleth is the *observer* and the grievous experience is that of the *observer* (9:3; 10:5); (3) Qoheleth is the *participant* in a vanity situation and the

42. Ogden, *Qoheleth*, 17.
43. Fox, *Time*, 366.

grievous experience is that of the *participant* (1:13–14; 2:21). Recognizing these different points of view will show that there is no pessimism on the part of Qoheleth as *speaker* with respect to vanity.

In the first category, the grievous experience is that of the participant of vanity and not Qoheleth the observer. So no matter how "pessimistic" the experience may be, the pessimism is that of the participant and not of Qoheleth the speaker. For instance in the first case (4:7–8) in this category, the one suffering the grievous experience is the workaholic miserably addicted to his "career" who would even ask himself why he works so hard and deprives himself of pleasure when he has no one to share or inherit his wealth. Similarly it is obvious in the other two cases (5:13–16; 6:1–2) that it is not Qoheleth who suffers the grievous experience but those pursuing vanities whom he observed.

In the case of the tragic workaholic, it may be appropriate to translate the *hebel* phrase as "This is indeed meaningless!" or even better, "This is really absurd!" In fact this translation makes better sense in the context than "This also is vanity!" The reason is that, as noted above, the "This" here refers not to the vanity of what is pursued (wealth), which is assumed, but to that of the toil involved in the pursuit. Wealth is vanity because it is ultimately profitless since death is inevitable, as well as immediately profitless when pursued or used to find satisfaction in life. Both aspects of the vanity of wealth are relevant to the futility of the workaholic's compulsive pursuit of wealth. This pursuit of vanity as described by Qoheleth the observer is not just vanity (futility) but since the toil is so obsessive and oppressive (which he labels "a grievous *obsession*"), the pursuit is absurd. The Hebrew word translated "obsession" here is *'inyan*, which ordinarily means a "business" (a task that occupies us), but in this context this business has become an obsession.

The meaning of *hebel* in this case is still "vanity (futility)," but in this particular context even Qoheleth the speaker would react: "This [the grievous futile pursuit] is *hebel* (absurd [vanity])!" Now this is not a pessimistic reaction as what Qoheleth observed is realistically absurd. Strictly speaking any futile business, as in 2:26 and 4:4, can be considered "meaningless." In this case the pursuit is so obsessive and oppressive, to do justice to the emotion of Qoheleth the observer and speaker, the more appropriate word to express it is "absurd" or even "tragic." In technical terms, "vanity" is the denotation (actual meaning) of *hebel*; in this particular context "absurd" or "tragic" is a connotation (additional sense) of *hebel*.

Here is a definition of connotation that is most helpful to understanding the connotations of *hebel* in Ecclesiastes: "Connotation is the array of emotions and ideas suggested by a word *in addition to* its dictionary definition [denotation].... The connotations a word carries may be different for different people [with different points of view], depending on a wide variety of factors, including their life experiences [and 'framework of expectations'], where they live, and when."[44]

44. Bulger, "Connotation."

The reason why there have been so many views on how to translate *hebel* is that this word not only has several denotations but also carries a range of connotations in the speech. In the context of the workaholic it may be appropriate to translate *hebel* with the connotation instead of the denotation as the context seems to require it. But it may not be appropriate in other contexts. We need to differentiate connotation from the point of view of the observer and speaker (Qoheleth) and that of the participant (whether Qoheleth himself or those he observed). In the case of the workaholic, the "absurd" connotation is from the point of view of Qoheleth the speaker himself.

In the case of the theme "all is vanity" discussed above, the connotation "ironic," "absurd," "meaningless," or "enigmatic" is not from the point of view of the speaker but that of the *reader*, who assumes that his own subjective reaction to the objective reality of vanity is that of the participant. In fact he identifies with, or even considers himself, the participant. Different readers have a different "framework of expectations" and hence different reactions to "all is vanity." The connotation of *hebel* they see or feel varies accordingly whereas the connotation the speaker sees or feels is fixed as there is only one speaker, who is reporting what he observed and expressing how *he* feels about it through his speech. Hence it is appropriate to translate using the speaker's but not the reader's connotation.

As for the second and third categories, where Qoheleth uses the expression "grievous experience" to describe a situation, the grievous experience is that of Qoheleth himself (as observer and participant respectively). In each of the two cases in the second category, Qoheleth had a grievous experience when he observed something that is realistically painful to observe. In one case (9:3a), it is painful to observe not only that the righteous share the same fate—certain death—with the wicked (cf. 9:2), but also that as a consequence, people "are full of evil, and stupidity is in their hearts throughout their lives" (9:3b). In the other case (10:5), it is painful to observe a king making a foolish decision that leads to upheavals in society (cf. 10:6–7). Again there is nothing pessimistic about Qoheleth's reactions to these observations.

In the first case in the third category (1:13–14), Qoheleth as participant found that when wisdom is used to try to solve the basic problem of life ("all is vanity"), this itself is vanity and he describes the vain attempt as a grievous experience. This is still objective realism and not subjective pessimism. For anyone who repeats what he did will also have a similar experience. The second case (2:21) is indeed a case of pessimism on the part of Qoheleth. But it is about his (past) negative reactions as *participant* of vanity in his experiment with pleasure (2:1–11), which included his experience with success and wealth (2:12–23). And now as *speaker* on vanity, he recounts his *past* discovery of, and reactions to, the vanity of pleasure and of success and wealth as a testimony in order to present his *present* admonition to his audience to respond realistically to vanity by enjoying what God has given (2:24–26).

Hence to appreciate the meaning and power of Qoheleth's profound speech we need to be sensitive to the different points of view and the various nuances of *hebel*, not just the denotations but also the connotations, and translate accordingly.

The statement above that "the connotation the speaker sees or feels is fixed" needs to be qualified. Consider the case of 8:14, where Qoheleth uses *hebel* twice to describe the situation where the righteous suffers while the wicked prospers. The denotation of *hebel* here is still "vanity," the "vanity" of righteousness as discussed above. But the situation is ironic even from the point of view of Qoheleth the speaker. While the connotation he sees or feels as speaker is fixed, we as reader still need to interpret what it is, whether it be on the side of "meaningless" (pessimism) or "enigmatic" (realism). Based on Qoheleth's overall viewpoint we have seen so far (realism), the appropriate translation of 8:14 is: "There is an *enigma* that takes place on earth, that there are righteous people to whom it happens according to the deeds of the wicked, and there are wicked people to whom it happens according to the deeds of the righteous. I say that this is indeed *enigmatic*." The burden of proof is on interpreters who see pessimism in Qoheleth's reaction.

Note that whether we translate *hebel* here as "meaningless" or "enigmatic," we are not dealing with the meaning of *hebel* since it involves a connotation and not the denotation of *hebel*. Like the connotations associated with the theme "all is *hebel*," the connotation here is based on a subjective reaction to an objective reality expressed through the denotation of *hebel* ("vanity"). So the connotations, no matter how "foul," have no bearing on the meaning of *hebel*.

Similarly a grievous experience associated with a *hebel* situation, no matter how "foul," has no bearing on the meaning of *hebel* as the experience is about a subjective reaction to the objective reality of *hebel* ("vanity"). Thus when Qoheleth says, "And I hated all my wealth for which I toiled under the sun [a rather "foul" experience], because I must leave it to the man who will come after me [wealth is vanity]" (2:18), the "foulness" arose from his (then) subjective reaction to the "vanity" of wealth. The "foulness" has nothing to do with the meaning of *hebel*, which expresses the reality. Hence contra Miller, there is no case where it requires "foulness" to be an aspect of the material sense of *hebel* so as to provide "the *rationale* for a metaphoric connection between vapor and foulness."[45]

We have looked at or referred to every occurrence of *hebel* in Ecclesiastes except 4:16, 6:9 and 8:10. These three verses are respectively about the (ultimate) profitlessness of power and popularity, the (immediate) futility of seeking to satisfy the insatiable appetite of the human soul with the things of this world, and the (immediate) profitlessness of a glowing eulogy and an honorable burial given to a wicked person. Thus *hebel* in these cases, as in every other case, also refers to an objective reality. Hence there is nothing pessimistic about *hebel* itself.

---

45. Miller, *Symbol and Rhetoric*, 96.

So whether Ecclesiastes expresses a pessimistic view of life depends solely on Qoheleth's subjective reaction *as speaker* to the objective reality of *hebel* ("vanity"). Now 8:14 is the only case where Qoheleth the speaker has a negative reaction to a "vanity" itself (and not to the senseless pursuit of a vanity as in cases like 4:8). Even in this case it is appropriately understood as realism and not pessimism. Therefore we can now conclude that there is no pessimism in Ecclesiastes on the part of Qoheleth as speaker. This means Ecclesiastes does not present a pessimistic view of the world.

The Meaning of "Under the Sun"

Strictly speaking, the meaning of the phrase "under the sun," which occurs twenty-nine times in Ecclesiastes and nowhere else in the Bible, is not at all controversial. For it is adequately attested in other writings of the ancient biblical world. In the Babylonian *Epic of Gilgamesh* we find this statement: "Only the gods [live] forever under the sun. As for mankind, numbered are their days; whatever they achieve is but the wind."[46] In the Babylonian text, the phrase translated "under the sun" is actually "with the sun" and is rendered by Assyriologist A. R. George as "in sunlight,"[47] which is equivalent to "under the sun." In two separate but similar Phoenician inscriptions the exact phrase occurs, contrasting "the living under the sun" with the dead who are "with the shades."[48] This phrase thus refers to the realm of human life and activities in this temporal world as opposed to the hereafter.

There is every reason to suppose that Qoheleth uses this phrase with the same meaning. This is rather clear when he describes the not-yet-born as those who have "not seen the evil deeds that are done *under the sun*" (4:3); the living as "those who move about *under the sun*" (4:15); and the already dead as those who "will no longer have a share in all that is done *under the sun*" (9:6). But interpreters and preachers who accept Ecclesiastes as Scripture inspired by God tend to give it a different meaning, which can change the meaning of the whole book as well as its application to believers in God. So it warrants an adequate response here.

The Views of Leupold, Eaton and Heim

To avoid reading pessimism in Qoheleth's assertion that "all is vanity," Herbert Leupold maintains that "the presence of the little phrase 'under the sun' *always* says in effect, 'What I claim is true if one deals with purely earthly values.'"[49] In other words, "Each time the phrase occurs it is as though the author [or speaker] had said, 'Let us

---

46. Pritchard, *Ancient Near Eastern Texts*, 79.
47. George, *Babylonian Gilgamesh Epic*, 201.
48. Pritchard, *Ancient Near Eastern Texts*, 662.
49. Leupold, *Ecclesiastes*, 43 (italics added).

for the sake of argument momentarily rule out higher things."[50] For if "*all* is vanity" includes spiritual or higher things, Qoheleth the speaker is indeed pessimistic.

We have seen that in the context of the theme of Ecclesiastes as represented in 1:2–3, Qoheleth is certainly dealing with purely earthly values and makes no reference to spiritual or higher things when he labels something as *hebel*. This is also the case with the whole speech. It is most obvious when he labels even righteousness as *hebel* ("vanity") because righteousness may not bring temporal or material profit (7:15; 8:14). Hence he ignores spiritual things even when considering the "profits" of righteousness.

However, Qoheleth did not use the phrase "under the sun" in order to indicate that he is ruling out higher things. There are contexts in which applying such a meaning to the phrase will be very awkward. In 8:15 Qoheleth commends the enjoyment of life, "for this will accompany him in his toil all the days of his life which God has given him *under the sun*." Two verses later he comments that we cannot discover "the work of God . . . which has been done *under the sun*." Not only is the "What I claim is true if one deals with purely earthly values" qualification out of place here, the phrase clearly refers to a realm (that of the living) rather than indicates a perspective (of ruling out higher values).

Michael Eaton also gives a different meaning to "under the sun" even though he acknowledges that the phrase "has links with other ancient writings."[51] He claims that Qoheleth uses it "for his own purposes,"[52] that is, in Ecclesiastes "under the sun" indicates a worldview[53]—secularism to be specific.[54] Thus for a person who is "*Under the sun* . . . To all practical purposes this man's life excludes God."[55] Why would he make such a claim?

Like most commentators, Eaton understands the term "vanity (*hebel*)" as basically an expression of pessimism.[56] And to him "All is vanity" (1:2) means "All earthly experience, seen as a unit, is 'subject to vanity' (cf. Rom. 8:20)."[57] So "All is vanity" (pessimism) applies to all humanity. However, "It is only to one seeking satisfaction in disregard of God [one 'under the sun'] that the Preacher's message stops at 'All is vanity' [that is, it is a message of pessimism]. . . . When . . . new factors are brought in (the generosity of God, divine providence, divine judgment), the 'vanity' of life is

---

50. Leupold, *Ecclesiastes*, 42–43.
51. Eaton, *Ecclesiastes*, 57–58.
52. Eaton, *Ecclesiastes*, 45.
53. Eaton, *Ecclesiastes*, 103.
54. Eaton, *Ecclesiastes*, 56.
55. Eaton, *Ecclesiastes*, 63.
56. Eaton, *Ecclesiastes*, 55–57.
57. Eaton, *Ecclesiastes*, 56–57.

not obliterated or forgotten; but the new factors transform the perspective and turn pessimism into faith."[58]

In other words, "All is vanity" remains pessimistic only to one who is "under the sun." To a person of faith it is no longer so. Thus Eaton concludes that "Ecclesiastes is . . . an exploration of the barrenness of life without practical faith in God";[59] it is an essay that "defends the life of faith in a generous God by pointing to the grimness of the alternative."[60] If this interpretation is correct, it would essentially remove the apparent pessimism attributed to Qoheleth as it limits the supposed pessimism of "All is vanity" to only those "without practical faith in God." It would also have a powerful message for secularists.

However, this interpretation is based on the supposition that people "under the sun" are secularists and thus people of faith are not "under the sun." This supposition cannot be consistently maintained. For instance, in 9:2–3 Qoheleth laments that under the sun there is one fate (death) for everyone: the righteous and the wicked, the (religiously) clean and the unclean, the one who offers sacrifices and the one who does not offer sacrifices. Thus according to Qoheleth even a man as pious as one who is righteous, religiously pure and who offers sacrifices—certainly not a secularist—is among those under the sun.

Like Leupold, Eaton disregards the straightforward and well-established meaning of "under the sun" in order to explain away the apparent pessimism of "All is vanity." To Leupold, "under the sun" indicates that Qoheleth is *limiting his message* to only matters that are secular (temporal as opposed to eternal). To Eaton, "under the sun" indicates that Qoheleth is referring to people who are *limiting their life* to only matters that are secular. All this is not necessary as "All is vanity" is realism and not pessimism.

Eaton's interpretation is very attractive to preachers because it not only removes the apparent pessimism of Ecclesiastes but also highlights the pessimism of a life built on secularism, which is a very relevant message for contemporary society.

Our interpretation also comes to a similar conclusion: most secularists in the modern world, because they put all their hopes in temporal things, will find life, to one degree or another, pessimistic because they cannot accept the vanity of temporal things. But it also gives room for secularists who are able to come to terms with the vanity of temporal things to have a realistic view of life. If Qoheleth indeed claims that secularists, just because their life "excludes God," will necessarily view life with sheer pessimism and without remedy, as Eaton's interpretation makes us believe, he is too pessimistic about secularists.

---

58. Eaton, *Ecclesiastes*, 57.
59. Eaton, *Ecclesiastes*, 45.
60. Eaton, *Ecclesiastes*, 44.

Eaton's commentary is the original volume on Ecclesiastes in the *Tyndale Old Testament Commentaries* series. It has been replaced by that of Knut Heim.[61] In an unexpected twist, Heim has given the phrase "under the sun" a peculiar meaning. Following Krüger,[62] he assumes that "The political context to which the book [of Ecclesiastes] responds is a period of foreign rule over Judea [where the book originated] under the Ptolemaic Dynasty of Greek rulers in Egypt."[63] Though he acknowledges that "The phrase initially appears to be a reference to 'life on earth' or 'the universality of human experience,'" he goes on to argue that, "Against the historical background of foreign rule under the Egyptian Ptolemaic kings, however, the phrase is also a cypher for Egypt: it means 'subject to the Egyptian foreign regime.'"[64] So "under the sun" does not just mean being alive in this world but specifically being alive under Egyptian rule. This difference, though relatively small, has relatively big consequences.

In a footnote, Krüger asks in passing: "Ptolemy V (204–180 B.C.E.) has himself worshiped as 'a king like the Sun (or the sun god Re)' . . . and his image put on coins with a sun crown. Could a contemporary reader thus also associate 'under the sun' with 'under the rule of the Ptolemies'?"[65] Heim has turned this speculation into a presupposition, for his view on "under the sun" is the paradigm that governs his interpretation of Ecclesiastes. Heim provides four arguments to support his view but concedes that "These arguments do not prove that the phrase is a cypher for Egyptian rule over Judea, and *this is precisely the point*. Qoheleth had to be careful, and this is why his oratory is so multivalent."[66]

Why had Qoheleth to be careful so that it cannot be proven from his speech that "under the sun" actually means "under Egyptian rule"? Heim claims that the speech was no different from how "comedians make veiled allusions to current affairs which are specific enough for the insider audience to recognize the reference to real-life events while carefully concealing what the talk is really about behind underdetermined [intentionally vague] language [so that the intended meaning can be easily denied to avoid persecution from the oppressive and repressive regime he was speaking against]."[67] Hence "Qoheleth's audience would have caught the political referent of the cypher, but for later readers the phrase appears to denote human existence in general. Its second, hidden meaning as a cypher for Jewish life under foreign rule will only become visible later, from 3:16 onwards [where the sub-theme of political oppression and undeserved suffering begins]."[68]

61. Heim, *Ecclesiastes*.
62. Krüger, *Qoheleth*, 19–21.
63. Heim, *Ecclesiastes*, 4.
64. Heim, *Ecclesiastes*, 4.
65. Krüger, *Qoheleth*, 53.
66. Heim, *Ecclesiastes*, 6 (italics added).
67. Heim, *Ecclesiastes*, 5.
68. Heim, *Ecclesiastes*, 48.

This view on the meaning of "under the sun" presupposes that the writer of Ecclesiastes was living specifically under the rule of the Egyptian Ptolemaic kings and not any other. Stuart Weeks, having evaluated the relevant materials cautions: "modern scholars have found no difficulty in reading Ecclesiastes against the background of various periods (just as their predecessors read the book against a Solomonic background), but little or nothing has been identified that points unequivocally to one specific period."[69] In other words, Heim's interpretative paradigm rests on a presupposition ("under the sun" = "living under Egyptian rule") which he himself says cannot be proven precisely because it rests on another presupposition (the writer was living under oppressive and repressive Egyptian rule) which Weeks says cannot be proven.

When a writer speaks through a persona, the historical setting of the persona need not be that of the writer. So even if the writer of Ecclesiastes lived under Egyptian rule as Heim presupposes, the political context of Qoheleth the Solomonic persona need not be that of Egyptian rule. And even if the political context of Qoheleth is that of Egyptian rule, without any indication from the writer there is no reason to conclude that he uses the phrase "under the sun" to mean not just living in this world (obvious meaning) but specifically living under Egyptian rule. If there is any indication given by the writer himself on the political context of Qoheleth, it is his choice of the persona—that of Solomon specifically as king over Israel (1:1, 12; 2:9) at its political peak ruling over even neighboring nations and receiving tributes from them (1 Kgs 4:21), which enabled Solomon to acquire the wealth which Qoheleth declares twice as *hebel* (vanity) and thus "there is no profit under the sun" (2:1–11). Hence even if the presupposition that Ecclesiastes was written during the period of the Egyptian Ptolemaic kings can be proven, it is still tenuous to suppose without proof that "under the sun" means specifically "being alive under Egyptian rule," let alone presuppose it as the interpretative paradigm.

Though Heim's view on "under the sun" retains the meaning of being alive in this world, how it differs from this established meaning cannot be treated as a small matter. In our discussion above on Heim's view of *hebel*, which he claims means "mirage" (illusion), we have seen how his view on "under the sun" is used to interpret 11:10 to support his claim that *hebel* always means "mirage" in Ecclesiastes. Consider now how it affects Heim's interpretation of the theme of Ecclesiastes as first expressed in 1:2–3, which we understand as, Everything is *hebel* (vanity) because there is no *yitrôn* (profit) under the sun (living in this world). Heim's view renders the theme as, Everything is *hebel* (a mirage) because there is no *yitrôn* (success) under the sun ("living under foreign rule"). But why would Qoheleth assert that there is no "success" living under foreign rule?

By presupposing his view on "under the sun," Heim supposes without evidence that the Hebrew word *yitrôn* used here and throughout Ecclesiastes has a peculiar

---

69. Weeks, *Ecclesiastes 1–5*, 75.

meaning: As "A neologism coined among Hellenizing Jews [living under Ptolemaic rule] specifically to express their aspirations to take advantage of the new opportunities, it meant to express economic and social success in the pursuit of personal happiness, something which, according to the foreign worldview, seemed obtainable without observance of the Jewish religion."[70] In other words, "In Qoheleth's time, many believed that this [success] was possible as a natural reward for hard work, *without* need for God."[71] Thus the *hebel* of life "under the sun" is about the pursuit of social and economic success "*without* need for God." Therefore, at least in the context of the theme of Ecclesiastes, Heim's view on "under the sun" is in practice that of Eaton's—leaving God out of one's thinking and living.

The Views of Longman, Bartholomew and Weeks

At least Eaton assumes that Qoheleth himself is not "under the sun" and thus not a pessimist. Longman claims that Qoheleth's "frequent use of the phrase *under the sun* highlights the restrictive scope of his inquiry. His ['under the sun'] worldview does not allow him to take a transcendent yet immanent God into consideration in his quest for meaning."[72] In other words, he goes so far as to say that Qoheleth is himself "under the sun," a pessimist who does not "believe that God has any relevance for the human realm."[73]

In his more recent and much shorter commentary on Ecclesiastes, Longman qualifies (or modifies) his view: "The Teacher's thought may be characterized as "under the sun" thinking, that is, thinking apart from the revelation of God. It is not that he completely leaves God out; after all, he reflects on who God is and gives advice about a relationship with him in ch 5. However, his thinking about life is restricted to what he sees happen on earth and is not based on what he learns from Israel's prophets."[74]

Longman, who argues that Qoheleth asserts "Everything is meaningless," himself asks, "if Qohelet's lengthy speech is [thus] pessimistic and out of sorts with the rest of the OT, why is it included in the canon?"[75] His answer: "Qohelet's speech is a foil, a teaching device used by the [assumed] second wise man [the 'frame narrator' who wrote and appended the orthodox 'epilogue' (12:9–14) to correct Qoheleth's unorthodox speech (1:2–12:8)] in order to instruct his son (12:12) concerning the dangers of speculative, doubting wisdom in Israel [represented by Qoheleth]."[76]

70. Heim, *Ecclesiastes*, 6–7.
71. Heim, *Ecclesiastes*, 39.
72. Longman, *Ecclesiastes*, 66.
73. Longman, *Ecclesiastes*, 66.
74. Longman, "Ecclesiastes," 264.
75. Longman, *Ecclesiastes*, 38.
76. Longman, *Ecclesiastes*, 38.

Hence though the views of Qoheleth are supposedly unorthodox, the teaching of the book as a whole is not since the orthodox epilogue provides the remedy to his views. This means almost the entire book of Ecclesiastes is useless in terms of authoritative teaching, and if one wants to preach from Qoheleth's speech, one would have to preach against Qoheleth's views. This would render Ecclesiastes useless to preachers as it makes no sense to preach against virtually the whole book.

Jerry Shepherd, who says "I have adopted Longman's main thesis"[77] that "Qohelet's speech is a foil"[78] asks, "Does it mean that it is wrong to preach a series of sermons from Ecclesiastes, since the only real word from God comes in the last few verses?"[79] His own answer is "yes."[80] He then qualifies that the answer "perhaps . . . can also be 'no'" only if the preacher bears in mind that "the speech of Qohelet in Ecclesiastes is not the word of God but is contained in a book that is God's Word. . . . So, can individual passages from Ecclesiastes be preached without always being qualified by the epilogue and the larger canon of Scripture? Perhaps, but I believe the warrant for such preaching is fairly thin."[81]

Like Longman, Richard Belcher understands "under the sun" to mean that "Qohelet's thinking is limited to this earthly life and the horizons of an earthly perspective without recourse to divine revelation."[82] The result is that, like Longman, he considers what we read in Qoheleth's speech (1:2–12:7) as "speculative wisdom."[83] Yet he seeks to help preachers preach through Ecclesiastes to the extent that he even provides "Homiletical implications" throughout his commentary of Ecclesiastes. Meredith M. Kline, in his review of this commentary asks, "What difference does Belcher's interpretation make when preaching from Ecclesiastes?"[84] He lays down the options:

> For the preacher who understands Qohelet's "under the sun" perspective as a presentation of deviant "speculative wisdom," which is corrected in the epilogue (12:9–14), Belcher's commentary is an excellent resource. For a pastor holding to the view that Qohelet is a believing realist, it becomes a question whether Belcher's perspective on Ecclesiastes so pervades his commentary that it is counterproductive to wade through all his details in order to arrive at an appropriate expository sermon.[85]

---

77. Shepherd, "Ecclesiastes," 258.
78. Shepherd, "Ecclesiastes," 257.
79. Shepherd, "Ecclesiastes," 269.
80. Shepherd, "Ecclesiastes," 269.
81. Shepherd, "Ecclesiastes," 269–70.
82. Belcher, *Ecclesiastes*, 48.
83. Belcher, *Ecclesiastes*, 51–55.
84. Kline, "Ecclesiastes: Review Article."
85. Kline, "Ecclesiastes: Review Article."

Craig Bartholomew rejects Longman's interpretation of "under the sun" as an expression "to indicate the restricted scope of Qohelet's inquiry."[86] To Bartholomew it only means "Qohelet is concerned with the whole range of human experience [and] his viewpoint certainly includes God and how belief in God bears on life 'under the sun.'"[87] Hence Qoheleth is not (entirely) unorthodox. Unlike Longman, Bartholomew recognizes that orthodox teaching in Ecclesiastes is found not only in the epilogue, but also in the body of the speech as well. According to him, "Qohelet is represented in a number of ways: as king in Jerusalem (the Solomonic fiction), as an explorer in the grip of an autonomous epistemology (Greek), and as a believing Israelite who affirms the meaning of life in the *carpe diem* passages and other sections such as 5:1–7. We ought to distinguish more closely between the [unorthodox] 'Greek' Qohelet and the 'orthodox' [Israelite] Qohelet. . . . The tension between these two Qohelets is central to the book and accounts for its dialogical nature."[88]

Bartholomew explains that this tension exists because "The postexilic [Greek] context of Israel, with what appeared to be the demise of the great Israelite experiment, must have led the Qohelet and his educated contemporaries to question the reality of the Israelite vision of life into which they were born and nurtured. Qohelet thus sets out to explore the meaning of life with the tools of his autonomous 'Greek' epistemology, while being unable to refute the genuine insights of his Israelite tradition."[89] Qoheleth then is the ancient counterpart to a modern biblical scholar who sets out to explore the meaning of the Bible with the tools of his autonomous Enlightenment epistemology, while being unable to refute (or reject) the "genuine insights" of his Christian (or Jewish) tradition.

Actually it is not difficult to see "two Qohelets" if one is so inclined. Whybray, who himself gives much weight to the "joy" (enjoyment) passages of Ecclesiastes, observes that, "Depending on the relative weight placed by the interpreters respectively on the negative and positive sides of statements . . . , a whole range of assessments of Qoheleth's outlook, from one of extreme pessimism and despair to one of courageous faith and radiant optimism has been made by ancient and modern scholars alike."[90]

Bartholomew is simply taking the middle ground by giving equal weight to both "the negative [Greek Qoheleth] and positive [Israelite Qoheleth] sides of statements." In the process he has to "allow the contradictory perspectives to stand side by side,"[91] even claiming that "The opposing perspectives are *deliberately* juxtaposed so that gaps

---

86. Bartholomew, *Ecclesiastes*, 108.
87. Bartholomew, *Ecclesiastes*, 108.
88. Bartholomew, *Ecclesiastes*, 78.
89. Bartholomew, *Ecclesiastes*, 59.
90. Whybray, *Ecclesiastes*, 28.
91. Bartholomew, *Ecclesiastes*, 153.

are opened up in the reading, and the book is precisely about how to resolve the tension between these contradictory juxtapositions."[92]

The first volume of Stuart Weeks's two-volume commentary on Ecclesiastes in the *International Critical Commentary* series came out when work on this book was essentially completed. Suffice it to note here that, based on his "Outline" of "Qohelet's Ideas,"[93] his views on Ecclesiastes are moderate compared to those of Longman and Bartholomew. Unlike Longman, Weeks understands "under the sun," which he renders as "beneath the sun" in the straightforward and well-established sense presented above. He rightly equates this phrase with "to see the sun" (7:11; 11:7), which he renders as "to look on the sun, i.e. to be beneath it, [which] is to be alive."[94]

And unlike Longman, who translates *hebel* consistently as "meaningless," Weeks translates this keyword as "illusion" and renders "All is *hebel*" as "It is all an illusion!"[95] Thus he does not necessarily introduce pessimism into the theme of Ecclesiastes. And though like Heim he translates *hebel* consistently as "illusion," his understanding of this term is rather nuanced.[96] He spells out that "It is difficult always to exclude other nuances in some places, and in 9.9, for instance, *hebel* surely carries some additional or even alternative implication that human life is ephemeral and transitory."[97] Thus unlike Heim, this will avoid introducing pessimism into contexts like 9:9 and 11:10, where *hebel* obviously means "fleeting." However by still translating *hebel* as "illusion" instead of "fleeting" in these contexts just for the sake of consistency, it will likely mislead readers of his translation.

Unlike Bartholomew, Weeks considers "the actual degree of contradiction and incoherence often to have been overstated" though he thinks that "the writer [of Ecclesiastes himself] does not intend us to find Qohelet entirely coherent."[98] In other words, "It should be very apparent . . . that we are not dealing with a carefully structured argument in the monologue, and even in the first three chapters there is sometimes more rhetoric than logic behind Qohelet's claims. It should also be evident, however, that Qohelet's ideas are cumulative: most of the assertions that he makes in later chapters depend on points that he has already made, and there is a deliberate effort early in the book to lay a groundwork, to which Qohelet himself not infrequently appeals."[99]

---

92. Bartholomew, *Ecclesiastes*, 81.
93. Weeks, *Ecclesiastes 1–5*, 14–20.
94. Weeks, *Ecclesiastes 1–5*, 259.
95. Weeks, *Ecclesiastes 1–5*, 248.
96. Weeks, *Ecclesiastes 1–5*, 20–29.
97. Weeks, *Ecclesiastes 1–5*, 27.
98. Weeks, *Ecclesiastes 1–5*, 53.
99. Weeks, *Ecclesiastes 1–5*, 18.

And for the content of Qoheleth's argument, Weeks goes so far as to say, "Qohelet behaves sometimes almost as an *idiot savant*."[100] So to be consistent with his view of Qoheleth, unlike Bartholomew,[101] Weeks has to read 12:9–12 against the grain to paint a negative picture of Qoheleth:

> It is more than a little disconcerting, therefore, when the last few verses of the book take pains to inform us that Qohelet was actually a writer and crafter of words [that goad us into fearing God]. . . . The problem is not simply that these statements seem out of step with all that has been said so far [1:2–12:8], but that they positively dismantle it: every effort [of Qohelet] that has been made to engage our sympathies, to provoke our laughter, anger or sadness, is revealed as deliberate manipulation by a clever writer, working in a tradition that specializes in such manipulation. With a metatheatrical flourish, this whole book, so concerned with illusion and misplaced belief, is shown to have been a sort of illusion itself.[102]

Weeks goes on to add, "Despite some praise for Qohelet's talents as a writer and a teller of truth, therefore, the epilogue . . . is hardly a ringing endorsement of his monologue, and seems more concerned that we should not worry about it too much. It is hard to believe that this is just clumsiness—the result, perhaps, of some later writer who wished to praise Qohelet inadvertently undercutting what had been said"[103] (for an elaborate discussion that 12:9–12 is indeed "a ringing endorsement" of Qoheleth's monologue, see "Exposition of Ecclesiastes" under "Excursus to 12:9–12"). Hence Weeks's commentary, though relatively moderate, also presents Qoheleth as an unreliable teacher and thus it is not advisable for preachers to preach through Ecclesiastes.

The Rhetoric of Ecclesiastes

We have shown that there is really no pessimism on the part of Qoheleth as speaker. To show there are also no contradictory perspectives in Ecclesiastes—whether those of Qoheleth versus the supposed frame narrator (Longman), or those of the supposed Greek Qoheleth versus the Israelite Qoheleth (Bartholomew), or those of Qoheleth a supposed *idiot savant* (Weeks)—we need to consider the rhetoric of Ecclesiastes.

Though we have seen that the theme "All is vanity" in itself is not ironic, we will no doubt encounter ironies in reading Ecclesiastes. The greatest irony is in the caution "Of making many books there is no end, and much study is weariness to the body" (12:12). Originally it was a warning about studying books other than those

---

100. Weeks, *Ecclesiastes 1–5*, 43.
101. Bartholomew, *Ecclesiastes*, 364–66.
102. Weeks, *Ecclesiastes 1–5*, 37.
103. Weeks, *Ecclesiastes 1–5*, 38.

like Ecclesiastes ("given by one Shepherd"); today it is also a caution about studying Ecclesiastes itself!

A student of Ecclesiastes is confronted with such an array of conflicting and thus confusing interpretations of Ecclesiastes that this caution amounts to saying we need to first look for the interpretive grid provided by Ecclesiastes itself to guide us in making sense of this otherwise enigmatic book. In fact unless guided by such an objective grid, it will be difficult for an interpreter, no matter how much research he does, to have a sense of assurance that his own interpretation is anywhere close to what Qoheleth is actually saying. In fact more likely, the more research one does the more difficult it would be for one to be assured.

Week's two-volume commentary is exceptionally massive—fifteen hundred pages for a relatively short biblical book. It has to be the most thoroughly researched piece of scholarship on Ecclesiastes so far. Yet it is candid about the tentativeness of its interpretations, or rather "opinions":

> It may be taken as a given that, since scholars disagree with each other on so many points, little that I say would win the assent of every other commentator, although I have tried to indicate where my opinions represent the view of a minority, or are cries in the wilderness. I should stress also, however, that even where there is some consensus with respect to the interpretation of specific passages, the fact of consensus does not always put that interpretation beyond question: some understandings survive, I think, more through their appeal to past authority than through any inherent credibility.[104]

The Interpretive Grid

Does Ecclesiastes actually provide an interpretive grid to make sense of the speech? If it does, to see it we need to come to Ecclesiastes without assuming the book is incoherent and look for signs in the text *taken as a whole* that may indicate how to make sense of it.

Firstly, except for the third person descriptions of Qoheleth (1:1 and 12:9–12), Ecclesiastes is a monologue and the three "says Qoheleth" (1:2; 7:27; 12:8) that punctuate the speech at the beginning, middle and end confirm that Qoheleth's words stretch from 1:2 all the way to at least 12:8. Secondly, Qoheleth makes it unmistakable that "All is *hebel*" (1:2; 12:8) is the theme of his speech from 1:2 up to 12:8, after which is the third person description (12:9–12). And immediately after that, we read "The end (conclusion) of the matter, all has been heard, fear God . . ." (12:13–14). We are here just making clear-cut observations of the text taken as a whole without prejudging whether the book is incoherent. These objective observations should form the basis for any valid interpretation of Ecclesiastes.

---

104. Weeks, *Ecclesiastes 1–5*, 3.

We have shown that "all is *hebel*" means "all is vanity." What then does "The end (conclusion) of the matter" mean and whose words are these? The Hebrew *noun* translated "end" occurs only five times in the Hebrew Bible, three times in Ecclesiastes itself. Two times it refers to the *physical* end of something (2 Chr 20:16; Joel 2:10). In Ecclesiastes, two times it refers to the *temporal* end or goal of something—"from the beginning to the *end*" (3:11) and "the *end* of every man (death)" (7:2)—and one time here in 12:13 in the Hebrew phrase, "the end of the matter." This Hebrew *phrase* occurs only here and nowhere else in the Hebrew Bible. However, it "is frequently employed by post-biblical writers for *in conclusion, finally*."[105]

In the context of 12:13a, "the end" then refers to the conclusion of "the all" (*hakkol* as in 1:2; see above) that "has been heard"—the speech from 1:2 to 12:8 (see further "Exposition of Ecclesiastes" in footnote on 10:19). No doubt "All is vanity" (1:2; 12:8) is already a conclusion in the speech; it is the conclusion of Qoheleth's investigation, upon which the speech is based. But this conclusion, like the conclusion of any factual investigation, requires a "So now what?" response, and thus cannot be the proper conclusion of the speech as such. Andrew Shead puts it excellently: "The [factual] conclusion 'Vanity' . . . is an indicative, the result of much observation and thought. The [logical] conclusion 'Fear God' is an imperative, the result (we must suppose) of the revelation of Israelite religion."[106]

This means, having concluded (factually) that "all is vanity" (1:2–12:8), Qoheleth further concludes (logically): "(therefore) fear God . . ." (12:13b–14). So to understand the book as a whole, the reader needs to answer the question: Why is it that because "All is vanity" (theme of speech), we are therefore to "Fear God . . ." (conclusion of speech)? This is to be done by intentionally and carefully looking for clues in 1:2–12:8 taken as a whole without assuming that Qoheleth is inconsistent or unorthodox until proven otherwise.

All this then provides the interpretive grid to read 1:2–12:8 and to read it with a sense of purpose and direction. The nature of Ecclesiastes is such that the content of each of the sections when taken in isolation can be comfortably and even convincingly read in different ways to the point that it contradicts not only other books of the Bible but also other sections of Ecclesiastes. So when we do not allow the grid provided by Ecclesiastes itself to constrain how we read 1:2–12:8, there will be no end to how this profound book is interpreted.

Without the objective grid, at the least we will not likely see how Ecclesiastes is a coherent speech from beginning to end, and we may even see Qoheleth not only as inconsistent but also as unorthodox. We may then have to argue that the orthodox ending (12:13–14) cannot be the words of Qoheleth but those of a supposed "frame narrator," who added 1:1 and 12:9–14 to the speech of Qoheleth (1:2–12:8). Since Qoheleth is now assumed to be inconsistent and unorthodox, we may also have to

---

105. Ginsburg, *Coheleth*, 477.
106. Shead, "Reading Ecclesiastes 'Epilogically,'" 68.

read 12:9–12 against the grain to conclude that it paints Qoheleth in a negative light (e.g., Longman)[107] when a plain reading of the text clearly shows the very opposite (see "Exposition of Ecclesiastes" under "Excursus to 12:9–12").

This is what can happen when an interpreter with prior assumptions read Ecclesiastes without the benefit of the interpretive grid: "The most important themes of the second wise man ['frame narrator'] and the book are found in 12:13–14, the last two verses of the book. Here the wise man tells his son (12:12) that the most important things in life are to 'fear God and obey his commands.' It is true that the Teacher [Qoheleth] used the same words (3:14; 5:7; 7:18; 8:12) *but with doubtful conviction.*"[108]

Now the interpreter does not deny that Qoheleth "used the same words" (fear God/him) in four verses (3:14; 5:7; 7:18; 8:12) as the "second wise man" in 12:13 and with the same meaning, but only "with doubtful conviction." Thus he recognizes that the "second wise man," who says Qoheleth is a "wise man" (12:9), is saying the same thing as what Qoheleth have been saying all along.[109] But when Qoheleth says it, somehow it has to be "with doubtful conviction" though there is no evidence in the respective texts to indicate that (see our interpretation of the four verses in "Exposition of Ecclesiastes").

This means we have a series of four verses (3:14; 5:7; 7:18; 8:12) as evidence to support the validity of the interpretive grid—the last two verses (12:13b–14) is the logical conclusion to Qoheleth's speech even if these were added by the "second wise man" to complete Qoheleth's otherwise incomplete speech. But this evidence can be easily missed or eagerly dismissed because of prior assumptions that rule it out. Actually one need not even be guided by the interpretive grid to see that 12:13b—"fear God and keep his commandments"—builds on those four verses. Commenting on 12:13b, Whybray says, "Qoheleth himself frequently advocates the fear of God (3:14; 5:7 [MT 6]; 7:18; 8:12 . . .), but nowhere makes any reference to keeping his commandments. In associating the two the epiloguist is deliberately interpreting Qoheleth's teaching in terms of the keeping of the Law and thus attempting to represent him as an 'orthodox' wisdom teacher."[110]

The Flow of the Argument

We will now show how the interpretive grid presented above enables us to recognize the rhetoric of Ecclesiastes, which permeates the entire speech. The flow of the argument can be readily discerned if we do not assume that it has to be presented linearly from beginning to end (for more details, see "Introduction to Ecclesiastes" under "Coherent Message"; what follows is a bare-bone summary of Qoheleth's argument).

107. Longman, *Ecclesiastes*, 277–81; Longman, "Ecclesiastes," 330.
108. Longman, "Ecclesiastes," 258 (italics added); cf. Longman, *Ecclesiastes*, 282.
109. Cf. Whybray, *Ecclesiastes*, 75.
110. Whybray, *Ecclesiastes*, 173.

As laid down by the grid itself, the basic argument is that because "all is vanity" (1:2; 12:8), we should therefore "fear God and keep his commandments" (12:13b). When we pay attention to the repetitions of the theme and sub-themes and consider how they move the basic argument forward, we will be able to see the flow of thought from "All is vanity (profitless)" all the way to "Fear God."

Firstly, "all is vanity" means that because of the certainty of death, everything we have in this world will ultimately be profitless. Thus the sensible or meaningful thing to do is to enjoy what we have while we have them (2:24–26). It is futile and does not make sense (it is meaningless) to pursue after more things and in the process fail to enjoy what we have (4:4–8). But we cannot enjoy what we have unless we are relatively free from the cares of this world (5:18–20). In fact it is possible to have everything we have ever desired and yet not enjoy what we have (6:1–2). In extreme cases of such a grievous existence it is better not to have lived (6:3–6; cf. 4:1–3; Job 3, 10); otherwise it is good to be alive (9:4–6; 11:7–10).

Failure to enjoy one's wealth is often due to covetousness (6:7, 9). For covetousness—a violation of the tenth commandment—in and by itself already robs us of the carefreeness needed to enjoy what we have; what more when it leads to telling lies, stealing, committing adultery or even murder as well as self-harming our body by not observing the Sabbath? In other words, to enjoy what we have, we need to "remember" our Creator (12:1) and his purpose for humanity, which is to fear God and keep his commandments (12:13). Only then can we avoid emotional anguish and physical pain that are a consequence of violating God's commandments (11:9–10). Otherwise, there is no way we can have the carefreeness to enjoy what we have, including our relationship with loved ones (9:9).

Secondly, "all is vanity" not only because death is certain but also because life is uncertain (3:1–9); we may lose all that we have even before we die. Life is so uncertain that a "righteous person" may lose what he has before he dies and may in fact die young (7:15; 8:14).

To be carefree in the face of the uncertainties of life, we need to have the assurance that a God who is sovereign (3:1–8, 11a) and just (3:17; 8:11–13) is watching *over* us (cf. Psalm 121). In order to believe that such a God is watching *over* us, we must first recognize that he is *watching us* (5:1–7; 11:9). And when we recognize that God is watching us, we cannot help but fear him and keep his commandments (12:13–14). So again "All is vanity" leads us to "Fear God." However it must be qualified that being carefree does not mean being complacent or careless. One needs to be proactive (9:10; 11:1–6), but since bad things can happen to even good people, we also need to be careful—but not full of cares—in what we do and how we relate to others (8:2–8; 10:1–20).

In other words, "God so works that men (people) should fear him" (3:14b). For he works through the reality that "all is vanity," which is the consequence of the certainty of death and the uncertainties of life, so as to prod us (12:11) to "fear God and keep his commandments." Why would God do that? Fearing God and keeping his commandments is what makes us human (12:13b). It is God's purpose for humanity. And it is on this basis that one day God will judge everyone (11:9; 12:14).

Therefore the entire speech is not only coherent but also consistent and orthodox (this is confirmed in "Exposition of Ecclesiastes," which demonstrates how the overall interpretation of Ecclesiastes presented and defended here works out in every section of the book).

"The End of the Matter"

Since, besides the meaning of "All is *hebel*," the meaning of "The end of the matter" is also crucial to the interpretive grid that we use to interpret Ecclesiastes, we need to respond to Fox and Seow,[111] who argue on the basis of a similar Aramaic phrase in Daniel that "the end (conclusion) of the matter" (12:13a) marks the (physical) end of what has just been said (in the written speech). This means Qoheleth's speech, which begins at 1:2, ends abruptly at 12:8 without a proper conclusion.

The interpretation of Fox and Seow seems convincing because the Aramaic phrase in the book of Daniel unmistakably marks the end of what has just been said: "Until here the end of the matter" (Dan 7:28a). On this basis Fox, who translates 12:13a as "(Here is) the conclusion of the matter. Everything has been heard,"[112] says that "the 'matter' . . . is not what is about to be said in vv. 13b–14 but what has been said so far."[113] We do not dispute that "the matter" is about what has been said and not what is about to be said. However the issue in question is what "the conclusion," and not what "the matter," is about. Does "the conclusion" mark the end of what has been said so far or point to what is about to be said?

Note that in the case of Daniel 7:28a, "the end of the matter" *unambiguously* marks the end of what has been said because "the matter" is specified by "Until here," which marks the boundary of what has been said. And the context clearly indicates that what has been said has indeed ended because what follows (Dan 7:28b) is about Daniel's response to what has been said. The word "end" by itself does not mark the end of what has been said.

In another biblical example cited by Fox,[114] where the word "end" does not even occur, it is again the phrase "Until here" that marks the end of what has been said: "Until here the words of Jeremiah" (Jer 51:64). And the context indicates unmistakably that Jeremiah's words have indeed ended. Seow notes two other biblical examples that clearly mark the end of what have been said: "The words of Job are ended" (Job 31:40) and "The prayers of David . . . are ended" (Ps 72:20). The respective *verbs* translated "are ended" *unambiguously* mark the end of what have been said. And again, the

---

111. Fox, *Time*, 358–61; Seow, *Ecclesiastes*, 390.
112. Fox, *Time*, 358.
113. Fox, *Time*, 360.
114. Fox, *Time*, 359.

respective contexts indicate unmistakably that Job's words and David's prayers have indeed ended.

The "concluding formula" in Sirach 43:27 noted by Seow does not mark the end of what has been said. Alexander Di Lella comments that the verse is about "Ben Sira's humble comment that he has said enough about the wonders of creation: 'More than this we will not add' (43:27a). 'The last word' (cf. Qoh 12:13) is 'He [God] is the all' (43:27b)."[115] The extant Hebrew text of Sir 43:27b reads, "And the end of the matter: He [God] is the all."[116] The Hebrew word translated "end" is a synonym of that in Ecclesiastes 12:13a, and the word for "matter" is the same and also without the expected article. So this example actually supports our interpretation of 12:13a.

Seow also cites three examples from Talmudic Aramaic: "the end of the verse," "the end of the book" and "the end of the *halakah*." These three phrases mark the end of something because of their precise *wordings* in their specific *contexts*. For instance, "the end of the *verse*" refers precisely to a specific *verse* that is ended. The same cannot be said of "the end of the matter" though this phrase shares the same form—"the end of the (. . .) ." If the three phrases cited by Seow were written as, "the end of the *matter*," it is like saying at the end of a quote, "end of matter" instead of "end of quote." Thus there would be no longer any indication that in their specific contexts they mark the end of "the verse," "the book" and "the *halakah*" respectively.

In contrast to the above four biblical examples, "the end of the matter" in Ecclesiastes 12:13a is not specified by "Until here" to mark the end of what has been said so far, and it does not say, "The words of Qoheleth are ended." Also unlike these examples, the context here has no clear-cut indication that Qoheleth's words have ended at that point. The question then is how we understand the Hebrew *noun* translated "end" in this context—is it the (physical) end of what has been said (written) or is it the logical end of "all (that) has been heard"?

Since the meaning of a word or phrase must be determined from the context it is used, the basic question is the relation of 12:13a to both 1:2–12:8 (what is before) and 12:13b–14 (what is after) and the relation, if any, between 1:2–12:8 and 12:13b–14. Our interpretation of 12:13a is based on, and fits perfectly, the supposition that 12:13–14 is integral to 1:2–12:8 and that it is in fact the logical conclusion to Qoheleth's speech. So 12:13a is functioning as the obvious bridge.

Unfortunately this supposition goes against the grain of current mainstream scholarship on Ecclesiastes, which is itself full of conflicting views on how Ecclesiastes in its parts and as a whole is to be understood. Even Weeks, who unlike biblical scholars like Longman concedes that "The closing lines of Ecclesiastes probably do not contradict Qohelet," still concludes that "it is unlikely that Qohelet himself would have represented his message in quite these terms."[117] Though Weeks has "reasons . . . to doubt

---

115. Di Lella, *Wisdom of Ben Sira*, 495.
116. Beentjes, *Ben Sira in Hebrew*, 76.
117. Weeks, "Fear God," 115.

that the closing lines are simply a secondary attempt to make the book acceptable," he also has reasons "to doubt that they can have been intended (either by the author or by some subsequent redactor) to summarize Qohelet's monologue faithfully."[118]

The question over how to interpret 12:13a is then how to understand 1:2–12:8 in its parts and as a whole and the relation, if any, between 1:2–12:8 thus understood and 12:13–14. Our bare-bone summary of the rhetoric of Ecclesiastes presented above shows that 1:2–12:8 flows naturally into 12:13–14 (this is fleshed out in "Introduction to Ecclesiastes" under "Coherent Message," which is itself a concise summary of "Exposition of Ecclesiastes").

And throughout the exposition of Ecclesiastes there is a built-in defense of the interpretation taken. As indicated in the many references, our interpretation of virtually every verse of Ecclesiastes that matters is corroborated by at least one biblical scholar who does not share our interpretation of Ecclesiastes as a whole. Hence the interpretation of the respective verses, which supports our interpretation of Ecclesiastes as a whole, is not necessitated though guided by this overall interpretation.

In fact the indications that 1:2–12:8 does flow into 12:13–14 are so evident that even Bartholomew, who assumes that Ecclesiastes is inconsistent and that 12:13–14 are not the words of Qoheleth but those of the supposed frame narrator, concludes: "In vv. 13–14 the narrator sums up Qohelet's journey. 'All has been heard'—this evokes the wide-ranging, comprehensive nature of Qohelet's quest. 'The end of the matter' refers to the ultimate conclusion to [and not marks the end of] the quest we have witnessed."[119]

The Interpretation of Peter Enns

Before we conclude this essay, we need to take a look at Peter Enns's interpretation of Ecclesiastes presented in his commentary.[120] For his interpretation is so similar to and yet so different from that of ours presented above. To compare and contrast the two interpretations will help solidify our interpretation.

Enns spells out his *overall process* of interpretation: "Understanding Ecclesiastes as being *a book*, the product of an intentional, skilled, creative, and above all sagely (12:9–10) mind, encourages readers today to presume the book's coherence, which is seen precisely through the tensions in the book and amid the conflicting struggles of life that are recounted for us there"; and "reading Ecclesiastes is an exercise in paying very close attention to recurring, and often confusing, mixtures of themes and phrases that drive forward the theology of the book."[121] This is similar to the overall process we have adopted in our interpretation of Ecclesiastes—reading Ecclesiastes as a coherent

---

118. Weeks, "Fear God," 115.
119. Bartholomew, *Ecclesiastes*, 370.
120. Enns, *Ecclesiastes*.
121. Enns, *Ecclesiastes*, 7.

whole, and paying attention to the repetitions of the theme and the sub-themes and how they develop the argument from the theme to the conclusion.

Based on his overall process of interpretation, Enns's interpretation of the *overall message* of Ecclesiastes[122] is basically in agreement with ours as summarized above except that he leaves out the sub-theme of God's judgment and introduces pessimism into Ecclesiastes due to his translation of *hebel* as "absurd." We have painstakingly argued above why *hebel* should be translated "vanity" when it does not mean fleeting, and why it should not be translated "meaningless" or "absurd" in the context of the theme.

Enns follows Fox not only in translating *hebel* as "absurd"[123] but also in seeing "self-contradictory statements of Qohelet."[124] And he affirms there is "friction created by Qohelet's unorthodox speculations and the frame narrator's declaration of Qohelet's wisdom."[125] Even then, contra Longman,[126] Enns affirms that according to 12:10, "the written words of Qohelet are 'words of truth' and have an 'upright' quality to them. And . . . we can conclude only that the frame narrator is making a very positive evaluation of Qohelet's wisdom."[127] And commenting on 12:11, he adds, "It is hard to escape the positive evaluation that Qohelet is given here by the frame narrator."[128]

What Enns means is that "the epilogue [which to Enns is not just 12:9–14 but also 12:8] fundamentally supports Qohelet's observations while at the same time offering a mild 'corrective' by placing Qohelet's observations in a broader (and traditional) theological context. In other words, there are elements of both confirmation and correction, but the latter is undertaken within the overall context of the former."[129] So the "frame narrator" is overall "positive" about and supportive of Qoheleth though Enns himself recognizes that Qoheleth makes "self-contradictory statements" and "unorthodox speculations."

Hence Enns's interpretation of 1:2–12:8 concerning Qoheleth and that of 12:9–12 concerning the frame narrator's evaluation of Qoheleth render the frame narrator himself less than orthodox when 12:13–14 (taken to be his words) shows how orthodox he is. This means the supposed frame narrator is like a modern biblical scholar who views the Old Testament as a book with "self-contradictory statements" and "unorthodox speculations"—just like how Enns views Qoheleth's speech—but still accepts it as Scripture inspired by God. Thus Enns's interpretation of Ecclesiastes

---

122. Enns, *Ecclesiastes*, 7–16.
123. Enns, *Ecclesiastes*, 31.
124. Enns, *Ecclesiastes*, 2.
125. Enns, *Ecclesiastes*, 16.
126. Longman, *Ecclesiastes*, 277–81.
127. Enns, *Ecclesiastes*, 112.
128. Enns, *Ecclesiastes*, 113.
129. Enns, *Ecclesiastes*, 6.

requires us to rethink the very nature of Scripture inspired by God—both Old and New Testaments.[130]

All this means that any interpreter who does not view the Old Testament the way Enns views Qoheleth, but concludes that there is either inconsistency or unorthodoxy or both in 1:2–12:8, faces a serious exegetical and theological dilemma—does 12:9–12 then paint a positive or negative picture of Qoheleth? Attempts to dress up a supposed inconsistent and unorthodox Qoheleth (such as the case of Bartholomew's Greek/Israelite Qoheleth) in order to justify the obviously positive evaluation of Qoheleth in 12:9–12 are unconvincing because they are nothing more than afterthought attempts to escape the dilemma. And these attempts are unnecessary when it can be shown that Qoheleth is neither inconsistent nor unorthodox.

Seen in light of the dilemma, the role of 12:9–14 is to constrain how one interprets Qoheleth's words. For it spells out that what Qoheleth has written are "honest words of truth . . . given by one Shepherd (God)." If there is inconsistency or unorthodoxy in words of *truth* inspired by *God*, what is at stake is not just the nature of Scripture, but also of truth itself and of God himself. It is as though the writer of Ecclesiastes, having explicitly laid out the theme and the conclusion as guardrails for interpreting Ecclesiastes—"All is vanity" (1:2; 12:8) *therefore* "Fear God" (12:13–14)—suspected that interpreters would still miss it because of what they read between 1:2 and 12:8. So he inserted 12:9–12 to warn them how not to read it (see further "Exposition of Ecclesiastes" under "Excursus to 12:9–12").

Now besides Enns's acceptance of Fox's translation of *hebel*, what could be the reason Enns's interpretation differs so much with ours though both use the same overall process? Could it be due to the entrenched bias in mainstream biblical scholarship that rules out the possibility that Qoheleth might be consistent and orthodox? Consider these words of Enns on the process of interpreting Ecclesiastes:

> Discovering the meaning and purpose of Ecclesiastes will likely continue as a back-and-forth journey between overarching concepts and smaller exegetical details, balancing the forest and the trees. In the end, the theory that presents the most cohesive picture of Ecclesiastes will gain assent, at least for the time being. What is disconcerting, however, is that confusion about the book's basic message may dissuade preachers and teachers from bringing its theology to bear on the life of the church. Or, perhaps more problematic, *ill-informed* or even *reckless* interpretation of the book—that which expects a certain kind of cohesion [read: consistency], or expects only certain things [read: orthodoxy] from biblical authors—could do more damage than simply avoiding the book altogether [emphases added].[131]

---

130. Enns, *Ecclesiastes*, 194–201.
131. Enns, *Ecclesiastes*, 4 (italics added).

Thus Enns has prejudged that in looking for a "cohesive picture of Ecclesiastes," an interpreter is not allowed—it is "ill-informed or even reckless"—to expect to see the things that have been ruled out. If one abides by this dictum, when he has discerned an objective interpretive grid embedded in Ecclesiastes and uses it to guide him in reading through the book, he will still end up not seeing the things ruled out even when they are starring at him. One needs to be willing to discard, or at least suspend temporarily, such a prejudice in order to both discern the interpretive grid and use it to read Ecclesiastes fairly.

Conclusion

Having taken this bumpy journey on a long and winding road in how Ecclesiastes should be interpreted, we can now conclude that "All is vanity" is not pessimistic and this translation of the theme of Ecclesiastes captures profoundly and powerfully the reality of life "under the sun" (in this temporal world). Whether this reality is pessimistic or otherwise depends on one's point of view. Qoheleth the speaker is himself not pessimistic but realistic. He is orthodox and his speech is both coherent and consistent.

Actually the speech is a sermon as the purpose and goal of its content and rhetoric are to persuade the audience to fear God and keep his commandments. Thus one can preach through it like one preaches through the Sermon on the Mount (Matthew 5–7).

Since there are so many different interpretations of Ecclesiastes as a whole and in its parts, the caution concerning the never-ending writing of books also amounts to saying that we need to evaluate with objectivity every interpretation, including ours as presented and defended above. Wherein lies that objectivity?

According to E. D. Hirsch in his classic book on literary interpretation,

> The root problem of interpretation is always the same—to guess what the author meant. Even though we can never be certain that our interpretive guesses are correct, we know that they *can* be correct and that the goal of interpretation as a discipline is constantly to increase the probability that they are correct. In the earlier chapters of this book, I showed that only one interpretive problem can be answered with objectivity: "What, in all probability, did the author mean to convey?" In this final chapter, I have tried to show more particularly wherein that objectivity lies. It lies in our capacity to say on firm principles, "Yes, that answer is valid" or "No, it is not."[132]

This means we need to evaluate an interpretation in terms of the validity of not only its overall process but also its final product. For two interpreters can use the same overall process that is obviously valid and yet come up with opposing products.

---

132. Hirsch, *Validity in Interpretation*, 207.

Based on an overall process of interpretation that is similar to that of Enns, our interpretation of the book of Ecclesiastes is guided by an interpretive grid that is discerned from and applied to the text of Ecclesiastes. However, the product of Enns's interpretation is that Qoheleth is pessimistic and unorthodox, as well as inconsistent, even self-contradictory. And the product of our interpretation is that Qoheleth says nothing that renders him pessimistic or unorthodox, or his speech inconsistent or incoherent. Hence we can count on Qoheleth as a reliable teacher and we can preach through the whole of Ecclesiastes as a reliable book.

Which interpretation is more likely correct? Can we "say on firm principles" our interpretation "in all probability" captures at least essentially if not entirely what Qoheleth did "mean to convey" in and through his speech? Now these are three facts about Ecclesiastes: Qoheleth's speech is a monologue *addressing the reader like a sermon*; the "epilogue" regards Qoheleth as "a wise man," who "taught the people knowledge," and what he presents in his monologue as "honest words of truth" which are "given by one Shepherd" and thus, "beyond these . . . beware" (12:9–12); Qoheleth's monologue is canonized as part of "Scripture," which the New Testament claims "is inspired by God and profitable for teaching, for reproof, for correction, for training in righteousness so that the man of God may be adequate, equipped for every good work" (2 Tim 3:16–17).

BIBLIOGRAPHY

Abbott, H. Porter. *The Cambridge Introduction to Narrative.* 2nd ed. Cambridge: Cambridge University Press, 2008.
Accettura, P. Mark. *Blood and Money: Why Families Fight Over Inheritance and What To Do About It.* Farmington Hills: Collinwood, 2011.
Adler, Mortimer J., & Charles van Doren. *How to Read a Book.* Revised and Updated. New York: Simon & Schuster, 1972.
Alberts, Ilze. *Passing the Torch: Preserving Family Wealth Beyond the Third Generation.* Hoboken: John Wiley & Sons, 2018.
Antonovsky, Aaron. *Health, Stress, and Coping.* San Francisco: Jossey-Bass, 1981.
Baird, Robert M. "Meaning in Life: Discovered or Created?" *Journal of Religion and Health* 24.2 (1985) 117–24.
Barrick, William D. *Ecclesiastes: The Philippians of the Old Testament.* Focus on the Bible. Fearn: Christian Focus, 2015.
Bartholomew, Craig G. *Ecclesiastes.* Baker Commentary on the Old Testament Wisdom and Psalms. Grand Rapids: Baker Academic, 2009.
Barton, George Aaron. *The Book of Ecclesiastes: A Critical and Exegetical Commentary.* The International Critical Commentary. 1908. Reprint, Edinburgh: T & T Clark, 1959.
Baumeister, Roy F. *Meanings of Life.* New York: Guiford, 1991.
Bebbington, David. *Patterns in History: A Christian Perspective on Historical Thought.* Leicester: Apollos, 1990.
Beentjes, Pancratius Cornelis. *The Book of Ben Sira in Hebrew: A Text Edition of All Extant Hebrew Manuscripts and a Synopsis of All Parallel Hebrew Ben Sira Texts.* Leiden: Brill, 1997.
Belcher, Richard P. Jr. *A Study Commentary on Ecclesiastes.* EP Study Commentary. Darlington: Evangelical Press, 2014. Also published as: *Ecclesiastes: A Mentor Commentary.* Mentor Commentary Series. Fearn: Christian Focus, 2017.
Bellah, Robert N., Richard Madsen, William M. Sullivan, Ann Swidler, and Steven M. Tipton. *Habits of the Heart: Individualism and Commitment in American Life.* Berkeley: University of California Press, 1996.
Berdyaev, Nikolai. *The Meaning of History.* New Brunswick: Transaction, 2006.
Berger, Peter L. "The Desecularization of the World: A Global Overview." In *The Desecularization of the World: Resurgent Religion and World Politics*, edited by Peter L. Berger, 1–18. Grand Rapids: Eerdmans, 1999.
Bridges, Charles. *An Exposition of the Book of Ecclesiastes.* 1860. Reprint. London: Banner of Truth, 1960.

Broadus, John A. *On the Preparation and Delivery of Sermons*. Fourth Edition. Revised by Vernon L. Stanfield. San Francisco: Harper & Row, 1979.

Brown, Francis, S. R. Driver, and Charles A. Briggs. *The New Brown-Driver-Briggs-Gesenius Hebrew and English Lexicon: With an Appendix Containing the Biblical Aramaic*. Peabody: Hendrickson, 1979.

Brown, William P. *Character in Crisis: A Fresh Approach to the Wisdom Literature of the Old Testament*. Grand Rapids: Eerdmans, 1996.

———. *Ecclesiastes*. Interpretation. Louisville: Westminster John Knox, 2000.

Bruner, Jerome. "Life as Narrative." *Social Research: An International Quarterly* 71.3 (2004) 691–710.

Bulger, Allison. "Connotation." *LitCharts*. 5 May 2017. https://www.litcharts.com/literary-devices-and-terms/connotation.

Bundvad, Mette. *Time in the Book of Ecclesiastes*. Oxford: Oxford University Press, 2015.

Cairns, Grace E. *Philosophies of History: Meeting of East and West in Cycle-Pattern Theories of History*. New York: Philosophical Library, 1962.

Calvin, John. *Commentary on the Book of Psalms*. Translated from the Original Latin and Collated with the Author's French Version by James Anderson. Volume IV. Edinburgh: The Calvin Translation Society, 1847.

Caneday, A. B. "'Everything Is Vapor': Grasping for Meaning Under the Sun." *The Southern Baptist Journal of Theology* 15.3 (2011) 26–40.

Clines, David J. A., ed. *The Dictionary of Classical Hebrew*. Volume IV: ל–י. Sheffield: Sheffield University Press, 1998.

———. *The Dictionary of Classical Hebrew*. Volume V: מ–נ. Sheffield: Sheffield University Press, 2001.

———. *The Dictionary of Classical Hebrew*. Volume VI: ס–פ. Sheffield: Sheffield University Press, 2007.

———. *The Dictionary of Classical Hebrew*. Volume VII: צ–ר. Sheffield: Sheffield University Press, 2010.

———. *The Dictionary of Classical Hebrew*. Volume VIII: ת–ש. Sheffield: Sheffield University Press, 2011.

Conway, Heather, and John Stannard. "The Emotional Dynamics of Property Law." In *Research Handbook on Law and Emotion*, edited by Susan A. Bandes, Jody Lyneé Madeira, Kathryn D. Temple, and Emily Kidd White, 229–47. Cheltenham: Edward Edgar, 2021.

Crenshaw, James L. *Ecclesiastes: A Commentary*. The Old Testament Library. Philadelphia: Westminster, 1987.

———. *Qoheleth: The Ironic Wink*. Columbia: The University of South Carolina Press, 2013.

Delitzsch, F. *Commentary on the Song of Songs and Ecclesiastes*. Translated by M. G. Easton. 1872. Reprint, Commentary of the Old Testament in Ten Volumes. Volume VI: Proverbs, Ecclesiastes, Song of Solomon. Grand Rapids: Eerdmans, 1980.

DeRouchie, Jason S. "Shepherding Wind and One Wise Shepherd: Grasping for Breath in Ecclesiastes." *The Southern Baptist Journal of Theology* 15.3 (2011) 4–25.

Di Lella, Alexander A. *The Wisdom of Ben Sira: A New Translation with Notes by Patrick W. Skehan, Introduction and Commentary by Alexander A. Di Lella*. The Anchor Bible. New York: DoubleDay, 1987.

Dunham, Kyle C. "A Time to Throw Away Stones: Qohelet's Enigmatic Reference to Stones as a Hinge for the Themes of War and Peace in the Time Poem." *Journal for the Study of the Old Testament* 45.3 (2021) 320–35.

Eaton, Michael A. *Ecclesiastes: An Introduction and Commentary*. Tyndale Old Testament Commentaries. Leicester: InterVarsity, 1983.

Edwards, Paul. "Life, Meaning and Value of." In *Encyclopedia of Philosophy, Vol. 5*, edited by Donald M. Borchert, 345–58. Detroit: Macmillan Reference USA, 2005.

Ellermeier, F. *Qohelet I/1, Untersuchungen zum Buche Qohelet*. Herzberg: Junger, 1967.

Emmons, Robert A. *The Psychology of Ultimate Concerns: Motivation and Spirituality in Personality*. New York: Guiford, 1999.

Enns, Peter. *Ecclesiastes*. The Two Horizons Old Testament Commentary. Grand Rapids: Eerdmans, 2011.

Epstein, Greg M. *Good Without God: What a Billion Nonreligious People Do Believe*. New York: HarperCollins, 2009.

Fernandez-Armesto, Felipe. "Century of Paradox May Lead to Lowered Expectations of New Millennium." 1999. http://www.cnn.com/SPECIALS/1999/millennium/20/histories/content1.html

Folberg, Jay. "Mediating Family Property and Estate Conflicts." *Probate and Property* 23 (2009) 8–12.

Fox, Michael V. *Ecclesiastes*. The JPS Bible Commentary. Philadelphia: The Jewish Publication Society, 2004.

———. "Frame-narrative and Composition in the Book of Qohelet." *Hebrew Union College Annual* 48 (1977) 83–106.

———. *Proverbs 10-31: A New Translation with Introduction and Commentary*. The Anchor Yale Bible. New Haven: Yale University Press, 2009.

———. *Qohelet and His Contradictions*. Sheffield: Almond. 1989.

———. *A Time to Tear Down and a Time to Build Up: A Rereading of Ecclesiastes*. Grand Rapids: Eerdmans, 1999.

Frankl, Viktor E. *Man's Search for Meaning*. Revised and Updated. New York: Washington Square, 1984.

———. *The Unheard Cry for Meaning: Psychotherapy and Humanism*. New York: Washington Square, 1978.

Fredericks, Daniel C. *Coping with Transience: Ecclesiastes on the Brevity of Life*. Sheffield: Sheffield University Press, 1993.

———. *Ecclesiastes*. Apollos Old Testament Commentary: Ecclesiastes & The Song of Songs. Nottingham: Apollos, 2010.

———. *Qoheleth's Language: Re-evaluating Its Nature and Date*. Lewiston: Edwin Mellen, 1988.

Friedman, Thomas L. *The Lexus and the Olive Tree*. New York: Anchor, 2000.

Frydrych, Tomáš. *Living under the Sun: Examination of Proverbs and Qoheleth*. Leiden: Brill, 2002.

Fuhr, Richard Alan Jr. *An Analysis of the Inter-dependency of the Prominent Motifs within the Book of Qohelet*. New York: Peter Lang, 2013.

Garfinkel, Stephen. "Qoheleth: The Philosopher Means Business." In *Bringing the Hidden to Light: The Process of Interpretation. Studies in Honor of Stephen A. Geller*, edited by Kathryn F. Kravitz and Diane M. Sharon, 51–62. Winona Lake: Jewish Theological Seminary and Eisenbrauns, 2007.

Garrett, Duane A. *Proverbs, Ecclesiastes, Song of Songs: An Exegetical and Theological Exposition of Holy Scripture*. The New American Commentary. Nashville: Broadman, 1993.

Gay, Craig M. *The Way of the (Modern) World. Or Why It's Tempting to Live As If God Doesn't Exist*. Grand Rapids: Eerdmans, 1998.

George, A. R. *The Babylonian Gilgamesh Epic: Introduction, Critical Edition and Cuneiform Texts*. Volume I. Oxford: Oxford University Press, 2003.

George, Login, and Crystal Park. "Meaning in Life as Comprehension, Purpose, and Mattering: Toward Integration and New Research Questions." *Review of General Psychology* 20 (2016) 205–20.

Ginsburg, Christian D. *Coheleth, Commonly Called the Book of Ecclesiastes: Translated from the Original Hebrew, with a Commentary, Historical and Critical*. London: Longman, Green, Longman, and Roberts, 1861.

Goldingay, John. *Psalms, Volume 3: Psalms 90–150*. Baker Commentary on the Old Testament Wisdom and Psalms. Grand Rapids: Baker Academic, 2008.

Good, Edwin M. *Irony in the Old Testament*. Philadelphia: Westminster, 1965.

Gordis, Robert. *Koheleth—The Man and His World: A Study of Ecclesiastes*. Third Augmented Edition. New York: Schocken, 1968.

Graham, Billy. "The Evangelist's Appeal for Decision." In *The Work of an Evangelist: International Congress for Itinerant Evangelists*, edited by J. D. Douglas, 171–76. Minneapolis: World Wide, 1984.

Greenberg, Moshe. "נסה in Exodus 20:20 and the Purpose of the Sinaitic Theophany." *Journal of Biblical Literature* 79.3 (1960) 273–76.

HarperCollins Publishers. *Collins Cobuild English Dictionary for Advanced Learners*, Glasgow: HarperCollins, 2001.

Heim, Knut Martin. *Ecclesiastes: An Introduction and Commentary*. Tyndale Old Testament Commentaries. London: InterVarsity, 2019.

Henry, B. V. *Forsaking All for Christ: A Biography of Henry Martyn*. London: Chapter Two, 2008.

Hirsch, E. D. Jr. *Validity in Interpretation*. New Haven: Yale University Press, 1967.

Holmstedt, Robert D., John A. Cook, and Phillip S. Marshall. *Qoheleth: A Handbook on the Hebrew Text*. Waco: Baylor University Press, 2017.

Horne, Milton P. *Proverbs-Ecclesiastes*. Smyth & Helwys Bible Commentary. Macon: Smyth & Helwys, 2003.

Isaksson, Bo. *Studies in the Language of Qoheleth: With Special Emphasis on the Verbal System*. Stockholm: Upssala, 1987.

Joüon, Paul, and Takamitsu Muraoka. *A Grammar of Biblical Hebrew*. Third Reprint of the Second Edition, with Corrections. Rome: Gregorian and Biblical, 2011.

Kaiser, Walter C. *Ecclesiastes: Total Life*. Everyman's Bible Commentary. Chicago: Moody, 1979.

Kautzsch, E. *Gesenius Hebrew Grammar*. Translated by A. E. Cowley. 2nd ed. Oxford: Clarendon, 1910.

Keefer, Arthur. "The Meaning of Life in Ecclesiastes: Coherence, Purpose, and Significance from a Psychological Perspective." *Harvard Theological Review* 112.4 (2019) 447–66.

Kline, Meredith M. "Ecclesiastes: Musings of an Unfaithful Solomon? A Review Article," 2019. https://opc.org/os.html?article_id=767&cur_iss=F.

Koehler, Ludwig, Walter Baumgartner, and Johann Jakob Stamm. *The Hebrew and Aramaic Lexicon of the Old Testament*. Translated and edited under the supervision of M. E. J. Richardson. 5 vols. Leiden: Brill, 1994–2000.

Kramer, Samuel Noah. *The Sumerians: Their History, Culture, and Character*. Chicago: The University of Chicago Press, 1963.

Krüger, Thomas. *Qoheleth*, Translated by O. C. Dean Jr. Hermeneia. Minneapolis: Fortress, 2004.

Kugel, James L. "Qohelet and Money." *The Catholic Biblical Quarterly* 51.1 (1989) 32–49.

Lasch, Christopher. *The True and Only Heaven: Progress and Its Critics*. New York: W. W. Norton & Company, 1991.

Leong, T. F. *Our Reason for Hope: An Exposition of the Old Testament on the Meaning of History*. CreateSpace Independent Publishing Platform, 2018.

Leupold, H.C. *Exposition of Ecclesiastes*. Grand Rapids: Baker, 1952.

Lewis. C. S. *Reflections on the Psalms*. New York: Harvest, 1958.

Little, Daniel. "Philosophy of History." In *The Stanford Encyclopedia of Philosophy*, edited by Edward N. Zalta, 2020. https://plato.stanford.edu/archives/win2020/entries/history/.

Lohfink, Norbert. *Qoheleth*. A Continental Commentary. Minneapolis: Fortress, 2003.

Longman III, Tremper. *The Book of Ecclesiastes*. The New International Commentary on the Old Testament. Grand Rapids: Eerdmans, 1998.

———. "Ecclesiastes." In *Job, Ecclesiastes, Song of Songs*, by August H. Konkel (Job), Tremper Longman III, 251–338. Cornerstone Biblical Commentary. Carol Stream: Tyndale House, 2016.

———. *Proverbs*. Baker Commentary on the Old Testament Wisdom and Psalms. Grand Rapids: Baker Academic, 2006.

Löwith, Karl. *Meaning in History: The Theological Implications of the Philosophy of History*. Chicago: The University of Chicago Press, 1949.

Martela, Frank, and Michael F. Steger. "The Three Meanings of Meaning in Life: Distinguishing Coherence, Purpose, and Significance." *The Journal of Positive Psychology* 11 (2016) 531–45.

McGrath, Alister. *Glimpsing the Face of God: The Search for Meaning in the Universe*. Grand Rapids: Eerdmans, 2002.

Miller-Naudé, C.L., & J.A. Naudé. "Is the Adjective Distinct from the Noun as a Grammatical Category in Biblical Hebrew?" *In die Skriflig/In Luce Verbi* 50:4 (2005), 2016. https://indieskriflig.org.za/index.php/skriflig/article/view/2005/3891.

Miller, Douglas B. *Symbol and Rhetoric in Ecclesiastes: The Place of Hebel in Qohelet's Work*. Atlanta: Society of Biblical Literature, 2002.

Montgomery, John Warwick. *The Shape of the Past: A Christian Response to Secular Philosophies of History*. Minneapolis: Bethany Fellowship, 1975.

Mostert, Christiaan. "Theodicy and Eschatology." In *Theodicy and Eschatology*, edited by Bruce Barber and David Neville, 97–120. Adelaide: ATF, 2005.

Murphy, Roland E. *Ecclesiastes*. Word Biblical Commentary. Dallas: Word, 1992.

Nagel, Thomas. "The Absurd." *Journal of Philosophy* 68 (1971) 716–27.

———. *What Does It All Mean? A Very Short Introduction to Philosophy*. Oxford: Oxford University Press, 1987.

Nash, Ronald H. *The Meaning of History*. Nashville: Broadman & Holman, 1998.

Neusner, Jacob, and Bruce Chilton, eds. *The Golden Rule: The Ethics of Reciprocity in World Religions*. London: Continuum, 2008.

Newport, John P. *Life's Ultimate Questions: A Contemporary Philosophy of Religion*. Dallas: Word, 1989.

Ogden, Graham S. *Qoheleth*. Sheffield: Sheffield University Press, 2007.

BIBLIOGRAPHY

———. "Qoheleth's Use of the 'Nothing is Better'-Form," *Journal of Biblical Literature* 98.3 (1979) 339–50.

Ogden, Graham S., and Lynell Zogbo. *A Handbook on Ecclesiastes*. New York: United Bible Societies, 1997.

Owen, John. *The Glory of Christ*. Chicago: Moody, 1949.

Percy, Walker. *The Message in the Bottle*. New York: Farrar, Straus and Giroux, 1984.

Pinker, Aron. "The Doings of the Wicked in Qohelet 8:10." *Journal of Hebrew Scriptures* 8.6 (2008) https://jhsonline.org/index.php/jhs/article/view/6204/5238/.

Polk, Timothy. "The Wisdom of Irony: A Study of *Hebel* and Its Relation to Joy and the Fear of God in Ecclesiastes." *Studia Biblica et Theologica* 6 (1976) 3–17.

Polkinghorne, Donald E. *Narrative Knowing and the Human Sciences*. Albany: State University of New York Press, 1988.

Pritchard, James B., ed. *Ancient Near Eastern Texts Relating to the Old Testament, Third Edition with Supplement*. Princeton: Princeton University Press, 1969.

Provan, Iain W. *Ecclesiastes/Song of Songs*. The NIV Application Commentary. Grand Rapids: Zondervan, 2001.

Ramachandran, V. S. and Sandra Blakeslee. *Phantoms in the Brain: Probing the Mysteries of the Human Mind*. New York: William Morrow, 1998.

Rankin, Oliver S. "The Book of Ecclesiastes." In *The Interpreter's Bible, Volume V*, edited by George Arthur Buttrick et al., 3–88. Nashville: Abingdon, 1956.

Rudman, Dominic. *Determinism in the Book of Ecclesiastes*. Sheffield: Sheffield Academic Press, 2001.

Salyer, Gary D. *Private Insight and Public Debate in Ecclesiastes*. Sheffield: Sheffield Academic Press, 2001.

Sargent, John. *Life and letters of the Rev. Henry Martyn*. London: Seeley, Jackson, and Halliday, 1868.

Sarna, Nahum M. *Songs of the Heart: An Introduction to the Book of Psalms*. New York: Shocken, 1993.

Schoors, A. *The Preacher Sought to Find Pleasing Words: A Study of the Language of Qoheleth*. Louvain: Peeters, 1992.

———. *The Preacher Sought to Find Pleasing Words: A Study of the Language of Qoheleth, Part II Vocabulary*. Louvain: Peeters, 2004.

Seachris, Joshua W. "Death, Futility, and the Proleptic Power of Narrative Ending." *Religious Studies* 47 (2011) 141–63.

———. "The Meaning of Life as Narrative: A New Proposal for Interpreting Philosophy's 'Primary' Question." *Philo* 12.1 (2009) 5–23.

Seow, Choon-Leong. "Beyond Mortal Grasp: The Usage of *Hebel* in Ecclesiastes." *Australian Biblical Review* 48 (2000) 1–16.

———. *Ecclesiastes: A New Translation with Introduction and Commentary*. The Anchor Bible. New York: Doubleday Dell, 1997.

Shead, Andrew G. "Reading Ecclesiastes 'Epilogically.'" *Tyndale Bulletin* 48.1 (1997) 67–91.

Shepherd, Jerry E. "Ecclesiastes." In *The Expositor's Bible Commentary, Volume 6: Proverbs–Isaiah*, edited by Tremper Longman III and David E. Garland, 253–365. Grand Rapids: Zondervan, 2008.

Shields, Martin A. *The End of Wisdom: A Reappraisal of the Historical and Canonical Function of Ecclesiastes*. Winona Lake: Eisenbrauns, 2006.

Silver, Morris. *Economic Structures of Antiquity*. Westport: Greenwood, 1995.

BIBLIOGRAPHY

Singer, Jefferson A. *Message in a Bottle: Stories of Men and Addiction*. New York: Free, 1997.

Stannard, Russell. "The Wave/Particle Paradox." Boundaries of the Knowable. Youtube video, 2010. https://www.youtube.com/watch?v=_nvgGk8A300.

Sternberg, Meir. *The Poetics of Biblical Narrative: Ideological Literature and the Drama of Reading*. Bloomington: Indiana University Press, 1987.

Stuart, Moses. *A Commentary on Ecclesiastes*. New York: George P. Putnam, 1851.

Stückrath, Jörn. "'The Meaning of History': A Modern Construction and Notion?" In *Meaning and Representation in History*, edited by Jörn Rüsen, 65–88. Making Sense of History. Volume 7. New York: Berghahn, 2006.

Talley, David. "חפץ." In *New International Dictionary of Old Testament Theology and Exegesis*, 5 volumes, edited by Willem A. VanGemeren, 2:231–34. Grand Rapids: Zondervan, 1997.

Tan, Sin Guan. "The Empirically Corroborated Theology of the Meaning of Life in Ecclesiastes: A Biblical and Empirical Analysis with Reference to Malaysian Businesspeople." PhD diss., Bangor University, 2016. http://e.bangor.ac.uk/9822.

Thagard, Paul. *Coherence in Thought and Action*, Cambridge: MIT Press, 2000.

Towner, W. Sibley. "The Book of Ecclesiastes: Introduction, Commentary, and Reflection." In *The New Interpreter's Bible*. Volume V, edited by Leander E. Keck, 265–360. Nashville: Abingdon, 1997.

"Vanity." *Lexico.com*. Oxford University Press, 2021. https://www.lexico.com/en/definition/vanity.

Veenhof, K. R. *Aspects of Old Assyrian Trade and Its Terminology*. Leiden: Brill, 1972.

———. "Prices and Trade: The Old Assyrian Evidence." *Altorientalische Forschungen* 15 (1988) 43–63.

Von Rad, Gerhard. *Wisdom in Israel*. London: SCM, 1972.

Walsh, W. H. *An Introduction to the Philosophy of History*. Bristol: Thoemmes, 1992.

———. "Meaning in History." In *Theories of History*, edited by Patrick Gardiner, 295–307. New York: Free, 1959.

Waltke, Bruce K. *The Book of Proverbs: Chapters 1–15*. The New International Commentary on the Old Testament. Grand Rapids: Eerdmans, 2004.

———. *The Book of Proverbs: Chapters 15–30*. The New International Commentary on the Old Testament. Grand Rapids: Eerdmans, 2005.

Waltke, Bruce K., and M. O'Connor. *An Introduction to Biblical Hebrew Syntax*. Winona Lake: Eisenbrauns, 1990.

Ward, Keith. "Religion and the Question of Meaning." In *The Meaning of Life in the World Religions*, edited by Joseph Runzo and Nancy M. Martin, 11–30. Oxford: Oneworld, 2000.

Weeks, Stuart. "Divine Judgment and Reward in Ecclesiastes." In *Goochem in Mokum, Wisdom in Amsterdam: Papers on Biblical and Related Wisdom Read at the Fifteenth Joint Meeting of the Society for Old Testament and the Oudtestamentisch Werkgezelschap, Amsterdam, July 2012*, edited by George J. Brooke and Pierre Van Hecke, 155–66. Leiden: Brill, 2016.

———. *Ecclesiastes 1–5: A Critical and Exegetical Commentary*. The International Critical Commentary. London: T & T Clark, 2020.

———. "'Fear God and Keep His Commandments': Could Qohelet Have Said This?" In *Wisdom and Torah: The Reception of 'Torah' in the Wisdom Literature of the Second Temple Period*, edited by Bernd U. Schipper and D. Andrew Teeter, 101–18. Leiden: Brill, 2013.

Bibliography

Whitley, Charles F. *Koheleth: His Language and Thought*. Berlin: Walter de Gruyter, 1979.

Whybray, R. N. *Ecclesiastes*. The New Century Bible Commentary. Grand Rapids: Eerdmans, 1989.

———. "Qoheleth the Immoralist? (Qoh 7:16–17)." In *Israelite Wisdom: Theological and Literary Essays in Honor of Samuel Terrien*, edited by John G. Gammie, Walter A. Brueggemann, W. Lee Humphreys, and James M. Ward, 191–204. New York: Union Theological Seminary, 1978.

Wolf, Susan. "The Meaning of 'the Meaning of Life.'" In *Routledge Encyclopedia of Philosophy*. Volume 5, edited by Edward Craig. London: Routledge, 1998. https://www.rep.routledge.com/articles/thematic/life-meaning-of/v-1/sections/the-meaning-of-the-meaning-of-life.

Wong, Paul T. P. "From Logotherapy to Meaning-Centered Counseling and Therapy." In *The Human Quest for Meaning: Theories, Research, and Applications*. 2nd ed., edited by Paul T. P. Wong, 619–47. New York: Routledge, 2012.

———. "Introduction: A Roadmap for Meaning Research and Applications." In *The Human Quest for Meaning: Theories, Research, and Applications*. 2nd ed., edited by Paul T. P. Wong, xxvii–xliv. New York: Routledge, 2012.

Wright, J. Stafford. "The Interpretation of Ecclesiastes." In *Classical Evangelical Essays in Old Testament Interpretation*, edited by Walter C. Kaiser Jr, 133–50. Grand Rapids: Baker, 1972.